GLOBALIZATION AND SUSTAINABLE DEVELOPMENT

GLOBALIZATION AND SUSTAINABLE DEVELOPMENT

A BUSINESS PERSPECTIVE

MARTIN OYEVAAR, DIEGO VÁZQUEZ-BRUST AND HARRIE VAN BOMMEL

First published 2016 by
PALGRAVE

Palgrave in the UK is an imprint of Macmillan Publishers Limited, registered in England, company number 785998, of 4 Crinan Street, London, N1 9XW.

Palgrave is a global imprint of the above companies and is represented throughout the world.

Palgrave® and Macmillan® are registered trademarks in the United States, the United Kingdom, Europe and other countries.

ISBN 978–1–137–44535–3 paperback

This book is printed on paper suitable for recycling and made from fully managed and sustained forest sources. Logging, pulping and manufacturing processes are expected to conform to the environmental regulations of the country of origin.

A catalogue record for this book is available from the British Library.

A catalog record for this book is available from the Library of Congress.

Printed and bound by CPI Group (UK) Ltd, Croydon, CR0 4YY

CONTENTS

LIST OF FIGURES

LIST OF TABLES

LIST OF BOXES

ACKNOWLEDGEMENTS

A heartfelt thanks to the many people who have generously contributed their time and efforts to the making of this book. A special thanks to Jim Gordon whose English translation of the Dutch text has had a direct influence on the readability of the text as it appears here. Others whose suggestions and input contributed significantly to the book's content include Josette Jilesen, Ankit Gaur, and Chris Buskes and Rosan Koops.

Publisher's acknowledgements

The author and publishers are grateful for permission to reproduce the following copyright material:

Figure 3.1: The UN's characteristics of good governance. From United Nations Development Programme (1997). *Governance for Sustainable Human Development.*

Figure 3.2: Mozambique. From MapsOpenSource, *Mozambique Location Map In Africa Black and White,* at http://mapsopensource.com/mozambique-location-map-in-africa-black-and-white.html.

Figure 3.3: Samora Machel, first president of Mozambique. From SABC (2011). *Mozambique remembers Samora Machel,* at www.sabc.co.za/news/a/d90ad38048be4ed a9abd9aee2cb4f1d1/Mozambique-remembers-Samora-Machel-20111910.

Figure 5.3: The Aral Sea before and after large irrigation projects took place. From The Earth Observatory (25 August 2000 and 19 August 2014). *World of Change: Shrinking Aral Sea,* at http://earthobservatory.nasa.gov/Features/WorldOfChange/aral_sea.php.

Figure 5.4: State of the world. From The Club of Rome: Meadows, D. H., Meadows, D. L., Randers, J. & Behrens, W. W. (1972). *The Limits to Growth.* New York, NY: Universe Books.

Figure 5.8: Rates of world energy usage. From BP (2013). *Data workbook (xlsx) – Statistical Review of World Energy 2013.* London: BP.

Figure 5.9: Wind power: Worldwide installed capacity. From Global Wind Energy Council. (2012). *Global Wind Report: Annual Market Update 2012.* GWEC.

Figure 5.11: Circles of Sustainability. From James, P., Magee, L., Scerri, A. & Steger, M. (2015). *Urban Sustainability in Theory and Practice: Circles of Sustainability.* London: Routledge.

Figure 6.4: Feelings of fairness, by Bram van de Groes.

Figure 9.1: The close relationship between supply chain and reverse logistics. From Kumar, S. & Putnam, V. (2008). Cradle to cradle: Reverse logistics strategies and opportunities across three industry sectors. *International Journal of Production Economics, 115*(2), 305–315.

Figure 9.3: Life cycle assessment according to ISO14040. From International Organization for Standardization (2006). *ISO 14040:2006: Environmental management – life cycle assessment – principles and framework,* at www.iso.org/iso/catalogue _detail%3Fcsnumber%3D37456.

Figure 9.4: The biological and the technical cycle. From Cradle to Cradle in Taiwan (2015). *Cradle to Cradle Terms & Definitions*, at http://www.c2cplatform.tw/en/c2c .php?Key=3. © EPEA Internationale Umweltforschung GmbH.

Figure 10.1: Schematic overview of ISO 26000. From International Organization for Standardization (2010). *ISO 26000:2010(en). Guidance on social responsibility. Introduction,* at www.iso.org/obp/ui/#iso:std:iso:26000:ed-1:v1:en.

Figure 10.3: Critical CSR in less-developed countries, from Yakovleva, N. & Vázquez-Brust, D. (2012). Stakeholder perspectives on CSR of mining MNCs in Argentina. *Journal of Business Ethics, 106*(2), 191–211.

Figure 11.3: The Bottom of the Pyramid, from Prahalad, C. K. (2006). *Fortune at the Bottom of the Pyramid: Eradicating Poverty Through Profits.* Philadelphia, PA: Pearson Prentice Hall.

Figure 11.7: Some aspects of the business model of Zipcar, based on Osterwalder, A. & Pigneur, Y. (2010). *Business Model Generation.* Hoboken, NJ: John Wiley and Sons. Based on template of Strategyzer AG. *The Business Model Canvas,* at www.businessmodelgene ration.com/downloads/business_model_canvas_poster.pdf.

Figure 12.2: Porter Hypothesis, from Ambec, S. et al. (2013). The Porter Hypothesis at 20: Can environmental regulation enhance innovation and competitiveness? *Review of Environmental Economics and Policy,* res016.

Table 10.1: Human resources management and human value management as a dichotomy, from Schoemaker, M., Nijhof, A. & Jonker, J. (2006). Human Value Management: The influence of the contemporary developments of corporate social responsibility and social capital on HRM. *Management Revue, 17*(4), 448–465.

PREFACE: USING THIS BOOK

Globalization and sustainability are both controversial concepts. The debate around these topics is highly polarized and despite the widespread use – and misuse – of both terms there is still little consensus, for instance, on what we mean by globalization and sustainability; for how long globalization has been in existence (if at all);[1] and how definitions of sustainability can be translated into policy and business practice,[2] let alone any consensus on what the priorities should be in sustainable policy; how cross-border sustainability challenges such as climate change can be addressed;[3] or whether globalization is a negative force for sustainable development, and to what extent it can be regulated or whether it is just inevitable.[4, 5] This book aims not to provide definitive definitions nor to bring closure to these debates but instead to approach the subject acknowledging its complex and dynamic nature, exploring the main ideas, ethical principles, actors and processes driving the growth and development of the international economy and its unsteady transition to a more globalized and sustainable economy. This perspective allows us to foreground many of the 'myths' and arguments surrounding globalization and sustainable businesses.

Globalization and Sustainable Development is primarily intended for students taking modules in international business courses or corporate sustainability courses at the undergraduate or masters level. Our goal in writing this book has been to provide an introductory text for understanding the role of corporations in the global economy from a sustainable development perspective. We believe that a common deficiency in many texts in international business is to ignore or downplay the relationships between economic processes and sustainability, as if climate change and the exhaustion of non-renewable resources has no consequences for business. Similarly, many books in sustainable business have paid insufficient attention to debates on globalization and the challenges of governance in the global economy and its implications for sustainable business. We attempt to address these omissions and aim to provide students with an overall picture of what it means to be a sustainable business in today's global economy.

The link between the chapters is the challenge of global progress towards sustainable development. It gives a red thread for such themes as the 'alleged worldwide success' of the market economy, the need for global governance to achieve more welfare worldwide, the inherent global nature of the sustainability problem, the role of business in the dissemination of globalization and the implications of 'more globalization' for the success of sustainability transitions. For rational policy, the agenda is clear: global collaboration to achieve more equality, allocating external costs of polluting activities, investing in renewable energy and changing consumption patterns.[6] But rational politics are an ideal concept. Vested interests and the dependency on past investment, infrastructure and past thinking about better paths to progress constrain our ability to change inertial and inefficient practice,[7] particularly the overreliance on oil and coal exploitation. The naturalist E. O. Wilson concluded the essay *In Search of Nature* (1996) by wondering if humanity is suicidal.[8] If the answer is yes, are we like lemmings blindly rushing on a pre-defined path of 'progress' towards self-destructive global development? This book has a moderately optimistic outlook. Human beings, with their natural habits of greed and aggression, but also respect, appreciation of fairness and empathy, have made progress towards sustainable development. There is still much to be done but the economic crisis has provided a unique window of opportunity for countries and organizations to try new economic and environmental policies and business models.[9] 'Struggling progress' seems to encapsulate the transition towards global sustainable development.

The biggest challenge in writing this book was the definition of its content bounda-ries, with the number of themes to be discussed restricted by necessity and parsimony. Any book on either sustainable business or business in the global economy must embrace a variety of different subjects and disciplines and must, by necessity, leave outside its boundaries some relevant concepts and topics. Our rationale in selecting what to include was to provide a common base for international business courses and sustainable business courses, and we hope more specialized courses will delve deeper into the concepts here presented. For that reason the structure of the book is wide and covers many topics in a way that requires no previous knowledge of economics. The clear choice from the beginning was to span a variety of concepts and trends; laying out with broad brush strokes the conceptual foundations of sustainability and the economics and politics of cross-border trade and investment at the macro, meso and micro level. Understanding is further aided by the introduction of relevant theoretical perspectives providing macro-level conceptual foundations to identify trends and chal-lenges in the global economy and in sustainable development. The book has aimed at a distinctive multi-disciplinary approach; drawing on economic, historical, sociological, management and geopolitical theories. Preferential attention is given to the role of cross-border aspects of market economies – particularly international trade and foreign direct investment – as a driving force in the integration of developing countries into the globalization process. The consequences of globalization in relation to the environment, social inequalities and poverty are also examined and other measures of welfare studied, highlighting the contribution of business models to global governance issues.

The four chapters in the first part of the book (Part 1: Foundations of economics, gov-ernance and society) are a 'primer', written to give business students a macro-level under-standing of main characteristics, ideologies and debates shaping the economic, political and social context in which global sustainable business takes place. Chapter 1 introduces two distinctive features of our times: the growing challenge of economic inequality and the rise of China and other developing countries as world powers. Chapters 2, 3 and 4 examine contemporary implications of three great conceptual breakthroughs, which interwoven provide the fabric of our current global economy: market economies, good governance and life in modern society. Chapter 2 focuses on the global dominance and regional varieties of market economy, Chapter 3 analyses the principles and challenges of good governance, Chapter 4 completes the analysis of foundational concepts providing insights into the ethical and psychological underpinnings of life in modern society.

The four chapters in the second part of the book (Part 2: Sustainable development and globalization) weave together concepts developed in the first part, in the examina-tion of two of the most powerful 'new' ideas – informing debates on politics, economics, development and society – that emerged out of the conceptual foundations discussed previously: sustainability and globalization. Chapters 5 and 6 examine sustainability and its macro-level implications for the global economy. Chapter 5 examines what is meant by sustainability and what are the main themes and principles embedded in sustainabil-ity debates; Chapter 6 brings together all the concepts discussed in the book until that point in order to understand how sustainability and market economies can be made compatible through enhanced governance and leveraged social capital. Chapters 7 and 8 examine globalization and its macro-level implications for sustainability. Chapter 7 first discusses differences between globalization and other global economic processes such as neoliberalism and internationalization, then presents the supranational institutions to which globalization has given rise, the World Trade Organization, International Monetary Fund and World Bank. Chapter 8 discusses the implications of globalization, internationalization and neoliberalism for sustainable development, with special attention to the unintended impacts of global institutions and the consequences for inequality and the governance of globalization.

The four chapters in the third part of the book (Part 3: Business implications of 'globalization' and sustainability) build on the first two parts to explore notions of 'globalization' and sustainability as regards their implications for business. To this end, Chapters 9 to 11 explore a selection of meso-/micro-level business concepts that we think essential to address the challenges of developing sustainable global businesses: corporate social responsibility, global supply chains and global business strategy. We end the book with a theme that summarizes our overall approach: the transition towards sustainable development as a dynamic and reflexive process of collectively managed creative destruction of past path dependency. A process where citizens, government, business and supranational institutions are closely intertwined in the creation of a new playing field where companies can make more sustainable products.

At the end of the book, students should be in a position to appreciate the genuine magnitude and significance of global economic forces, principles and processes for global sustainability, national economies, industries and firms.

PART I

FOUNDATIONS OF ECONOMICS, GOVERNANCE AND SOCIETY

1

THE WORLD ECONOMY: TRENDS AND INDICATORS

Overview and learning objectives

The world economy has undergone radical changes in the last few decades. The end of the Cold War in the late 1980s triggered the acceptance of market economies world-wide. New economic giants such as China and Brazil emerged and changed the balance of economic power, which has been steadily shifting from West to East, and – to a much lesser extent – from North to South. Simultaneously, growing economic internation-alization and globalization increased interdependencies between national economies through cross-border networks of production and consumption. Since 1978, US, UK and global institutions such as the World Trade Organization (WTO) and the International Monetary Fund (IMF) promoted so-called neoliberal economics, aimed at removing barriers to free movements of capital, goods and services across national boundaries. Pressure mounted on developing countries to deregulate business activity, cut welfare spending and dismantle the apparatus of state intervention in the economy.

This chapter provides a glimpse of antecedents of such shifts in trends in policy and their consequences on worldwide welfare and well-being. It takes a look at historical pat-terns of worldwide economic growth and inequality using China, the rising star in the world economy, and Africa, the poorest region of the world, as focal points to explore trends, indicators and reasonable expectations for welfare growth and the direction it is taking. In addition to economic growth figures, a more holistic view of economics is used to understand how the economy affects our well-being: inequality, freedom and envi-ronmental sustainability are as influential to well-being as they are to economic growth.

Learning objectives

At the end of this chapter, readers will be able to:

- Recognize the world economy's well-being and growth indicators.
- Acknowledge the growth and pivotal role of China in the world economy.
- Understand recent trends in economic growth and well-being.
- Acknowledge reasonable expectations for future trends.

1.1 Worldwide economic growth in the last century

This section will provide a basic overview of growth trends in the past century. The most commonly used indicator of growth is gross domestic product (GDP): the total value of goods and services produced by a country in a year. GDP is a measure of a country's 'value added'. It aggregates the yearly value added to the economy of a country by each productive unit residing in it (the value of its output minus the value of goods that are employed in producing it).[1]

Growth of GDP is dependent on the following:[2]

1. Population growth.
2. Investment ratio (relation between investment and GDP).
3. Employee education level.
4. Foreign investment and trade.
5. Monetary policy.
6. Use of resources such as mined materials, energy and land.

Worldwide economic growth experienced a period of continuous expansion after the end of the Second World War (WWII) in 1944. The post-war period from 1945 to 1980 was characterized by the dominance of the welfare state, with a focus on redistribution of wealth through state investment in education, health and infrastructure.[3] During WWII (January 1941) US President Franklin D. Roosevelt announced plans to end poverty. His famous 'Four Freedoms' speech touched on the minimum living standards necessary for well-being and health.[4] World leaders were anxious to fight poverty not only in their own countries but also globally, although possibilities for real coordinated global action began only at the end of the Cold War.[5] Figure 1.1 shows results for population index and the GDP per capita of world population. When both indexes are multiplied the result is the increased GDP for world population.[6]

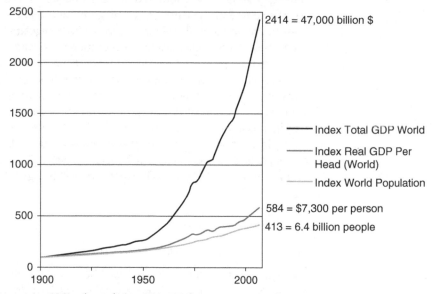

Figure 1.1   GDP and population 1900–2005[7]

It can be concluded that population indices and GDP per capita have increased dramatically and as a result GDP for the world population has risen from 100 to 2414 in only 100 years.

Much has changed in the past 20–30 years. Since 1980, neoliberal policy – discussed in detail in Chapter 8 – increasingly dismantled the allegedly inefficient and overgrown welfare state, reducing welfare budgets and promoting free trade and unrestricted foreign investment as drivers of growth.[8] A significant step towards worldwide welfare improvement was the 1990 UN Conference which focused on education for all the world's children, and this item remained on many agendas throughout the decade. A series of economic social crises in the late 1990s led to mounting criticism of the social impacts of neoliberal policy.[9] As a response, the new century gave birth to what Peet (2008) termed as an 'augmented and benevolent' neoliberal agenda. This new agenda maintained the focus on free trade and deregulation but also accepted the need for social welfare budgets and condoned the external debts of the least developed countries.[10] This new approach for liberal as well as more socialism-based economies led to increased funding not only for education, but for health care and poverty relief as well.[11] Despite fluctuations, a period of sustained growth ensued until 2007 when the world economy entered into the worst economic downturn and longest lingering recession since 1930.[12] The crisis shattered the dominance of neoliberal ideas and triggered the partial resurgence of state intervention, some degree of capital control and welfare state policies worldwide.[13] Uneven economic recovery started again in 2009, but ever since the advanced economies have had to deal with sluggish growth, averaging 2% in the US, 1% in Europe and 0.5% in Japan from 2009 to 2013.[14] On the other hand, although it was reduced compared to pre-recession figures, emerging countries still enjoyed inertial growth. Growth in Eastern Asia, China and India was on average above 6% during the same period, 4.5% in Africa and 5% in Latin America.[15]

This dual nature of growth in the world economy today raises questions about the continuity of these trends. Are wealthier economies entering a maturity phase of stagnant growth or even de-growth? If consumption continues to fall in the West, the world economy is likely to experience a cooling process; will productivity and welfare continue to increase for the world's poor countries in the future?[16] Alarmingly, both relatively stagnant and relatively booming economies share a common feature: the incessant rise of economic inequality, which may prevent long-term welfare and even, as Nobel Prize winner Joseph Stiglitz argues, eventually lead to the collapse of capitalism.[17] On the other hand if consumption returns to pre-recession patterns we will also have to ponder the future of our natural resources, the developmental impacts of climate change and inequality, and the success of sustainable development as well as human rights, democracy and international trade issues.

1.1.1 Growth in China and the law of increasing and decreasing economic growth

For a better insight into trends in economic growth during the last 30 years, it is instructive to look at China. With more than one billion people, China has been fast outpacing other world economies and its gradual transition to a relatively open market economy provides a unique opportunity to examine the evolution of growth patterns. From 1979 to 2013 average Chinese growth rates were 9.5% of GDP increase per year. In the 1980s GDP growth averaged 8% but rose fast in the 1990s. GDP growth peaked in 2007 at 14.2%, but subsequently fell to 9.6% in 2008 after the global economic crisis hindered Western demand for Chinese products. Despite fluctuations – such as a 10.4% GDP increase in 2010 – the trend continued downwards to 7.1% in 2015.

The pattern of 30 years of growth in China closely responds to the law of increasing and diminishing growth rates. In the early stages of development, low growth percentages are the norm, as in the early 1980s in China, because the implementation of new laws and reforms needs considerable time to take effect. After a while, when new policy begins to take effect, growth margins increase. In China between 1983 and 2008, percentages remained high and stable with no discernible changes. Finally, according to the law of increasing and diminishing growth rates, when desired goals are achieved the growth decreases. This phase of decline is inevitably happening in China.

To ascertain the pattern that China's growth will follow in the coming years, we can look at the six factors influencing GDP that were outlined on p. 4, Section 1.1.

Expectations for the Chinese job market indicate that *workers' migration to the cities from the country* will continue to increase at its present pace. The number of workers for the industrial sector will also grow.[18] China has also been enjoying a *high level of foreign investment*. In 2005 it had already reached 40%.[19] China has a high investment ratio; much higher, for example, than Germany, whose investment ratio declined between 1960 and 2002 from 27% to 19%.[20] In fact, between 2007 and 2008 developed countries recorded a sharp decline in foreign investment of around 29% but developing and transition economies showed an increase in total investment of around 37% and 17% respectively. However, China experienced a continued decrease in foreign direct investment (FDI) levels from 2009 onwards. In 2013 only, FDI in China dropped by 18%.[21] The Chinese are also working to *develop their educational skills*. Since 1999, the number of students completing Masters Degrees has increased yearly by 30%.[22] China's membership of the WTO led to relaxed restrictions on imports and exports which stimulated further growth helped by *China's monetary policy* which increased the competitiveness of Chinese exports.[23] By 2007 the yuan exchange rate was undervalued by 27.5% according to a study by the Peterson Institute commissioned by the US Congress.[24] However, the value of the yuan is tied to the US dollar by Chinese law (the yuan cannot move more than 2% a day against the US dollar). Therefore, with an increasingly strong dollar, by 2014 the yuan appreciated by more than 30% compared to 2008 values. By 2015 the yuan was the world's second most overvalued currency after the US dollar.[25] The Chinese government corrected the situation with small devaluations in August 2015. Although only amounting to 4.5% depreciation, the devaluation triggered three things: panic within global markets, hysteria within the media and fears of currency wars within political circles. The global overreaction – a clear sign of the pivotal role of China in the world economy – stunned Chinese leaders, who assured world leaders that there would be no further currency adjustments.[26]

Production of Chinese raw materials is also enjoying a boom, with the mining industry producing more than ever before. Aluminium production, for example, increased by 60% between 2005 and 2006 and steel production is also on the increase with a 30% rise in 2015.[27] Energy is also profiting due to the immense Chinese coal reserves, but this is becoming less popular because of the hazardous CO_2 emissions produced during coal mining.

Despite positive figures, many economists feel that China is headed for a decrease in growth in the coming years which correlates with the law of diminishing returns. Less traction is expected for individual investments, schooling and migration and there is increasing pressure on the Chinese to revaluate the yuan which would have an immediate effect on exports. Decreases in growth are also expected for land, water, raw materials and energy and these should stabilize or even go into negative figures. The mining and traditional energy sectors will almost certainly have less growth with decreasing yields and it will be imperative that China finds new environmentally friendly energy and raw material sources. Productive growth will diminish but still remain above Western levels. Expectations for the future are a 5%–7% yearly rise, which is still more than the 1%–2% growth figures predicted for the West.[28, 29, 30] See Box 1.1 for some thoughts on how China's growth curve is reflected in its opening of new museums.

> ### Box 1.1 Modern Chinese museums and the growth curve[31]
>
> Growth is a 'natural' process and can be easily visualized using a curve. The trick is to determine the critical point of entry on the curve and to take into consideration the linear or exponential factors. For China, increased exponential growth can be shown in many areas. The beginning of China's opening to the West was marked 30 years ago, with culture developing as fast as the economy. Before the 2008 Beijing Olympic Games, 100 new museums were opened and by 2015 another 900 were expected, with at least one museum for every city in the People's Republic of China.
>
> A new era of openness and freedom is slowly taking hold as long as there is no embarrassing public criticism of the ruling party. Chinese society is offering greater diversity for media expression. Experts claim that the increased demand for information has rendered state control ineffective in some areas and public service broadcasting does not follow a clear uniform policy.[32] The censor has scissors at the ready but at the same time people are striving for quality, independence and impartiality.[33] The Internet is also offering increased options for gathering news and information.[34] Chinese bloggers are now an integral part of the social fabric and have assumed the role of criticasters for non-politically tinted messages as well as supporting central government policy in the battle against red tape and corruption.[35]

1.2 Welfare, well-being and sustainable development

In order to see the results of development it is necessary to look at different indicators of welfare. The growth of GDP on its own is not a solid indicator of economic progress and well-being.[36] Well-being refers to an experience of a 'good life' which also depends on input from income distribution, environmental protection, health care and education, among other factors. This section will examine the different indicators that are used to create an image of welfare and well-being that not only apply to today's world but also look ahead to the future.

1.2.1 Distribution of welfare and well-being worldwide

Income gap between rich and poor countries

The income gap between rich and poor countries has increased steadily through the centuries but came to a halt in 1992 in the West. In 1700 the comparison was roughly equal because Western society was relatively as poor as its Eastern counterparts. The awakening of Eastern Asia, and now also Africa to a certain extent, has brought more income inequality which can be represented by what is called the Gini coefficient. The Gini coefficient ranges from 0, representing perfect equality, to 1, representing perfect inequality. If the wealthiest 1% of residents in a country have 100% of the income, the Gini coefficient approaches 1. If everybody has the same income, the Gini coefficient approaches 0. We see that the gap increased from 0.48 to 0.67 from 1700 until 1992.[37] From 1992 to 2008 there was a decrease, and the value of the coefficient in 2008 was 0.62. However, new research from Joseph Stiglitz has argued that these figures are misleading because fast-developing Asian economies are included in the group of poor countries. His calculations of the income gap between poorest countries (excluding East Asia) and wealthiest countries show that income inequalities between the two groups have been steadily increasing.[38] Additionally, Gini coefficients have been criticized because of the complexity of their calculations and because the index is heavily influenced by the proportion of middle-income citizens. The higher the percentage of middle-income citizens, the lower Gini is. This makes Gini a weak indicator of extreme poverty and the differences between the poorest and the richest residents. An alternative indicator of inequality is gaining international consensus: the Palma ratio, named after its creator, the Chilean economist Gabriel Palma. Palma ratios are easy to calculate and very effective for conveying extreme inequality. Palma ratios are calculated as the aggregated income of the richest 10% divided by the aggregated income of the poorest 40%.[39]

Income differences within countries

Scores for income inequality vary from country to country. From 1970 to 1985 this inequality decreased on average but increased afterwards due to several large countries' shift to a market economy. China, Russia and India experienced this first-hand but so did developing countries with a strong export trade or dependence in natural resources investment.[40] Inequality, in turn, also increased in countries with a long-standing market economy. The income increase has been particularly pronounced in the US and to a lesser extent in most European countries.[41] Chapter 8 will explore in more detail the causes and consequences of inequality.

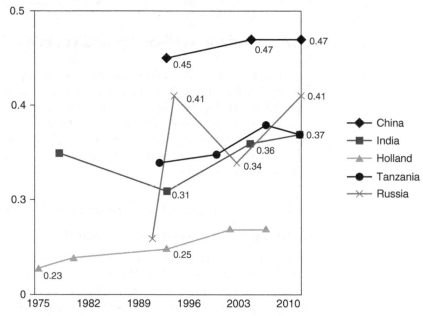

Figure 1.2 Gini coefficient, China, India,[42] Holland,[43] Tanzania[44] and Russia[45]

Box 1.2 Well-being worldwide: United Nations Millennium Development Goals

After the Cold War, fighting poverty became a major goal of the United Nations (UN). After years of ideological trench warfare between capitalism and communism, new ideas emerged putting the state in a favourable light, and allowing it to intervene in the market in a friendlier and more sociable manner. The process towards global welfare received a strong boost in 2001 when the leaders of

(Continued)

185 countries signed up to the UN Millennium Development Goals (MDGs), a set of quantifiable targets to improve welfare and well-being in developing countries.

The eight goals were established following the Millennium Summit of the UN in 2000, following the adoption of the UN Millennium Declaration. All UN member states at the time and many international organizations, such as the World Bank, committed to help achieve them by 2015.

In order to develop a concrete action plan to achieve the MDGs and to reverse the grinding poverty, hunger and disease affecting billions of people, the Millennium Project was commissioned by the UN Secretary-General in 2002. In 2005, the independent advisory body, headed by Professor Jeffrey Sachs, presented its final recommendations to the Secretary-General in a practical plan for achievement.[46]

The Millennium Development Goals

1. To reduce extreme poverty and hunger
2. To achieve universal primary education
3. To promote gender equality and empower women
4. To reduce child mortality
5. To improve maternal health
6. To combat HIV/AIDS, malaria
7. To ensure environmental sustainability
8. To develop a global partnership for development

In 2012 the UN Secretary-General established the UN System Task Team on the Post-2015 UN Development Agenda, bringing together more than 60 UN agencies and international organizations to focus and work on sustainable development. A yearly report kept track of how the involved countries were getting on and substantial improvements have been noted in almost every goal. The exception is goal 7 – 'To ensure environmental sustainability' – where some targets improved, such as access to drinkable water, but other targets drastically worsened: pollution, emissions and extinction of species increased.[47]

Moreover, progress has been uneven between countries, with only one country – Brazil – achieving all targets. The only goal where targets were globally achieved was goal 1, the aim to reduce extreme poverty by half. In 1990 almost 42% of people were classified as living in conditions of extreme poverty and in 2010 this percentage dropped to 22%.[48]

In 2015, the MDGs were replaced by a new set of indicators: the Sustainable Development Goals (SDGs), which will be discussed in Chapter 5.

1.2.2 Future of the economy

Though there is a disagreement among economists, Piketty (2013) has presented inequality theory in a unified way by integrating it with income, economic growth and income distribution between capital and labour. Simply put, in a free market economy the rent of capital (profit) grows much faster than the rent of labour (salary) and therefore the owners of capital such as firms' owners and investors receive a higher share of growth than workers. Piketty's work predicts future exponential growth of inequality if preventive measures are not implemented globally.[49] Statistical evidence suggests that inequality hinders long-term growth, fuels violent conflict and triggers migrations.[50] Therefore, among the crucial economic conundrums confronting private sector–led development and requiring collective action is how foreign investment in developing countries may increase growth but also increase income inequality, a key global challenge for the next decades.[51] The situation is particularly acute in natural resource economies such as those in African countries which might otherwise be flourishing according to macroeconomic indicators. Poverty alleviation from an investment in natural resources appears to get concentrated within certain strata of society and further increases inequalities between the genders despite various corporate efforts of linking such investment to development outcomes.[52] (See also Chapter 8's discussion on globalization and inequality.)

Moreover, worldwide welfare and distribution of income are not the only development indicators to be examined. Two centuries of increased productivity have given Europe and other parts of the world a dramatic improvement in welfare and well-being but at the same time environmental concerns have begun to assume more prominence. Scientists, politicians, policy makers and concerned citizens have pointed out the downside of unchecked consumption. Recycling, renewable energy, clean air policy, toxic emissions and water purification have all become agenda points for international environment meetings. Politics, science and pressure groups have become more involved and reached an important goal with the United Nations' 1987 publication of *Our Common Future*. This work, also known as the Brundtland Report, coined the definition of 'sustainable development' (SD) as 'development that meets the needs of the present without compromising the ability of future generations to meet their own needs'.

SD acknowledges that control of our natural resources should be an essential part of policy making. A one-sided focus on short-term welfare growth can lead to irrevocable pollution and serious depletion of raw materials. Scientists and citizens alike are becoming seriously concerned about the future. SD discussions – analysed in detail in Chapter 6 – often point to the limited amount of fossil fuels, CO_2 emissions and global warming, much of which has been created by humans themselves.[53] The current economic system is coming under increased pressure. Many naturally obtained goods are traded for unrealistically low prices resulting in the fact that natural resources are mined or acquired with little regard for reuse or regeneration of the sources from which they were taken. To avoid a future welfare disaster scenario, economies will have to be equipped with the power to use natural resources in a responsible way. Humans should use their knowledge and creativity in an economy with new, smarter rules (more details in Chapters 9 and 11). For the future, it is not an option to create wealth based solely on fossil fuels. Indeed, as we will see in Chapters 5 and 12, some argue that in the future economic growth will be neither desirable nor achievable and the world economy will either collapse dramatically amid social and economic disruption or experience a transitional period of gradual de-growth until a sustainable economic system, in balance with nature, is reached.

Box 1.3   Africa in the global economy

The failure of a substantial number of African countries to achieve MDGs is a poignant reminder that Africa is still lagging far behind the rest of the developing world in too many development indicators, despite substantial decrease in maternal mortality rates and the number of people dying of AIDS-related diseases.[54] Foreign investment in Africa has been growing and continues to be dominated by natural resource firms.[55] Since more than 80% of Africa's mineral potential may be still untapped, mining can be a key source of revenue for the continent and can

(Continued)

help to guide its human development initiatives.[56] Increased FDI in mineral-rich countries did help to bring about economic growth in terms of macroeconomic indicators, but the key challenge it brought alongside it was rising inequality.[57] Inequalities in income and health increased in the majority of Africa's resource-rich countries.[58] Based on conventional Gini measures, Africa is the world's second most inequitable region after Latin America; sub-Saharan Africa houses six of the ten countries with the largest income inequality in the world, some of the world's highest values of extreme inequality as captured by Palma ratios,[59] and the bottom 11 countries in the inequality-adjusted Human Development Index.

Inequality is not a new phenomenon in Africa. Even after the colonial regimes were replaced, power was passed into the hands of the elite few who did not reform the structures put in place during colonial times and failed to redistribute the assets in a fair manner.[60] Natural resource endowment seems to exacerbate this structural bias against less privileged groups of society.[61] One of the reasons is that the benefits obtained from foreign investment are not being transmitted widely throughout the population: mining sites and factories sometimes become privileged enclaves reinforcing inter-regional and inter-ethnical inequalities, and in turn fuelling conflict and migration.[62] Mining, farming, manufacturing and service companies from all nationalities have also been accused of creating environmental damage and violation of human rights, while sector-specific pay structures have been linked to increases in income inequality.[63] Bonsu (2014) argues that colonialism and its trappings were reborn through foreign investment; colonialism now assuming the contemporary form of neoliberalism that maintains the racial and economic imperialism that sustained colonial exploits.[64]

1.3   Learning tools 🔧

1.3.1   Summary

- This chapter looked at current trends in economic growth and well-being.
- Growth is measured using gross domestic product (GDP).
- Growth follows the law of increasing and diminishing returns. It is low in early stages of development, then it increases faster and eventually declines. This pattern can be seen in the Chinese economy.
- China's growth has stabilized at around 7% per year since 2012 and it is not expected to increase further in the short term.
- Growth on its own is not a solid indicator of development and welfare. GDP is only a monetary figure and needs to be supported with information relating to how money is earned, how it is spent and what percentage of the population is benefited by growth. Income inequality is measured using Gini coefficients. Extreme inequality is measured using Palma ratios. Welfare inequality is measured with the inequality-adjusted Human Development Index.
- Inequality within countries has been increasing in the last decades. Inequality between countries decreased overall, but the gap between the poorest and richest countries widened.
- Sustainable development (SD) views welfare as the coexistence of economic prosperity, equity, well-being and environmental protection. It is not only concerned with the present situation but is also directed towards welfare in the long term.

(Continued)

1.3.2   Further reading

Mahbubani, K. (2008). *The New Asian Hemisphere: The Irresistible Shift of Global Power to the East* (pp. 144–150). New York, NY: Public Affairs.

Stiglitz, J. (2012). *The Price of Inequality: How Today's Divided Society Endangers Our Future.* London: Penguin.

1.3.3   Assignments

 Assignment 1.1 Growth patterns

Compare and contrast worldwide patterns of growth in the period 2003–2013. Identify groups of countries with similar growth patterns. Your essay should investigate differences between linear and exponential growth.

 Assignment 1.2 Inequality

In the last five years, Tanzania, Canada and Russia have achieved contrasting levels of economic growth and inequality. Discuss to what extent differences can be linked to different patterns of population growth and investment ratios (relations between investment and GDP; employee education level; limits to free trade; monetary policy; and use of resources such as mined materials, energy and land).

 Assignment 1.3 Well-being and growth

Discuss to what extent continuous decrease in worldwide growth will result in decreased welfare and well-being.

 Assignment 1.3 MDGs

Critically discuss the weaknesses and strengths of MDGs to improve worldwide welfare. Why do you think only one out of the eight goals was fully achieved? Justify your answer with theory and examples.

1.3.4   Self-test questions

 Self-test Questions

1. Explain the law of diminishing returns.
2. What are Gini coefficients? What is the meaning of a high Gini value?
3. Give examples of countries with low and high Gini coefficients.
4. What causes inequality?
5. What indicators would you use to assess well-being?
6. Is well-being improving globally?

2

MARKET ECONOMIES AND GOVERNMENTS

Overview and learning objectives

The concept of market economy is fairly recent. Only in the last three to four centuries have governments implemented policy to create, in a more structured way, conditions favourable to business.[1] The development of the market economy has contributed strongly to improved welfare and its principles rule in almost all the world's countries. Its premise is the availability of goods whose price is determined by supply and demand. Government plays a limited role in the market economy when it comes to offering goods and services to the general public. The degree of government intervention in the market varies per country but in general the differences across the globe are smaller compared with 30 or 40 years ago.

The advance of the market economy owes much to expectations of increased prosperity. Extensive academic research has concluded that market systems are dynamic by nature and contribute to the innovative output of society.[2] This occurs when government ensures that the basic structure is in place for the market to function. Global institutions such as the International Monetary Fund (IMF), World Trade Organization (WTO) and the World Bank (WB) have indefatigably promoted the virtues of free markets and pushed reform in reluctant countries. During the last four decades many developing countries have embraced, with varying degrees of conviction and success, a process of restructuring their economies to develop well-functioning markets.

Russia and China have incorporated many aspects of market economy into their command economies. However results in these two countries could hardly be more different. China transitioned from being a mostly agrarian economy to become an industrial and technological power rapidly catching up with the most developed countries. Russia's gross domestic product (GDP) shrunk by a third during its decade of transformation to a market economy (1989 to 2000).[3] Russia quickly transitioned from being an industrial and technological titan – Russia put the first satellite into orbit – into a natural resource producer. In the same period, 1989 to 2000, Moldavia and the Ukraine fared worse: their GDP was reduced by two-thirds in their transition to market economies. Hungary, Slovenia and Slovakia successfully transformed their economies but their GDP did not increase substantially during the period.[4]

The market economy remains a subject of discussion. One criticism is its inability to create sustainable welfare. The issues of dispersion of resources and pollution come immediately to mind. A second important factor that causes headaches for policy makers concerns the complex relationship between the physical economy and monetary policy which can lead to 'bubbles', recessions and unemployment.[5] The third arrow of criticism which will be covered in this chapter is the fact that inequality is inherent in a neoliberal market economy. Those on the lowest rung of the ladder are often not in a position to generate a basic income.[6]

Despite such disadvantages market economies are often seen as a good thing. This chapter will first review the fundamentals of economic systems: how markets work, and their potential limitations and impact on welfare. It will also explore differences between the ideals of the free market and the realities of market economies, including the measures that governments have to take to allow the economy to function smoothly. Because market economies are themselves not capable of solving all problems, the tasks and measures which require government control will be emphasized, and to what extent government intervention should go beyond creating conditions for a well-functioning market. The chapter ends with a discussion of the causes of financial crises, which, according to XIXth century economist Karl Marx, are an inevitable consequence of capitalism which will eventually lead to its self-destruction.

Learning objectives

At the end of this chapter, readers will be able to:

- Understand the basic principles of economics and types of economic systems.
- Understand differences between the free market and the market economy.
- Understand alternative views on roles of the state in market economies.
- Understand the impact of market economies on welfare, distribution of wealth and occurrence of economic crisis.

2.1   Definitions and basic concepts

Economics' central problem is scarcity: human wants exceed the resources available to satisfy such wants. As a consequence, societies must make three basic choices about allocation of resources: what to produce (product mix choice); how to produce (factor combination choice); and for whom to produce (income distribution choice). They are difficult choices because scarcity implies a trade-off between alternatives. Whatever the alternative chosen by society in terms of using resources, there will be groups that would have preferred the others. The value of these alternatives that have been foregone is known as the opportunity cost of the chosen use.[7] For instance, when a firm invests in a new marketing campaign, the opportunity cost of such a decision is the value of the best alternative use of the investment (for instance buying additional machinery, hiring more employees or developing new products).

Societies differ in the methods and systems used to make allocation choices. Methods reflect the values, beliefs, traditions and goals of each society. Choice is therefore a very complex task. Economics aims to simplify choice by providing principles to improve methods of allocation of resources. The first simplification is that a decision must result from rational choice. Choice is rational when perceived benefits exceed opportunity costs. The second simplification is that choice should maximize society's net value. Net value is maximized when there is productive and allocative efficiency. Productive efficiency exists when production of outputs is maximized with minimal use of resources. Allocative efficiency is achieved when it is not possible to produce more of a good without producing less of another. Economic systems are methods used by society to allocate resources rationally and efficiently.[8]

Free markets and hierarchies (or command economies) are alternative economic systems. In hierarchies all decisions are made by a central planning authority which owns resources and decides what is to be produced, how and for whom. Today, only North Korea is a pure example. In the free market, economic resources are privately owned while customers and producers are free to decide by themselves what to produce, how and for whom. Markets are decentralized because allocation of resources is the outcome of aggregating many individual decisions, each of them based on self-interest. This is called the invisible hand. Although the invisible hand has proven distinctly more efficient than command economies, there are no pure free market economies. Real-world market economies combine free market and hierarchy. Governments still play an important role for two reasons: a) the inability of markets to deliver some types of goods (for instance police protection) and b) to correct imperfections of the market system (for instance marginalization of the needs of those with low incomes).[9] A particular type of market imperfection is 'boom' and 'bust', the cyclical economic and financial crisis affecting capitalist economies.[10]

The extent to which governments should intervene is controversial. Three main views can be identified. *Neoclassical economics* (also called neoliberal) argues that many problems labelled as 'market imperfections', such as monopolies, are due to a lack of the right conditions for well-functioning markets. Governments must 'get the basics right' for the creation of such conditions, providing macroeconomic stability and a reliable legal framework to promote competition while protecting property rights. *Revisionist views* contend that a wide range of market failures are likely to happen even in well-functioning markets. For instance, in 1993, a landmark World Bank report on the 'East Asian miracle' stated that markets have shown systematic failure to channel investment to those industries that can generate highest growth for the economy as a whole.[11] Therefore, non-market coordination mechanisms are needed when markets fail. Governments must have a vigilant role and selectively intervene to prevent crises and failures. At the other extreme, *Austrian economics* rejects all kind of government interference and sees market imperfections as virtues; waves of prosperity are followed by painful but necessary adjustment, where those previously marginalized have chances to benefit from change (as in the French Revolution). Intervention in a crisis only prolongs agony. Austrian economics informs Joseph Schumpeter's theory of creative destruction, which will be discussed later in this chapter.[12]

2.2 Welfare and the market economy

2.2.1 The forward march of the market economy

The market economy is the result of laws, tax, subsidies, grants and the existing political regime. Some countries choose to exert major influence in areas such as education, health service and public utilities. They also tend to maintain strong control over social services. Other countries choose less stringent controls, permitting the fluctuations of supply and demand to determine market buoyancy. This section will be examining free market theory. 'Free market' is a purely theoretical concept and is contrary to the market economy whose parameters are determined by governments themselves. Before delving into free market theory we will examine the history of the market economy.

Fifteenth-century Europe saw the first improvements in public welfare but similar developments were not taking place in China. This may sound strange, because in the 1400s China and Middle Eastern societies were technologically more advanced than Europe. China already had firearms, printing presses, hydraulic clocks, a magnetic compass and ships capable of sailing long distances. Within China there were also good roads, an expansive waterway network and irrigation and canals. People used currency for trading, and economic traffic was largely regulated by the market. Far ahead of its time, China was producing goods that can be categorized as mass production. In the fifteenth century, China also had a well-developed and functional bureaucratic regime.[13] Public education was widespread and for a time almost 20% of the population resided in cities.[14]

European growth from 1500 was due to other reasons. Fierce rivalry existed between many countries. Economic improvement was the main objective of growth with little emphasis placed on political expansion.[15] The nineteenth- and early twentieth-century sociologist Max Weber first coined the term capitalism. He declared that capital accumulation was an integral aspect of the creation of the market economy. In this system the propertied middle and upper class invested their money in production methods. This led to a situation where societies were more capable of providing essential goods, resulting in more products being mass-produced but requiring less labour. Weber goes on to state that capitalism can only develop when a governing body is appointed which functions effectively with clearly definable objectives. Capitalism can succeed when government leaders invoke a rational administration which includes implementing laws that make a contribution to the general welfare.[16] Weber sees capitalism as the successor to feudalism, a system where wealthy landowners maintained power by leasing parts of their immense lands to others according to specific conditions. He shows that such systems were not conducive for capital accumulation, as the development of improved production methods was not seen as a way of creating a better functioning society. European countries also had different attitudes towards savings. Max Weber explains that hard-working Calvinist countries such as Switzerland attached more importance to investing for the future than producing for direct consumption which led to a higher national percentage of money being saved. For a country's economic development this is an important point because higher national savings sets capital accumulation in motion. This relatively high level of 'average propensity to save' (APS) in the nineteenth century was the catalyst for investment in infrastructure, buildings, ships and many other goods for the general public, and led to the increase in mass production for future generations.

2.2.2 Liberalism and the market economy

We can safely assume that the market economy provided society with the rational groundwork for improved and more efficient operation although this was not an automatic consequence. John Locke (1632–1704) and John Lilburne (1614–1657) were early proponents of government's role in promoting welfare and freedom. They pleaded for the concept of 'liberalism' which arose in response to poor governing policies of ruling kings and emperors. Strong emphasis was placed on individuals' right to express their opinion and the freedom to conduct business.[17]

Carrying the argument a step further, Adam Smith (1723–1790) published *An Inquiry into the Nature and Causes of the Wealth of Nations* in 1776. This famous book presents a strong plea for the market economy and contends that society is best served when people can freely pursue their own interests. It is also an encouragement of competition in business with individuals and companies striving for increased efficiency. The division of work whereby tradespeople and factories provide specialized products and services using modern techniques is a major point of the book.

Adam Smith believed that the 'profit motive' had a positive effect on everyone. His famous quote, 'It is not from the benevolence of the butcher, the brewer or the baker that we expect our dinner, but from their regard to their own interest'[18] alludes to ample freedom being provided in the creation of laws and rules which should not only be seen as ways of correcting negative aspects of the human condition. Every individual has an inborn desire for personal success and attaining higher goals. Rich and poor must be allowed access to the market. Effective laws must also include provisions for property rights so that business and professionals are not subject to unfair bias, decided behind closed doors, by courts and governments either on local or national levels.[19]

2.2.3 The market economy and citizens' well-being

Nineteenth-century German economist Karl Marx (1813–1883) proposed radical new theories about the role of economics in society. He was critical of the inhuman work ethic of the Industrial Revolution and its effect on the working-class poor.[20] He introduced the word 'proletariat' for people with no tangible possessions and pointed out discrepancies between the 'haves' and the 'have nots'. Adam Smith's ideas came under scrutiny in his work as Marx believed that the free market was not a guarantee that everyone would be able to earn a decent wage. Marx demonstrated that the proletariat (working class) had few rights and were heavily dependent on the wealthy. In the event of any economic downturn, the working class were the first to lose their jobs. He pointed out that within a capitalistic structure, this group formed the largest revolutionary opposition. Marx also contended that capitalism was intrinsically instable and prone to cycles of growth (boom) followed by depression (bust).[21] He prophesied that crises would be increasingly severe and become capitalism's undoing. Marx's solution was the rejection of capitalism and 'citizens' democracy' and replacing it with a centrally controlled social economy. His ideas were embraced by several countries, notably Russia and China. During the Russian Revolution of 1917, Vladimir Lenin (1870–1924) successfully exploited Marx's ideas during his rise to power. Production was determined by the government. Business and the private sector were not granted free access to the market. This concept became known as a 'command economy' or 'planned economy' and is diametrically opposite to the principles of the market economy.[22] These are theoretical concepts and, just like the market economy, they do not exist in pure form. The twentieth century provided much debate about the advantages and disadvantages of each system, especially for the lower classes, and which system offered the most welfare. At the end of the millennium there was hardly any further debate because by that time both Russia and China had embraced the market economy. Marx's theories also played an important role in western European countries.[23] The creation of organized trade unions marked a major step for better working conditions. Safety nets such as social legislation, affordable communal housing, the minimum wage and health insurance also owe their existence to Marxist ideas. As we will see in Chapter 8, the IMF and WTO were also created with the explicit objective of proving Marx wrong in saying that capitalism was doomed.

2.3 Neoclassical free-market framework

Many governments advocate the market economy for the simple reason that they consider it to be the best system for welfare improvement, but there are differences in its degree of application. The United States, for example, has a stronger belief in the free market than Germany or China.[24] The extent of the free market's endorsement is dependent on cultural and historical factors but also on governments' weighing of positive and negative elements of the free market and their willingness to bestow power on other parties. Supporters claim that a relaxed approach ensures a smoother flow of goods without suffocating rules and regulations. Free trade creates improved welfare through optimal allocation of scarce resources, whether land, labour or technological know-how, into a coherent whole. Successful business ventures prove their worth by providing high returns and efficient management. Those who operate inefficiently or are unaware of market trends either go bankrupt or cease operations. These elements will be examined in the following sections. The differences between neoclassical (neoliberal) theory and reality will be covered so as to present a clear picture of the market economies' pros and cons.

2.3.1   Gross national product

In primitive economies without foreign trading partners, consumption is roughly at the same level as production. Abundant land for hunting and planting, simple tools and the input of human labour provide goods which are meant for direct consumption although some of the produced goods are set aside for use at a later date.[25] In our own history, during successive centuries, humankind learned to make useful instruments such as tools and machines. In the early years, with a simple economy, the labour involved in making an instrument or tool was in itself a form of savings. When society developed better production methods, increased output and consumption were the result. The term 'technology/know-how' refers to the combination of skilled workers, modern techniques and the same working hours leading to increased production. Today's welfare owes a large debt to technology, know-how and also to the reserve capital that has been invested in machinery, housing, factories etc.

At the time of writing some societies are still in a savings and investment mode, with consumption relatively low. This is the current situation in China where business, government and the private sector manage to save quite a bit and the average propensity to save is more than 50% (according to 2008 figures).[26] In these types of societies a high amount of goods and services are produced that do not contribute to present-day welfare but prove their worthiness in the future. Examples include business investments for the future and parents who willingly provide for their children's education hoping that their eventual success will generate improved welfare for succeeding generations.

Gross national product (GNP) is the way in which welfare improvement can be measured per individual and is to a great extent determined by labour participation and labour productivity. In a country where children, students and elderly are relatively sparse, the labour participation is conversely higher. Labour productivity comes from capital invested in machines and houses, the level of technology and the level of skills (education). Countries with a high productivity produce more goods and services per person.

Box 2.1   Personal income at the end of the nineteenth century in the Netherlands[27, 28]

In 1898 a good weaver working a 60-hour week could expect to earn a monthly wage of around €17.73. From this amount 17% went towards a two-roomed dwelling with no sanitation, gas, light or shower facilities. The leftover income was spent on food and drink. A loaf of bread was 9.0 euro cents, a kilo of potatoes 5.3 cents and an egg 1.3 cents. Coffee and sugar were seen as relatively expensive. A half pound of coffee was 32 euro cents and 250 grams of sugar was 52 cents.

(Continued)

In today's world the net income of skilled craftsman is around €1,612 monthly.[29] Using the same percentage of income for the identical expenditures, the breakdown would look like this.

- A very modest two-room house or apartment: €268
- 1 loaf of bread: €8.34
- 1 kilo of potatoes: €4.91
- 10 eggs: €9.49
- Half pound of coffee: €29.85
- Half pound of sugar: €48.15

In the nineteenth century productivity was low and people worked longer hours for modest rewards. Most people lived in rented accommodation. Meat was a luxury and most meals consisted of stews and spuds (potatoes). The main furniture was limited to a high table, a few chairs and a wooden bench. People slept on straw mattresses with oat-filled pillows. Leisure activities took place close to home. A 'holiday/vacation' was an unknown concept. People joined choral societies or amateur theatre groups. In those days productivity and wages were much lower and this meant that people had to work long and hard to provide for their families.

2.3.2 Freedom and equality for market participants

Freedom and equality for all market participants is a major theme of the free market because one's position in society has no bearing on the right to do business. The realization of an ideal free market goes hand in hand with fair laws, unambiguous rules and a minimum of corruption.[30] The government has the power to enforce property rights and is responsible for ensuring that every participant is treated fairly and this leads to a situation where more people are encouraged to enter the market economy. Hence, government is necessary to facilitate a 'level playing field'.

Box 2.2 Bureaucracy: Friend or foe?

Bureaucracy is a fact of life in many developing countries. It is not enough when well-meaning central governments rationalize laws to decrease red tape for entrepreneurs. National and local government often work together and the interests of each are not always represented but they both owe their existence to bureaucracy. To begin with, it creates jobs and spawns conditions for mild and serious forms of corruption. For many educated people the government means a coveted civil service job and bureaucracy serves as valued ally although there is an important difference between central and local government. Central government has a direct interest in limiting corruption because its legitimacy is strengthened if welfare improves. Local government, on the other hand, benefits less from decreased corruption and red tape because the larger local government organizations have the possibility of assuming powerful positions which makes it possible to generate income through corruption.[31]

A good example of how this works in a developing country is the government of Tanzania which has for over two decades made a concentrated effort to decrease

(Continued)

bureaucracy to benefit the market. This gives businesses a better chance of an entry or exit strategy. In 2004 any requests in Tanzania for business grants or permission involved 26 different stages and took at least 313 days to complete.[32] By 2010 this was reduced to 12 stages and 29 days.[33]

2.3.3 Invisible hand

An advantage of the free market is that government does not dictate what goods are produced and by whom.[34] Companies decide for themselves which products and services are to be made available. Government provides continuity. This non-regulatory concept is called the 'invisible hand'. The price level has an influence on supply and demand. Overproduction can lead to a decrease in price and can force companies to curtail or stop production. In other words the 'glut' of goods disappears without government intervention. The opposite is also true: when demand exceeds supply, prices will rise and this becomes a more appealing option for business. Again, no government assistance is necessary.

The mechanisms of supply and demand and market transparency provide goods that the public wants. Adam Smith stated that the invisible hand is self-regulatory. This is an advantage of a market economy and it is good that the government has a limited role. But it would be a mistake to assume that Smith is pleading for a fully free market. He realized early that even in a totally free market, situations can occur that conflict with general interests, especially if trading partners are dealing with a view to personal gain.[35]

2.3.4 Market discipline

In well-functioning transparent markets with limited entrepreneurial risk, the profit margin is lower because competition dissipates profit margins.[36] In other words, the price of goods and services is equal to production costs multiplied by compensation for invested capital and the production process. This implies that high profit margins are the exception to the rule especially when it comes to goods with a technology that can easily be reproduced by competitors. Businesses in this sector must ensure that their production costs are in line with market parameters, otherwise losses will occur. Government has the challenge of creating policy to encourage competition. India put this into practice with the trade liberalization laws passed in the 1990s and this led to production growth.[37] But there were also negative effects. Research on the Indian economy has shown that unemployment did increase in the short term but it seems that trade liberalization has not worked negatively on total employment in the long term. Parallel research studies have concluded that Indian liberalization did have a negative effect on wage inequality.[38]

Michael Porter's 1990s study on 'market discipline' and economic growth stated that companies are compelled to continuously innovate and keep prices low in order to stay ahead of competitors. This means that competition is a driver to produce identical or similar goods for less which has a positive effect on welfare.[39]

2.3.5 Money streams to profit

The invisible hand plays a role not only in what is produced but also where it is made. Companies with good profit margins and savings-minded consumers create fluidity in the money market. With the banks as intermediaries, money is targeted to enterprises with the most potential and which are most likely to progress. This 'money streams to profit' motive was responsible for Western businesses' and banks' investment in China in the 1980s.[40] The money was targeted for labour-intensive industries (toys and clothing) which were capable of reducing costs with a minimum of investment.

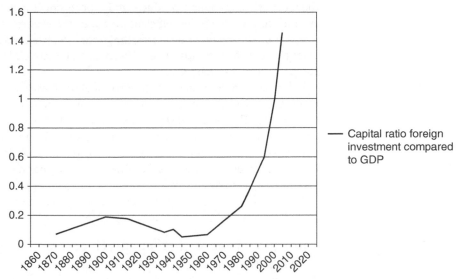

Figure 2.1   Average domestic assets owned by the non-resident worldwide
Data: Obstfeld and Taylor; Lane and Ferretti[41]

2.3.6   Comparative advantages

The WTO encourages freedom of international trade and says this is a good thing for economic development and well-being.[42] This has resulted in governments having to strive for good import and export procedures while at the same time remaining alert to denying subsidies to companies so they can better compete with goods produced abroad. This vision constitutes a basic principle when government sets down rules for international trade. Foreign business gives by nature a more dynamic competition. Governments tend to stimulate such competition based on the assumption that protection has drawbacks because welfare lags behind and there is insufficient stimulus for business to be innovative. But not every country can deal with international competition and in the short term and sometimes even in the long term this can lead to less employment.[43]

One of the first nineteenth-century scientists who commented on the link between welfare and open borders was David Ricardo (1772–1823). He formulated the theory of comparative cost advantages and argued that trade between countries is a key to prosperity even if one country has more efficient production methods than the other. If all goods and services are more efficiently produced in one country than in another with less capacity, international trade can still benefit the less and the more efficient country, while at the same time expanding consumption. This will happen because even the most inefficient country has a comparative advantage in the production of some goods if it is relatively more efficient than others in the production of such goods. The comparison of productive efficiency is made in terms of opportunity costs. When a country uses resources to produce one good, it can't use the same resources to produce another good. The opportunity cost of producing a certain quantity of Good A is the quantity of another Good B the country could have produced with the same resources it deployed to produce Good A. As long as the opportunity costs of producing A and B differ among countries, there are potential benefits from trade. The term 'comparative cost advantages' is thus a conscious choice and suggests that a poorer country can benefit from trade even though it is less efficient in absolute terms. This will happen if the more efficient country produces and exports only the goods which it is 'most best' at producing, while the less efficient produces and exports the goods which it is 'least worst' at producing (in other words, the goods in which it has relatively less opportunity costs and therefore comparative advantage).[44] See Box 2.3 for a further exploration of comparative cost advantages.

In his day Ricardo pleaded for international trade within the UK, then a very controversial topic promoted by the Conservative government and resisted by the opposition Whig Party.[45] This type of discussion still goes on today, especially in times of recession when business must deal with a shrinking market.[46] Governments tend to lend less support to struggling local businesses and resist the pressure from business to introduce import duties, quotas and subsidies. This non-intervention policy is based on the law of comparative cost advantages.

Box 2.3   Theory of comparative cost advantages applied to East and West[47, 48]

Imagine two countries called East and West. East is considerably larger than West and has 150 hours per day available for work (15 workers working a 10 hour day). West only has 100 hours (10 workers working a 10 hour day). Both countries produce rice and potatoes. It takes East 5 hours to produce a kilo of rice while West can do the same job in 4 hours. Time plays an even more important role for the potato crop, with East taking 15 hours to produce 1 kilo of potatoes and West taking only 5 hours.

If the two countries do not do business with each other, East will only be able to produce 30 kilos of rice and no potatoes. If it would rather plant potatoes, the maximum output is 10 kilos. Without a trading partner East must decide if rice, potatoes or a combination is best suited to its needs. In Figure 2.2 you can see the consumption line if East does not trade with West.

A similar consumption line can be shown for West. Without a partner West can produce 25 kilos of rice or 20 kilos of potatoes or a combination of both and the internal harvest will be the same as required by the public.

A simple mathematical formula can demonstrate the advantages if both countries trade with each other. The improved positions are dependent on the prices that are agreed upon. Price policy and price fixing are not subjects for discussion in this book. The following table and Figure 2.2 will highlight the results of the contrasting systems.

	East	West
Work needed for 1 kilo of rice	5 hours	4 hours
Work needed for 1 kilo of potatoes	15 hours	5 hours
Maximum available hours	150 hours	100 hours
Maximum rice consumption without trade	30 kilos	25 kilos
Maximum potato consumption without trade	10 kilos	20 kilos

(Continued)

East is less efficient than West in the production of both rice and potatoes. However, when West allocates resources to produce a kilo of rice, it is giving up the opportunity to produce 0.8 kilos of potatoes (the opportunity cost is 0.8). For East, the opportunity cost of producing 1 kilo of rice is 0.3 kilos of potatoes. Therefore, East has a comparative advantage in the production of rice: it has to give up less production of potatoes than West. We can calculate the comparative efficiency for rice and potatoes as the ratio between work needed to produce the good in East divided by work needed to produce the good in West. For rice such a ratio is 5/4 = 1.25. That means that producing a kilo of rice in East requires 25% more work than producing it in West. For potatoes the ratio is 15/5 = 3, thus producing 1 kilo of potatoes in East requires 300% more work than producing the same amount in West. Therefore, West is the 'most best' at producing potatoes (it has both absolute and comparative advantage as rice producer), while East is the 'least worst' at producing rice (it has a comparative advantage as rice producer). Therefore West should allocate all its resources to producing potatoes while East should allocate all its resources to producing rice.

If they do so, then the total production of rice will be 30 kilos (150 hours divided by 5 hours/kilo), whereas the total production of potatoes will be 20 kilos. If West allocated all its resources to producing rice and East to producing potatoes then total production of rice would be 25 kilos whereas the total production of potatoes would be 10 kilos. You are invited to try different combinations. You'll see that every combination yields less total production than the allocation of resources following comparative advantages.

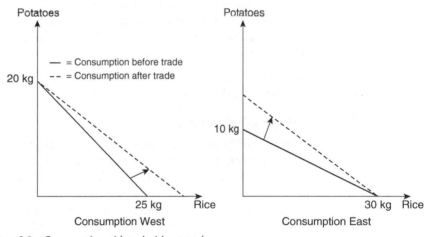

Figure 2.2 Consumption with and without trade

2.4 Limitations of market regulation through supply and demand

In the 1980s and 90s a number of Asian, Latin American and African countries initiated reforms to give better meaning to the market economy. They did this by allowing more freedom with less government intervention in areas of investment and price forming. China and the Soviet Union, the strongest advocates of Communism, also began cautiously to look in the other direction.[49] The fall of the Berlin Wall in 1989 was a milestone in the demise of Communism and state-controlled economics. Many East European countries were quick to introduce major reforms. The idea that a free market is in a better position to increase prosperity with less government control became gradually accepted worldwide, although there are some obvious drawbacks. One of the causes of market failure is the absence of the correct information.[50] The market is not transparent and buyers had limited insight into the price/quality of suppliers. Another aspect of market failure is the lack of competition if one or a limited group of suppliers can get a dominant position in the market.[51] A third aspect of market failure which will be covered in Section 2.4 concerns the instability of economic growth.[52] This uneven growth has had to deal with bouts of recession and even depression. Themes examined in Sections 2.4 and 2.5 include the question of the markets' ability to provide a solution for the allocation of scarce materials and whether all aspects are considered when determining the price of goods. Obviously, the payments for goods and services provided by market participants are not reflecting the total economic spectrum.[53] Many things that we take for granted such as clean air, safety, health care and education do not fall under the realm of the free market. Sections 2.4 and 2.5 will therefore consider the disadvantages of the 'free market'.

2.4.1   Perfect information

How the market economy functions is dependent on rational decisions taken by participants and therefore it is important that all the necessary information is available.[54] Only when the market offers clear insight into possibilities for the present and future can people negotiate rationally and take the best decisions when it comes to investment or purchasing. Theorists proclaim 'perfect information' as a pipe dream and consider its lack to be one of the reasons for market failure.

There are several reasons why perfect information remains in the realm of theory rather than an actual concept. The following paragraph will discuss two factors that have a negative effect on transparency:

- Incomplete insight into price/quality relations.
- Changing conditions.

Price/quality relations

Without sufficient transparency in the market, buyers do not get a complete picture of the relationship between price and quality in the goods being offered. Different methods are used to correct this. For instance, the Dutch government has introduced an energy efficiency rating which requires house owners wishing to sell their properties to conduct an 'energy check' to confirm if the house meets current standards of energy use. A classification of seven levels (A to G) is given to the house after the inspection and this gives potential buyers a clearer picture of what they can expect in the form of expenses for gas, water, electricity etc.

In business, transparency also benefits the seller especially when a good product is on offer. Potential customers will make quicker decisions to buy and have less doubt.[55] Companies provide additional transparency by offering guarantees, seals of approval and extensive documentation.

Changing conditions

Changing market conditions also mean that participants do not possess the information needed for rational, good decisions. Trying to predict how products will fare in the future is often a waste of time for investors and market participants. Supply and demand factors can change with little or no warning and market trends can take unexpected detours. Government can also play a role by imposing new legislation and lower or higher taxes. Any combination of these factors can lead to poor decision making, resulting in a disappointing return for the investor. For the market economy, optimal distribution of resources remains a 'fixed idea'.[56]

Box 2.4   Command economies have also problems with resource allocation

Many countries have opted for a form of market economy whereby the price of the goods offered is, for most of the goods, an indication of their scarcity. These economies cannot function optimally for several reasons such as the lack of 'perfect information'.[57] The allocation of resources could, theoretically considered, be better, which is easily observable in the many countries with severe unemployment. The alternative, the 'command economy', was experimented with in several communist countries. However, this type of economy does not function optimally, either. Those governments who adopted it took it upon themselves to control resource allocation and government bureaus decided how resources were to be used. Quotas determined what the industrial and farming sectors should produce which led to imbalances in supply and demand.[58] The citizens of these countries had, for example, access to large supplies of toilet paper but staples such as grain were hard to come by.

2.4.2   Forms of monopoly

Whether markets function well is, among other things, dependent on whether or not companies compete with each other without creating artificial or natural monopolies.[59] An 'artificial monopoly' exists when businesses make deals to mitigate competition. Artificial monopolies are also referred to as cartels and define secret deals that are made behind closed doors. A 'natural monopoly' exists when there is only room for a single provider and this is often the case when large investments are made for services yet to be introduced to the public. Electricity and water supply are good examples. They require huge financial input for the setting up of networks and the consumer benefits from the fact that one provider is responsible, thus eliminating the need for competition. A natural monopoly implies that the company must invest heavily in costly infrastructure but has the benefit of keeping prices lower because expenses are divided among thousands of consumers. This concept of a single provider offering low-priced services to a large population is referred to as 'economy of scale'.

All forms of monopoly put any provider in a strong position. There are few obstacles to bringing low-priced goods to the market because there is no competition. Inversely, market strength can lead to companies asking a higher price which, because of the lack of competition, means higher profits. Therefore, monopoly is diametrically opposed to the purpose of the market economy: increased prosperity for all citizens.

There is a role for government in assessing companies' misuse of market power with the means to limit unbridled market power by anti-trust legislation.[60] There are many countries where large enterprises with considerable clout can be forced to turn down a merger proposal with other large companies operating in a similar market. Also there are governments that are capable of limiting the freedom of the pricing of goods produced by natural monopolies.

Market economies such as the US and European Union (EU) have strong anti-trust laws to prevent the formation of monopolies. The US Sherman–Clayton Act regulates practices that may violate fair competition. These include, for instance, setting prices too low to get rid of competitors, exclusivity agreements with distributors or merging with competitors to dominate a market. The US prosecution of Microsoft on these grounds is an example of the seriousness of the matter for governments. An initial ruling by Judge Jackson decided that Microsoft should be split in two. After a lengthy process of appeals a settlement was agreed. Microsoft did not split but had to accept several changes in its policies. Computer manufacturers were allowed to use competing software with Microsoft's operating system. Microsoft was forbidden to retaliate against customers supporting competing software and exclusivity contracts were banned. In the EU, Coca-Cola anti-trust laws were applied, for instance, to prevent Coca-Cola from having exclusivity agreements with retailers which would have restricted their sale of Pepsi-Co products.

The application of anti-trust laws has sometimes been used politically to further national interests and prevent foreign companies from taking over markets. A landmark case was the EU versus Boeing/McDonnell Douglas. The merge of aircraft manufacturers Boeing and McDonnell Douglas had been approved by the US anti-trust commission. However, the European Commission determined that this was anti-competitive in the European commercial aircraft sector. But rather than blocking the merger in Europe they asked Boeing to cancel an exclusive sales agreement with US airlines. This agreement would have excluded EU company Airbus from selling in the American market. The case shows how globalization has changed the rules of the game. EU legislation was used to prevent an American company excluding European competitors from the American market.

2.4.3   Long- and short-term pricing

A smoothly running market economy is dependent on price being a reflection of scarcity. Questions are now being asked about the long-term effects of short supply. Analysts assume that short-term supply and demand in the market is self-regulatory. Prognoses for long-term scarcity are not concerned with major fluctuations. It seems that future shortages have little influence on the owners of the gas, oil and metal industries. Analysts have demonstrated that the price of crude oil rose in 2000–2008 from $30 per barrel to more than $100 due to a large extent to increased demand from China, among other countries, and the fact that refineries were not able to keep up with the demand on a worldwide level.[61] It seems that long-term shortages of oil for about 20–30 years are not an important factor in the price. It could mean that current oil prices are lower than is theoretically necessary. This results in less investment by people and industry in alternative energy forms because oil is considered relatively cheap. This long-term prosperity scenario could come under pressure especially if predictions about the limits of future oil reserves are proven true and there are insufficient alternatives at hand.

Box 2.5   Forecast of the oil peak 40 years ago

The predictions of author Donella Meadows (with colleagues) in the 1972 book *The Limits to Growth* still apply today.[62] Their thoughts about decreased future natural resources have not needed new interpretation. According to their theory, oil production will start to decline around the year 2020 which matches the current

(Continued)

predictions of the International Energy Agency (IEA). Insiders in the field of oil exploration agrees with these statistics. The 'oil peak' is the moment when day-to-day oil production starts to decrease. From that moment supplies will decrease despite new discoveries and improved drilling methods. The oil peak is an important issue for policy makers because the economy must be ready with alternatives to fossil fuel.

2.4.4   Unbalanced growth

Advocates of the market economy state that its success is largely due to the rational behaviour and self-interest of humans as 'homo economicus', but in the real world such a concept is purely theoretical.[63] Human emotions have a strong influence on the market economy. John Maynard Keynes referred to it as the animal spirit and described how this affects purchase and investment decisions to the extent that these choices are dependent on emotions, instinct and preferences.[64] Animal spirit is one of the causes of unbalanced growth.[65] The emotional influence on unbalanced growth can be better understood through the concepts of 'bubbles' and 'self-fulfilling prophecy'.

Bubbles occur when investors expect a higher than average return on future profits and therefore invest more than good sense would dictate. Incorrect allocation of capital is the consequence. Bubbles limit prosperity because high expectations are not always fulfilled and this wastes, among the more obvious resources, human energy.

The Internet bubble

Between 1995 and 2000, investors poured huge sums of money into start-up Internet companies. They envisioned a 'get rich quick' return from this new branch of technology but were not prone to take a critical look. Money invested in the new companies was proportionally higher than projected profit margins. As time progressed many of these start-up companies failed to meet expectations and made little profit or suffered losses, which led to closure and bankruptcy. In 2003 many educated people who went to work for Internet companies found themselves unemployed which led to a dip in economic growth.[66]

Investors get caught up in bubbles when poor decisions are made about putting money into areas such as land, labour, machinery and technological know-how. The invested resources are not wisely spent. Many Internet companies produced goods that the general public had little use for. More patience and rational thought on the part of investors could have stimulated production of more useful products which would have increased prosperity.

In addition to investor over-enthusiasm in supporting new ventures, the consumer can also be responsible for uneven economic development. The US housing market is a good example. From 2000 to 2009 house prices soared.[67] The price increases were more than ten times higher than average inflation and price developments like this are often unsustainable and/or irrational. Potential buyers felt that all property would increase in value within a reasonable time. These types of sentiments can induce a bubble, and when a bubble bursts this can have severe consequences for the particular industry or the economy as a whole. In the case of the British housing sector this resulted in fewer transactions and houses being sold for less than their perceived value. Many potential buyers were scared away by the insecurity in the market.

Self-fulfilling prophecy

The market economy also has to deal with the idea of 'self-fulfilling prophecy' or self-confirmed predictions.[68] The term is used in situations that do not initially appear to be true but later gain credibility because the public as a whole believes them to be so. Consumers and investors can be upbeat about the economy even if facts and figures present a less florid picture. Money changes hands rapidly, providing an impulse to demand in the economy, and employment, technology, land and production thrive. Because of the tangible buoyancy, people are positive about the economy and spend their money quickly. Banks are also important players in this upbeat scenario and money is widely available for consumers. People are encouraged to make use of it and, all in all, the velocity of currency circulating in the economy increases. This would seem to have a positive effect on welfare but the negative side of the self-fulfilling prophecy should not be neglected. When people are pessimistic about the economy it can result in stagnation and slow-down which can lead to recession or, in the worst case, depression. Self-fulfilling prophecy is an intrinsic part of the market economy and contributes to its unstable growth (see Figure 2.3).

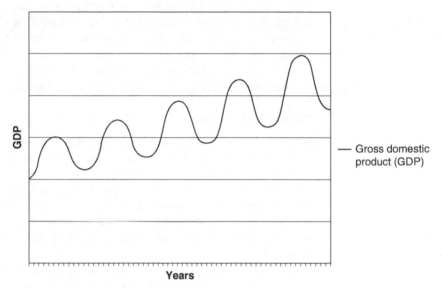

Figure 2.3   The typical unstable growth of the market economy

Creative destruction

Competition is by nature national and international which creates dynamics that can often be experienced as a hard reality. Opportunities exist, although not every business is capable of surviving in the international market. At the end of the 1970s ship building and the textile industry were heavily represented in the Dutch economy but had difficulties competing with Asian companies. Despite government subsidy, many of these enterprises failed. The demise of these operations caused a major policy rethink for the Dutch government. Subsidy was granted to innovative companies and was diminished for or denied to those unable to keep pace. This change of policy was based on the theory of 'creative destruction' that was proposed by Joseph Schumpeter in 1913.[69] Schumpeter used the term to indicate that the innovative companies which make use of new technology replace the ones still adhering to old ideas and so not able to compete effectively. Schumpeter believed that technical improvement is the only true source for economic growth and pleaded for governments to stop subsidies for old-fashioned companies even though closure and unemployment were obvious consequences. Successful innovation leading to higher productivity equals improved welfare. Note that the neoclassical economics free-market framework advises against any type of subsidies, regardless of a company being innovative or not. Schumpeter's ideas are representative of a group of economists broadly labelled as the Austrian school of economics.

2.5 How the market economy affects prosperity, well-being and environment

Those countries with well-regulated property rights and limited bureaucracy within the market economy framework often can point to success but this is by no means the total picture.[70] A market cannot solve all the problems of prosperity, well-being and environment. We will look at some of these topics in this section.

2.5.1 Collective goods

When goods (products and services) are offered to the market it is important to recognize that the government can be a valuable partner. For some goods, government intervention is essential otherwise the good would not be produced or only marginally.[71] These type of goods are called collective goods. We will now discuss governments' contribution to prosperity, well-being and environment in the areas of useful products and services.

Public goods

This concept refers to products and services not offered through the market. Think of public order, administration of justice and flood mitigation works. The government is the initiator of this type of service which must be offered to everyone and it is difficult to exclude any single individual. Everyone has certain obligations and participation can be required. Citizens for example, do not have a way to opt out of the justice system if they have committed a crime or major violation. A strong feature of pure collective goods prevents incurred extra costs being applied when an individual uses the services. Any humanitarian exclusion is also undesirable. The concept of collective goods forms one of the main building blocks of contemporary society.

Quasi-public goods

Education, health care, social services and some insurance fall under the category of quasi-public goods. The 'quasi' aspect comes into play when the good can be offered through the market but government has a role in supply and demand, which occurs for different reasons. Compulsory education is seen to benefit the general interest. If large segments of the population are well educated, society benefits as this group makes a strong contribution to the economy.[72] Humanitarian concerns in the form of social services also fall under the same heading. A third reason for quasi-government intervention is to discourage the free-rider problem. An example is the premium payment for health insurance that some countries demand of their citizens. The government in these countries has made this mandatory because the small percentage of people who are uninsured will eventually be treated at the cost of the insured. In this way the government is able to keep the free-rider problem to a minimum.

2.5.2   Goods with an incorrect price

Some items in the free market are not fairly priced because not all costs and profits are part of the price forming.[73] Externalities are positive or negative impacts on society that result from the production of an item which are not accounted for in the price of the item. The price is incorrect because it does not reflect society's interest in the product. The incorrect pricing means that either too much or too little of the product is being made available. Government's role in this type of situation is essential in order to ensure that the supply and demand does not have negative side effects for prosperity, welfare and well-being. Goods with external costs (negative externalities) and external benefits (positive externalities) and items with a negative value will be analysed further.

Goods with negative externalities

Negative externalities are uncompensated costs generated by the production of an item. Underpriced goods exist when the asking price of an item being brought to the market is too low and the seller has not included the costs of externalities. In the oil industry, the consumers' demand for gasoline has many consequences. Minerals needed to make gasoline are limited and often found in vulnerable eco-systems. Toxic fumes are released during the refining process and when the end product is used by the consumer.[74] In this situation society benefits from the government's role in overseeing supply and demand in order to curb environmental damage.[75] The extra regulatory guidelines such as excise and environment taxes put a price tag on products with harmful side effects.

Goods with positive externalities

Health care, education and social services are sectors that enjoy goods' external benefits. Good health is not only advantageous for the person concerned but it benefits family and employers as well. The same applies to education. Society benefits from offering education at a low price, so that the average educational level of the population increases. Positive externalities also play a pivotal role when applied to social services geared to combating income inequality. Results of different studies have shown that public health declines and the crime rate rises when income inequality increases.[76, 77] If market prices of services with high positive externalities are too high, the government has good reason to ensure that prices are kept within sensible limits by providing subsidy or a lower rate of tax.

Box 2.6   Educational investment in developing countries

Many developing countries see investment in education as a desirable goal but few bother to question whether the investment will be rewarded. Research by Adam Szirmai (1946–) sheds light on the subject.[78] He showed that many developing countries spend too much on general and university education. The range of the training is limited because the skills learned have little practical use in the developing countries. He makes a case for a more practical approach to include professional emphasis on technical skills for agriculture, steel, textiles and the construction industries. Such an approach was applied by East Asian countries such as Taiwan, South Korea, China, Taiwan and Malaysia in the initial stages of their development, later upgrading into technical skills for the electronics and telecommunications industries.

Goods with a negative value (bads)

Goods have a negative value (and are also known as bads) when the owner would rather get rid of them than try to make a profit. Old batteries, computers and refrigerators fall into this category and government strives to provide for their environmentally friendly disposal.

Merit goods and merit bads

Merit goods are those regarded by the state as having a special merit that is not fully understood by customers who would not buy as much of the product as needed to assure overall welfare. For instance, it is argued that primary education would not be bought by low-income customers even if they could afford it. For that reason primary education is free and subsidized by governments in the majority of countries. Merit bads include tobacco and drugs, judged to have harmful consequences which are underestimated by customers. Governments act to discourage consumption of 'merit bads'; the UK government, for instance, forced cigarette producers to include prominently in their packaging images of the ravages of tobacco-induced cancer and a banner warning about effects of tobacco on health.

2.5.3   Redistribution of prosperity

The options for providing equal rights for everyone in the market economy are limited.[79] Consumption is dependent on market insight, trade and barter capacity and available cash. Individual wealth, intelligence, social skills, health, clear thinking and the countries where people live are also major influences that, with the mechanics of pricing, allow goods to be evenly distributed. In societies where equality and solidarity are important, people realize that corrective measures can be applied beyond market boundaries. Think only of social services, changing tax structure, insurance companies and education subsidy. Redistribution of prosperity is supported by several ideas. Solidarity and protection of the weak is a major topic but other arguments can play a role. There is less tension when societal differences are kept to a minimum. The underprivileged do not participate in the official economy. A structure that promotes inequality has a high crime rate.[80] Prosperity suffers because increased budgets are needed for the police and the prison systems and people in general feel less safe. Income equality (see Box 2.7) creates a greater sense of trust but large income discrepancies do not contribute to a feeling of well-being and produce negative effects.[81] The final argument for increased equality is based on the principle of rational choice theory and the premise that wealth is a state of mind. A raise in salary of €100 for a low earner has more value than the same amount for someone earning a lot more.[82]

Box 2.7   Income equality[83]

The industrialized countries of the OECD (Organization for Economic Cooperation and Development) conducted a survey in 2011 comparing rich and poor and their effects on society. Average individual prosperity (based on GDP per person), was high in Sweden and Denmark, countries with a high income equality, though there are also poor countries with high income equality.

(Continued)

A country's income equality is determined using the Gini coefficient. In the OECD analysis of the 26 countries who were members for more than 20 years, results showed that 6 of the 10 richest scored highest in the category of income equality and hardly felt any effects of a lower level of prosperity. The two top scorers were Luxembourg and Norway with respective gross individual incomes of $113,000 and $94,400. Based on the previous figures, we can conclude that income equality is more likely to have a positive than a negative correlation to wealth.

2.5.4 The free market: Prosperity, well-being and environment

Since countries like Brazil, China and Russia have taken steps to liberalize their economies we can cautiously conclude that the market economy is slowly gaining acceptance as a way for countries to create prosperity.[84] However it is clear that in its purest form, many social questions have not been dealt with well by free markets. The market simply has too many rough edges for long-lasting welfare and well-being. Countries impose rules to suit their individual needs and do not strive for the purest interpretation of the idea of the free market. Governments intervene in varying degrees of intensity for environmental concerns, social security, health care, housing and income equality. On the other hand, misguided or chronic government intervention is counterproductive. Studies in France, for example, have shown that excessive government protection of employees has limited prosperity and the ability of the market to be flexible.[85] However, it would be foolish to use the idea of market freedom as a mantra for all problems. The minimum wage in UK has been an important element in increased productivity and changing tax laws have also assisted in creating more income equality and a better lifestyle.[86] Government watchdogs steer the market towards a more compact and coherent society, and non-market coordination mechanisms should be in place to prevent environmental and economic crisis when markets are working badly.

2.6 Economic and financial crises

An economic crisis is a market disruption. It occurs when the economic system is no longer able to allocate resources to satisfy the needs of society. Examples are recession and hyperinflation. A financial crisis is a particular type of economic crisis where investors lose confidence in the financial system and withdraw resources in mass. A main consequence of an economic crisis is a drastic increase in unemployment. As people withdraw money from the financial system and restrict consumption, aggregated demand falls, in turn causing reductions in welfare, growth and prosperity. Economic crises often have political, social and institutional consequences.

2.6.1 Crisis and economics schools

The market economy is to some extent unpredictable. Academic and policy makers have long debated to what extent crises are an intrinsic part of the capitalist system (therefore unavoidable) or if it is possible to prevent them with policy. This issue is discussed in this section on the basis of the crises in Argentina (2001, see Box 2.8) and the US (2008)

Box 2.8   Argentinian crisis in 2001

During the last decade of the twentieth century Argentina was praised for its effort to transform into a free market economy. Neoliberal policies included privatizations; currency pegged to the dollar; reduced bureaucracy; and complete de-regulation of trade and capital flows. A property and consumption bubble, low inflation and a focus on exporting natural resources and agro-products (in demand in a growing global economy) had sustained growth.[87] However, by 2000 demand for commodities fell in the context of global 'cooling' of the economy and Argentina's growth halted. Internal consumption slowed down and exports fell as Argentina's currency became more and more overvalued. Argentina's shrinking local industry (already substantially reduced by its inability to compete with cheaper foreign imports) took advantage of de-regulated labour markets to reduce employment costs. The aggregate result was a deep recession with unemployment rising to 20%.[88] Declining government revenues and the need to repay a mounting external debt led to austerity measures including further reduction of public employment, cuts in social services and assistance to the poor. Investors lost confidence in the country's growth prospects and withdrew capital from the country. As unemployment increased, Argentina could not devaluate because its currency (the peso) was pegged to the dollar by law. Thus, Argentina's Central Bank had to use its reserves to buy all pesos sold in the currency market. Speculators saw an opportunity to benefit from imminent collapse if they could force devaluation. They continued selling pesos hoping the Central Bank would run out of dollar reserves. At the same time investors withdrew deposits in foreign currency and moved them abroad. Economic and political downfall accelerated after 30 November 2001. To protect the banking system, the government decided to close all bank accounts and seized deposits in foreign currency. Social unrest led to protests and violence ensued when the government used military force to repress opposition. On 5 December the International Monetary Fund (IMF) withheld a $1.24 billion loan instalment. On 7 December Argentina announced it could no longer pay its external debt. By 18 December supermarkets were being looted, the unions called a general strike, the minister of finance resigned and the president declared state of siege amid mounting violent riots. On 20 December, the killing of protesters by armed police forced the president to resign and flee from the presidential mansion in a helicopter, leaving 28 people dead. Institutional chaos followed with five presidents in a week and police forces unwilling to deter rampant violence, theft and vandalism.[89]

What caused Argentina's crisis? Could have been it avoided? In general terms, nowadays the answer seems simple enough: Argentina's transformation just went too fast and disregarded the limitations of the ideal free market model, thus creating a bubble economy. Unfortunately, the reality is more complex, there is no simple answer in terms of explaining mechanisms linking market economies to crisis, and how the situation could have been avoided.

The debate on causes of economic crisis

The causes of economic crisis and how the government should act in a crisis has been the subject of much debate between economic schools. We discussed in Section 2.4 some of Schumpeter's ideas. Schumpeter's views about how governments should act in an economic crisis are similar to the perspective of scholars adhering to the Austrian economics school: governments should not intervene at all! Indeed, the Austrian economics school argues not only that governments are incapable of modifying the development of economic crises, but also that all type of government intervention in a crisis only 'socializes' private losses and creates moral hazard.

Other economic schools believe that government can and must act in crisis. Following Roubini – an economist who predicted accurately the USA sub-prime crisis – four main views can be identified in terms of focus and extent of intervention.[90]

Neoclassical view

In the neoclassical view, crises are a mechanism to 'cool down' a booming market. When demand increases, firms need to keep up with supply and wages increase because there is more demand for labour. When wages get too high, the economy will necessarily contract because firms will not be able to afford maintaining full employment. As unemployment rises wages will start to fall and entrepreneurs will hire again. The role of the government is to avoid indebtedness by being austere in its spending and to prevent large firms from using the crisis to create monopolies. Social and economic losses will be compensated when the economy peaks again.[91]

Keynesian view

In the Keynesian view, employment levels are the result of aggregate demand. If demand falls and wages are cut, the economy plunges into recessive 'underemployment equilibrium', a state of suspended animation in which workers remain unemployed and factories shuttered. Then, as demand falls below the aggregate supply of goods, firms are forced to cut prices to sell the inventory of unsold goods. This price deflation – which was severe in the great depression – leads to a further fall in their profits and cash flows. As profit falls, more people are made redundant, customers spend less and consumption falls. All this makes entrepreneurs reluctant to invest, which dampens demand even further. This is called the 'paradox of thrift', requiring government intervention to stimulate demand through spending.[92]

Monetarist view

The monetarist view is advocated by Nobel Prize winner Milton Friedman: recessions are caused by decline in money supply. Contraction of capital supply causes aggregate demand to collapse. For monetarists, states are needed to 'buffer' fluctuations in the money supply. Government intervention is required only to cut the rates at which banks could borrow from federal reserves and act as 'lender of last resort', making lines of credit available to faltering banks and financial institutions.[93]

Neo-Keynesian view

The neo-Keynesian view is represented by Hyman Minsky who contended that instability is an inherent and inescapable flaw of capitalism. Instability originates in the very financial institutions that make capitalism possible. Capitalist economy is fundamentally flawed, because the financial system furnishes the potential for unfettered expansion. Expansion without control is always negative. As the economy expands without limits, accumulated financial change makes the system fragile. Financial intermediaries bind creditors and debtors in complex financial networks which – as they grow in complexity and interdependence – bring the entire system crashing down. Minsky classified debtors into three categories corresponding to increasing levels of financial fragility: hedge, speculative and Ponzi. Hedge debtors' income is enough to pay both the interest and the principal of their debts while speculative debtors can cover only the interest. Ponzi debtors' income can neither cover the interest nor the principal. They mortgage their future finances with more borrowing, betting on a rise in the value of the assets they acquired with borrowed money.[94]

2.6.2 Financial crisis

A financial crisis is a type of market failure that can be defined as a situation of massive withdrawal of investment from the financial system as a result of investors' loss of confidence in a country's currency, its banks, or its government's ability to repay debts and prevent economic crisis. When savers do not believe that banks can return their deposits, we have a bank crisis. We have a currency crisis when currency holders fear devaluation and do not believe the currency will maintain its purchasing power. We have a debt crisis when foreign investors lose confidence in the ability of a country to repay the interest and principal of its debt.[95]

Loss of confidence is based on sentiment, since information asymmetries prevent a fair assessment of the financial system situation based on factual evidence (particularly when new information surfaces). Information asymmetry is an economic term indicating differences in access to information between actors. Investors do not have complete access to up-to-date information about a bank's state of affairs. Therefore they have to trust in their instinct or sentiment. From the perspective of the financial system, loss of confidence can result in a solvency crisis or liquidity crisis.[96]

Solvency crisis

A solvency crisis happens when loss of confidence is justified and the system does not have resources to repay all debtors. For instance if banks have used customer deposits in bad loans, or governments have squandered reserves or emitted currency not backed by reserves. Solvency crises are the result of intrinsic economic weakness in the system. Typical weaknesses include the end of a bubble that had inflated market values, making values much higher than it should be given the economic actors' actual incomes. Solvency crises are also caused by macroeconomic imbalances, such as large budget deficits caused by excessive governmental spending, or a high relative price inflation rate, or excessive expansion of domestic borrowing, or economic stagnation due to contractionary policies.[97]

Liquidity crisis

On the other hand we have a liquidity crisis if such a loss of confidence does not have a sound basis and the financial system is robust. This is the case of self-fulfilling prophecy. Most banking financial crises have been about lack of liquidity: the ability to raise cash at short notice. When rumour spreads and investors lose confidence, they run to get their money out of the banks (herd behaviour). Even if the rumour is false, it can bankrupt the bank. If everyone demands their money at the same time banks have no liquidity and will have to raise cash selling assets at fire-sale prices. If the bank does not have enough assets to cover its debts, then a bail-out can solve the problem until things calm down. This happened in US in 1998 when the large hedge fund Long-Term Capital Management collapsed.[98] In practice, most crises are a result of a combination of liquidity and solvency causes, which mutually reinforce each other in vicious circles.[99] Liquidity crises are likely to be worsened in countries with capital liberalization policies (lack of barriers to entry and exit of capital) exposing the economy to volatile capital flows. Interestingly, the 'freer' the capital market, the more dependent it is on temporary loans from the government to navigate crises.[100] In countries with free-floating currencies such as the USA, investors' nervousness is triggered when there is currency volatility: changes in the value of a currency during a specific period of time (calculated as the deviation from the mean during the period). High volatility implies a high variation (and frequency) of peaks and lows. It is a measure of uncertainty and risk. Monetary reserves allow a government to influence the exchange rate. These reserves can be used to purchase a country's own issued currency and therefore reduce the levels of liability.

2.6.3   Central banks and liquidity crisis

Central banks are able to stabilize the country's currency in response to excessive volatility if they have enough reserves and they are willing to use them. Reserves are foreign currency deposits held by central banks. Reserves also protect the monetary system from currency traders engaged in buying an asset and quickly reselling it for profit. When a country has a fixed exchange rate, the government is signalling its commitment to use its reserves to maintain the exchange rate, buying all the currency that investors put up for sale.[101] Large reserves are an indicator of currency strength. Under a flexible exchange rate system, the exchange rate is determined by market forces. If there is an excess of offer (everybody is selling) the currency devaluates (loss of exchange values). A crisis means an uncontrolled, rapid depreciation of the currency.[102]

Low or falling reserves may be a signal of an imminent financial crisis, which will be more severe if the country has a fixed exchange rate. Under a fixed or pegged exchange rate system, as in Argentina from 1998 to 2001, the government is obliged to maintain the exchange rate by buying the local currency if foreign exchange dealers are selling. A crisis entails the loss of international reserves and devaluation. Countries with a pegged exchange rate may be more vulnerable to a crisis because there are more opportunities for speculative attack.[103]

 2.7   Case Study: The US sub-prime crisis

In 2002, US consumption was at a historical low after the internet bubble crashed. US Central Bank drastically reduced interest rates to increase borrowing and stimulate consumption. The result was an unprecedented increase in housing mortgages and a property boom fuelled by public belief – hyped up by the media and economists – that 'housing prices never fall'. The construction industry rapidly increased its capacity while mortgage brokers and banks created innovative financial instruments to expand the demand base. Lack of financial regulation allowed banks to spread the risk of sub-prime loans to other investors. Sub-prime are loans offered at higher interest rates to individuals who do not qualify for prime rate loans. Sub-prime borrowers have low credit ratings, insufficient income or other factors that suggest a high risk of defaulting on the debt repayment.

Sub-prime borrowers often did not have enough income to pay either prime or interest, betting that house prices would rise and they would be able to re-mortgage or sell their houses to pay the interests on their loans. Alan Greenspan, the former chairman of the US Federal Reserve Board from 1987 to 2006, admitted in an interview with Newsweek: 'The big demand was not so much on the part of the borrowers as it was on the part of the suppliers who were giving loans which really most people couldn't afford. We created something that was unsustainable. And it eventually broke.'[104] One year later, summoned to testify at a US congressional hearing about his role in the crisis, Greenspan conceded that his staunch opposition to stronger financial regulation had been a mistake. He had put too much faith in the self-interest of banks and the self-correcting power of the market and was now in 'a state of shocking disbelief' (The New York Times, October 2008).

As Krugman (2008) noted,[105] these were bad loans that were likely to go very, very bad. Banks were willing to take risks thanks to the introduction of ABS (asset

(Continued)

based security) which allowed banks to sell hidden sub-prime debt to investors. A security is a financial instrument that can be traded. Securitization is the name given to the process of pooling assets (i.e. debt, real state, or infrastructure) into financial instruments which are subsequently offered for sale to general investors. Securitization allowed the risk of investing in the underlying sub-prime mortgages to be diversified because each security represented a fraction of the total value of the diverse pool of underlying debt portfolio. Using this so-called financial engineering, banks pooled 'good' and 'bad' loans and sold their debts in the form of securities called collateralized debt obligation (CDO). CDOs are distinctive in that they purport different types of debt and credit risk. Each of these different types of debt and risk are called 'slices' or 'tranches'. Each tranche is associated to a different level of risk. The lower the risk, the more 'senior' a tranche is. Both principal payments and interest are made following seniority. Junior tranches are paid last, therefore they are offered at lower prices or attract higher interest payments to compensate for additional default risk.[106]

In a nutshell, a CDO is a commitment to repay investors and paid dividends in a prearranged sequence, depending on the amount of cash flow the CDO obtains from the portfolio of debts it owns. If the amount of money collected by the CDO is not enough to pay all of its investors, those in the lower layers are the first to bear losses.

The financial securities industry was left largely unsupervised by the US government. De-regulation of capital markets lead to reliance on 'financial watchdogs' that gave the banks AAA and BBB ratings despite clear evidence of 'overcapitalization' (the banks were selling more 'commitments to pay' that they were able to repay with their current assets and cash flow). Banks sold the toxic investment hidden in CDOs to other banks, cities, pension funds, insurance companies and speculative/ Ponzi borrowers, many overseas.[107] Sub-prime and CDO sustained an enormous housing bubble and fed huge levels of borrowing into the bubble. Houses were bought with almost no money deposited and sub-prime borrowers repaid their loans by re-financing their mortgages, thus making cash out of rising property prices. Eventually, demand reached its ceiling and housing prices started to fail. Many homeowners found themselves with a debt higher than their houses were worth (negative equity) and failed to repay. As more homeowners defaulted, big losses for lenders ensued.[108]

Lack of transparency meant that investors in CDOs did not know the extent of bad loans in their underlying pool of assets. Confidence fell and investors panicked and rushed to get rid of their CDOs. Banks did not have enough assets to cover their debts, CDOs were not paid. Dollar and stock prices plunged. Total collapse of the system was only avoided with four government bail-outs to banks in five months, but several institutions went bankrupt and investors all over the world were affected.[109]

 Case Study Questions

1. What type of borrowers are sub-prime borrowers, hedge, speculative or Ponzi?
2. Were CDOs a Ponzi scheme?
3. What limitations of the market can you identify in the case study?
4. How could they have been avoided?
5. Why do you think the US government did not prevent the crisis?

2.8 Learning tools 🔧

2.8.1 Summary

- Scarcity of resources mean that societies face three basic choices: what to produce, how and for whom. Economic systems are the systems used by societies to make allocation choices. Economics provides principles to make such choices rational and efficient.
- There are two extreme economic systems: free market and command economies. These are ideal types; in practice most countries have a mix of command and market systems. The market economy (free market with some government intervention) has become the dominant economic system but the free market remains a subject of discussion.
- Opponents of free market 'fundamentalism' argue that sustainable welfare is not attained with such a system and is less justifiable in times of crises. Discrepancies in supply and demand lead to unemployment, 'bubbles' and recession. A third point of criticism is the creation of social imbalance. Those on the lowest rung of the ladder are often disadvantaged and inequality grows.
- Crises are the result of intrinsic market failures to sustain aggregated demand. Economic crises are disruptions in the economic system. Financial crises are disruptions in the financial system (banks and exchange rate).

2.8.2 Further reading

Congdon, T. (2011). *Money in a Free Society: Keynes, Friedman, and the New Crisis in Capitalism*. New York, NY: Encounter Books.

Lewis, M. (ed.) (2008). *Panic!: The Story of Modern Financial Insanity*. London: Penguin.

Stiglitz, J. (2002). *Globalization and its Discontents*. London: Penguin.

Stiglitz, J. (2010). *Freefall: Free Markets and the Sinking of the Global Economy*. London: Penguin.

Szirmai, A. (2005). *The Dynamics of Socio-Economic Development*. Cambridge: Cambridge University Press.

2.8.3 Assignments

 Assignment 2.1

The US sub-prime crisis is proof that Marx was right and capitalism is doomed to fail. Discuss.

 Assignment 2.2

Compare and contrast the processes of transformation in China, Russia and India. Which country do you think has been most successful and why? Use conceptual arguments and empirical evidence.

Assignment 2.3

Who are the winners and losers in the market economy? To what extent can market economies deliver benefits for all and how?

2.8.4   Self-test questions

 Self-test Questions

1. What are opportunity costs? How would you use the concept to assess a case in your own country's policies?
2. What are the differences between the free market and the market economy?
3. Is bureaucracy good or bad?
4. Give three examples of limitations of regulation through supply and demand
5. What are bubbles and self-fulfilling prophecies? Why do they happen?
6. Describe the differences between monetarist, neoclassical, Keynesian and neo-Keynesian views of crisis.

GOOD GOVERNANCE

Overview and learning objectives

As far back as 306 BC Aristotle claimed that a healthy state (political community) occurs when the middle class is involved in politics but that a strong middle class is not the only criterion.[1] The healthy state also depends on government's knowledge and implementation of good management. Are the right tools being used? Is there a long-term vision of how to create durable welfare and well-being? This chapter will take a close look at 'good governance'.

How does governance differ from government? Governance refers to the procedures, traditions, social norms and institutions by which authority in a country is exercised. Simply put, governance is the process by which authority is conferred on rulers, by which they make the rules, and by which those rules are enforced and modified.[2] Rulers include those holding formal authority (government) but also informal rulers such as market actors (companies) and non-governmental civil society organizations.

In turn, good governance is the type of governance that is more effective and equitable in the delivery of public services and rule of law, while ensuring that 'political, social and economic priorities are based on broad consensus in society and that the voices of the poorest and the most vulnerable are heard in decision-making over the allocation of development resources' (United Nations Development Programme, cited by World Bank, 2014).[3] According to social scientists following the ideas of twentieth-century French philosopher Michel Foucault (1926–1984),[4] good governance involves a network of relationships of cooperation between the governed and the governing.[5] In short, good governance is the set of processes and conditions (well-functioning markets, empowered social actors, efficient governments) enabling the achievement of compliance with social objectives through free conduct, self-awareness and self-limitation. Good governance concerns aspects that we often take for granted such as the combating of corruption, democracy, an independent functioning central bank, human rights, a positive investment climate, independent jurisprudence and government budget policy. In the World Bank's view, 'good governance' is demonstrably an important stimulus for welfare and well-being.

At present most countries agree that some form of market economy is needed for good public governance. However, there are still differences of opinion regarding the most effective tools and the extent of government involvement needed to make market economies work for all citizens in each country. Since the 1990s the notion of 'good governance' has become a key factor in the United Nation's (UN's) policies. These policies have been mirrored by the World Bank who also created guidelines for government. Some elements of these guidelines include the question of what the primary government tasks are and which of them could be relegated to a secondary position. 'Neoliberal governance' is a view of governance based on the predominance of market mechanisms and restriction of state involvement in the economy.

Neoliberals argue that the state is inherently inefficient when compared to markets in terms of delivery of public services.[6] In the neoliberal (also called free-market) view of good governance one of the primary tasks is to create the laws that enable a good investment climate. The government should not interfere too much with business but it is crucial that some conditions are met so that investors and companies dare to take the risk to make investments. On the other hand, the revisionist view of good governance (represented, for instance by economics Nobel Prize winner Joseph Stiglitz) is more cautious in terms of the outcomes of free markets. Revisionists believe that markets have imperfections requiring constant government intervention to assure efficient and just allocation of resources to satisfy social objectives. This view of good governance gives more prominence to regulations and controls that minimize negative impacts of investment (for instance, pollution, human rights abuses, monopolies), while emphasizing the role of governments to ensure that markets work well and the benefits of market economies are fairly distributed among citizens.[7]

Neoliberal and revisionist views both agree that it is important to establish a government that is operating at a high level of professionalism and has the capacity to maintain a high level of performance. But which tools and indicators should be chosen to measure the public administration's performance? Several different organizations undertake studies in this area but there are still discrepancies since the selection of tools is strongly influenced by each organization's view of what good governance entails. Since 1996, for example, the World Bank has published bi-annual reports showing how countries score according to governance indicators. The indicators are currently based on good performance scores in the areas of 1: Voice and accountability; 2: Political stability; 3: Government effectiveness; 4: Regulatory quality; 5: Rule of law; 6: Control of corruption. Aligned in its inception with the neoliberal view of governance, governance indicators were updated in the twenty-first century to take on board revisionists' concerns with fairness in the distribution of risks and benefits between the most advantaged and disadvantaged sectors in each country.

This chapter focuses both on the principles and philosophical foundations underlying the notion of good governance and on the tasks required by national governments and international organizations to implement 'good governance'.

Section 3.1 examines liberalism and 'the Enlightenment' and why they have both exerted a strong influence to the present day. Section 3.2 discusses national government responsibilities and the tasks that must be defined and carried out to achieve 'good governance'.

Learning objectives

This chapter will enable the student to:

- Know the principles of good governance that have directly been influenced by the ideas of the Enlightenment and liberalism.
- Understand the essential tasks that must be implemented by a government in order to survive at a basic level.
- Be familiar with the government duties aimed at stimulating citizen participation in society so that as many people as possible benefit from increased welfare and well-being.
- Have gained insight into government's redistribution of capital schemes to create opportunities for disadvantaged citizens as well as new business initiatives.

3.1   Starting points for good governance

3.1.1   Introduction

Prosperity flourished in many countries in the final decades of the twentieth century and the start of the twenty-first because measures were introduced that gave structure to the market economy while creating facilities to encourage business development. This could be seen as a (partial) surrender of power to the private sector, but the case of China – since 2014 the world's largest economy, ahead of the US – shows that market economies can flourish under strong interventionist governments. China's revisionist approach to market openness demonstrated that investment can be induced without substantial surrender of power and controls. However, regardless of their level of intervention in markets, more than ever before governments are aware that being an efficient, predictable and trustworthy partner is crucial in permitting business and citizens to actively take part in improving their own lives. Authorities that are unable to create a favourable investment climate soon realize that this has a limiting effect on citizens and business with negative consequences for prosperity. Countries understand that they should develop governing bodies that keep corruption and the abuse of power from gaining a foothold and that they need dedicated cooperation from important groups. This principle came into existence in Europe in the seventeenth and eighteenth centuries and is commonly known as 'the Enlightenment'. The movement was characterized by intellectual and cultural ideas that were based on rational thinking. The elite, but also the middle class, began to incorporate the concept of rationality into their everyday thoughts. Power and hierarchy were debunked. In society, discussions were fuelled by reasonable arguments instead of dictates.[8] This had a marked influence not only on science but also on the set-up of society as well. The seventeenth-century Enlightenment philosophers pressed the – at the time – innovative idea that governments are responsible for the protection, welfare and well-being of their citizens.[9] The movement created a new vision of humanity and society and formed the basis of the modern state that we know today. In this section we present the main ideas that have made an important contribution to the modern state and good governance.

3.1.2   The Enlightenment and liberalism

The Enlightenment was a movement which took rationality as its guiding principle and had its roots in the emergence of individualism in sixteenth-century Europe. As a result, people in society began to increasingly adopt personal beliefs and to be less dependent on the opinions of others.[10] This led to fierce resistance from religious and political authorities who were not pleased with the idea of 'rational thinking' as a basis for analysis because the accepted hierarchy and dictated rules could then be questioned.

The Englishman John Locke (1632–1704) based his ideas on the principles of the Enlightenment. He was one of the first philosophers who looked at the relationship between rulers and the public, claiming that leaders should act responsibly towards all citizens. From the Middle Ages until late in the Renaissance, rulers had been seen as being chosen by God.[11]

Box 3.1   Meddling with the power of absolute authority

The Dutch Rebellion in the sixteenth century was one of the first instances of citizens challenging the authority of the monarch in Western Europe. The economic and cultural urban middle class rose up against King Philip II who governed the Netherlands from Spain, serving Spanish interests. In 1581 several Dutch provinces formed an 'Act of Secession' and rejected the rule of King Philip II. The act gained legitimacy by claiming Philip to be a tyrant. The provinces claimed the throne to be vacant and stressed that citizens were not created by God to be obedient to the whims of a decadent ruler. The proclamation went on to say that the monarch has the right and reason to rule, but by calling Philip II a tyrant who abused the freedom of his citizens, Dutch administrators won moral legitimacy to choose another leader.

The ideas that Locke and other Enlightenment philosophers presented were considered controversial and their writings were a threat to the ruling elite.[12] By making citizens' rights a central issue, it became clear that absolute power was a poor basis for kings and emperors. The ideas of these philosophers formed the roots of liberalism with freedom and individual rights as its central points. Liberalism is in fact social innovation because its premise paved the way for society to improve and caused governments to validate its legitimacy in a new framework. Locke stated that the legitimacy of a government is only acceptable when there is a social contract with the people.

The broad implications of the Enlightenment changed in seventeenth- and eighteenth-century Europe for good. Education became an important objective and the movement caused major changes in politics, philosophy, science and religion.

Box 3.2   Immanuel Kant

Immanuel Kant (1724–1804) wrote about the most essential aspect of the Enlightenment, 'rationality'. He demonstrated that good decisions should be supported by rational arguments. 'Freedom of expression' was a condition for an 'enlightened' society. Kant was often angry with people who could not think for themselves but realized that this was caused by constraints on freedom placed by the authorities.[13] He stated that the average citizen placed little trust in his or her own thought and was expected to be told what to do by the governing powers. Kant blamed this immaturity on both citizens and the authorities.[14] He detested it when people had insufficient courage and convictions to think for themselves and pleaded for individuals and organizations to make more use of the power of rational thinking.

3.1.3   Democracy

The concept of electoral democracy, a form of democracy founded on the principle of elected officials representing a group of people, took full flight after the Second World War; not only for Western Europe but also for a number of former colonies such as India. Because of the deplorable situation in Europe at the time there were only 12 fully fledged electoral democracies after the Second World War.[15] In 1972 there were 44 electoral democracies and in 2013 the number of electoral democracies was 117.[16]

According to Lake and Baum (2001) democracy is good for the poor because democratic governments have more 'public goods' on offer than their non-democratic counterparts.[17] However, it does have its detractors, from critics of the failures of representative systems to give voice to the most disadvantaged or sustain long-term development objectives (Acemoglu, 2006)[18] to traditional ruling elites reluctant to relinquish 'God-given' powers to the masses and trying to keep control divided among a small group.

Democracy as a political system takes its cue from the city state of Athens in ancient Greece and the first inklings of the democratic process were already evident in 500 BC. Administrators followed 'official' rules that allowed the majority of Athenians to take part in the decision-making process. Different variants of democracy have evolved considerably since those early days but a limited number of countries and territories worked with a comparable system. When this was the case, it was basically a watered-down version allowing a limited group access to administrative decision making. The system only began to evolve in the eighteenth century due to the arrival of the Enlightenment which played a crucial role. People began to use rational thought when discussing government, and the rule of the absolute monarch was no longer taken for granted. The prestige and power that was nestled in the hands of the aristocracy became a talking point in many countries. This culminated in a genuine revolution in France that commenced with the storming of the Bastille in 1789. The ruling elite in other European states was also forced to make concessions. This was likely to have been more easily achieved in countries with a relatively large middle class:[19] because they (the middle class) had something to lose their demands were less extreme, making it easier for the wealthy to divide power.

Looking at the situation in the nineteenth century, we see that development of democracy in many countries was a gradual affair. In countries of north-western Europe, for example, voting rights were initially only available for male taxpayers at the beginning of the century, but this changed in due course. The poorest segment of society also became restless and began to protest, fired up by the ideas of German economist Karl Marx. The working classes were urged to revolt so that a new society could be created without the rich controlling the purse strings. In an attempt to avoid revolution, many north-western European rulers introduced voting rights for the male population which were finally extended to women in the early twentieth century.[20] It should be noted, however, that the right to vote is not a universal phenomenon, and rules still vary throughout the world.

Box 3.3   Democracy in crisis?

Crisis in democracy is a recurring theme in the media and in scientific debate. Observers write that the link between politics and voters is losing strength and talk of electoral volatility.[21] Political parties have come to expect short-term provisional support from the voters at best. Loyalty to a party is not a characteristic of today's undecided voter who does not hesitate to switch sides when new elections are looming. It is becoming more and more evident that elections can cause a political landslide with 10, 20 or sometimes 30% of the voters changing sides.[22]

In Europe and the US, voter turnout has also noticeably decreased in the last decades of the twentieth century and the beginning of the twenty-first, with 60%–70% now often being considered the norm.[23]

(Continued)

We might ask ourselves if the current system, known as electoral representative democracy, whereby voters feel allied to a political party, is a concept for the twenty-first century because of its basis in loyalty and hierarchy.[24] Does the new century, with its emphasis on globalization and social media, offer us another 'playing field' in which decision making contains a different dynamic?[25] Scientific debate is flourishing on the subject of whether or not a form of direct democracy could partially or entirely replace the existing system. Some new ideas are emanating from a surprising source: ancient Greece in the fourth century BC. This society used the concept of direct democracy known as sortition in which deliberation played an important role. Sortition's primary method was that members of the political body were selected on the basis of a lottery. The appointed members of the group were designated at random based on their involvement in the political system. If such a system were applied today in the US, for example, the political body could exist of around 500 people. The make-up of this group would be based on a random sampling and include 51% women, 16% Hispanics/Latino, 13% African American, poor and rich, old and young.[26]

Economist Fishkin sees a positive side to the possibilities.[27] The first aspect of this is selection. Because representatives would no longer be accountable to their supporters, they have little concern about their future election prospects. They are basically there to pitch their own interests and contribute to problem solving. In this model the political body is not an opinion poll. With polls is measured primarily what the people thinks if it does not think.[28] In a poll, respondents often choose for a position without analysing the pros and cons first. In a direct democracy the problem of 'not thinking' is avoided because the 'at-random' selected political groups will intensely be involved in the policy-making process concerning the societal topic. They work, for example, regularly for two months on a certain policy issue. The second positive aspect is consensus. When people come together to solve a problem they are obviously seeking consensus. This aim differs hugely from that of political parties based on representative democracy whereby elected leaders continuously seek to strengthen bonds with their constituents who are often excluded from the information loop. To improve the system, Fishkin suggests the incorporation of 'deliberative democracy' in which gathering of information, discussion and constructive arguments form the basis of the decision making. Successful deliberations are also reliant on participants being able to call on the advice of experts. Assertive participants must also not be given too much leeway to disrupt proceedings and, finally, working together in small groups, professional discussion leaders and an outlined agenda are elements that can all contribute to a well-functioning political body.

3.1.4 Human rights

Human rights are directly related to liberalism.[29] It has taken more than two centuries to bring these ideas to a reasonable level of acceptance within Western society. The institutionalizing of 'human rights' has been a painstaking process. The abolition of slavery in nineteenth-century England was an important step. In 1787 more than 390,000 people had signed 519 petitions to end slave trade, but it took 20 years of anti-slavery campaigns for slave trade to be banned in 1807. Although trade was outlawed, slavery itself was still legal until the Slavery Abolition Act in 1833.[30] Other branches on the tree of human rights are equal rights for women, freedom of speech and the right to a fair trial, with an emphasis on the rights of the 'maverick' or loner. Through the human rights movement individuals and minorities get fairer treatment to protect them from becoming victims of powerful authorities or pressure groups. An important element for the enforcement of human rights is that majority opinion can have strained relations with individual rights. Human rights in the context of the law means that limits apply for the tyranny of the majority. Today human rights are part of many constitutions and its laws are firmly implanted in the public consciousness.

3.1.5   Trias politica

The political thinker Charles-Louis Montesquieu (1689–1755) bitterly criticized irresponsible authorities, dictators, despots and tyrants in eighteenth-century Europe and pleaded for demands to be made on government.[31] One of his most important interests was the organization of the state. Montesquieu embraced liberalism and with it he sought ways to increase citizens' freedom and limit the power of despots. His most famous book 'On the Spirit of the Laws' contains essays on division of power now commonly known as 'trias politica' (separation of powers). The concept of 'trias politica' implies three different tasks for governments. These three tasks should be executed by three independent bodies. The first task is legislative power which comprises the institutions which enact laws. In the UK, this power is in parliament. The executive power is the second task that is performed by the government. It takes care of the enforcement and maintenance of the legislation. The third task of Montesquieu's treatise is judicial power, which interprets the law and applies it to the cases of individuals. This is the task of the Supreme Court, Courts of Appeal and District Courts in the US. The misuse of power must be prevented and arbitrary decisions by governments limited through evenly spread distribution. To stop tyranny and omnipotence the three concepts must be administered by three separate governing bodies. Furthermore the regulatory task must be entrusted to a representative body in order to give the people a voice.

Separation of powers is a practical social innovation and appears in many parts of our society, not only in the context of trias politica. Business and associations also use division of power which brings into perspective the positions of those who make decisions and those who enforce them.[32] The different portfolios within an organization mean that representative individuals have their own obligations but must qualify their actions to a third party. Large businesses with boards of directors, boards of commissioners and planning committees also incorporate role division by specifying in their charters who is in charge and who carries out the decisions, which can lead to improved quality and general performance.

The role division provides countervailing power. A counterforce exists for each power. Every party has its own responsibility. In this way a critical attitude is institutionalized.[33] A well-run supervisory board will be critical of ambitious projects proposed by the board of directors. The supervisors, appointed by the shareholders, will want to see figures pertaining to yield and risk calculations. Institutionalized countervailing power produces a more thorough analysis of questions and helps to avoid tunnel vision.

3.2   Good governance of a state

3.2.1   Introduction

After communist countries such as China and the former Soviet Union began participating in free-market economics, official organizations like the World Bank and the UN lent a hand to create new criteria for government based on neoliberal governance.[34] The end of communism in these countries led to the idea that quality of governance is more or less a scientific question. Based on experiences in the past, governments in general have gained more insight concerning the best tools a state can use to provide welfare and well-being for its citizens. Today many countries have similar views on the basics of effective administration. Solid research has offered a more convincing argument than individual opinions and part of the discussion is based on the idea of civil society. This is a concept that is often highlighted and refers to a society where government serves the people and allows individuals, groups and organizations the freedom to pursue personal interests and improve their lives.[35] To set up a modern and stable society, the government's role must be clear in the creation of standards of safety, welfare and well-being.[36]

Box 3.4   The state

The state is an authority with a prevalence of power which is used to regulate community life. Whether or not it is successful depends on its laws, rules and regulations and how they are enforced. During the ancient eras, providing security for citizens was the main task, and power was in the hands of a limited few that made and enforced the laws.[37] German sociologist Max Weber (1864–1920) wrote about state-building and suggested that the state is the only authority that can use physical violence as a right and that has a monopoly on violence, and that this characteristic is one of its most important aspects. The police and the army are examples of how this power is institutionalized. A second feature of the state is its monopoly on taxes.[38]

3.2.2   The definition of good governance

Good governance is a concept disseminated in the 1990s by neoliberal think tanks and supranational organizations such as the World Bank. Neoliberals distinguish between the task of making policy decisions ('steering') and the activity of delivering public services ('rowing'). They distrust governments' ability to deliver public services. The concept of governance offered neoliberalism the opportunity to differentiate between bad government (too much bureaucracy and involvement in 'rowing') and necessary good governance (focus on steering to enable efficient markets). Good governance sees pared-down governments working with individuals and organizations outside of government (markets, civil society)[39] to steer the structural conditions required for the success of actions to improve social well-being. The concept was promoted as a main enabling condition for economic growth and well-being in developing countries. At the end of the 1980s the decolonization of Africa had entered a new phase. Financial aid for developing countries had decreased, amid growing concerns about its effectiveness to promote long-term economic development in countries with weak institutions and corrupt governments. African decolonization had in fact begun 20–30 years earlier (1960s) and already seemed like a long time ago. The taboo concerning criticism against the former colonies was decreasing. It was not seen as a surprise that international organizations cast a critical eye on the quality of government in developing countries. This was a fortunate coincidence for the World Bank, which was formulating its criteria for 'good governance' at the very same moment. Former World Bank President Barber B. Conable criticized the quality of governmental bodies in developing countries. In the report 'Sub-Saharan Africa: From Crisis to Sustainable Growth' published in 1989 the word 'good' in relation to governance was used unconcealed.[40] 'Weak economic performance' was directly linked to the failure of public institutions.

By putting 'good governance' on the agenda of international organizations the role of the world community became stronger. It also gave impetus to the discussion that a state's autonomy is not absolute. This rebuke from the World Bank can be seen as a clear signal that world societies are prepared to intervene when signs of poor administration are evident in independent countries. Globalization is the trend, reciprocal dependence is increasing and international organizations are assuming added responsibility. The same development took place in the 1990s at the UN with its champion, former UN Secretary-General Kofi Annan (term of office 1997–2006) at the helm. As secretary-general, Kofi Annan gave priority to revitalizing the UN. He was keen to strengthen the organization through a comprehensive programme of reform and as a result was awarded the Nobel Peace Prize in 2001. Among other things he directed the spotlight towards international peace and security, the advocating of human rights, the rule of law and the universal values of equality, tolerance and human dignity. Good governance was also on the secretary-general's agenda and in his 1999 report 'Preventing War and Disaster' he wrote:

> In practice good governance involves promoting the rule of law, tolerance of minority and opposition groups, transparent political processes, an independent judiciary, an impartial police force, a military that is strictly subject to civilian control. A free press and vibrant civil society institutions, as well as meaningful elections. Above all, good governance means respect for human rights.[41]

The UN distinguishes eight aspects in its definition of good governance.[42] These are:

1. **Participation**
    All men and women should have a voice in decision making, either directly or through legitimate intermediate institutions that represent their interests. Such broad participation is built on freedom of association and speech, as well as the capacity to contribute constructively.
2. **Rule of law**
    Legal frameworks should be fair and enforced impartially, particularly the laws on human rights.
3. **Transparency**
    Transparency is built on the free flow of information. Processes, institutions and information are directly accessible to those concerned with them, and enough information is provided to understand and monitor them.
4. **Responsiveness**
    Institutions and processes try to serve all stakeholders.
5. **Consensus orientation**
    Good governance mediates differing interests to reach a broad consensus on what is in the best interests of the group and, where possible, on policies and procedures.
6. **Equity**
    All men and women have opportunities to improve or maintain their well-being.
7. **Effectiveness and efficiency**
    Processes and institutions produce results that meet needs while making the best use of resources.
8. **Accountability**
    Decision makers in government, private sector and civil society organizations are accountable to the public, as well as to institutional stakeholders. This account-ability differs depending on the organization and whether the decision is internal or external to an organization.

Figure 3.1   The UN's characteristics of good governance[43]

3.2.3   The extent of government involvement

Looking at different governments shows that some are more involved than others. Heavy involvement in areas such as the environment, infrastructure, social services, health care and education, however, has not been found to be automatically better for the people. In the beginning of the 1990s it became clear that governments were loosening their grip on some of these areas and many policy makers claimed this should be reflected in more market freedom. It was seen as common sense, and influential institutions like the International Monetary Fund (IMF), the World Bank and the US Treasury felt that less interference was a good way forward.[44] This agreement on a neoliberal ideology promoting unfettered market liberalization, 'back to core business' and 'hollowing out' of the state became known as the 'Washington Consensus' (see more detail in Chapter 8). Washington Consensus policies included privatization of state assets, lower direct taxation, unrestricted trade and financial flows and a reduction of the state's welfare role.[45] This approach was not uniformly successful and in several developing countries, chaos and financial instability were the result. Nowadays, neoliberal policies are strongly criticized both in developed and developing countries. For many (such as Nobel Prize economists Joseph Stiglitz and Paul Krugman)[46, 47] the Washington Consensus has been responsible for growing global inequality and social unrest. Global dissemination of neoliberal policy has also been blamed as the main factor behind the global financial crises escalating since the end of the twentieth century and the economic depression in the new millennium. Indeed, social scientists argue that neoliberal policy has actually achieved very little in terms of reducing the state. Instead 'the neoliberal reform fragmented service delivery and weakened central control without establishing markets' (Bevir, 2013).[48]

Many countries had stepped back from excessive regulation but failed to realize how remaining tasks should be executed. In order to build, governments must clearly show a 'pecking order' to indicate which tasks are most important and also to create the external conditions to allow the market to function. What happened in Russia is a classic case. State businesses were privatized but legal aspects were neglected and the role of the Central Bank was not reinforced. The banking, oil and gas industries gained excessive power with decreased service to society as a result. This was accompanied by a significant increase in corruption and Mafia activities.

After 2008's US sub-prime crisis and the ensuing global depression many governments realized that the hands-off approach to free markets (particularly financial markets) had gone too far. This heralded a return of what is called Keynesian economics: the view that 'states really do matter' (Dicken, 2011).[49] More government intervention was needed to foster aggregated demand, reduce poverty, control market excesses and prevent unequal or unfair accumulation of wealth.[50] This economic trend, termed neo-Keynesian or post-Keynesian, inspired measures such as partial nationalization (the case of the UK's Royal Bank of Scotland), large bail-outs of ailing industries (for example, the US bail-out of its bankrupt automotive and financial industries), increased government spending in infrastructure and research, quantitative easing (emission of currency by central banks beyond levels guaranteed by reserves), and stronger market controls. Even the IMF has softened its approach to hard core neoliberal 'market fundamental-ism', acknowledging the importance of more government spending on social policies and more slowly paced approaches to market liberalization.[51] However, a stumbling block remains the effective regulation of the highly globalized financial industry.[52] As Peter Dicken noted in 2011: 'Quite how this will play out over the next few years is not yet clear. However, there is a generally held view that things will never be quite the same again'.[53]

In this context of returning powers to states, Krugman (2013) argues that government should increase its levels of intervention in markets but that it is of the utmost importance that government does not retain total control in the execution of some of its tasks.[54] In many cases, neoliberal ideology was taken to damaging extremes, but the cases of economies such as Cuba and Venezuela clearly show that interventionism taken to extremes is equally damaging. Governments have facilitating duties to make sure that markets' outcome is citizens' well-being. The effectiveness of the 'facilitating duties' are referred to as 'power of the state'. The 'extent of state functions' should contain limitations. By this we mean that government's 'facilitating' arm must not be omnipresent so that business and social organizations like schools and hospitals are able to function well on their own.

3.2.4   Areas of government involvement

Introduction

Governments aiming for greater prosperity, welfare and stability for their citizens should have a clear picture of their own role and also the needs of individuals, groups and organizations to achieve their goals. The World Bank (1997) defines three levels of involvement of the state/government.[55]

1. **Minimal functions**
   The role here relates to public trust and humanitarian issues. Winning public confidence is important because it encourages participation from business and the private sector. This 'minimal function' stimulates investment from both groups who trust that their actions are approved by the authorities. It leads to more business investments plus educational and social initiatives.
2. **Intermediate functions**
   Intermediate function is the government's hand in bringing participation to a higher level and is related to direction-orientated tasks such as lifestyle improvement.
3. **Activist functions**
   Government's role is considered activist when it is directed towards the future, such as investment so that an industry can develop. An activist function is future orien-tated and authorities retreat from the existing situation. New tax laws are made (for limited periods) to curb the lopsided growth rate of assets between rich and poor. The activist functions of the state are a main area of controversy between

neoliberal economists – seeking to minimize activist functions – and neo-Keynesian economists, viewing the activist role of the state as crucial and unalienable to avoid inequality (across and within countries) and to ensure long-term sustainable development.[56]

Table 3.1 The three functions of a state defined by the World Bank[57]

	Addressing market failure			Improving equity
Minimal functions	**Providing pure public services**			**Protecting the poor**
	Defence			Anti-poverty programmes
	Law and order			Disaster relief
	Property rights			
	Macroeconomic management			
	Public health			
Intermediate functions	**Addressing externalities**	**Regulating monopoly**	**Overcoming imperfect information**	**Providing social insurance**
	Basic education	Utility regulation	Insurance (health, life, pensions)	Redistribution of pensions
	Environmental protection	Antitrust policy	Financial regulation	Family allowances
			Consumer protection	Unemployment insurance
Activist functions	**Coordinating private activity**			**Redistribution**
	Fostering markets			Asset redistribution
	Cluster initiatives			

Table 3.1 contains the key areas of responsibility for the various state functions. Now we will explain the content in more in detail.

Minimal state functions

Concerning the main external tasks of a government, the World Bank (1997) recognized five minimal state functions:[58]

1. Defence
2. Law and order
3. Property rights
4. Public health/protecting the poor (anti-poverty programmes, disaster relief)
5. Macroeconomic policy

These five areas will be explained more in detail now.

Defence & Law and order

Defence is an essential function of government and with it comes the responsibility to protect the population against aggression from abroad. Also "law and order" is an essential activity for the state. This function ensures safety and trust. For society it is important that there are clear rules in the area of human rights and crime and that these are maintained. Law and order should be of a high standard and governmental policy should retain its integrity. Respect for authority, unbiased justice and judicial efficiency work together to ensure that crime does not go unpunished.[59] The public should feel that they are being well served and that no one can take the law into his or her own hands. If certain sections of the population condone crime because they feel social or economic discrimination, the government will have a harder time maintaining law and order. Respect for the power of the law is therefore seen as essential.

Property rights

Confidence in the state shows to be strongest when business and the private sector have the possibilities of improving their fate by participating in the economy. 'Property rights' encompasses a broad field which offers, among other things, a good public justice system for solving business conflicts. Business and investors should have the confidence to initiate activities even though profit margins, sales, corruption, new laws and breach of contract are not part of the preliminary equation.[60, 61] As an example, in England and Wales property rights are regulated by the English Property Law System. The property law system deals with issues such as legal owners, business rights, contract law and capital law. In addition, it regulates the field of patents and purchase and sale of real estate matters. Think of the work of the land registry office and the civil law notary who provide clarity in property transfers while keeping misunderstanding and conflicts to a minimum.

Public health, equal rights and poor relief

Public health is an essential government responsibility, because the private sector does not have a direct interest in offering such services. Public health topics such as sports promotion, correction of health-damaging situations, and prevention of illness through public surveys and public flu shots fall in this category. Parallel with public health, the government is also charged with caring for the poor, emergency assistance and, in worst-case scenarios, financial support for disaster situations.

Box 3.5   Hygiene and public health in the nineteenth century

The nineteenth century saw the first major advances in public health. In 1847, the Viennese physician Ignaz Semmelweis (1818–1865) discovered that infection was not only transmitted through the air.[62] Hospital mortality rates plummeted sharply when people washed their hands and cleaned surgical instruments. During the second half of the century the relationship between hygiene and public health became more important and was promoted by leading medical professionals. People came to realize that clean tap water, refuse disposal and sanitation were public issues and the government was bound to invest in these collective goods.

Macroeconomic policy

The fourth area necessary for the state to function well is macroeconomic policy. This implies that the government should make prudent decisions to keep the economy moving to improve the welfare and the well-being of its participants. The following four divisions of the macroeconomic policy area have been shown to play an important role:

1. Labour participation and productivity
2. Monetary policy
3. Balance of payments policy
4. Government budgeting

We will now take a closer look at these four divisions.

Labour participation and productivity   When the government succeeds in stimulating people's participation in the economy with increased productivity, the result is a higher GNP and increased prosperity. The UK government has implemented measures to limit unemployment benefits but at the same time is providing opportunities to those who are affected by unemployment to retrain for new professions. This stimulation is also seen in the government's decision to raise the retirement age in order to keep more people in the workforce.

Monetary policy   Keeping a growing economy in balance without creating inflation is a major function of macroeconomic policy. In most countries this task is delegated to a central bank. For the UK this is the Bank of England and for the USA the Federal Reserve (Fed). These banks are monetary watchdogs. In the early part of the twenty-first century these central banks have had more focus on price stability because it has a positive impact on the investment climate.[63]

For example, the European Central Bank strives for a scenario where sufficient capital is available in the market for goods and services being produced, while keeping inflation at 2% over the medium term.[64] In previous centuries, individual governments had more control of their monetary policy and sometimes created money to develop industrial sector and finance government spending.[65] After the Second World War more countries were inclined to put their monetary policy in the hands of independent central banks, hoping that lower inflation expectations would have a positive effect on foreign investors' confidence.

To give some perspective into the strange and difficult relationship between money and reality, Box 3.6 tells a classic tale:

Box 3.6   The desirable amount of virtual money

The gold standard

Gold and silver were the forerunners of currency. Because everyone felt that these precious metals had great value, they were universally desired. For royalty, the search for gold was especially important. It financed armies and enforced power but was also used for building castles, art purchases and festivities. Some kings even employed alchemists who attempted to make gold from other materials. The sixteenth-century gold discoveries in Latin America inspired Spanish royalty to send ships and explorers to the New World to retrieve the gold and silver, thus outfoxing the alchemists, but the search for precious metals did not end there. Leaders were always looking for ways to bring more money into the economy, often by using artificial methods to increase the amount of gold and silver. The Swedish royal family was directly involved in the setting up the Riksbank. It was the first bank that experimented with paper money, although in the form of certificates.[66] The first banknotes were issued in 1661 with gold remaining in the vaults as collateral. The experiment was successful and more banknotes were printed while the level of gold in the vaults remained unchanged. Soon, doubt arose about the value of the banknotes and history's first 'run on the bank' followed shortly afterwards. The bank failed in 1664 and the Swedish government assumed all debts. At the end of the seventeenth century the British tried a similar approach. The Bank of England was founded in 1694 and started issuing banknotes.[67] The public trusted the bank because of the text printed on the paper currency: 'I promise the bearer on demand

(Continued)

the sum of ... [golden] pounds.' The system worked this time and many countries started issuing their own banknotes which quickly replaced gold and silver coins. The fault coverage became an important barometer to ensure that not too much currency was printed in relation to the actual supply of precious metals and this policy was still in use as late as the 1930s. People trusted the system but there was an important disadvantage. Friction can arise between the real economy and the desired amount of money that society needs. An example is when the gold reserve remains stable while increased growth and demand in annually produced goods and services increases.

The fiduciary system

Today's central banks determine how much money society needs and this is commonly referred to as 'monetary policy'. The banks are independent from government and have their own responsibilities. Almost every central bank in the world relies on a fiduciary system.[68] Fiduciary money is paper money that is circulated by central banks but is no longer convertible at the central bank to a certain amount of gold, which was a possibility until relatively recently; however, after the 1970s, this changed. Fiduciary is a synonym for trust: trust in the value of paper money. For example, the European Central Bank (ECB) is responsible for the amount of money being circulated in the Eurozone. Its main objective is to keep inflation below but close to 2%. To achieve this target, it is important to closely monitor the amount of money circulating in the economy. Too much money can lead to inflation but too little can have a negative effect on economic growth and can even cause a slowdown.

The ECB is responsible for the amount of money being created. This is not always an easy task and is influenced by many factors. A country's money supply can be increased to encourage foreign investors to lend with government bonus of high interest returns. Private banks also make use of their option to create money although on a limited scale. The supply of money is automatically increasing because cash transactions and cash circulation occur at a more rapid pace, creating trust in the economy, but the direction of cash flows can change quickly. Because billions are at stake, small percentage changes in currency movements can be enough to cause dramatic changes in the amount of money available to society. To keep credit creation in check the ECB uses 'refi-interest'. This is interest that banks and other financial institutions pay to the ECB. When the interest rate changes most 'commercial' banks will be able to borrow more or less from the ECB. This has an immediate effect on society because interest rates determine the spending patterns of the business and private sectors.

Balance of payments policy   The balance of payment consists of the current account and the capital account. The balance of trade is an essential element of current accounts and indicates the balance between imports and exports which gives information about competitive ability. Banks and government exert influence on the balance of trade. For example, the interest rates offered by banks affect the exchange rate by making currencies more or less expensive. Devalued currencies make foreign products more expensive to buy, slow down imports and cause prosperity to stagnate. The inverse impact is true for local goods, which become cheaper on the foreign market.

Stable economic development also depends on input from the capital account.[69] This provides, inter alia, information on the strength of foreign direct investment (FDI) into the country. FDI gives countries the opportunity to grow. Money that is well spent increases earning power. In certain cases FDI can increase the recipient country's foreign debts. Whatever choice governments and central banks make concerning current and capital accounts is strongly dependent on the situation and is determinative for economic development.

Government budgeting   The government budget forms an important part of macro-economic policy. Governments must know not only where money is to be spent but also how the expenses are accounted for. Major themes for any budget proposal include government debt and deficit. In the EU, growth guidelines were established in 1997 which aimed to limit budget deficits to 3% with public debt limited to 60% of GDP. In 2011 the so-called 'Six Pack' was applied to EU member countries and allows sanctions to be enforced for national governments who do not have their house in order.[70]

Box 3.7   The rationality of another budgetary discipline

Some Southern European euro countries have not adhered to the criteria set up when the Maastricht Treaty came into effect, feeling them to be a disruption of established monetary policy.[71] Greece has since become the bad boy of the EU and the question has been raised if it should have entered the eurozone in the first place.

Research has shown that there is an argument for a less severe monetary policy: a country's individual currency offers more possibilities to solve its own budget shortages and inflation issues without creating big problems.[72] Monetary policy coupled with money creation often resulted in higher inflation accompanied by a devaluation of local currency on the foreign exchange, but also made it possible for relatively easy repayments of government debts. The higher inflation brought in more (nominal) tax revenue to the treasury and this made it fairly simple for old outstanding loans to be repaid. With a large amount of banknotes put in circulation, the government authorities had an additional benefit because the newly printed banknotes remained in hands of the society and they were not coming back to central bank (seigniorage income). Also, the business community was not much affected by higher inflation and currency deflation because its competitive edge improved as long as employee salary increases could be kept to a minimum.[73] The disadvantages of this type of policy may seem obvious but for some countries this approach helps to avoid political polarization and instability.

Intermediate state tasks

The intermediate tasks are close behind the minimal state functions when it comes to areas of government responsibility.[74] The basic government responsibilities relate to security, property rights, macroeconomic policy and protection of the less fortunate. The intermediate tasks are concerned with public goods and the legislation that has a direct connection with market failure. The World Bank has stated that governments cannot choose whether or not to perform these tasks but are expected to determine the way in which they are applied. Government policy must be aimed towards combating market failure so that the market economy can better contribute to welfare and well-being.[75] The enforcement of intermediate tasks by the government ensures that necessary public goods are not in short supply, it increases public and business confidence and it allows for a more professional participation in the market economy. Themes relating to this are discussed in Sections 2.4 and 2.5 in Chapter 2.

The World Bank has defined these intermediate tasks:

- Regulating monopoly.
- Externalities.
- Providing social insurance.
- Overcoming imperfect information.

Section 2.4 in Chapter 2 concentrated on the theme of 'regulating monopoly', whereby governments enact measures to combat improper collaboration between companies and to limit the power of those enterprises with monopolistic tendencies. The same section discussed externalities, a market failure that is the direct reason why allocation of resources does not find its proper course. It has led to government legislation destined to benefit the environment, education and health care. The third and fourth intermediate tasks described by the World Bank are 'providing social insurance' and 'overcoming imperfect information'. In Section 2.4, these two subjects were not discussed in detail. The concept of imperfect information was, however, examined from the viewpoint of business and entrepreneurs and the importance of market information related to a reduction in market insecurity. The subject of uncertainty and the market economy also has an influence on ordinary citizens. This insecurity is a determining theme for the working of the market economy because 'willing to participate' goes hand in hand with 'reliance'.[76] An advanced economy where division of labour has reached a mature state is characterized by mutual dependency. The keyword here is "trust" which gives courage to participants on both sides to invest in development and further participate in an anonymous society.[77] The government can improve this concept of trust by providing required services with its major contributions being 'overcoming imperfect information' and 'providing social insurance'.[78]

Overcoming imperfect information

The level of the private sector's participation in society is largely dependent on trust and risk taking. Government plays an intermediate role in promoting insurance and financial services. Companies are more likely to invest if the risk factor can be split with a third party, the lenders. The banks play an important role by bringing lenders (savers) and investors together. Insurance comprises the final element; companies tend to invest more easily when they have the possibility of assigning risks to third parties.[79] Insurance is also in people's interest. When people can insure themselves for health bills, senior care and pensions, stability increases. If tragedy or illness strikes, the risks are limited. It gives people the opportunity to plan ahead and invest in themselves. Being able to save for a child's higher education is a good example.

The question of 'incomplete information' must also be considered when examining how the market works. The government should play an intermediate role by creating legislation that is geared to standards concerning transparency of product information and certification.[80]

Providing social insurance

The market economy has its own dynamic. Businesses are set up and expanded but they can also go belly-up. In the dynamic of the market people become stimulated to do their best. The market economy has a hard shell and rewards are often dependent on competence and intellect. The downside also implies that people have to face the realities of unemployment and reduced income. In this scenario government also has an intermediate role in regulating pension redistribution, family allowances and unemployment insurance.

Activist state tasks

The third and final task area for governments is an activist one as related to the fields of 'redistribution' and 'coordinating private activity' (World Bank 1997).[81] Redistribution becomes the chosen path if a situation has gone off course and needs to be set straight.

There are countries where the upper classes retain a disproportionate amount of personal wealth but their riches do not contribute to the economy.[82] For example, if families have amassed huge amounts of land and capital but these resources are under used. Their received richness is because of laws which were enacted for the benefit of the elite centuries ago, but there has been no correction of this situation. This is certainly the case in some South American countries where in the past, governments sold land for next to nothing to a very limited group of people.[83]

An activist approach from government can also be applied to the support of new economic activities. This question was addressed in the World Bank's Development Report under the title 'Coordinating private activity'.[84] If a fledgling industry has not developed sufficient initiatives, the government can step in to lend a helping hand to boost the sector. This can include assistance to get a failing business back on its feet or to provide adequate harbour facilities for companies specializing in the transport of bulk chemicals and raw materials. Other areas where activist intervention can stimulate growth include the placing of fibre-optic networks for the tech sector and creating start-up subsidies for companies investing in green energy. Activist state tasks are crucial to prevent growing inequality and polarization between the most advantaged and disadvantaged members of a society, which may result in social conflict and political instability.[85] We will now look at these tasks in detail.

The World Bank has defined these activist tasks:

- Coordinating private activity.
- Redistribution of capital.

Coordinating private activity/industrial policy

Coordinating private activity, which is also called industrial policy, is a controversial topic. Neoliberal economics views industrial policy as undesirable, a distorting interference in market behaviour with questionable long-term effects. Therefore, Washington Consensus policies advise against its implementation.[86] On the other hand, Neo-Keynesian economists such as Stiglitz argue that clear-headed industrial policy has been successfully achieved by many governments, with Japan and 'East Asian Miracle' countries (Taiwan, South Korea (Box 3.8), Singapore) as shining examples.[87] The basic thought is that fledgling industries need time to start up and develop before being able to hold their own against foreign competitors. By protecting these new businesses against the competition, the government creates some 'breathing room' but on the condition that the new enterprises will be able to keep pace with their rivals in the future.

Box 3.8   South Korea

South Korea has worked with an active Keynesian industrial policy for more than 60 years. Five-year plans supported certain active industrial sectors and were regulated with varying tax laws for the different branches.[88] The policy was a success. Individual GNP rose from $100 in 1960 to $20,000 in 2004.[89] Heavy industry such as fertilizer, PVC and cement were supported in the first phase and the focus later shifted to textiles, a labour-intensive light industry. Research and development took over in the late 1980s. This policy led to the outburst of manufacturing in the automotive and semi-conductor fields with Samsung, Hyundai and Daewoo at the head of the pack.

Redistribution of capital

Policy that is directed toward capital redistribution is considered 'socially motivated' and refers to subsidy or income transferal for basic products as food and water but also to investment in social housing, health, universal education and infrastructure. The progressive tax system ensured that those who earned more paid more.

Capital redivision also exists in property transfers and can stimulate economic participation while also correcting inequality between population groups. But not all redistributions contribute to the general interest. The land reform programme in Zimbabwe serves as a good example. The expropriation of land from predominantly white farmers is a clear violation of human rights and, to add insult to injury, the reclaimed land was not allocated to black farmers but was presented to the undemocratic black elite of the country.[90] On the one hand it is a good thing that historically created unfair policy of the past has been rectified but it is the quality of the legislation that determines in the end if the changes are viewed positively.

Box 3.9   South African black economic elite

After the end of apartheid blacks claimed political power with the African National Congress (ANC) getting more than 50% of the vote, but for the economy little changed. Most big business and much of the land remained in white hands.[91] To stabilize society it was important to have more blacks running industries and this was a considerable challenge for the authorities. On the one hand, the economy benefited from a solid legal system and managers were held responsible for their performance. On the other hand, growth was dependent on the support of the people and could not develop if blacks did not participate on an equal footing. South Africa took measures to create a black managerial class.[92] Start-up endeavours got easier credit and could look to the government for extra training. A point system was also introduced to determine if a company followed an emancipation policy. The 'Black Business Supplier Development Programme' kept track of the number of black managers and whether blacks could invest in a company.[93] Businesses meeting the criteria got extra points and became government suppliers but were able to offer their wares at less competitive prices. Price fluctuation was dependent on the number of points. It is too early to tell if this system has been effective and many whites have complained of corruption and unfairness, but at the same time the number of black and white enterprises doing business with each other has increased.

3.3   Case Study: Governance in Mozambique

3.3.1   Introduction

Throughout this chapter the ideas and historical events that play an important role in creating a good administration in a modern state have been discussed. Putting these principles into practice however, is another matter. In previous centuries insufficient knowledge of 'governance' was not the only reason. People thought differently as well.

Rulers were not terribly bothered by war, colonialism or the abuse of power. In many countries the elite and ruling class were firmly in charge and did their best to make sure that it stayed that way.[94] But even today, the institutionalizing of 'good governance' is complicated. It depends on items such as cultural values, administrative know-how and the abuse of power by the elite, not forgetting that the people themselves can constitute an obstacle. This can occur, for example, if different ethnic groups or segments of society have conflicting interests or if there is little public support for measures designed to come into effect in the long run. The following case study presents an analysis of the situation in Mozambique. Using historical and socio-economic developments as a framework, it illustrates how events dating back several centuries have played an important role in the development of the present state.

3.3.2 History of Mozambique

A Portuguese colony

Mozambique (see Figure 3.2) is situated in south-east Africa and shares a common border with the country South Africa. It also has a coastline stretching some 2700 kilometres. The population is around 21 million people and the surface area is more than three times the size of the UK. Mozambique was for many years a Portuguese colony.[95]

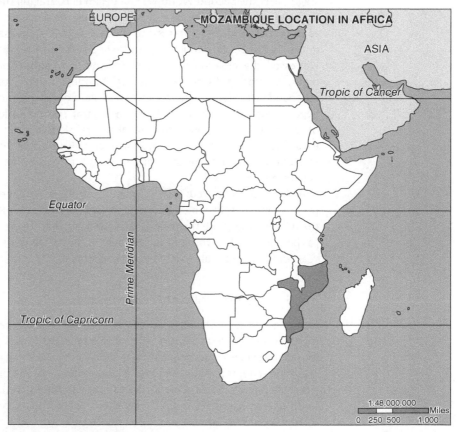

Figure 3.2 Mozambique[96]

At the end of the fifteenth century the explorer Vasco da Gama discovered the coast of present-day Mozambique during a voyage to India. By the beginning of the sixteenth century small trading posts had been established, as well as a military garrison. For the next 300 years Portugal implemented a pragmatic policy to retain control of the country.[97] It was in complete control of a number of trading posts but was increasingly forced to negotiate with powerful tribal chiefs and local sheiks. By the nineteenth century things started to change, mainly due to the increasing colonization of Africa by Western countries.[98] It became necessary for Portugal to consolidate its influence in the region. Despite the fact that Portugal was itself not a wealthy country, it proceeded to extend large concessions to business. Huge tracts of land, some as large as an entire county, were granted to plantation holders. Some of these became mini-kingdoms with their own regimes. One of the largest operations was the Mozambique Company, which specialized in mining, sugar and coconut plantations. The mines on the plantations employed thousands of black workers who were officially considered contracted employees but in actual fact were nothing more than slaves. Mozambique was first and foremost a Portuguese colony. Like other colonial powers, Portugal reaped material benefits for the mother country but failed to structurally invest in colonial administration and public education.

This all changed in 1932 when Antonio Salazar came to power in Lisbon and literally turned the country into a dictatorship. He was a dedicated imperialist and wanted absolute submission from the colonies in order to gain more influence on the world stage. After the Second World War he began encouraging the Portuguese middle class to emigrate to Mozambique and he sweetened the deal by offering fertile plots of land to potential candidates. This led to thousands of Portuguese moving to Mozambique in the 1950s and 60s, which in turn fuelled resistance from the black population and witnessed the creation in 1962 of Frelimo, a Marxist–Communist guerrilla movement. Operating from neighbouring Tanzania, which itself had recently gained independence, Frelimo guerrillas crossed the border into northern Mozambique and began their own struggle for freedom. Salazar reacted furiously and sent thousands of troops to Mozambique to control the rebels but his strategy failed. In time the entire north of Mozambique was in rebel hands costing Portugal a large number of killed and wounded. The surviving soldiers returned home and were ignored by the government.[99]

At the end of the 1960s Salazar suffered a stroke and stepped down, leaving the country in chaos. In 1974 a bloodless coup called the Carnation Revolution took place and the military sided with the people. Rumour has it that the people passed out carnations to the soldiers who promptly placed them in the barrels of their rifles, thus bringing 400 years of Portuguese rule to a symbolic, abrupt end.[100]

3.3.3   The Republic of Mozambique

Mozambique gained independence on 25 June 1975. At the time Frelimo was led by the charismatic leader Samora Machel (Figure 3.3). He was the successor of Eduardo Mondlane who was murdered in 1969, allegedly by the Portuguese Secret Service.

At the time of its independence Mozambique was one of the poorest countries in Africa with few schools, a black population with little governing experience and thousands of Portuguese nationals fleeing the country. The Marxist-leaning Frelimo looked to the West, East Germany and the Soviet Union in order to get economic support. Mozambique opted for a command economy. Many of the old plantations were taken over by the state but it hardly took measures to create a good/stable investment climate for the private sector. Samora Machel had chosen a communist regime. He was an effective speaker in pointing out that exploitation was a thing of the past. He encouraged people to pool together for the benefit of the common good.

Figure 3.3   Samora Machel, first president of Mozambique[101]

The new government was particularly focused on education and health care.[102] The old Portuguese plantations became government property and aid workers (not much older than 30) were called on for advice. Even though there was little corruption and a naïve optimism, the economy just couldn't get moving. Lack of administrative experience and manipulation of the wrong economic model led to the plantations producing less than had been expected. At the same time Frelimo was being opposed by a new resistance group called Renamo which was largely supported by South African whites. Mozambique became a dangerous place. Renamo set fields ablaze and attacked lorries carrying supplies. Towards the end of the 1980s the capital Maputo was little more than a filthy ruin and production came to a halt. Lack of parts and mismanagement caused havoc on the plantations and in the factories. During this time the Berlin Wall fell and the Soviet Union informed Frelimo that it was withdrawing its support.

Simultaneously in South Africa significant change was occurring. The white population realised that apartheid was not the way forward and this eventually led to Nelson Mandela's release from Robben Island in 1990. Whites entered into discussions to regulate a smooth handover of power to the ANC, the black South African guerrilla movement.

Back in suffering Mozambique, Frelimo finally rejected all aspects of Marxist ideology. As a consequence of this gesture, white South Africa declared its intention to withdraw support for the right wing Renamo movement. The West intervened as well and put pressure on Frelimo to enter into direct talks with Renamo. This was followed by UN resolutions relating to the situation. A new peace agreement was reached in 1992 and elections followed several years later. After 20 years of independence Mozambique was ready for a new beginning. The economy was comatose and the thousands of landmines in the countryside made work impossible, but there was peace. The new beginning had its expected ups and downs. Government organizations were not effective and investors had little confidence. The opposition party Renamo also felt banished from the proceedings and boycotted the 1998 local elections. This led to a redefinition of voting rights and Mozambique was lent a helping hand by the international community. National elections were held in 1999 and this time the process was well organized with more than 85% of citizens registering to vote.[103] National elections were again held in 2004, 2009 and 2014 with the same party remaining in power. The new government embarked on a process of economic transformation towards a market economy with the support of

World Bank loans and Western donors.[104] With untapped oil, gas and titanium reserves, the country became attractive for foreign investment which fuelled GDP growth.[105]

However, despite increasing wealth, most of the population of Mozambique are peasants relying on subsistence farming instead of commercial farming. The number of people below the poverty line in Mozambique is one of the highest in the world and the country is plagued by droughts, pests and famine.[106] As recently as 2014, 300,000 people were affected by famine. The government promised to help peasant farmers produce more food, providing financial packages to buy fertilizers and agricultural equipment and to build irrigation systems. The Brazilian Development Bank contributed a loan of $100 million to acquire agricultural machinery.[107] However, critics pointed out that the government had promised agrarian modernization several years ago, when large expanses of indigenous lands were given in concession to coal-mining companies. A key undertaking in the transformation process had been agrarian reform as the pathway to capitalist development in the region. Agrarian reform aimed to improve land productivity and attract foreign investors.

Today, Mozambique's land ownership system is a hybrid where the government is still the sole owner of land as in command economies, but rights to exploit and manage lands are given to a variety of actors both local and foreign. Since 2008 the government has been granting land concessions for large-scale farming to foreign multinationals. This way, the government obtained much-needed capital, but also expected to disseminate managerial know-how and technology to fast-track agrarian reform among the majority of peasants. The results have been increased overall productivity and a boom of exports, but famines remain a problem and modernization remains locked in the areas exploited by foreign companies.[108]

Why did agrarian reform not spill over? The answers include inadequate and too-expensive imported technologies that farmers could not afford, lack of specific know-how for small-scale production and a focus on crops which are not staple foods in Mozambique. For instance, many land concessions are focused on sugar cane harvesting for export-focused biofuels production following the example of Brazil, which agreed to transfer know-how and technology. Although biofuel production is expected to reduce poverty, it has been criticized as putting food security at risk. Mozambique still has problems putting food on the tables of its people but its lands are being used to satisfy the needs for fuel in foreign countries. Large expanses of fertile land are taken up by biofuel production, thus raising the price of food and reducing the income of poor communities relying on food markets for sustenance (these communities are extremely vulnerable to food price fluctuations).[109] In addition, since the 2008 financial crisis there has been growing concern amongst activists, academics and journalists that companies and foreign governments are increasingly engaging in 'land-grabbing' interventions in sub-Saharan Africa.[110] Land grabbing is considered a new form of colonialism; it refers to the dispossession of indigenous people of the lands they had for centuries inhabited and used for small-scale farming to support their livelihood. Mozambique is considered second-most targeted country for land grabbing in the global land market. Land-right disputes have already emerged as a result of biofuels projects and the obscure management of ownership. A specific case is the ProCana project, in which the same area inhabited by local tribes has been granted by the Mozambique government for both biofuel production and a transnational park.[111] Arnal and Talhada (2014) conclude that land grabbing is a serious concern threatening traditional lifestyles. However, they warn that foreign actors operating in international financial markets only partially explain the phenomenon of land appropriation. They identify a genuine national desire for rapid agricultural modernization which is hindered by corruption. Government-based elites give away state-owned land to political supporters in exchange for political and economic favours, while development donors such as Brazil give loans in exchange for land concessions and use of machinery imported from donor countries.[112]

3.3.4 Good governance in perspective

Developments in Mozambique during the nineteenth and twentieth centuries is the story of governance in a nutshell. It highlights worldwide administrative trends, and that countries sometimes do not always entirely adhere to them.

The Portuguese vision of colonialism was generally accepted in the nineteenth and early twentieth centuries.[113] Portugal wanted to be a colonial power even though its governmental instruments were relatively weak. Thus Portugal allowed large businesses to colonize Mozambique but retained little control over the colony. After the Second World War Portugal took a hard stance on democracy and decolonization. While major Western European countries were involved in implementing good principles of government, Portugal, Spain and Greece were still ruled by dictators. However, the trend towards democracy did not go unnoticed in Lisbon. Sub-standard economic performance and Portugal's isolation in Europe resulted in support for the dictatorship fading from different groups in society.[114] A crisis often presents opportunities for political and social change. Enforcement becomes dubious in a system that does not enjoy public support. People are restless and leaders search for solutions that usually end up encompassing known frameworks. For Portugal the framework was Europe and the democratic market economy.[115] In Mozambique it was a different scenario. After the country's independence from Portugal in 1975, the black elite felt that good administration began by combating exploitation and had little interest in the instruments of good governance such as market economy, macroeconomic management and property rights. Because the concept of exploitation lies at the heart of Marxist theory, communism became an understandable choice.[116] Only after five years of independence, when it became clear that underperforming state businesses, bureaucracy and right wing rebel movements were going nowhere, did the elite start searching for new solutions. The fall of communism in Eastern Europe plus the changing political climate in South Africa helped Mozambique to distance itself from old ideologies. Added pressure from the West and UN resolutions also played a major role in the setting up of a modern government. A crisis makes the economic and political elite weak. When the old rules are no longer effective, it becomes time for a change.

However, as we see by the end of the case study, the result of the change seems to have been a country where large sugar cane plantations and mining sites are exploited and managed by foreign companies, while an elite of government officials, urban dwellers and employees of multinationals accumulate wealth. This in a context where the countryside lacks infrastructure and education, hundreds of peasants are dispossessed of their traditional land and famines ravage the poorest regions of the country.[117]

 Case Study Questions

1. Go back to the beginning of the case study and compare this to its end. To what extent do you think today's Mozambique is different from its period as a Portuguese colony?
2. Were poor farmers better off during the period of centralized economy or during the colonial period?
3. To what extent has market transformation solved the peasants' problems?

(Continued)

4. Compare and contrast governance structures and their strengths and weaknesses across the colonial, centralized and market-orientated periods. Who were the winners and losers in each period?
5. What governance problems can you identify in Mozambique today? How can they be solved?
6. If you were the manager of a multinational company with strong business ethics, would you invest in Mozambique?

3.4   Learning tools 🔧

3.4.1   Summary

- The cultural movement called the Enlightenment that began in the seventeenth and eighteenth centuries encouraged people to use rationale, argument and research to find solutions. The movement proved to be an important change for science as well as a redefinition of society for all participants.
- Liberalism, the political–social trend, emphasizes individual freedom as long as the freedom of others is not impaired. Liberalism sets limits on 'majority rule' and is based on human rights.
- Trias politicas is a method of organizing authorities to provide quality-based governance. The governments split themselves into three separate independent bodies and each have their own power (executive, legislative and judiciary). The interaction by three basically autonomous bodies makes sure that they will correct each other faster (countervailing power) when a standard is not met.
- The role of government in the economy has been the subject of heated debate in the last 50 years. Despite controversy, there is growing agreement that governments must have an active role in correcting market imperfections, managing public goods and distributing wealth.
- In order to achieve efficient and effective administration, a report from the World Bank provides a clear definition of government tasks, which are divided into minimal, intermediate and activist functions.
- Minimal tasks are the basic functions that all governments must fulfil to ensure stability. The intermediate tasks are concerned with public goods and the legislation that has a direct connection with market failure. The World Bank has stated that governments cannot choose whether or not to perform these tasks but are expected to determine the way in which they are applied.
  - Minimal functions include basic tasks directly related to 1. Defence/law and order; 2. Property rights; 3. Macroeconomic management; 4. Public health; 5. Anti-poverty programmes and 6. Disaster relief.
  - Intermediate government functions encourage citizens to actively participate in society and link directly to education, the environment, control of monopolies, social insurance, insurance, the transparency and redistribution of pensions, and income and unemployment insurance.
  - The activist function is future orientated and encourages society's retreat from the existing situation while the government takes control of long-term aims. Important activist functions are industrial policy and the redistribution of capital.

3.4.2 Further reading

Easterley, W. (2001). *The Elusive Quest for Growth: Economists' Adventures and Misadventures in the Tropics.* Cambridge, MA: MIT Press.

Fukuyama, F. (1992). *The End of History and the Last Man.* Harmondsworth: *Penguin.*

Fukuyama, F. (2004). *State Building: Governance and World Order in the 21st Century.* Ithaca, NY: Cornell University Press.

Meadows, D. H., Meadows, D. L., Randers, J. & Behrens, W. W. (1972). *The Limits to Growth.* New York, NY: Universe Books.

Stiglitz, J. (2012). *The Price of Inequality: How Today's Divided Society Endangers Our Future.* London: Penguin.

Szirmai, A. (2005). *The Dynamics of Socio-Economic Development.* Cambridge: Cambridge University Press.

Wright, R. (2001). *Nonzero: The Logic of Human Destiny.* New York, NY: Vintage Books.

3.4.3 Assignments

 Assignment 3.1

Prepare a defence using arguments (for and against) and a conclusion to determine to what extent, in a country like the UK, business should have a human rights policy and what aspects should be included in such policy.

 Assignment 3.2

Market economies require government intervention to prevent market failures but poor governance results in government failure to control the negative effects of markets. Discuss the extent to which you think this statement is true and to what extent you think countries with poor governance can still benefit from a market economy.

 Assignment 3.3

Hugo Chavez was, until his death in 2013, the long-time president of Venezuela and clearly focused on certain areas of government interest. Describe the areas of interest 'macroeconomic management' and 'public health' (see Section 3.2), where Chavez's influence can clearly be seen, and discuss the positive and negative influences that his policies have had on Venezuelan society.

 Assignment 3.4

Critically discuss to what extent the World Bank approach to governance needs to be updated to address modern global challenges such as terrorism, migration crisis, inequality, climate change and financial crisis.

3.4.4   Self-test questions

 Self-test Questions

1. What is the trias politica and how does it apply to business?
2. A famous quotation from Immanuel Kant is:

    > But I hear calling from all sides: Do not argue! The officer says: Do not argue but rather drill! The tax collector: Do not argue but rather pay! The clergyman: Do not argue but rather believe![118]

    Discuss to what extent this quote characterizes the spirit of the Enlightenment.
3. Discuss the concept of human rights and provide an example to demonstrate how it can be at odds with 'democracy' where a majority of votes can carry certain decisions.
4. Briefly describe the concept behind ownership rights and give examples of two laws from your country that shed light on the subject.
5. To what extent should governments intervene in economic activities? Provide arguments for and against the 'hollowing out of the state'.

LIFE IN MODERN SOCIETY

Overview and learning objectives

In a developed modern society, relationships between people are, in many instances, limited to restricted roles.[1] Apart from immediate family ties, people are often perceived by others as employees, football supporters, volunteers, church members, voters, consumers, etc. The basis for this type of society owes much to the principles of the Enlightenment.[2] Innovations, productivity, social legislation and human rights all emanate from this important source. Society is, simply put, a form of social interaction between people that justifies itself through the harmonization and implementation of doctrines. The term 'modern' applies if the doctrines are directed towards values such as production, division of labour, usefulness and 'rationality'.[3]

Today's post-industrialized, tech-orientated society demands advanced political and judicial systems.[4] Something worthwhile must be on offer to attract participants. For government, this means always being alert to aspects of human behaviour in the areas of psychology, ethics and culture. Good functioning ground rules and laws are imperative for societies to function effectively.

One of the key players of the Enlightenment was Adam Smith who has already been mentioned in Chapter 2. His ideas on the market economy were based, among other things, on a government that ensured property rights and good administration of justice.[5] Using these ground rules, Smith was able to use the human trait of 'self-interest' to encourage a focus on welfare in society instead of it leading to destructive and negative consequences. Montesquieu, another important Enlightenment philosopher, contributed to this process by focusing on people as the basis for good legislation and his main concerns targeted characteristics of dominance, power struggles and esteem. The concept of 'trias politica' (Chapter 3) is neither more nor less than the institutionalizing of countervailing power. This is the case when people see narcissism as a quality associated with many powerful leaders.[6] For society to function well, 'trias politica' is an effective instrument to limit this power.

This chapter will focus in detail on the differing aspects of human behaviour with special emphasis on ethics and human nature. Section 4.1 will look at the nature of the human being. Nature can be defined as the characteristic aspects of personality that originate in our genetic DNA.[7] Biological implications relating to human behaviour can be included in nature. Components of brain chemistry that affect or dictate personality serve as a prime example. Character traits such as empathy, adaptability, justice, esteem and self-interest will be discussed. It will become clear that a prosperous modern society has rules designed to neutralize human characteristics that result in negative output, and to stimulate them when they benefit society.

Section 4.2 will deal with ethics. This subject is related to the concepts of good vs. evil and can arouse deep emotions.[8] We will examine different ethical systems and how they have evolved through the centuries. Many of today's successful societies incorporate principle ethics in their laws.[9] In traditional societies where religion, family and historical bonds play a major role in relations, the tendency is to rely more on ethical values such as empathy, loyalty and historically based commitment.[10] We will demonstrate that ethical systems can be conflicting and can be crucial in determining if a society is capable of addressing and solving problems effectively.

Section 4.3 will cover the concept of modern society and the laws, systems and organizations that have been established to encourage participation by the general public. Government faces definable challenges especially in the area of creating social capital. This implies a society based on the individual's trust of the system which, in turn, stimulates initiative taking. This happens when individuals feel they have been given a fair reply from the people and organizations with whom they are dealing.

Learning objectives

At the end of this chapter, readers will:

- Have learned about the ethical developments that have influenced the creation of 'modern society'.
- Appreciate the different animal- and human-based psychological experiments which have helped to explain primary behavioural patterns such as conformism, empathy, justice and self-interest, all of which are embedded in the human gene system and are also known as human nature.
- Better understand different ethical points of departure and realize that they can partially be explained through behavioural elements existent in our DNA.
- Have gained insight into different ethical principles and that the choice of one of these concepts has direct influence on how ethical questions are dealt with.
- Be aware of society's necessary preconditions so that individuals take their own initiative to participate in society.

4.1   Nature

The media confronts us on a daily basis with tales of human behaviour and subjects such as status and the abuse of power, but solidarity and justice also provide headline news. When human behaviour is approached from the standpoint of nature, the emphasis shifts to characteristics determined by our DNA. The tell-tale signs of who we are and what we will become are in place at birth and are classified in different forms. The psychologist Cloninger, with his colleagues, has placed these inborn temperaments into four groups: 1. harm avoidance; 2. novelty seeking; 3. perseverance; 4. reward dependence.[11] This chapter will examine nine aspects of nature that play a prominent role in discussions about governance, politics, economics, culture and solidarity. These are: 'homo economicus', 'status', 'aggression', 'authority mindedness', 'exploratory impulse', 'empathy', 'fair treatment', 'conformism' and 'kin selection'. Many concepts show that competitiveness is inherent in man. But non-competitive behaviour also exists. This last view has gained support in recent years especially in the fields of neurobiology and behavioural sciences. Loyalty, affection, empathy etc. are inherent in our genes, and surroundings play a minor role.[12]

The concept of 'nature' is often coupled with its counterpart 'nurture'. The main points of nurture comprise ethics, culture, upbringing and experience. Section 4.2 of this chapter will look at this concept in detail using elements of ethics. Human behaviour depends on the interaction between nature and nurture.

4.1.1   Homo economicus ('calculated self-interest')

Adam Smith's enthusiasm for the market economy also implies that government should make more use of individuals' desire to improve their lot. Nineteenth-century philosopher John Stuart Mill coined the phrase 'economic man' to clarify Smith's hypothesis and we know this today as homo economicus.[13] Its premise is that humanity prefers a combination of minimum effort and rational decisions in the quest for increased income, welfare and comfort, with human differences as part of the equation. A good example is of people who are prepared to work for low wages as long as they can work, as opposed to those who postpone their income to study first, for better paying jobs later.

Box 4.1   The Marshmallow Experiment[14]

In the 1960s, Walter Mischel conducted the Marshmallow Experiment with small children to see how they dealt with reward. The study has become a classic with far-reaching implications.

Four-year-old children were placed in a small room with a table and on the table was a dish with one marshmallow (a soft white candy with a gooey centre). Before leaving the children alone in the room, they were told if they didn't eat the single marshmallow, they would get two when the researcher came back. Cameras filmed the children during their time alone which varied from 10–15 minutes. Some toddlers were able to wait patiently while others couldn't resist the temptation and ate the marshmallow straight away. One-third of the group had the perseverance and patience to restrain from eating and wait for the researcher, but this was not the main point of the experiment. The children were monitored into adolescence and results showed that those who were patient to wait achieved greater success, with intelligence and self-control playing an important part. The degree to which you as a child and later as an adult are capable of controlling your thinking and desires influences your decision-making ability and interaction with people.

You can see the Marshmallow Experiment on YouTube.

Homo economicus and policy research

Homo economicus, the rational being, always on the lookout for personal improvement, has been the subject of countless studies. The basic assumption is the pursuit of money supported by positive and negative feelings all relating to the end goal. Variations on this theme include, for example, deciding between free time and overtime where a subject can decide if a €15 hourly wage is sufficient enough to decline extra work. The concept of homo economicus is important for government policy. Alcohol duties, road pricing, traffic tickets and carbon dioxide taxes are measures based on the idea that financial incentives have an influence on human behaviour.

4.1.2   Status

Status, the state of being admired, is something that most people desire at a certain level.[15] Status is easily visible in society and can best be seen in hierarchy. It shows your progress in the climb up the social ladder. Fields of endeavour contribute as well. Think only of those aiming for success in a sporting career as opposed to those who are happy to be promoted to higher functions in the workplace. Although status has a strong link with financial reward and power, this is not always the case. Artists and writers can become world famous while not always having an income that reflects their status.

Box 4.2   Honours list[16]

Status plays an important role in society, therefore the government in several countries around the world tries to add to the status of its citizens by recognizing their contributions via annual honours lists. In India, the government grants four types of awards to its citizens: the leadership, civilian, particular and patriotic awards that are given every year. The highest civilian award is the 'Bharat Ratna' that is awarded to individuals in recognition of their exceptional service to the nation in any field. The recommendations for the award are made by the prime minister directly to the president of India. Since it was first started in 1954 until the time of writing, 43 awards have been granted.

Status in relation to societal interests

Status does not have a clear relationship with 'good and bad' in the moral sense. The best president, the best hacker and the cleverest thief all have a sense of esteem. Although esteem is an important facet of nature, achieving it is closely related to culture and trends or hypes. Balance in society is dependent on a good mix of individual status and general interest but this can also go wrong, with the recent bank crisis being a prime example (see Box 4.3).

Box 4.3   Do banking 'gurus' have the wrong nature?

Many high-level bank employees are there to increase the bank's profits through lucrative deals. The esteem accorded to these young banking 'gurus' is based on their daring, the creation of strong profits and their willingness to take risks. The banks thought that these types of banking professionals were best suited to make good financial deals but in the end they shot themselves in the foot. Many of these 'high flyers' took foolish risks and reverted to fraudulent banking practices.[17] The banks brought the proverbial Trojan horse into the office. The initial successes were indeed due to daring, decisiveness and cleverness, and the air of superiority was tangible, but few, if any, of these new 'deal makers' had the capability of coupling the new esteem to values such as integrity and dependability. These are values that require courage, especially when profit margins are lower than predicted.

4.1.3   Aggression

Aggression, the feelings of anger or antipathy resulting in hostile or violent behaviour and the readiness to attack or confront, has a functional origin.[18] In a threatening situation, people's urge to protect themselves is primary and they use their energy to deal with the perceived problem. Society in general frowns on aggressive behaviour and expects that people have the capacity to control themselves. Aggression is not easily explainable and learning to control it is important. Aggression increases with power and can be seen in the ways bosses treat their employees and in soldiers who mistreat and humiliate captives. In order to control aggression at administrative levels, there must be limits of rules and regulations for people in power and authorities must also be trained in mental and ethical aspects. Escalation of aggression by those in power was classically demonstrated by Philip Zimbardo in the famous 1971 Stanford Prison experiment (Box 4.4).

Box 4.4   The Stanford Prison Experiment[19]

For this experiment two groups of males were selected, one for the prisoners and one for the guards, 18 in total. The purpose was to see how people would adjust to role division within the prison system. The candidates for prisoners received a letter asking them to report to the test centre, but to make the circumstances more realistic, 'staged' arrests were planned without informing the participants. After the nine prisoners had assembled, an arrest team appeared made up of real police officers. They were taken to the university where they were lectured by the nine guards who had been briefed a day earlier. They were told to address the guards as 'correctional officers', stating their prison number as well. The guards also set up house rules including which uniform was to be worn during the experiment.

Prisoners were informed that they had committed a serious crime and were briefed about the life they could expect behind bars including proper conduct and the treatment they would be given. The prisoners were then forced to strip and were sprayed with disinfectant. Prison garb was also kept to a minimum with no underwear allowed and everyone wearing long numbered shirts that closely resembled a dress. The prison cells were three small rooms at the university with bunk beds and very little space.

The first day passed without incident with everyone seemingly happy but circumstances changed unexpectedly on day two. As part of the game playing, the prisoners challenged the guards. At first the guards failed to act decisively but soon afterwards order was restored and the inmates were locked up in their cells. From then on things got worse. Because all nine guards could not be constantly on duty, a rotation system was set up. The guards partially blamed themselves for being too lenient during the uprising and soon began a tougher regime. One prisoner in particular lost control when he was told his smoking rights were to be curtailed. The guards made his life miserable, knowing that the man wanted to smoke when he felt like it. Further prisoner protests followed when the guards limited use of the toilets and placed buckets by the beds but some of the men became lifeless followers of the guards' orders. To stop things from getting out of hand and for security reasons, the experiment came to a halt after six days. The level of tension and escalation had increased to such an extent that the experiment was never repeated again.

Several films, videos and YouTube clips about the experiment exist, all of which make a strong impression on the viewer.

Important lessons can be learned from the Stanford Prison Experiment. For a society that wishes to contain aggression it is important to bear the following themes in mind:

- Surroundings and aggression.
- Aggression and the escalation of violence.

The Lucifer Effect and aggression

Philip Zimbardo, who conducted the Stanford Experiment, analysed his findings in a book entitled 'The Lucifer Effect.'[20] One of the most important conclusions was that good people can become aggressive in specific surroundings. He felt that in questions of guilt, the justice system is inadequate in only dealing with the accused. Because the behaviour of the accused is caused by the system, society can benefit in the end, as the system itself becomes vulnerable to criticism and suggestions for improvement can be directed at those in charge; both the system and the authorities come under scrutiny.

Aggression and spiralling violence

The Stanford Prison Experiment shows us how closely action and reaction are related and how things can rise to a boiling point in a tense situation when rules are poorly conceived. In daily life we refer to this as the escalation of violence. The Stanford study demonstrated that an aggressive dynamic is not an easy thing to control.

4.1.4   Respect for authority

Nowadays parents in UK (and elsewhere) complain that young people have little or no respect for authority. A 'negotiation-orientated' culture is emerging and police, parents, teachers and doctors are expected to accept it. The government is also confronted with this trend but despite this there are voices in society (authority-sensitive ones) who would like to see more respect for those with power. We see this in more hierarchy-orientated societies. Many people are motivated to do their work or duties when supported by a person in charge or an authoritative body. Authority gives government a good opportunity to influence behaviour. The description of the Milgram Experiment (Box 4.5) will illustrate how strong the instrument of 'authority', the legitimation or socially approved use of power, can be.[21]

Box 4.5   The Milgram Experiment

In 1961, psychologist Stanley Milgram conducted research to measure sensitivity to authority. He wanted to determine if people would discard accepted standards and values if told to do so by the authorities. Participants responded to advertisements but were not told the real purpose of the experiment, rather that it was an attempt to see if punishment had a positive effect on learning behaviour. When the candidates arrived at the test location they were introduced to another participant who in reality was an actor who was hired to play the role of a student. The researcher explained that a teacher–student relationship would be set up. The teacher would recite a series of word combinations and the student had to remember as many as possible. For every incorrect answer, the teacher would punish the student by administering a small electric shock which would increase in intensity for further mistakes. This supposedly would demonstrate if severe punishment had a positive or negative influence on learning behaviour.

The electric shock device was placed in the room with the teacher and had a scale of 45–450 volts. The machine obviously did not give any electric shocks but the real participant was unaware of this.

(Continued)

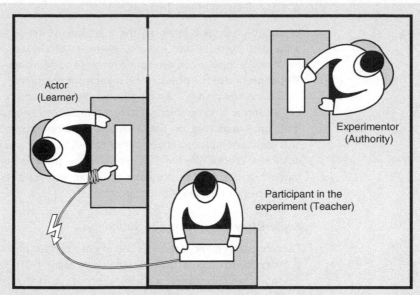

Figure 4.1   Milgram Experiment set-up

The actor gave more and more incorrect answers and the voltage was increased with the actor/student starting to scream when a 135 volt shock was given. Most participants wanted to stop but the researcher, dressed as a doctor, insisted that the experiment continue by using expressions as 'The experiment requires that you continue' and 'You have no choice, you must carry on.'

After that most candidates did continue while having to listen to screams and banging on the walls of the adjacent room when the shock device was used. When the voltage reached 300 watts the actor stopped screaming and gave no further answers and silence ensued but the pseudo doctor demanded that the participants continue. In the end many participants obeyed directions despite the eerie silence from the student room. 26 of the 40 candidates (65%) followed instructions to the end and pushed the button with a strength of 450 volts.

YouTube has a selection of films about the Milgram Experiment.

Currently, much animal research is being conducted in areas of obedience, co-operation and domination.[22] Our genes and genetic make-up influence the production of the brain substances serotonin and oxytocin which in turn influence our behaviour as cooperative, obedient or aggressive. Psychologist Simon Young predicts that the field of genetic origins will soon be a prominent field of study.[23]

The idea of 'authority' is an instrument that carries considerable weight in society.[24] Hierarchy is institutionalized and respect for rules and decisions made by governments, judges and experts are usually obeyed. 'Authority' can have legal status but softer forms, such as the power of knowledge, can also be included. Power is a sensitive issue and comes with pros and cons; the Milgram experiment demonstrated that sensitivity to authority can backfire. For society, it is important that people learn to form their own independent judgements during their upbringing based on inherent and accepted ethical principles.[25] This gives citizens better possibilities to confront the abuse of power. It is no accident that the expression 'Befehl ist Befehl' (orders are orders) has a negative association with Nazi Germany, as it was used to silence dissenting soldiers.

4.1.5   Exploratory impulse

Exploratory impulse refers to the pleasure we derive from research, discovery and expanding horizons and includes elements of courage and curiosity. The degree of exploratory impulse can determine success and flourishes when there is a basis of trust.[26] This concept also has physical and mental connotations.

The businessman is exercising his physical exploratory impulse when he decides to pay a supplier or takes the necessary steps to acquire new machinery or construct a new building. Researchers, on the other hand, concentrate more on independent thinking. This approach is characterized by flexibility, creativity and mentally unscrambling previously held taboos. We see that people in the arts and leaders who take new directions have a high degree of this courage, but in fact everyone has it to some degree with some people being more ambitious than others.

Exploratory impulse and surroundings

Passion, engagement, openness and intense perception are also closely associated with the exploratory impulse and help to release energy.[27] The released energy has a link with, among others, dopamine, a chemical produced in the brain.[28] The degree of curiosity is thus related to genetic make-up, not forgetting the importance of surroundings. The level of ambition is dependent on an individual's perception of his/her chances for success and whether a clear image can be formed to achieve desired goals. Think only of the special training programmes for talented young players organized by professional football.

Box 4.6   Safe surroundings and exploratory impulse[29]

During a primary school experiment two groups of children were presented with a series of assignments and had the option of an easy or a difficult choice. Both groups received feedback. If the task was done well, the kids of the first group were told that they were smart. In the other group, children who participated in the assignments were told that the results verified the hard work that was done. The results showed that children who were praised for their intelligence only tended to choose easier or slightly challenging tasks. Those who were told that they had done good research and achieved an admirable result opted for more complex tasks.

Society must make good use of individual exploratory impulses, and when conditions are in place to encourage this the rewards can be substantial. New, vigorous forms of art, expression, technology, business and science are among the many contributions possible.

4.1.6   Empathy

Charles Darwin's theory of evolution states that the 'survival of the fittest' takes precedence over natural selection but the expression should not be interpreted as referring to physical strength alone.[30] Darwin is saying that living beings need certain characteristics to survive in a pre-determined situation. Strength, dominance and aggressiveness are necessary but there are many other considerations. Flight prowess, camouflage capabilities and empathy can be valuable survival assets. Empathy means being aware and sensitive to the feelings of others without having to communicate in an explicit manner. Many recent studies have focused on this and have concluded that empathy is the primary reason for the success of the human race and is not only learned (nurture), but is also a part of our genetic make-up (nature). Taking care of your own 'kind' is a primary part of 'nature' and this theory has been reinforced through animal experimentation.

Box 4.7   Sociable birds are not always losers

Researchers Dingmanse and Both and their colleagues studied character traits of great tits, a common bird species, and concluded that they could be divided into two groups: aggressive and sociable.[31] The degree of aggressiveness was determined by genetic structure. Further results showed a stable level of coexistence between birds with a dominant character and those who were more frightened and cautious. Natural selection has not caused the more frightened birds to die out but it was proved that the more aggressive and dominant ones did better in difficult situations such as harsh winters, drought and periods of food shortage. By contrast, favourable conditions allowed the frightened and cautious birds to thrive by being less hectic, with normal conditions increasing survival chances. They were less prone to search for new hunting grounds, were content in familiar surroundings and better able to raise their chicks. Despite different conditions, relations between the two types of great tits have remained stable through the years. One harsh winter accounted for a surplus of aggressive birds while several years later the balance was restored. In succeeding years a mathematical average could be applied and the relation between 'social' and aggressive' birds remained constant.

Besides the bird experiments described in Box 4.7, much research has been done into primate behaviour by the well-known Dutch scientist Frans de Waal. His work has provided keen insight into nature and nurture and proved that upbringing and culture are only a part of social values. During more than 200 million years of primate evolution, the development of empathy, caring and sensitive emotions have made a critical difference to the success of apes at the highest end of the species and parallels have been drawn with humans.[32] De Waal stated that humans had a great degree of aggressiveness but also a great degree of empathy.[33] Compared to other creatures, humans are socially inclined and capable of reacting to the feelings of others. A mother's care for her young is often used as an explanation for the instinctive feelings of loyalty and empathy and is seen as an automatic response. This form of empathy, which belongs to the nature category, is triggered by the limbic system, a part of the brain with a long evolutionary history. A human's prefrontal cortex, which developed much later, does not control this behaviour. It means that the feeling of joy that is felt when caring for someone else is created through an automatic 'reward mechanism' generated in the brain itself. With the exception of extreme psychopaths and very seriously autistic people, all of us have this type of empathy. When this study is translated to the realm of 'good governance' it is obvious that government must stimulate empathy. The encouragement of volunteer work, for example, is not only a method for achieving government tasks inexpensively but also serves to enrich the experience of the person offering his or her time.

4.1.7   Feelings of fairness (justice)

The Monkeys Reject Unequal Pay Experiment observed apes' behaviour when they were unequally treated. Two monkeys were given equal slices of cucumber for performing certain tasks. All went well until one of the monkeys got a juicy grape. The behaviour of the other one changed instantly and besides refusing to cooperate, it threw its remaining slice of cucumber out of the cage. On YouTube there are video clips about the monkeys that reject unequal pay. [34]

The experiment showed that monkeys are not always out for their own interests and cannot be considered as homo economicus. The cucumber is at first satisfactory but is soon rejected. This irrational behaviour, which has no relation to task and reward, has to do with judicial sentiment and the anger that ensues due to unfair (unequal) treatment. The judicial sentiment is related to frustration, anger and discrimination and caused one of the chimps to reject its reward; humans have reacted in a similar fashion.[35] Tests have proven that people in group situations are not necessarily after the top prize but are more concerned about prize division. Alternatively, people react negatively in a group if they think they are not getting an equal share. Even the prospect of a higher reward is not always satisfying if people perceive that others are getting something better.

4.1.8   Conformism

People differ in the degree to which they are prepared to adjust to norms, values and behaviour in groups. When a large company of friends goes out for a drink and the first three order a beer, it is likely that the rest will order the same. If you are the last to order and decide on something else, comments will surely follow. Group pressure is often sufficient to change individual behaviour; many psychological and neurological studies have examined this. Research and experiments have proved that feelings for adjustment/conformity are present at birth.

In 1951 social psychologist Solomon Asch developed the well-known study described in Box 4.8.[36]

Box 4.8   Conformity Experiment

In this experiment a 'guinea pig' was selected and asked to compare the length of a drawn line with three others via a simple multiple choice answer. Eight to ten actors also played a part but the 'real' person assumed that they were all participants. The candidates were called into a room with a long table and the actors were told to always take a place at the ends of the table ensuring that the real subject always sat somewhere in the middle. The test leader entered with 18 sheets of paper. A line was drawn on each sheet followed by three others lettered a, b and c. The correct answer was easy to see but the actors were told to uniformly give the wrong answer for 12 of the 18 examples. In general the test subjects were able to adjust. On average they gave the wrong answer one-third of the time and conformed to the rest of the group.

There are video clips on YouTube about the Conformity Experiment.

Conformity of society

Conformist tendencies are not only limited to small groups but apply to larger numbers as well. Values in society change and the majority of people adjust accordingly. A good example is smokers vs. non-smokers. In the UK at the end of the 1960s at least 70% of the men and 40% of women were smokers.[37] Ashtrays were everywhere: in the office, factories, cafes and restaurants and many public buildings. Fifty years later things were different. Now, smoking is prohibited in most public places. It all began with scientific evidence showing the connection between smoking, cancer and heart and vascular disease. The media and health organizations joined in soon afterwards, together with doctors and health professionals, and the perception of smoking began to change. More people 'kicked the habit' and public opinion demanded clarification of existing policy towards smoking. It has taken 50 years for these adjustments to affect society in the UK and elsewhere. It would be fun to speculate how values and standards will change 50 years from now in the area of sustainability and which national and international organizations will play a major role.

Neurological studies have also played a part in clarifying humanity's conformist tendencies. Scans of sections of the brain that process conflict have indicated a higher degree of activity when people don't conform.[38] The part of the brain that triggers euphoria and reward becomes by contrast less active. Final thoughts on the subject have shown that a feeling of loyalty creates a comfortable situation and this helps avoid conflict scenarios. Adjustment/conformity tendencies remain closely linked to 'nature'.

4.1.9   Kin selection

It would be wrong and a bit naïve to think that evolutionary theory is only based on survival of species. Competitive instinct also exists within a species. Male chimpanzees, wolves and lions are renowned for their tendency to eliminate the competition by killing newborn cubs (infanticide).[39] This becomes an advantage for the aggressor, as a female without offspring is more easily prone to mate again, even if the male partner is the one who killed the first litter. Humans, too, compete with each other on a global scale but also in microcosms. Statistical research has shown that stepchildren face a far greater chance of being abused or even killed by one of their stepparents than children born from two biological parents.[40] This implies that we must look for another theory to understand cooperation within the same species.

We could assume that survival of the individual remains the principal goal, that despite everything 'looking after number one' remains the primary objective. However, this does not always coincide with observations that we make about ourselves and nature. People and animals exhibit behaviour that is not always associated with personal survival or gain and this suggests that the assumption that living creatures only care about producing offspring from their own seed is imperfect. Think only of social insects such as bees, wasps and ants who have a distinct separation of tasks, almost like a caste system that includes workers, feeders and guards. The lowest members of the hierarchy show a remarkable degree of altruism. The individual sacrifices itself for the benefit of the group. Workers in bee and ant colonies are born infertile but, because of the tasks they perform, are able to provide the Queen with the chance she needs to reproduce.

The phenomenon of kin selection can be described as helping to ensure the success of the next generation. In human terms, family ties come first to mind but there are broader implications. Factors such as skin and eye colour and even body shape can play an underlying role and culture itself helps to create 'family ties'.[41] The human nature aspect 'kin selection' makes it clear that people use numerous criteria to classify groups. Religion, ethical values, but even the sport that you practise and the car brand that you choose provide a basis for discrimination.

Box 4.9   Us versus them

Scientists have stated that people have the unenviable character trait of dividing the world into groups.[42] This 'us vs. them' thinking is based on natural, primal instinct, and serves to quickly put the enemy into perspective. Many people have a sharply tuned 'enemy recognition system' and this makes it difficult to create a multicultural society. Globalization does not imply that people can automatically get on well with other cultures and 'us vs. them' attitudes have deep roots. This was demonstrated in an experiment by Iowa teacher Jane Elliot who wanted her students to feel what it was like to experience discrimination. She did this after feeling uncomfortable during student discussions about the murder of Martin Luther King.

The dialogue between Ms. Elliot's students was weak and espoused politically correct platitudes. With student approval, she decided to create an actual discrimination condition. Her students were all white and she divided them into two groups: blue and brown eyed. The brown-eyed students wore a brown board on their chest to distinguish them as 'workers'. The students were then told that blue-eyed people had more melanin in their bodies: the chemical substance that makes eyes blue but also has a positive influence on intelligence. After being told this, student behaviour changed. The blue-eyed students achieved better results on their assignments and later on refused to use the same drinking fountain as their brown-eyed contemporaries.

Despite the inborn trait of us vs. them, society does have possibilities of combatting discrimination. An important factor is that people must have the courage to enter into and develop alliances outside of their own group. It means for example that a government ensures a good enforcement policy in the area of discrimination. For instance, the immigrants have just as much chance of getting a job as the native population. Creating a feeling of security is essential. People who feel discriminated against suffer from stress and heart palpitations and are less productive. When people feel they are not included, counterproductive tendencies arise with an accompanying downward spiral. A positive spiral results when we encourage people's desire to belong to a group and helps to create a feeling of safety when dealing with those who are not in your own group. The availability of halal meat in office canteens has contributed to acceptance and has stimulated Muslims to share the lunch table with others not conforming to their dietary laws. When this is applied to cultural aspects, it works the other way around. Participants in society readily accept 'generic' demands that apply to everyone when discussing honesty, responsibility, care for each other and acceptance.

When the study in Box 4.9 is translated to the realm of 'good governance' (see Chapter 3) and inequality it is obvious that government must have instruments to create a sphere of cooperation between people of different cultural backgrounds. It is also important that government has the necessary tools to intervene in the event of conflicts between different ethnical and cultural groups. It was no coincidence that 'human rights' assumed a prominent position in legislation after the Second World War.[43]

4.1.10 'Nature' and the human brain

Section 4.1 has so far examined different human traits, with some indication that people are generally able to stand up for themselves, and has considered other factors demonstrating inherent social interaction. Human beings have inborn empathy, strive for equality, adjust fairly easily but are also influenced by aggressiveness, status and calculated behaviour. The degree in which these characteristics manifest themselves is wholly dependent on the individual (see Box 4.10 and Figure 4.2).

Box 4.10   Nature perspective on homo sapiens

The primate research of Frans de Waal is often used to discuss the relevance of homo economicus. Rational and calculated behaviour provides a very limited view of mankind. He demonstrated that there is more empathy (homo empathia) in us than is generally assumed. Nevertheless homo violentus (aggression) and homo oboedientia (respect for authority) are also part of our genetic makeup. The arsenal of motivations we possess is enormous. Some people can be conformist (homo conformo) while others pursue status (homo honoro). The behaviour of a human rights activist, for example, can easily be explained by a sense of fairness (homo justus) and exploratory impulse, because of the urge to change the world (homo exploratio). The need to choose people based on skin colour or status (obviously a form of discrimination) can be explained through the phenomenon of kin selection (homo electio).

The social traits which are part of 'nature' are concerned with uncalculated self-interest. People tend to help others faster when there is no forethought of personal gain or other consequences. Behaviour is in large part based on emotions and rationality plays a relatively small part in human reactions. This means that a majority of people are more inclined to be helpful and the rational tendencies of the homo economicus have little or no effect on feelings.

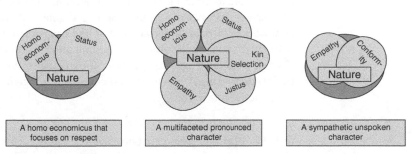

Figure 4.2   Nature aspects and personality

Box 4.11   Uninhibited good deeds[44]

A positive frame of mind and increased optimism have been linked to increased propensity of helpful acts. A study was conducted at a busy train station in a large metropolitan city located in the Netherlands. The experiment aimed at analysing the helpful tendencies of individuals towards a fellow passenger who had dropped some pens from his briefcase. Initially, a group of people was asked to describe the kind of day they had had. These individuals became more self-conscious and inhibited in their outlook, and, as a result, only 7% of this group of people offered to help the passenger who had dropped his pens. On the other hand, another group of individuals was asked to describe a positive situation where they had felt no inhibitions. From this group of people, 53% individuals helped their fellow passenger who had lost his pens. This study suggested that an uninhibited feeling of happiness is enough to prompt people to be helpful and spontaneous.

For a better understanding of human behaviour, it is helpful to know that the brain is divided into three sections: the reptile brain, the limbic system and the new cortex.[45]

The *reptile brain* is the oldest. More commonly known as the brain stem, it accounts for cold-blooded behaviour, lack of empathy, territorial control, desire for power and aggression. It reacts immediately and helps us to survive dangerous situations but has no capacity for feelings or thoughts and has no learning capabilities.

Surrounding the brain stem is the *limbic system*. It also has a long evolutionary history and shares basic characteristics with the brains of dogs and countless other mammals such as fear, aggressiveness, satisfaction and empathy.

The *new cortex* is the part of the brain that separates humans from animals. It is not well developed for animals high on the evolutionary ladder but for humans it is the key to abstract thinking and controls vision and hearing functions.

Ethical behaviour and nature

Recent studies have caused a re-evaluation as to how human behaviour has developed. It is now clear that the limbic system is responsible for feelings of sympathy and empathy and that much social behaviour is driven by genes, hormones and neurological impulses.[46, 47] Cooperative behaviour is only partially influenced by the cortex. Today we know that ethical behaviour such as justice, empathy and respect for authority can be partially linked to 'nature'. Culture is not the only factor with a bearing on ethics and the old saying 'culture is just a coat of paint' is no longer valid. Humans do not tend to live at others' expense but expect fair treatment and the chance to increase status (social standing).[48] In general an individual is not a true homo economicus and most of us prefer a comfortable existence with modest rewards instead of aggressively searching for fame and fortune. Quite a number of human beings, however, do like to distinguish themselves. When this doesn't happen, shame and frustration is often the result.[49] Behavioural scientists are aware of this and have advised governments on how to work with frustration, aggression and discrimination in order to improve behaviour. They have pointed out that young people in particular must be steered away from destructive tendencies and be given assistance and encouragement to put them on course for a constructive role in society.[50]

4.1.11 Nature and contemporary society

After Russia, China and India began to embrace and endorse principles of the market economy in the 1980s and 1990s the World Bank became a principal benefactor by being able to offer a more uniform concept of effective government.[51] This does not imply that all affected states are doing well and there are still many challenging questions about reduction of poverty, improved health care and sustainable development. Despite this, modern society has a number of instruments available to it that have proven their worth.

Contemporary society and the institutionalization of participation

We can make clear connections to show whether the tools of modern society are in tune with people's needs (see Figure 4.3). The idea of safety and security are essential provisions but government also has effective methods to encourage participation.[52] In an ideal situation, government, business and social organizations all contribute to improve welfare and well-being. In addition, individual curiosity and exploratory tendencies are paramount. A person chooses a course of study and often looks for work beyond a familiar environment, and is less concerned with family ties and ethnic groups.[53] In a modern society people can take risks and explore knowing that there is a social safety net if things don't work out.[54] Society offers institutionalized empathy and people are less dependent on family and friends. Contemporary society also stimulates participation because our 'sense of justice' has been institutionalized in different ways.[55] Everyone is equal before the law. The fact that people as citizens can vote for political parties has a direct relation to justice. Every individual has equal influence concerning his or her political opinion. The institutionalizing of co-decision whereby politicians act on behalf of citizens strengthens participation.[56, 57]

Another aspect with a positive influence on participation has been the institutionalization of the free market. 'Property rights', an essential aspect of the market economy, offers human beings the chance to explore, create and innovate and people are motivated to participate because society appeals to 'nature' factors such as 'homo economicus' and the exploratory impulse.[58]

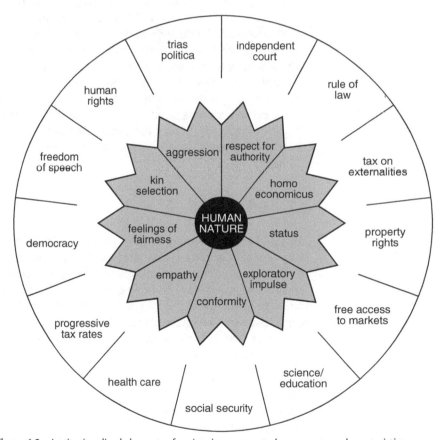

Figure 4.3   Institutionalized elements of society in response to human nature characteristics

The development process of the modern state

The modern state has had a long development and in many countries the individual freedoms which limit the power of the elite are institutionalized in a better way. Privileged members of these societies have learned the rules of governing not only by addressing division of power issues and advancement but also by debating the best ways to improve welfare. The elite in government were often acting in their own interests and positive change occurred as a result of general discontent, press freedom, international context and people's protests.[59] Welfare and well-being have often benefited (or not) through governmental trial-and-error policies; an example of this is the position of the central bank.[60] In the twentieth century, governments delegated some aspects of monetary policy to an independent central bank which gave them less influence over their own pocketbook. This gives investors (as well as ordinary citizens) confidence in monetary policy, because issues such as inflation remain under control.

Box 4.12   Nonzero[61]

In his book *Nonzero*, author Robert Wright examines human history through the lens of 'game theory'. *Nonzero* implies that many situations have nothing to do with the 'zero sum game', which happens when one person's welfare improves and is directly related to a decline in the welfare of another. The object of the game (society) is to avoid creation of zero sum scenarios. This can be partially achieved with a well-functioning free market economy. Trade between countries results in improved conditions for both partners. A zero sum situation also exists when a country regulates free trade within its borders to improve productivity.

Wright considers 100 years of history in a nutshell and emphasizes that the results of the 'nonzero concept' are often positive. Societies using the concept of 'nonzero' as a starting point often do better than those with stifling restrictions. Creativity in people is best motivated when government has rules to stimulate their participation and this is the best way to avoid playing the zero sum game.

4.2   Ethics

Ethics deal with the question of good versus evil, right versus wrong. Through individual interpretation of society's values and standards, it becomes possible to assume a position in the community without causing disrupting problems.[62] Tensions arise when people are not capable of accepting existing ethical codes. When unacceptable conduct occurs, people place themselves outside the boundary of community norms. Many people have sensitive antennae when the issue of acceptable behaviour is raised. People are often concerned with the question 'is what I do acceptable?' Related questions that hold importance for individuals are:[63]

- Will people accept it?
- What's in it for me?
- What do others get from it?
- Have I offended others?

In this section we will be examining ethics and the role they play in society. The constant re-tuning of expectations to society's guidelines will be covered. Rules in a society have more legitimacy if people from the entire spectrum of society feel assured that pre-set standards and values apply to everyone. This gives individuals and groups more confidence in knowing that they can challenge the actions of those who abuse present standards.[64] Ethics are the reflection of our morals, of the standards and values that we expect to be reasonably accepted by others in an attempt to maintain balance in everyday life.

4.2.1 Ethics and society

In multicultural societies consisting of different ethnic and religious groups it is important that governments develop clearly defined ethical guidelines.[65] What part of ethics should be put into law and which elements are better left untouched? The field of ethics has made enormous strides in the last few centuries.[66] The regulation of social traffic in large societies with people of diverse backgrounds implies that a guarantee of freedom is imperative.[67] To get an idea of distinguishing ethical features in contemporary life we will now look at tribal and religious groups.

Tribal ethics

The regulation of human interaction plays an important role in tribal cultures. There is a wonderful film that has focused on this subject. 'The Fast Runner' by director Zacharias Kunuk examines passion, love and jealousy among the Inuits, a community of Eskimoes living in northern Canada. The ins and outs of daily life are presented in microcosm because the tribe consists of only 20 people. When two people fall in love, the story turns into one of vengeance and manslaughter. The ethical question here is extremely sensitive as feelings of jealousy and revenge are weighed against the constant struggle of a small community to survive together in the harsh conditions of the Tundra. We see that the ethics of a close-knit community are different. The primary focus of such groups is working together and they know that their future is dependent on cooperation.[68] Values and standards are based more on mutual loyalty and less on anonymous justice. Although mutual cooperation is a key aspect of tribal life, it does not imply that it is written in stone. Rules of loyalty, solidarity, justice and tolerance vary.

When different groups come together in a certain sphere, a new situation arises. The ethical system for a specific group in society, known as 'particularism', is a tension-creating concept which exists when different groups come together and the dominant group demands more rights and privileges for its members.[69] When group interaction intensifies, it is important that an ethical system is developed which applies the same rules to everyone.[70] This is called 'universalism' which is a basic building block for a modern society.

Ethics and religion

There is an important place for ethics in organized religion. From the human perspective this is a rich field of thought. By bringing the crucial concept of good versus evil into religion the question of ethics can distance itself from the populace.[71] Standards and values are placed in a different category and the layperson has less control. Religion provides ethical authority. The ethics that underpin religion are less susceptible to critical discussion, giving them a legitimacy which results in a more stable ethical system.[72] Societies that possess an ethical system that is not called into question, because people believe in its principles, generally have less insecurities which is usually considered an advantage.

Religion is an important medium for implementing ethics in society. Clearly definable actions such as theft and murder are areas where ethical considerations apply but less obvious situations such as relations between men and women, attitudes towards tolerance, and hospitality and solidarity fall under the same umbrella. Organized religion also has rules to deal with acceptable and unacceptable convictions concerning belief in a supreme being. This last aspect can often lead to problems in developing societies especially as the ethics system begins to take shape through the creation of laws. Communal tension can increase when law dictates how people are supposed to think about God.[73]

4.2.2   Ethics and the state

Government plays a major role by creating laws with fixed ethical standards for the general public and citizens are expected to obey the rules. Theft, violence and discrimination don't require much thought to determine what is right and what is wrong. Other ethical concepts also find their way into law. Think for example of the government's role in the taxation of pensions or in development aid.

The modern state has distanced itself from 'personal beliefs'.[74] Government keeps, with good reason, appropriate distance in the realm of acceptable and non-acceptable religious convictions. This position has evolved through trial and error. Religious wars and recurring conflicts contesting personal beliefs has led to freedom of religion being a highly valued item in many countries, and so governments began to see the importance of non-interference. The separation of church and state was an important doctrine in setting up the rules of society and had its heyday in nineteenth-century Europe.[75]

Many countries are engaged in discussions about the separation of church and state. Spiritual leaders in Iran are debating whether Islam and all its personal beliefs should be compulsory for all citizens. At the moment many imams in Iran favour this position although a minority of religious leaders are pleading for the opposite approach. Their argument is that Islam is losing strength because politicians use religion as ideology which happens to be a convenient method for rallying support.[76] This results in a situation where people cannot develop an honest relation with their religion and has often resulted in people turning against their Islamic faith.

Box 4.13   Sharia law in Malaysia[77]

In 2007 the federal court of Malaysia forwarded a case to the Islamic court concerning a woman who converted from Islam to Christianity. Defection is covered by Islamic law and falls under the jurisdiction of the Sharia court. It should not be interfered with by civil courts.

The judgement was presented, even though one of the judges supported the woman's case and stated that it was unreasonable to send the case to the Sharia judge as she would almost certainly be found guilty for her actions. Defections from Islam are punishable with a fine and jail sentence. The woman, who changed her name from Azlina Jailaini to Lina Joy, argued that Sharia law could not be enforced as she was no longer a Muslim. None of the arguments were helpful. The Sharia judge who was allowed to decide on this case did not grant her request.

Countries differ significantly when it comes to deciding which aspect of ethics should be put into law. In the last few centuries the general trend has been to emphasize freedom of speech and freedom of religion. This way of thinking has resulted in an easier way of including ethical considerations in the law of the land.

By including freedom of speech in the law, a solution has been found to give state ethics a general validity which applies to all inhabitants of a country.[78] Personal convictions of a few or of a certain religion no longer play a role in state ethics but the state does guarantee that everyone is entitled to personal or religious beliefs. Freedom of speech and religion provide space for irrationality.[79] People are allowed to have ideas and beliefs you can't prove. This ethical code (rule) is a social innovation that is used to avoid conflicts. In addition it is reasonable that this ethic applies to everybody regardless of religious beliefs, orientation or political convictions. This is universalism in the truest sense of the word.

4.2.3   Ethical starting points

Different starting points can be applied to solve ethical questions. One of the most commonly used in discussions about right and wrong can be linked to the question about *whether something gives 'utility'*. This can be found in thoughts pertaining to good infrastructure, a good income and what is the best buy. Another frequently used spring-board for the question of good versus evil is that of *fairness and justice*. Moral behaviour is then linked to rules and principles, and the dividing line between right and wrong is clearly defined. A third alternative will also be covered in this chapter: *virtue ethics*. This starting point takes the wider situation into account and also considers the character of the person involved and whether there is a historically based commitment. It explains, for example, why one comes to a tougher verdict when strangers are involved, because you don't have a common history together. These three starting points form the primary approaches in discussions relating to 'normative ethics.'[80]

We will now look at the pros and cons of different ethical starting points. When groups examine ethical questions, differing ideas tend to create confusion and many people have conflicting opinions. One view is pragmatic, the other is based on principle and yet another is based on solidarity. During a conflict it is important to recognize the opponent's approach. This can cause you to have respect for your adversary. Together you determine which strategy offers the best chance for success. If it is clear which different ethical principles form the basis of discussions, it is easier to differentiate the main and secondary issues.

We will now examine three different ethical points of view in detail. The topics are:

- Consequence ethics (utilitarianism).
- Principle ethics (deontology).
- Virtue ethics.

Consequence ethics[81]

Jeremy Bentham (1748–1832) is regarded as the founder of the concept originally called modern utilitarianism which later became known as consequence ethics.[82] Its premise is 'public utility'. In order to determine if conduct, projects or social change are ethically acceptable, it is first necessary to ascertain who will be affected in a positive and negative way. The sum of the plus and minus factors will determine if the ethics serve the general interest. The tools of consequence ethics can be effectively applied to business as well. 'Pro' and 'con' elements of projects can be expressed in financial terms but this approach can be laborious especially when dealing with unknown quantities. A good example would be the unavoidable noise created during road construction. To form an ethical judgement it is necessary to take an inventory of all the other facets involved in building the road. If the public benefit of the road outweighs the noise aggravation, the end result will justify the means and the activity is perceived to be ethically acceptable.

Consequence ethics as a starting point for ethics has its limits. Whether or not a certain activity is ethically justified cannot always be determined on the basis of maximizing a utility.[83] For example, the principle of 'being useful' becomes problematic if people are harmed in a fundamental way. The example from Michael Sandel, professor of political science, in Box 4.14, will illustrate this.

Box 4.14   Christians fed to the lions [84]

In the Colosseum of ancient Rome, Christians were thrown to the lions for public entertainment. Try to imagine the value of such a spectacle, especially when the poor victims suffered unbearable pain while being ripped to shreds and eaten by the animals. But think also of the collective ecstasy of the cheering public in a packed amphitheatre. If enough people took pleasure from such an event how could it be defended by the principles of consequence ethics? Could this sort of 'game' expand outside the theatre into the streets of Rome and could unsuspecting citizens be scared to death that they might be the next victims to be sacrificed for public enjoyment? If the disadvantages increase it could weigh against the pleasure received by the public. The advocate of consequence ethics could argue for discontinuation of the public event.

The example in Box 4.14 demonstrates clearly that consequence ethics has its limits. It is often hard to justify public satisfaction when human rights are involved. Nonetheless, consequence ethics remains popular especially with rational people. It remains useful in situations where questions of principle and personal interest are not an issue.

The case study in Box 4.15 provides an example of how consequence ethics can be applied and the practical problems that can arise from it.

Box 4.15   Application of consequence ethics to the CO_2 question

Proponents of reduced CO_2 emissions are quick to point out the dire consequences if current levels remain unchanged. The 'greenhouse effect' resulting from excess CO_2 will cause world temperature increases, rising water levels and melting polar icecaps.[85] If the higher water levels are linked to costs related to dike reinforcement, flood danger and loss of income, then consequence ethics can be applied (because harbours could be permanently flooded). The homo economicus has a responsive chord when the potential outcome of a problem is pointed out. Costs and returns are brought into play and, if the costs are too high, alternative measures must be taken. The path you choose can be crucial. For example, it makes a difference for the time frame in which the revenues of the solution are being taken into account.

If climate changes result in a yearly decline in food production, then it becomes important to know if the lower production has been calculated for 20 or 200 years. Proponents of CO_2 reduction have not arbitrarily taken the long-term view concerning the projected food shortages due to occur in the coming centuries.

Definition of the area being targeted is also a factor because public involvement is different when analysing smaller and larger projects. Rising water levels, flood danger and melting polar icecaps will affect some harbours more than others. The city of Cork in southern Ireland, for example, is at increasing risk. This port is at a low-lying location and its geographical position within the River Lee's catch basin means that the city is at risk of flooding as well as smaller towns close to the main harbour.[86]

(Continued)

Other harbours will be less susceptible to these flood danger problems and could even benefit depending on their geographical position. Finally, any analysis has to consider the involvement of the stakeholders and if the prognosis and analysis is looking at one particular harbour or all harbours in a certain area.

Principle ethics[87]

The concept of fixed principles lies at the heart of principle ethics, also known as deontological ethics. Dealings are morally accepted as long as they adhere to present principles regarding which choices are morally required, forbidden or permitted.[88] The strength of this approach lies in its clarity. Society runs smoothly when easily understandable norms and values are maintained and can be illustrated by laws that guarantee equal rights for men and women. Governments are fond of principle ethics because a minimum of explanation is required.[89] Honouring of contracts, respect for property, self-determination and non-discrimination constitute the major points of departure.

Uniformity has led to countries creating laws that apply to all citizens. Universal principle ethics has become a powerful government tool for gaining societies' trust in an institutionalized situation and serves to measure welfare and well-being in a complex societal existence composed of people with different religious and ethnic origins.[90]

Box 4.16   Kant's universalism and groundbreaking social innovation

Philosopher Immanuel Kant (1724–1804) devoted considerable time to the creation of a valid general explanation of principles. He was far ahead of his time. When Europeans were busy making laws to limit the rights of the people in their conquered colonies, Kant was searching for the 'Golden Rule', a universal set of ethical principles that could be applied to everyone.[91] He wanted a practical, flexible, thoughtful philosophy that could serve as the basis for 'principle ethics'. He himself described it as 'duty-based ethics', meaning that everyone in the world would be bound by the rules in a general sense, regardless of religion, ethnic background or gender. He even envisaged world peace and the role that duty bound principles could play in its establishment.

To express his ideas, Kant used a phrase borrowed from religion that he called the 'categorical imperative'. In essence it said 'deal with others using integrity and fairness so that your methods will be accepted by all concerned'.

In the hope of convincing countries and religions to accept his ideas, Kant formulated the necessary preconditions to get everyone to agree. Freedom and respect were the main ideas. He stated that people should be prepared to adjust their behaviour and inclinations if they prove unacceptable to others and have no rational argument behind them. Reasonable argument is the only device available to limit freedom of another and this freedom can only be limited if included in a general rule that affects everyone.

Immanuel Kant's philosophical writings concerning the 'categorical imperative' have become an important basis for the law in modern society with freedom of religion, freedom of expression, and non-discrimination sitting at its core.

Virtue ethics[92]

Last, but not least, virtue ethics is the third major field in discussions concerning normative ethics (the other two being the principle ethics and the consequence ethics that we have already discussed). It is concerned with virtue and its focus is placed on character.[93] In contrast to the basic tenets of principle and consequence ethics, the approach of virtue ethics is more concerned with feelings. Imagine an emergency situation where someone clearly needs help. A utilitarian definition would point to the consequences and conclude that assistance should be forthcoming as a means of improving social well-being. Also, if applying the theory of principle ethics to 'do the right thing' help would be offered, but here is the difference: the helper would justify his or her actions based on the principle 'treat others as you would like to be treated', whereas providing assistance when seen through the perspective of virtue ethics is done from a feeling of benevolence and charity.

Virtue ethics has a much older pedigree than its two partners and although the ancient Greek philosopher Aristotle is considered its founding father, there is evidence of its existence in an even earlier period in Chinese philosophy. Two of the major supporting viewpoints concerning virtue ethics will be covered in the succeeding paragraphs: the narrative and intention perspectives.

Narrative perspective of virtue ethics

Using history as a template, it is fair to say that people have a prominent role in the 'big picture'. Every inhabitant of the UK has a place in its society and cannot opt out. His or her part in the story concerns daily life in the UK as opposed to a Hindu or Sikh's daily life in India. Context plays an important role within the narrative perspective. Judgement on ethical questions can be linked to precedents or be related to the community of the person in question. Moral considerations are dependent on time and situation. Narrative perspective can be applied, for example, to define loyalty and solidarity. The moral obligation to extend a courtesy to another is also dependent on the relation with the person concerned. This hypothesis also embraces loyalty and solidarity for specified groups.[94] A pervading vagueness persists about the value of applying context ethics and critics feel uneasy when it is serves as a point of departure. Nonetheless, there are positive elements. Ethical questions are harder to approach when a person's position and his or her character in the community are ignored. A narrative perspective offers possibilities for dealing with dilemmas relating to the borders of solidarity. It is legitimate to deal differently with people who are on the edge of your existence from those who are close by. The answer to the question 'What should I do?' is dependent on the situation in which you are involved.[95] Ethical conduct between people strongly determines how relations will develop in the future. The old expression 'kindness reciprocates kindness from others' applies here.

Intention perspective of virtue ethics

The intention perspective associated with virtue ethics is also referred to as intentionalism.[96] Using this approach we can link it directly with empathy, a natural characteristic.[97] It allows us to make a general statement saying that loyal and generous people are 'good'. Intentionalism is concerned with the role motivation plays in human interaction. If someone dies in hospital due to a medical fault, it is considered just that the medical intentions are discussed when examining the case. Intentionalism also plays an important role in Islam and Christianity and incorporates the term 'fallible man'.[98] Intentionalism suggests that people are not always aware of the consequences of their dealings and if this is questioned, consideration must be taken of whether or not the person has acted in good faith. This occurs less in the areas of consequence and principle ethics which assume that people deal in a rational manner. Intentionalism, however, is not always applicable. In a court of law judges do not always take the intentions of a defendant into account because they can be unreliable. The only available option is to stick to the facts. Nonetheless, intention remains an important consideration for most ethical judgements. Organizations or individuals with good intentions must be able to count on positive and trusting local support for what they are trying to achieve.[99] Societies incapable of creating a climate where good intentions are not taken into consideration end up with an untrustworthy scenario.

Box 4.17   Business and intentionalism

An example of how intentionalism can play a role is when businesses make purchases abroad. If an company takes sufficient measures to ensure a product's safety and the product turns out to be unsafe because the supplier knowingly and wittingly traded an unsafe item, it is important that the intentions of the enterprise are known and considered if it is taken to court for negligence.[100] In any court case involving business, judges will consider if the company has acted in good faith, and if this is proven sanctions will not necessarily be applied.

4.2.4   Development of ethical systems

Ethical insight depends on people's ability to predict and explain feelings, thoughts, ideas and intentions of others as well as themselves, with personal empathy towards others included.[101] Ethical capabilities in humans are strongly developed and can be partially attributed to the significant role of mirror neurons located in the brain.[102] The development of ethical codes (systems) between people with frequent contact relies on the interaction of these brain neurons and related reward mechanisms. An empathetic reaction from one individual elicits a similar response from the other with feelings of solidarity being stimulated by the mirror neurons. This results in a real need for conformity and has led to the development of ethical systems using logical thought construction as a premise.[103] People link loyalty, justice and calculated behaviour to 'perceptions of good versus bad'.[104] Darwin was also interested in this field and wrote in his autobiography that it was difficult to change attitudes in systems where strong convictions applied. He compared humans' reluctance to depart from principles with the monkey's instinctive fear of snakes.[105] Ethical convictions are often supported by rationale and emotion. The brain-computer cannot delete thoughts, principles and memories with the push of a button. The brain is a biodynamic, fluctuating, living organ. Rationale, feelings and emotions play a role in the storing of information.

It has been proven that when memory and emotions combine, the related synapse connections get priority above all other chemical responses if the right conditions exist. Daniel Goleman, who has written on the subject, refers to it as 'emotional piracy'.[106] The amygdala, a section of the brain next to the hippocampus, is largely responsible.[107] When taking emotional decisions, the brain gives priority to certain preconceived thoughts and people do not have the openness to always use these as discussion points. In particular we are referring to principles, beliefs and opinions as points of departure for dealing with a specific situation. If you consider that the brain needs no more than one-tenth of a second to discern the emotional weight between good and evil, it will come as no surprise that people are inclined to rely on pre-accepted truths. Therefore, many people have difficulties to deal with different ethical starting points.

4.3 Modern society

Humanity was enthusiastic about its future after the fall of the Berlin Wall in 1989.[108] The demise of communism with its planned economy was a fact and people hoped that more countries would choose for market economies, human rights and democracy. This was described in Fukuyama's book *The End of History and the Last Man* and he wrote that a new 'boring' era was beginning because all countries chose the market economy and elements of democracy were institutionalized. He was partially correct. In the 1990s the market economy made big strides but history, of course, is fickle. Development is not a linear process and the realization of the modern state is a complex affair. The final section of this chapter will discuss themes that have given further insight into the characteristics of the modern state.

4.3.1 Social capital

Social capital is the result when, in society, institutionalized standards and values respond fairly. Encouraging everyone to participate, regardless of ethnicity or religion is how this social capital is created. Participation increases when citizens can expect a quick response from societal organizations and business acting on their behalf. Fukuyama's description of social capital states that informal, institutionalized standards create cooperation between people, business and organizations based on trust and reciprocity.[109]

'Social capital' pervades several layers of society and includes education, economic traffic and social organizations among other elements, to ensure that the concept of trust is not limited to family and friends (see Figure 4.4).[110] It gives a tourist the courage to ask a passer-by for directions and can also generate an investor's desire to do business with an unknown bank. Social capital exists when farmers have the courage to invest in their land and also when a patient trusts the competence of an unknown physician.[111] It is created when individuals make a positive connection with society.

Figure 4.4 Social capital framework

4.3.2   Social capital and Trompenaars

The question of 'social capital' can be well illustrated through the case study of 'the car and the pedestrian', a test carried out by Trompenaars and Hampden-Turner.[112] This dilemma is used to explain the dimension of 'universalism vs. particularism'. Trompenaars and Hampden-Turner started with the question of whether people were loyal to institutionalized principles or to the people they live with.

To test this question they formulated a dilemma called 'the car and the pedestrian', and it was proposed to participants in different countries. The participant is theoretically a passenger in the car of a close friend. In a quiet neighbourhood, the driver hits a pedestrian. The speed limit was 35 km per hour but the car was travelling at 60 km. There are no witnesses and the case goes to court. Your friend's lawyer says that he will have a serious problem unless you are willing to testify under oath that he was not exceeding the speed limit.

The participant is asked to provide an explanation of innocence, and can choose one of the following three responses:

1. Your friend can always count on you to testify for his innocence.
2. Your friend has a right to legal defence because you have attested to his innocence.
3. Your friend has no right to assume that you will provide testimony confirming his guilt.

Results showed that North Americans and north-western Europeans chose options two and three while Asians and Latin Americans had a preference for options one and two (see Table 4.1).

Table 4.1   Percentage of people with a preference for answer options 2 and 3

Country	Percentage	Country	Percentage
Venezuela	32	Czech Republic	83
Korea	37	Germany	87
Russia	44	The Netherlands	90
China	47	Australia	91
India	54	United Kingdom	91
Japan	68	United States	93
Singapore	69	Canada	93
France	72	Switzerland	97

The research proved that 'universal' values differ significantly. Trust is not only based on culture but also on faith in government and societal organizations. To use an anecdote, the test results were shown to a Korean manager. The manager found the Americans untrustworthy as they were willing to betray their best friends.[113] The Americans had a similar opinion of the Koreans saying they were prepared to lie under oath. There is no easy solution for this dilemma, but in general countries do better when there is an abstract trust of rights and jurisdiction. Governments who fail to fulfil these requirements will discourage participation in the official economy and help to create grey areas and undefinable situations.

Box 4.18   Civil society

Civil society is a term used to describe a contemporary society strongly based on liberal, democratic values.[114] This concept implies that citizens are the principal actors or players and the freehold characteristics of the society are freedom of speech and independent jurisprudence. A civil society allows citizens to express themselves through organized groups that can directly influence the outcome of an unclear or unsatisfactory situation. Non-governmental organizations constitute a substantial part of the system. A civil society is democratic at heart because its citizens are free to express their interests. Non-governmental and other organizations represent the wishes and desires of the common man.[115] This can be in the form of trade unions but other examples are representatives for ethnic minorities, associations for nature preservation and clubs that add content to solidarity and justice issues. In a civil society the citizen becomes an important player with his/her own domain, adjacent to the government and business world. Civil society differs from other communities where power is in the hands of the elite. The opposite end of the spectrum includes communism, where government controls and dictates the entire setup of society in minute detail and items such as social services, health care and the economy are controlled by a small group of powerful individuals. Civil society can come under pressure when certain actors ascend to a dominant position. Think only of countries where the clergy, the bourgeoisie or the military are in ruling positions.

4.3.3   The modern state and sustainable development

concept of the modern state becomes viable when power is regulated through law with property rights, security and equality.[116] Skilful legislation deals with 'nature' characteristics such as esteem, aggression, justice, empathy and 'homo economicus'. The market economy, through social security, justice and equality, has created a high level of welfare and well-being, but some of the tools governments use in modern society have weak points.

Long-term government fitness tools

Government must be ready to intervene in the market economy to preserve its environmental elements. Many entrepreneurs possess the 'animal spirit' and strive to generate profit and improve their products and innovate them but this does not automatically assume that they are environmentally friendly.[117] Animal spirit may improve welfare in the short term but it is not concerned with the question of long-term solutions. Populist democracy, too, is not always a willing partner in sustainable development.[118] Politicians use attractive slogans to entice voters but election victories do not necessarily make it possible to implement new laws destined to improve long-term welfare and well-being. Governments are struggling to form policies for the long term, somewhat similar to the behavioural dichotomy behind the Marshmallow Experiment (Box 4.1).[119] In such scenarios sustainability suffers, as well as other policies.

Box 4.19   Institutionalizing good governance

This chapter has tried to provide food for thought about human beings and what is needed to establish a workable society. There are many questions to ponder: Is modern society with democracy, property rights and social services at its core a basis for social capital? Is social capital created when the state effectively institutionalizes

(Continued)

aspects of human nature? Is social capital directly related to welfare? There are no presupposed 'yes' answers to these questions. A thorough analysis requires additional research. The dynamic processes in society are complex but even though good governance can lead to welfare and well-being, not every country has chosen to embrace the concept. Why, in today's Russia, can a man like Vladimir Putin be elected and questions of human rights and the institutionalizing of 'feelings of fairness' be relegated to the back benches?

When compared to the UN's and World Bank's definitions of good governance, Russia has a long way to go. The creation of a civil society and social capital are an imperative for creating welfare and well-being and require a government which is fair in its response to its people. Many well-functioning societies have partially achieved this and governments have succeeded in creating nonzero-sum situations (see Box 4.12). The rules are effective and purposeful and human characteristics such as competition, exploratory impulse, authority sensitivity, empathy, feelings of fairness and conformism contribute more to prosperity and well-being rather than they have a negative impact.

 ### 4.4   Case Study: Tit-for-Tat[120]

The fact that no other creatures on earth have an intelligence equal to humans is pure coincidence. Evolution does not have a goal or purpose. New species thrive through gene mutations and favourable conditions for their survival and procreation.[121] This randomness factor has meant that creatures have evolved with a myriad and often remarkable set of differing characteristics. An excellent example is the peacock with its vibrant plumage. Despite its handicap with flying, the peacock's feathers are essential to its survival because females choose their potential mates on the basis of the beauty of their plumage. This selection criterion is also pure coincidence. Other bird types can be attracted to beaks and in other animal species aesthetic plays no role whatsoever. Female peacocks, though, do use the criterion of the most impressive plumage to choose a mate and have little or no concern for the fact that the male's colourful display also makes him an easy and obvious target for hungry foxes.

Certain characteristics are functional but this does not necessarily imply that they are always effective. The functionality of the sense of smell and vision need little explanation but other aspects of functionality are more difficult to define, referring specifically to the human characteristic called 'collaboration' or 'cooperation'. If collaboration is deemed a natural character trait then it should be spontaneously duplicated if the evolution process is copied or simulated.

In 1979, political scientist Robert Axelrod devised a way to test this based on game theory. In his theory, disputes or interactions between two or more parties are considered to be a 'game'. If 'cooperation' is beneficial, both sides must have an advantage. But the opposite can also be true. If egoism is a functional characteristic in living beings, it must have an advantage for the participants and it stands to reason that this trait should reappear in future generations. Axelrod tested his hypothesis using a computer tournament.

Game theorists, evolutionary biologists and other scientists were invited to participate in and devise software for a computer program. Every program was meant to have an independent character, just like people. Fifteen entries were submitted, all of which were copied twice so that all software programs could compete with the others but also with themselves. In total there were 225 games (15 x 15) and

(Continued)

each game consisted of 200 rounds. During each round, the computer program had to decide if he/she preferred to be selfish (defect) or collaborate with others. If a program did well against an opponent it was considered a survivor and had a good chance of carrying on. The rounds were tallied with a maximum of 5 points and the maximum for one game was 1000 (200 x 5).

Table 4.2   Robert Axelrod's computer tournament

		Program A	
		Cooperate	Defect
Program B	Cooperate	Both 3 points	A: 5 points B: 0 points
	Defect	A: 0 points B: 5 points	Both 1 points

The maximum score that a program could achieve in the tournament with 15 players (computer programs) was 15,000 points. Those programs (players) that competed with each other and opted for collaboration received 600 points per game. All of the programs had different strategies. Some were designed to cheat from the beginning while others chose cooperation. To avoid exploitation, most of the programs included built-in retaliatory measures in the event that collaboration was not rewarded. This retaliation was achieved by an immediate attempt to cheat in succeeding rounds so as to score at least 1, but hopefully 5, points.

The winning program turned out to be Tit-for-Tat created by the Russian mathematician and game theorist Anatol Rapaport. The program was simplicity itself and began with the instruction to always collaborate and do what the opponent had done in the previous move. Compared to other entries, Tit-for-Tat was never threatening unless the opponent had been threatening beforehand and in this way it differed sharply from other programs that incorporated devious methods to score points. These methods failed in the end even though it sometimes meant a loss for the Russian mathematician to all opponents reverting to dishonesty. Tit-for-Tat easily compensated for this when playing against itself and was capable of earning 600 points.

Some of the opposing programs did indeed have a better game strategy but were less successful on average. One of the main advantages of the winning program was its predictability. Competitors knew that they would always score fewer points by failing to collaborate.

 Case Study Questions

1. What is the purpose of the computer tournament and what conclusions can be drawn from it?
2. What parallels can you observe between the computer experiment and the case study about the great tits discussed earlier in this chapter?
3. Which of the nature characteristics 'homo economicus', 'empathy' and 'conformity' best describes the Tit-for-Tat rule that states that it's okay to work together with someone else as long as you have not been deceived in the previous session? Present your arguments.
4. Which of the three ethical starting points (consequence ethics, principle ethics and virtue ethics) is most important for 'institutionalizing' in a society where the focus is on the Tit-for-Tat approach? Defend your arguments.

4.5   Learning tools 🔧

4.5.1   Summary

- Human nature refers to the human characteristics determined by our DNA which are independent of environmental conditions. The sections covered in this chapter that are determined by 'nature' include 'calculated self-interest', 'status', 'aggression', 'respect for authority', 'exploratory impulse', 'empathy', 'feelings of fairness', 'conformism' and 'kin selection'.
- Aspects of human nature can be demonstrated through psychological experiments and behavioural testing of people and animals. The experiments and tests described in this chapter are 'Marshmallow', 'Honours list', 'Stanford Prison', 'Milgram', 'Safe surroundings and exploratory impulse', 'Sociable birds are not always losers', 'Monkeys Reject Unequal Pay', 'Conformity of Solomon Asch' and 'Us versus them'.
- Ethics are the reflection of our morals, of the standards and values that we expect to be reasonably accepted by others in an attempt to maintain balance in everyday life.
- An important departure point for close-knit community ethics is mutual loyalty.
- State ethics requires verifiable rules to implement justice in a simple manner with measurable elements and that is a reason why virtue ethics with aspects such as intention and historically based commitment play a less prominent role.
- The result of an ethical decision is strongly dependent on the point(s) of departure chosen. Among these are consequence ethics, principle ethics and virtue ethics.
- Social capital is evident in societies when individuals feel they are being treated fairly by people and organizations.
- Universalism in society is achieved when the same values and standards apply to everyone. Particularism results when laws, values and standards are altered to benefit specific groups.
- Universalism in society is institutionalized when a witness declares before a court of law that a friend has committed an offence, fully realizing that it can have dire consequences for the defendant (for example in the dilemma 'the car and the pedestrian').

4.5.2   Further reading

De Waal, F. B. M. (2001). *The Ape and the Sushi Master: Cultural Reflections by a Primatologist* (1st ed.). New York, NY: Basic Books.

De Waal, F. B. M. (2009). *The Age of Empathy: Nature's Lessons for a Kinder Society*. New York, NY: Harmony.

Goldschmidt, T. (1998). *Darwin's Dreampond: Drama on Lake Victoria*. Cambridge, MA: MIT Press.

Hofstede, G. J., Pedersen, P. B. & Hofstede, G. (2002). *Exploring Culture: Exercises, Stories and Synthetic Cultures*. Yarmouth, ME: Intercultural Press.

Rachels, J. & Rachels, S. (2009). *The Elements of Moral Philosophy*. New York, NY: McGraw-Hill.

Sandel, M. J. (2009). *Justice: What's the Right Thing To Do?* New York: Farrar, Straus and Giroux.

Trompenaars, F. & Woolliams, P. (2003). *Business Across Cultures*. Capstone.

4.5.3 Assignments

Assignment 4.1 Nature, culture and participation in society

Make a study of the research of Helena Helve: 'Re-thinking youth and citizenship. Value groups and citizenship types of young Finns'[122] (inclusive of Appendix 2), which you can find as a pdf file on Google Scholar.

a) Discuss for the group 'nationalists' which of the nine different concepts stated in the paragraph on nature is most applicable. Present and defend your arguments.

b) Determine which government measures could be taken for the 'nationalists' to give them a more active role in society. Present and defend your arguments.

c) What two groups named in Helena Helve's study have characteristics which can be linked to the 'nature' aspects of 1. 'empathy' and 2. 'respect for authority'? Present and defend your arguments.

d) What type of people as described in Helena Helve's research are most likely to 'feel at home' in a civil society? Present and defend your arguments.

Assignment 4.2 Corruption

Make a study of the different research you can find on 'Google Scholar' about factors that encourage corruption in Indonesia which are based on the starting points of culture, history and socio-economic developments and the 'role of government'.

a) Summarize the results of your investigation and show those aspects which have influenced Indonesian corruption.

b) Explore the steps currently being taken and state your opinion as to whether Indonesian corruption will increase or decrease in the future.

Present and defend your arguments.

Assignment 4.3 'Mugabe and the White African'

a) Which ethical principles do the leading players refer to in the documentary "Mugabe and the White African" when expressing their interests and point of views? Present and defend your arguments.

b) Demonstrate which of the three ethical starting points (consequence ethics, principle ethics and virtue ethics) has had the most influence for the creation of social capital. Present and defend your arguments.

c) What are the possible negative consequences of the institutionalizing of ethical values to create social capital? Present and defend your arguments.

4.5.4   Self-test questions

 Self-test Questions

1. Marshmallow Experiment

   - Describe the Marshmallow Experiment in your own words.
   - What did the experiment prove?
   - What similarities can you see between the large groups of participants in the Marshmallow Experiment and the voters that make up a democracy (Section 4.3.3)?

2. Principles of ethics

   - What three ethical starting points can be used to form an opinion on an ethical question? (Provide a short description of each one.)
   - What ethical starting point(s) can best be applied to the environmental movement's standpoint that biodiversity must be maintained because of the place every plant and animal has within the ecological system and that reduction of biodiversity could result in decreased human food supply? (Defend your arguments.)
   - Discuss the ethical starting points used by the UN to advocate antidiscrimination laws for the improvement of 'human rights'. (Defend your arguments.)

3. 'Social capital'

   - Elaborate on the concept of 'social capital'.
   - Is the level of social capital in Switzerland better or worse than that of Venezuela? (Present your arguments.)

PART II

SUSTAINABLE DEVELOPMENT AND GLOBALIZATION

5

SUSTAINABLE DEVELOPMENT: ENVIRONMENTAL AND SOCIAL ASPECTS

Overview and learning objectives

Everybody is talking about sustainable development these days and the word "sustainability" is becoming more and more an integral part of societal debates, governmental policies and business strategies. But what is the history of sustainable development? How is it defined, and what are the people, planet and prosperity aspects of sustainability that are so often mentioned?

Sustainable development starts with the awareness that the economic development of the last 50–60 years causes societal (social and environmental) impacts that might become so big that further economic development will be influenced by it. The economy is built on the resources of this earth (planet) and uses labour (people) for creating products and services. Not taking care of these two pillars of the foundation of our economy could be seen as a type of cannibalism, a short-term focus without a long-term strategy. Sustainable development places the horizon at the long term and asks for strategies and choices concerning future generations. Is there a survival strategy for the human population on this planet? Some believe that technology will solve our environmental problems while others feel that production and business models will have to change and relate to realistic production and consumption patterns while being culturally relevant. Working on sustainable development will also have social implications.

The first part of this chapter explains the societal debate on sustainable development and presents the definitions, international institutions and agreements related to it. In the second part, the environmental dimension of sustainability is looked at and four environmental aspects are, as examples, explained more in detail. These aspects are: water resources and management, natural resources, sources of energy and ecosystems and biodiversity. These topics are not representative of all the other environmental aspects but do show the dilemmas society is facing. In the third section of this chapter the social dimension of sustainable development is discussed.

Learning objectives

At the end of this chapter, readers will be able to:

- Know and understand the historical development and the present definition of sustainable development.
- Understand landmark conceptual and policy developments shaping sustainability practices: triple bottom line (three *P*s); green growth; planetary boundaries, sustainable development goals.

(Continued)

- Have basic knowledge of and insight into the environmental themes of water resources and management; natural resources, resources for energy and ecosystems and biodiversity and understand their relation with sustainable development.
- Understand the importance of the social dimension of sustainable development and its relation with the environmental and economic dimensions.

5.1   Prosperity, well-being and the environment

The Industrial Revolution of the nineteenth century was an important catalyst for welfare improvement and can be seen as the starting point for two centuries of increased productivity. Europe and other parts of the world benefited from a dramatic improvement in welfare and well-being. The 1960s were pivotal years for welfare in many countries. Industry had largely recovered from the ravages of the Second World War and in Japan and Western Europe gross national product (GNP) rose to more than 5% annually. The consumer society was alive and well and at the same time environmental concerns began to assume more prominence. Scientists, politicians, policy makers and concerned citizens pointed out the downside of unchecked consumption. Recycling, renewable energy, clean air policy, toxic emissions and water purification all became agenda points for international environment meetings. After the 1970s national and international environmental concerns attained significant prominence. Politics, science and pressure groups became increasingly involved. It is obvious that discussion on the environment has a strong link to welfare and prosperity; political debate on this theme has received differing levels of priority, but in periods of economic crises it drops quickly to the bottom of the main agenda.

Increased prosperity does have a downside however. The scarcity of raw materials, clean water and fossil fuels is growing. In addition more space is being used for agriculture, urban planning, infrastructure and business parks. The chemical composition of earth, water and the atmosphere is also changing due to emissions from human activities into the environment. The changing use of space coupled with these chemical mutations has created diverse undesirable effects such as loss of biodiversity, eutrophication, erosion, deforestation, deterioration of public health, acidification, climate change etc. These developments have contributed to the fact that the number of governmental controls pertaining to environment has increased sharply over the past 50 years. This has been coupled with increasing attention to one of the greatest achievements of our time, technology. Budgets are increasing for ideas that lead to less harmful and, if possible, environmentally neutral solutions. Optimists are convinced that environmental problems can be controlled but their opponents have also presented convincing arguments. Their point of view contends that the earth's general health has been decreasing since 1984 because of the insufficient possibilities for restoration. This is certainly true when considering the emissions of CO_2 and other greenhouse gases but it also applies to mined materials and increased pressure on nature itself.

The consumption-orientated society is a social-economic plan dedicated to stimulating needs so that people continuously feel the desire to purchase more.[1] It is often seen as a consequence of two centuries of industrialization coupled with the diversity of the market economy. Many environmental groups object to this, stating that the system is undesirable because its primary aim is to encourage consumption and there are many more goods available than we really need. Environmental groups became active in the

1990s and their pleas to set limits on growth became known as the 'de-growth movement' (less consumption).

Politics took little notice of the de-growth movement and calls for restrictions on GDP for the simple reason that any negative growth corresponds to unemployment and decline. Current debate is focusing on sustainable economic growth and political parties are choosing measures to encourage this. There are differences, however, in the ambitions of the parties and the speed to which they are committed to putting changes into practice.

5.2 Sustainable development

5.2.1 Introduction

The concept of sustainable development was launched in 1987 even though decades before (the 1960s) the relation between economic growth and environmental impact was already much discussed in society. In this section the historical development of the concept is explained in a worldwide UN context, and related to three important summits and to the Millennium Development Goals.

5.2.2 Definition

In 1987 the UN World Commission on Environment and Development (WCED) published the report *Our Common Future*.[2] The commission was requested by the UN to develop a future-orientated long-term view on the relation between economic development and the environment. The chair of the commission was the former Norwegian prime minister Gro Harlem Brundtland and the report is often referred to as the Brundtland report. In this report the principle of sustainable development was defined as: 'Development that meets the needs of the present without compromising the ability of future generations to meet their own needs.'

The Brundtland Commission started from the environmental perspective but concluded that human resource development in the form of poverty reduction, gender equity and wealth redistribution would be crucial for formulating environmental strategies. It found that environmental limits to economic growth in industrialized and industrializing societies exist. The report also stated that the different crises this planet is facing are *interlocking crises* and that is why active participation of all sectors of society in consultation, and decisions relating to sustainable development are needed.

5.2.3 Triple bottom line (triple *P*)

The triple bottom line framework contains three parts: social, environmental (or ecological) and economic/financial. These three dimensions are often called the three *P*s: 1. People, 2. Planet and 3. Profit; or the 'three pillars of sustainability'. This framework illustrates the balance needed between these three pillars for long-term sustainable development.

In traditional business accounting and common usage, the 'bottom line' refers to either the 'profit' or 'loss', which is usually recorded on the very bottom line of a statement of revenue and expenses. Over the last 50 years, environmentalists and social justice advocates have struggled to bring a broader definition of bottom line into public consciousness by introducing full-cost accounting. The triple bottom line adds two more 'bottom lines': social and environmental (ecological) concerns. The phrase 'triple bottom line' was first used by John Elkington.[3] The framework states that a company's responsibility lies with stakeholders rather than shareholders. In this case, 'stakeholders' refers to anyone who is influenced, either directly or indirectly, by the actions of the firm. According to the stakeholder theory, the business entity should be used as a vehicle for coordinating stakeholder interests, instead of only maximizing shareholder (owner) short-term profits.

At the 2002 world summit in Johannesburg, it was decided to replace the word 'profit' with 'prosperity'. This was done to make clear that this pillar should be seen as the general economic pillar, not only focusing on short-term 'profit'. But in many businesses and publications this third 'p' is often still being defined as 'profit'.

Figure 5.1   The three types of bottom line

5.2.4   Green growth

In 2011 the OECD published a strategy for green growth.[4] The term green growth has been used to describe national and international approaches. As agreed at the fifth Ministerial Conference on Environment and Development in Asia and the Pacific (Seoul, 2005), it is a strategy for achieving sustainable development. It focuses on changing the economy in a way that synthesizes economic growth and environmental protection, and building a green economy in which investments in resource savings as well as sustainable management of natural capital are drivers of growth and in which governments collaborate in the phasing out of unsustainable technologies and modes of production. An economy which is in balance with sustainable development objectives will provide opportunities for using financial resources and be better able to meet development needs and reduce the vulnerability of socio-economic systems to environmental change and resource constraints.[5]

The Global Green Growth Institute was first launched as a think tank in 2010 and was later converted into an international treaty-based organization in 2012 at the Rio+20 Summit in Brazil.[6]

5.2.5   Planetary boundaries

Green growth theorists argue that growth can continue as long as it relies on non-renewable resources and respects the capacity of the planet to renew ecological services and natural resources (see more in Section 5.3.3). Since the carrying capacity of our physical world is unambiguously limited, it follows there must also be a specific limit to growth, albeit of the green variety. However, a longstanding issue in debates regarding the limits to growth has been the paucity of scientific research providing quantitative indicators and precise standards to determine when the planet's capacity is being threatened beyond recovery. This shortcoming was addressed by a groundbreaking paper published in 2009 in *Nature* by a team of 28 renowned scientists led by Johan Rockstrom from Sweden's Stockholm Resilience Center. The paper quantifies the safe operating space for economic activity, indicating nine distinctive natural 'ceilings' for growth, seven of which are precisely calculated.[7] Rockstrom et al.'s paper generated a strong debate with more than 60 papers commenting on limitations and areas for improvement. The criticisms elicited an updated and refined framework which was published in January 2015.[8]

The nine planetary boundaries 2.0[9]

1. Climate change.
2. Change in biosphere integrity (biodiversity loss and species extinction).
3. Stratospheric ozone depletion.
4. Ocean acidification.
5. Biogeochemical flows (phosphorus and nitrogen cycles).
6. Land-system change (e.g. deforestation).
7. Freshwater use.
8. Atmospheric aerosol loading (microscopic particles in the atmosphere that affect climate and living organisms). Not yet quantified.
9. Introduction of novel entities (e.g. organic pollutants, radioactive materials, nano-materials and micro-plastics). Not yet quantified.

The planetary boundaries are ceilings for vital-sign-style parameters such as levels of biodiversity loss and greenhouse gases. The ceilings are danger warnings. Trespassing the first 'danger signal' means we are moving out of our safety zone. We move into a zone of uncertainty with increasing risk of causing irreversible environmental change. Uncertainty zones have also a lower and upper limit; once the upper limit is reached, we move into a high risk of irreversible change compromising safe levels for other processes and ceilings. Such are the 'planetary boundaries'. The good news is that as far as we stay within the safe zone – now clearly defined – we know that civilization can expand and thrive. The bad news is that we have already moved into the uncertainty zone in two of these boundaries: the percentage of total land covered by natural forests and the level of CO_2 concentration associated with climate change. More worryingly, we have trespassed the high impact ceiling in two other boundaries: flows of human-generated nitrogen and phosphorus, and the rate of biodiversity loss.[10]

5.2.6   Sustainable development summits and organizations

In 1992 the first United Nations Conference on Environment and Development (UNCED), known as the Rio Conference or Earth Summit, raised public awareness of the need to integrate environmental and economic development based on the report *Our Common Future*. This first Earth Summit influenced later UN conferences and set a clear agenda. Important outcomes of the conference were the Climate Change Convention – a climate-change agreement that led to the Kyoto Protocol, the Convention on Biological Diversity (see more on biodiversity in Section 5.3.4) and Agenda 21.

Agenda 21 is a non-binding, voluntarily implemented action plan of the United Nations with regard to sustainable development.[11] It is an action agenda for the UN, other multilateral organizations, and individual governments around the world that can be executed at local, national and global levels. The '21' in Agenda 21 refers to the twenty-first century.

This first summit also created new international institutions, among them the Commission on Sustainable Development, tasked with the follow-up to the Rio Conference, the United Nations Framework Convention on Climate Change (UNFCCC) and it led to the reform of the Global Environment Facility.

Ten years later the Earth Summit 2002 (Rio+10) was held in Johannesburg, South Africa with the goal of again bringing together leaders from government, business and non-governmental organizations (NGOs) to agree on a range of measures to achieve similar goals. At this summit sustainable development was recognized as an overarching goal for institutions at national, regional and international levels. The need to enhance the integration of sustainable development in the activities of all relevant UN agencies, programmes and funds was highlighted. Major outcomes of that conference include the Johannesburg Declaration and almost 300 international partnership initiatives meant to help achieve the Millennium Development Goals (MDGs) (see Chapter 1).

Ten years later in 2012 The United Nations Conference on Sustainable Development (UNCSD), also known as Rio 2012, Rio+20 or Earth Summit 2012 was held.

It aimed at reconciling the economic and environmental goals of the global community. The official discussions had two main themes:

- How to build a green economy to achieve sustainable development and lift people out of poverty, including support for developing countries that would allow them to find a green path for development.
- How to improve international coordination for sustainable development by building an institutional framework.

The primary result of this third conference was the non-binding document, *The Future We Want*.[12] In this document the states renewed their political commitment to sustainable development and declared their commitment to the promotion of a sustainable future. The document largely reaffirms previous action plans like Agenda 21. The text includes language supporting the development of Sustainable Development Goals (SDGs), a set of measurable targets aimed at promoting sustainable development globally.[13] It was thought that the SDGs would pick up where the MDGs left off and examine criticism that the original goals failed to address, namely the role of the environment in development. As seen in Chapter 1 'environmental sustainability' is (only) one out of eight MDGs.

5.2.7   Sustainable Development Goals

The SDG set of 17 goals and 169 targets is influenced by triple bottom line, planetary boundaries and green growth ideas. SDGs are noticeably more ambitious and comprehensive than MDGs.

The Sustainable Development Goals[14]

1. End poverty in all its forms everywhere.
2. End hunger, achieve food security and improved nutrition and promote sustainable agriculture.
3. Ensure healthy lives and promote well-being for all at all ages.
4. Ensure inclusive and equitable quality education and promote lifelong learning opportunities for all.
5. Achieve gender equality and empower all women and girls.
6. Ensure availability and sustainable management of water and sanitation for all.
7. Ensure access to affordable, reliable, sustainable and modern energy for all.
8. Promote sustained, inclusive and sustainable economic growth, full and productive employment and decent work for all.
9. Build resilient infrastructure, promote inclusive and sustainable industrialization and foster innovation.
10. Reduce inequality within and among countries.
11. Make cities and human settlements inclusive, safe, resilient and sustainable.
12. Ensure sustainable consumption and production patterns.
13. Take urgent action to combat climate change and its impacts.
14. Conserve and sustainably use the oceans, seas and marine resources for sustainable development.
15. Protect, restore and promote sustainable use of terrestrial ecosystems, sustainably manage forests, combat desertification, and halt and reverse land degradation and halt biodiversity loss.
16. Promote peaceful and inclusive societies for sustainable development, provide access to justice for all and build effective, accountable and inclusive institutions at all levels.
17. Strengthen the means of implementation and revitalize the global partnership for sustainable development.

It should be noted that SDGs specifically promotes sustainable growth (goal 8) rather than de-growth. Major improvements with respect to MDGs are the inclusion of specific goals related to equality (5 and 7) and a range of environmental issues (12, 13, 14, 15). Another improvement is that SDGs are goals for both developed and developing countries, whereas MDGs were aimed at developing countries only.

However, debate is already growing regarding: a) to what extent the goals are well developed and conceptually grounded; and b) to what extent they provide clear guidance to policy makers in terms of indicators of progress.

Table 5.1 shows our evaluation of the SDGs according to these two aspects. Our evaluation builds on the report 'Review of target for the SDG: The science perspective' (2015)[15] which evaluates all 169 targets with a traffic light colour scheme. Green means a well-developed target. Yellow indicates that overall the target is satisfactory but needs improvement to insure it will contribute to SDGs. Red means the target is weakly conceptualized, misses key aspects or uses inadequate indicators, thus requiring major revisions. Seventeen multidisciplinary teams evaluated how well conceptualized, relevant, comprehensive and unambiguous the goals and targets are.

We classified targets into three categories: economic and social, environmental, and integrated (targets explicitly addressing interdependencies between environmental social and economic dimensions). The latter are extremely important, since in our view a crucial gap in the MDGs was the lack of integrated indicators. Lack of integrated indicators can create trade-offs between economic and environmental aspects and ignores the interrelated nature of sustainability challenges. We identified 111 economic and social, 38 environmental and 20 integrated targets.

Furthermore, we identified targets accounting for each of the nine planetary bounda-ries. Examples are goal 14: oceans (planetary boundary 4) and targets about sustainable agriculture in goal 5 (hunger) which refer to geochemical cycles of phosphates and nitrogen (planetary boundary 5). Therefore, in theory at least, fulfilment of SDGs will keep the planet safe from irreversible ecological changes.

However, the International Council for Sciences contends that only targets with explicitly quantified indicators and standards will help policy making achieve precise objectives and enable comparison of progress across countries. Many of the targets in the SDGs are likely to remain unfulfilled since they are generic, non-quantified and ambiguous[16] (for instance 'achieve substantial reductions in greenhouse emissions' is ambiguous and non-quantified as opposed to 'achieve 50% reduction in CO_2 aggre-gated emissions by 2050, compared to 2015 baseline'). Only clearly quantified targets can ensure that the fulfilment of a goal will result in the outcomes needed to prevent planetary boundaries being trespassed. Therefore, we also carried out a content analysis to identify goals and targets specified in a quantitative and unambiguous way. As we can see in Table 5.1, substantial improvements are needed: whereas 30% of economic and social targets are fully quantified (a disappointing finding in itself) only 8% of envi-ronmental targets are fully quantified with goals related to sustainability of oceans and climate change among the less well quantified, thus casting a doubt onto the suitability of SDGs to deal with critical environmental challenges.

Table 5.1 Analysis of Sustainable Development Goals based on 'Review of target for the SDG: The science perspective' and own content analysis

	Total targets	%	Economic + Social targets	%	Environmental targets	%	Integrated targets	%
Green	49	29%	36	32%	11	29%	2	10%
Yellow	91	54%	58	52%	25	66%	8	40%
Red	29	17%	17	15%	2	5%	10	50%
Total	169		111	99%	38		20	
Goals quantified with specific indicators and targets	38	22%	33	30%	3	8%	2	10%

5.3 Environmental sustainability

5.3.1 Introduction

As we have mentioned in Section 5.2, the environmental aspects are one of the pillars of the definition of sustainable development and they are also the seventh MDG. In this section, four environmental aspects have been selected to be described, to analyse and to be discussed. They are: water resources and management, natural resources, biodiver-sity ecosystems and the use of energy. Water, materials and energy were selected because they are the main driving (planet) forces for the economy, and biodiversity was chosen because of its big impact on our ecosystems. Many other environmental aspects like erosion, human health problems (cancer, lung diseases etc.) related to emissions of toxic chemicals, noise and odour nuisance, external safety, radioactivity, etc. could also have been selected. The four selected aspects are not fully representative of all environmental problems but their impact in terms of planetary boundaries is substantial.[17] They give a good overview of the problems and dilemmas our production and economic systems are facing now and in the future.

Box 5.1   Anthropocentrism vs. ecocentrism

Many conflicting points of view exist when discussing the environment. Some feel that the environment must offer something and others see it as an autonomous entity that must be preserved by people. These opposing philosophies have been divided into anthropocentrism and ecocentrism. The 'anthros' feel that the environment exists to serve mankind. The 'ecos' believe that nature is central and humanity is part of the total eco system. They value nature for what it is and not for its functionality for man. Ecocentrics are among those who fight for animal rights, the Waddenzee (Wadden Sea), and the preservation of unique coral reefs or habitats.

The world of the anthropocentrists revolves around limiting depletion of natural mined minerals, scarcity of good quality drinking water and fishing quotas; not to protect nature as an independent entity but to protect the planet's resources for future generations. The Brundtland definition of sustainable development is very anthropocentric because it focuses on the next generation of the human population.

5.3.2   Water resources and management

Introduction

Global freshwater use is one of the planetary boundaries. Universal access to water is one of the SDGs.

Water resources are sources of water that can be used now or in the future for agricultural, industrial, household, recreational and environmental activities. The majority of these processes require fresh water. However, only 3% of total water is fresh water and two-thirds of fresh water is frozen in glaciers and polar ice caps. The remaining unfrozen freshwater is found mainly as groundwater, with only a small fraction present above ground or in the air (see Figure 5.2).

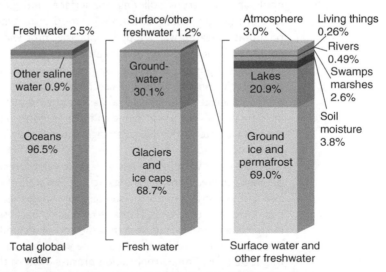

Figure 5.2   A graphical representation of the distribution of Earth's water[18]

Fresh water is a renewable resource but the world's supply of groundwater is proving to be steadily decreasing, most prominently in Asia and North America. It is unclear how much natural renewal balances this usage, and whether ecosystems are threatened. The framework for allocating water resources to water users (where such a framework exists) is often known as water rights.

In some regions a big shortage of water with the right quality can occur and in other regions too much water causes flooding and damage. The increasing amount of flooding worldwide is seen as an impact of climate change and will require adaptive measures in many places in the world. Because the water conditions can change drastically during the year, from extreme shortages to flooding related to the seasons, water measures are hard to implement and water management is a complex matter.

Water quality for consumption

It is estimated that 8% of water used worldwide is for household purposes.[19] This includes drinking water, bathing, cooking, sanitation and gardening. Basic household water requirements have been estimated at around 50 litres per person per day, excluding water for gardens.

Drinking water is water that is of sufficiently high quality so that it can be consumed or used without risk of immediate or long-term harm. Such water is commonly called potable water. In most developed countries, the water supplied to households, commerce and industry meets drinking water standards even though only a very small proportion is actually consumed or used in food preparation.

In 2000, the world population was 6.2 billion and the UN estimates that by 2050 there will be an additional 3.5 billion people with most of the growth in developing countries where there is already suffering due to water stress. Thus, water demand will increase unless there are corresponding increases in water conservation and recycling of this vital resource.[20] Access to water for producing food will be one of the main challenges in the decades to come. Access to high quality drinking water will need to be balanced with the importance of managing water itself in a sustainable way.

Waste water, pollution and treatment

Water pollution is an important concern in the world today. Waste water from households and industry is polluting the surface- and groundwater. This water frequently isn't of the right quality any more for food processing, drinking and irrigation. Many pollutants threaten water supplies, but the most widespread, especially in developing countries, is the discharge of untreated sewage water into natural waters; this method of sewage disposal is the most common method in underdeveloped countries, but is also prevalent in countries such as China, India, Nepal and Iran. In addition to sewage, nonpoint source pollution such as agricultural run-off is a significant source of pollution in some parts of the world, along with urban storm water run-off. This is an overflow of the sewage systems that brings sewage water directly into the surface water when heavy rainfall occurs.

Waste water with high levels of organic materials will need a lot of oxygen (oxygen demand) to break down the organic material in in the surface water. This waste water also brings nutrients into the surface water and this causes the so-called eutrophication process in the water. Plants grow quickly because of the increasing availability of nutrients and after some time they die and biodegrade, absorbing oxygen. This lowers the concentration of oxygen in surface water at specific moments so much that fish might be killed. The eutrophication process disturbs the finely tuned balance between nutrients and oxygen in natural aquatic ecosystems.

Treating the waste water before diluting it into the surface water is increasingly done in developed countries but even if the sewage is treated, problems might still arise. Treated sewage water forms sludge, which may be dumped in landfills, spread out on agricultural land, incinerated or dumped at sea.[21] Moreover, the sludge often contains high concentrations of pollutants like heavy metals.

In addition to organic material, waste water can also contain many different chemical pollutants that will not be removed by the regular water treatment plants. Industries increasingly are forced to install specific treatment technologies but many of these pollutants are still being diluted into the surface water.

Water quantity: Shortage and flooding

Besides the existing shortage of water for consumption in households in some regions and some periods of the year the shortage is also felt in agricultural and industrial processes.

It is estimated that 22% of water worldwide is used in industry.[22] Major industrial users include hydroelectric dams, thermoelectric power plants (for cooling), oil refineries (in chemical processes), manufacturing plants (water as a solvent) and food processing industries (for example water for beer brewing).

But this consumption is generally much lower than that of agriculture because it is estimated that 70% of water worldwide is used for irrigation. It takes around 2000–3000 litres of water to produce enough food to satisfy one person's daily dietary needs.[23] This is a considerable amount, when compared to that required for drinking, which is between two and five litres daily.

Agriculture is not only producing food but, increasingly, crops that are used for all kinds of other functions like animal food for meat production, biomass for energy production, cotton for the textile industry etc. These crops also need a lot of water and compete with other functions like drinking water, recreational water and water for nature/ecosystems. A well-known example of this competition is the impact of the use of surface water for agricultural irrigation of cotton fields near the Aral Sea.

Box 5.2   The Aral Sea

The Aral Sea was a lake lying between Kazakhstan and Uzbekistan. The name roughly translates as 'Sea of Islands' and refers to over 1100 islands that once dotted its waters. Formerly one of the four largest lakes in the world with an area of 68,000 km^2, the Aral Sea has been steadily shrinking since the 1960s after the rivers that fed it were diverted by Soviet irrigation projects. By 2007, it had declined to 10% of its original size, splitting into four lakes – the North Aral Sea, the eastern and western basins of the once far larger South Aral Sea, and one smaller lake between the North and South Aral Seas. By 2009, the south-eastern lake had disappeared and the south-western lake had retreated to a thin strip at the extreme west of the former southern sea. Satellite images taken by NASA in August 2014 revealed that for the first time in modern history the eastern basin of the Aral Sea had completely dried up. The eastern basin is now called the Aralkum desert. The shrinking of the Aral Sea has been called 'one of the planet's worst environmental disasters'. The region's once-prosperous fishing industry has been essentially destroyed, bringing unemployment and economic hardship. The Aral Sea region is also heavily polluted, with consequent serious public health problems. The retreat of the sea

(Continued)

has reportedly also caused local climate change, with summers becoming hotter and drier, and winters colder and longer.

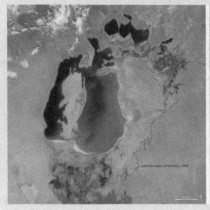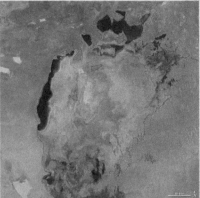

Figure 5.3   The Aral Sea before and after large irrigation projects took place[24]

Floods can be caused by many different factors: heavy rainfall, highly accelerated snow-melt, severe winds over water, unusual high tides, tsunamis or failure of dams or other structures that retained the water. Climate change is also seen as an important factor for the increasing number of floods all over the world because of the rising sea levels and the heavy rainfalls that cause more flooding of river basins. Floods can damage property and endanger the lives of humans and other species. Rapid water run-off causes soil erosion and sediment deposition elsewhere (such as further downstream or down a coast). The spawning grounds for fish and other wildlife habitats can become polluted or completely destroyed. Some prolonged high floods can delay traffic in areas which lack elevated roadways. Floods can interfere with drainage and economic use of farmlands.

Europe is often seen as at the forefront of flood control technology, with low-lying countries such as the Netherlands and Belgium developing techniques that can serve as examples to other countries facing similar problems.[25] After Hurricane Katrina in 2005[26] the US state of Louisiana sent politicians to the Netherlands to take a tour of the complex and highly developed flood control system already in place.[27] The Netherlands has one of the best flood control systems in the world and new ways to deal with water are constantly being developed and tested, such as the underground storage of water, and storing water in reservoirs in large parking garages or on playgrounds. Rotterdam started a project to construct a floating housing development of 120 acres (0.49 km^2) to deal with rising sea levels.[28]

International water management and policy

At the Johannesburg World Summit for Sustainable Development in 2002 governments approved a plan of action to halve by 2015 the proportion of people unable to reach or afford safe drinking water. The Global Water Supply and Sanitation Assessment 2000 Report (GWSSAR) defines 'reasonable access' to water as at least 20 litres per person per day from a source within one kilometre of the user's home. The summit also agreed on reducing the number of people without access to basic sanitation to half the proportion. The GWSSR defines 'basic sanitation' as private or shared but not public disposal systems that separate waste from human contact. In 2025, water shortages will be more prevalent among poorer countries where resources are limited and population growth is rapid. In December 2003, the United Nations General Assembly proclaimed the period 2005–2015 International Decade for Action 'Water for Life'. The decade officially started on World Water Day, 22 March 2005.

5.3.3   Natural resources

Introduction

Many different materials/resources are extracted from the earth by mining, harvesting, catching or cutting. Metals/oil etc. are being mined, cotton/coffee/corn etc. are being harvested, fish is caught in the seas and oceans and wood is being cut in the (tropical rain) forests. But will there be enough of these resources/materials for the increasing demand and growing population in the future?

As far back as 1972 Massachusetts Institute of Technology (MIT) researcher Donella H. Meadows published, with colleagues, *The Limits to Growth*[29] which became a groundbreaking treatise for convincing governments to take a more active role in environmental issues. The findings made a strong impression not only because the study came from a renowned scientific institution, but also because its findings suggested population and welfare growth were not without limits. The report included many graphic tables with prognoses for the coming 50 to 100 years. Almost all contemporary environmental discussions were systematically categorized and discussed including oil, gas, coal and precious metals. Not only were the decreased resources analysed but also the increased harmful emissions (pollution) were examined in detail. At the time of writing 40 years later it can be said that although some of the report's fine points have not turned out to be valid, the main hypotheses were correctly predicted and science presented society with much food for thought.[30]

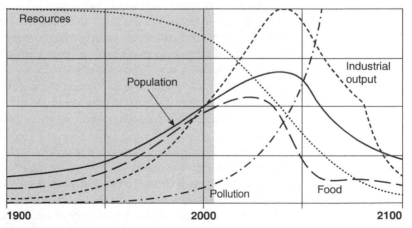

Figure 5.4   State of the world
Report 'The Club of Rome 1972'[31]

Looking at resources it is important to distinguish the difference between renewable and non-renewable resources.

Renewable resources can restore their capacity (using solar energy) in a short time (years/decades). Agricultural crops, wood from forests and fish from the oceans are renewable but the amount that is taken from the system should be in balance with the reproduction speed to prevent the ecosystem being damaged. Forests can restore their capacity but a forest can, of course, not be cut every year, while agricultural crops can be harvested annually.

Non-renewable resources are resources that have been accumulated on our planet for millions of years and can be found in sinks in deep layers of the earth. These resources have to be found with advanced technologies, and be mined and processed by industries before they can be used. Fossil fuels, many different metals, phosphate and also uranium are examples of non-renewable sources. The resources in Figure 5.4 are only non-renewable resources and the graph shows that using them in 200 years while it took millions of years to create these sinks will cause their scarcity and depletion.

The situation concerning the scarcity of the non-renewable fossil fuels is discussed in 5.3.5 in relation to their mainly being a source for energy. But these fossil fuels do not only contain energy. They are also a source of carbon molecules that are used to produce artificial materials (plastics). These plastics can replace natural materials like wood and metals in many products. Recycling of these plastics is very possible and this will help to reduce the scarcity. The impacts of wood cutting on the forests (a renewable resource) will be discussed in the ecosystems and biodiversity section, 5.3.4. In the present section the non-renewable resources phosphate and metals are used as examples of resources becoming scarce and recycling projects and experiments being offered in response.

Phosphates

In 2008, 1.1% of the extractable phosphate reserves were mined (see Figure 5.5).[32] A very important economic function of phosphates is their use as fertilizer. Increased agricultural production depends very much on phosphate although this mineral is not being mined in Europe. All the phosphate used in European agriculture as fertilizer is being imported as phosphate rocks from outside Europe and is processed in industry. The phosphate as a nutrient makes, together with other nutrients in the fertilizer, the crops grow faster so the farmer will produce more kilograms per hectare.

Parts of the phosphate are not absorbed by the plants but dilute as phosphorus into the ground and surface water where it can cause eutrophication (see also 5.3.2).

Phosphate is also a very important nutrient in our food and leaves our bodies after consumption. This suggests that high concentrations of phosphates are being found in urban sewage systems and traditional waste water treatment plants have not removed them, so it dilutes into the surface water where it contributes to the eutrophication process.

Phosphorus flow in ground and water is one of the planetary boundaries already trespassed and urgent action is needed to scale it back.[33] As phosphate reserves decline (it cannot be mined in Europe) while phosphate waste flows are causing eutrophication the question arises: why not recycle the phosphate?

Phosphate recycling will prove to be critical in the long term, because there is no biochemical replacement for phosphorus. Oil could be replaced by solar or biofuel energy, but without phosphates cells cannot function, crops simply cannot grow, and humans cannot live.[34]

Water treatment plants in the Netherlands started removing phosphate and the phosphorus factory of Thermphos International uses sewage sludge as a replacement for phosphate rock as a raw material.[35]

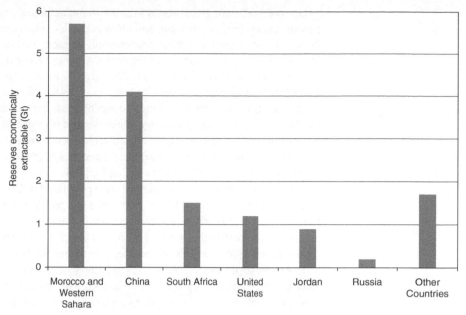

Figure 5.5 Reserves phosphate rock 2008[36] (1 Gt = 1,000,000,000 tons)

Metals

Demand for all kinds of different metals is increasing as the global population grows. The variety of metals we use has also expanded as technology has advanced. As a result, fears regarding metal scarcity and resource depletion have returned during the past ten years.

Concerns focus on the future supply of metals such as indium, lithium, rare-earth elements, tellurium and germanium, all of which are crucial to delivering new digital and low-carbon energy technologies including photovoltaics and electric cars. In 2009, the issue received high priority when China reduced its exports of rare-earth elements as the government sought to maintain the supply to its rapidly expanding domestic manufacturing sector. Most technology metals are mined in only a few places. In 2011, for example, 72% of global cobalt came from the Democratic Republic of the Congo and 57% of indium originated from China (see Figure 5.6).[37] Such metals are produced in low quantities.

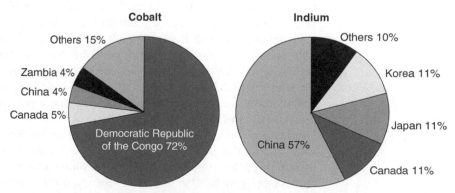

Figure 5.6 Production of cobalt and indium according to British Geological Survey[38]

Up to 60 different elements go into the manufacture of microprocessors and circuit boards, usually in tiny quantities and often in combinations that are not found in nature. Recycling these metals is most economically attractive when they are highly concentrated, for example in manufacturing scrap. Around 70% of the indium used in producing flat-screen displays, for example, finds its way into scrap, which is then recycled.[39] To fix bottlenecks and inefficiencies requires understanding how they flow through the whole supply chain – from mining to concentration, extractive and process metallurgy, manufacturing, use, reuse, recycling, dispersal and disposal.[40] In theory, more than 90% of platinum-group metals used in auto catalysts could be recovered but in practice only 50%–60% is retrieved from European scrapped cars because many vehicles are exported second-hand to places that lack recycling facilities.

More than 1.8 billion mobile phones were purchased in 2013 but only 3% will be recycled. Each phone contains about 300mg of silver and 30mg of gold. Between now and the end of 2020, 10 million tons of electronic products will be purchased in the UK. This includes silver, gold and platinum group metals with a high estimated total market value. Of the 20 different materials in a phone, only a small fraction are ever recuperated, even in the most sophisticated electronics recycling plants such as the huge smelting and electrolysis facility run by metals firm Umicore in Antwerp.[41] In developing countries, where manual disassembly of electronics often takes place, the recovery rate is far lower and comes with the added risk of exposure to hazardous chemicals. Private companies are developing systems[42] to make phone recycling easier, cheaper and less hazardous and they are also working on designs for extending the useful life of phones, such as modular phones featuring replaceable components and 'skins' that look better with age.

Use of land and the ecological footprint

As the use of land/space is also seen as a resource for production and is necessary for the regeneration of exploited ecosystems (absorbing CO_2, recovering of fish population, wood etc.) the method for calculating the ecological footprint is also presented in this section.

The term 'ecological footprint' is used to describe how individuals in different countries make use of the environment. In order to determine a personal profile, it is necessary to know the patterns of consumption for each person. Everything that is consumed should be reduced for use as biological consumption. It can be determined how much an individual uses in the form of oxygen, CO_2 and food. When the ecological footprint was being developed it was assumed that the earth was capable of reproducing its riches.

The basic premise implied that consumption could continue for centuries as long as the earth was able to replenish itself. To determine the ecological footprint, it is necessary to calculate the number of hectares the average person needs in order to live, plus the amount of land that is actually available. The earth will continue to regenerate itself if the average citizen uses less than his prescribed hectares. The use of fossil fuels and the accompanying CO_2 emissions can be used to calculate how much space an individual needs to absorb CO_2 at a safe level. The same methods apply to a different type of consumption and we can calculate how many hectares a person needs for eating meat or vegetables. In this way we can see if people have a small or large ecological footprint. Using this method, different quantities are combined into one unit using either land or water as a starting point. If we take the 2007 world population of seven billion people as a starting point, this translates into approximately 1.8 hectare per person. The actual figures (see Figure 5.7)[43] show that people now use 2.7 hectares per person which puts the condition of the earth in a weaker position.

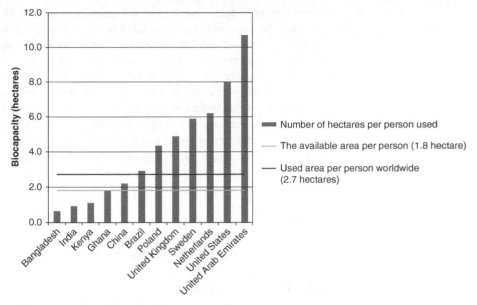

Figure 5.7 Ecological footprint for 12 countries[44]

The ecological footprint has attempted to categorize the taxing of the environment using one prefix, which is unprocessed data and gives a little insight into the different environment and scarcity problems that exist. In actual practice we tend to make more use of specific environmental indicators and are more concerned with accurate measurements of air, water and ground quality including mined materials, fossil fuels and biodiversity.

5.3.4   Ecosystems and biodiversity

Ecosystems

An **ecosystem** is an integrated community of moulds, bacteria, plants and insects that live collectively with each other while retaining a certain form of independence. Together they form an interactive system of living things which feed and thrive with non-living entities (a-biological) such as water, earth, air and temperature. There are staggering differences between them. Think only of the tropical rainforest, the desert, the steppes of Central Asia and city environments as basic examples. Ecosystems differ in fragility. Diversity within the group can be a crucial factor for revitalization in cases of unpredicted circumstances. Plant diversity, for example, can be a deciding element for vitality and growth when related to carbon and nitrogen cycles and minerals in the earth. In general, ecosystems in desert-like conditions are more vulnerable and have a harder time adjusting to disturbances than those in areas which enjoy moderate to plentiful rainfall. Ecosystems in drought-ridden territories experience less growth and minimal development. Land masses in periods of extreme drought suffer the most and offer little fertile ground, which in turn inhibits the variety of plant life, resulting in less developed moulds, with insect and animal life being relegated to a primitive status.[45]

Ecosystems are important for the renewable sources we use daily in our economic systems. The systems provide us with fish, wood and all kinds of other natural resources. The cutting of wood is threatening the tropical rainforests because too much timber is being cut and the forests do not have the time to recover. Not only will the trees in these forests fail to recover but the whole ecosystem with its related species will not be able to regenerate. Estimates vary about the extent of tropical deforestation but approximately one-fifth of the world's tropical rainforest was destroyed between 1960 and 1990.[46] It was claimed that rainforests 50 years ago covered 14% of the world's land surface, now only 5%–7%, and that all tropical forests will be gone by the middle of the twenty-first century.[47] The NGO Forest Stewardship Council (FSC) was founded in 1993 to protect tropical forests from being destroyed and create transparency about the forests where wood for international trade comes from. The organization promotes responsible forest management throughout the world and the consumer can see by the FSC logo on the product if the wood comes from a forest that is managed in a sustainable way and conforms to the ten principles of the Council[48].

Not only are the big ecosystems like the tropical rainforests very important as resources (natural forest coverage is another planetary boundary) but the agricultural land we use is also dependent on smaller, less visible, ecosystems for remaining fertile.

Ecosystems and agriculture

Soil is considered fertile when it offers the possibility of feeding and sustaining crops and when nutrients in the soil evaporate or wash away with difficulty. The chemical substances in the soil are another important element, with the various combinations of moulds and bacteria serving to break up spent organic material from plants and animal waste. A critical process must be in place to ensure that the decomposition of complex organic materials into simple nutrients allows plant life to regenerate its growth with ease. The available bacteria and moulds in the earth determine if organic and plant waste is turned into water, CO_2 nitrogen, phosphates or other simple nutrients. Earthworms, mites and single cell micro- organisms also play a pivotal role as food for larger animal species who spread genetic diversity by planting seeds in different areas. A healthy soil composition is thus dependent on a varied ecosystem and the vitality of each system is dependent on the balance of eating and being eaten. The condition of the soil is important for the available nutrient cycle. The agricultural sector cannot always count on fertile conditions and it is constantly looking for methods to ensure continuous cycles of replenishment.[49]

Loss of biodiversity

Biodiversity loss and species extinction is another planetary boundary already tres- passed and in need of urgent action.[50] The World Wildlife Fund (WWF) announced in a study released on the state of our planet in 2014 that the world has lost 52% of its biodiversity since 1970.[51]

According to the *Living Planet Report 2014*[52]:

> The number of mammals, birds, reptiles, amphibians and fish across the globe is, on average, about half the size it was 40 years ago. This is a much bigger decrease than has been reported previously, as a result of a new methodology which aims to be more representative of global biodiversity.

Scientists studied trends in more than 10,000 populations of 3038 mammal, bird, reptile, amphibian and fish species and calculated a 'Living Planet Index' (LPI) that measures the health of species in various environments and regions. While the LPI in temperate regions declined by 36% from 1970 to 2010, in tropical climates the index dropped 56%. Latin American biodiversity took the biggest hit globally, plummeting 83%.

The enormous loss of biodiversity has diverse causes. Through the relatively rapid temperature increases of 0.2 degrees per decade (see 5.3.5), ecosystems are forced to readjust to the new situation much faster than ever before and often plants and animals are not able to adjust quickly enough and will disappear. The availability of less space and the mixed functions spaces have also play an important role. The decrease of woodland areas, especially the rainforest, has had major consequences. The third factor is the availability of water. Many ecosystems rely very much on the water systems being part of the ecosystem. When water is used on a large scale for industry or agriculture the ecosystem might suffer a shortage of water (see the example of the Aral Sea in 5.2.2) and species will not survive. Another important factor is the pollution of the ecosystems with nutrients and chemicals that increase the regular levels of the nutrients and/or are toxic for specific species. Nutrients like phosphates and nitrogen, used as fertilizer in agricultural fields, can spread over neighbouring natural areas and disturb the nutrient balance in the ecosystem. For example, when pesticides are used on agricultural land to combat insects, it can affect small birds, and when they in turn are eaten by predatory birds the pesticides can accumulate and kill them.

The Convention on Biological Diversity

The Convention on Biological Diversity (CBD) is an international legally binding treaty with three main goals: conservation of biodiversity; sustainable use of biodiversity; and the fair and equitable sharing of the benefits arising from the use of genetic resources. Its overall objective is to encourage actions which will lead to a sustainable future. The conservation of biodiversity is a common concern of humankind. The CBD covers biodiversity at all levels: ecosystems, species and genetic resources. The convention covers all possible domains that are directly or indirectly related to biodiversity and its role in development, ranging from science, politics and education to agriculture, business, culture and much more. In 2010, parties to the CBD adopted the Strategic Plan for Biodiversity 2011–2020, a ten-year framework for action by all countries and stakeholders to safeguard biodiversity and the benefits it provides to people.

The United Nations General Assembly declared 2011–2020 the UN Decade on Biodiversity (Resolution 65/161). This incentive serves to support and promote implementation of the objectives of the Strategic Plan for Biodiversity and the Aichi Biodiversity Targets,[53] with the goal of significantly reducing biodiversity loss.

5.3.5   Use of energy and its impacts

Energy sources

Energy is needed for all processes in our economy, industry, households and transport. Many different energy sources could be used but after the Industrial Revolution the so-called fossil fuels became the dominating source. Fossil fuels are substances like coal, oil and gas that were formed millions of years ago from decayed plants and due to high pressure beneath the soil, transformed into liquid-oil, solid-coal or gas/natural gas. Sophisticated technology is used to find these fossil fuels, mine and process them so they can be used as petrol in your car, kerosene in aeroplanes or gas for your heating or cooking. They can also be used not to produce energy but to produce artificial materials like plastics as discussed in Section 5.3.3. All the energy that the fossil fuels contain originates from the sun because the plants as the source for the fossil fuels have captured solar energy in their biomass during their lifetime. The enormous amount of CO_2 that was captured by these plants caused the CO_2 levels to decrease and the oxygen levels increased so that life for many species (like the human population) became possible.

As Figure 5.8 shows, the main sources of energy in the world are very much based on the fossil fuels oil, coal and natural gas. Hydro power and nuclear energy cover only a limited part and the part that is covered by energy based on renewable sources like wind, sun, biomass etc. is only recently increasing very slowly.

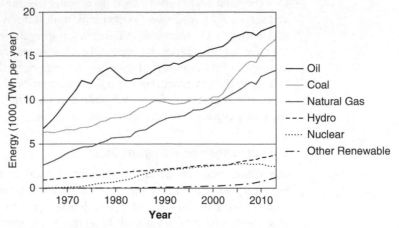

Figure 5.8   Rates of world energy usage[54]

As mentioned in 5.3.3, resources can be divided into renewable and non-renewable and this also counts for energy resources. Fossil fuels are not renewable and one day they will run out. Easily obtainable fossil fuels have already been exhausted. That is why industries put a lot of effort into developing new technologies for exploitation of fossil fuels in these more difficult places and conditions. Many countries depend on the import of fossil fuels and they often import from countries they do not like to depend on because of unstable governments and wars. And last but not least the burning of fossil fuels causes the emission of CO_2 and its increasing levels are being held responsible for the climate change. Because of these three aspects, governments and business are increasingly looking for alternative energy sources. Countries with mountain areas and a lot of water often invest in large hydro power stations while other countries have built many nuclear power plants. After a Tsunami in Japan caused the Fukushima nuclear disaster accident in 2011 the government decided to close down all its nuclear power plants.[55] Germany also decided to close down all its nuclear plants and changed the focus in its energy policies towards renewable sources. And it proved to be very successful because in 2014 in Germany 31% of all the energy used was produced by renewable energy sources like solar, wind and biomass.[56] Decades ago Brazil was already producing the biofuel ethanol based on agricultural production of sugar cane. In 2011 Brazil produced 21.1 billion litres (5.57 billion US liquid gallons), representing 24.9% of the world's total ethanol used as fuel.[57] Producing biofuels with crops that have grown on agricultural land causes a dilemma, because it often concerns land that is also used for food production (see Section 5.5).

Globally the percentage of energy from renewable sources is increasing very slowly, but also countries like China, Italy, Japan, and the US invest significantly in renewable energy sources. Figure 5.9 shows the development of the global wind power capacity from 1996 until 2013.

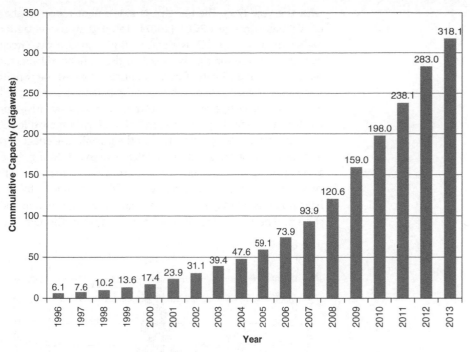

Figure 5.9 Wind power (Worldwide installed capacity[58])

Renewable sources for energy seem to be promising for the future but the technological changes and the economic systems connected to it will need time to adapt.

The 'fossil fuel period' in our history might not end because of the climate change it causes, or because we run out of fossil fuels, but because the use of renewable sources for energy will be technologically possible and from a societal point of view much more rational. Like the former Saudi Arabian minister of oil, Sheik Ahmed Zaki Yamani, said: 'The "stone age" did not end because they ran out of stones'.[59]

Carbon dioxide (CO₂) and climate change

The huge release of CO_2 into the atmosphere during the last 200 years has been due to the use of fossil fuels for heating, cooling and transportation. Strong criticism, especially from the scientific community, is protesting the undesirability of switching from an era of dependence on oil to an era dependent on coal and natural gas even though there are enough reserves for 100 years. In the future, individual countries will also grant concessions to oil companies. We can expect extensive exploration in countries bordering the North Pole where huge reserves are suspected which could be easily obtained should a significant melting of the polar ice occur. In 2010 it was expected that crude oil production would reach its peak in the next decade.[60] In other words, estimated oil production for the future would then have reached its highest point. Fewer new oil fields would be discovered and the production of oil would decrease. But this has proved to be more fiction than fact.

Fossil fuel era

The fossil fuel era (see Figure 5.10) began around 1800, when the first steam locomotives were powered by coal. Scientists have developed scenarios to put the CO_2 concentration into perspective. In the worst-case scenario, CO_2 emissions will double compared with the year 1750. The fourth UN assessment report of the Intergovernmental Panel on Climate Change (IPCC) (2007) stated that concentration levels are already 35% higher than in 1750. CO_2 is a so-called greenhouse gas. Greenhouse gases capture the warmth from the sun that has reached the planet and heats the atmosphere to a certain temperature and climate. This has in history created the conditions in the atmosphere of our planet to make life possible. But the balance between the level of these greenhouse gases and the temperature and climate is a very sensitive one. Small changes in these levels can have big impacts. The emission of carbon dioxide (CO_2) by burning fossil fuels accounts for a 50% intensification of the greenhouse effect. A second gas receiving more and more attention is methane which is released during the digestive process of cattle and the piling up of dung heaps. The atmospheric increase in the concentration of these two greenhouse gases is directly related to human activities. Greenhouse gases that have no human influence are gases that rise in swamplands and volcanoes but they have shown to be less significant than those that occur through human participation.

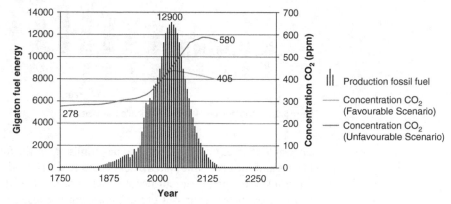

Figure 5.10   Fossil fuel era[61, 62]

Climate change

Climate change is one of two planetary boundaries currently in the uncertainty zone. The increase of the greenhouse effect is seen as a serious problem because it is changing the climate and this can have drastic impacts on people living in areas sensitive to flooding, storms, droughts etc. Today's levels of CO_2 are increasing further and the average earth temperature will rise accordingly and change the climate. People will have to adapt to these changing climate conditions, build protection against flooding and sometimes even move activities from sensitive areas. Nature is also responding to these changes by shifting flora and fauna to other regions trying to create a new ecological balance.

Today we are becoming acutely aware of the increasing amount of greenhouse emissions and the problem is emerging as one of worldwide concern with the increases happening in a relatively short period of time. Global warming has taken flight in the last decades and is predicted to increase by 0.2°C every ten years.[63] It means that all of us, including the animal and plant worlds, must prepare for a new situation. Weather will be more extreme, with dry periods lasting longer and rainy periods being shorter and more intense. The number of hurricanes is also expected to increase along with a rise in sea level, and this will affect the lives of a large group of people living in coastal regions with deltas and high population concentrations.[64] Holland with nine million coastal residents and Bangladesh with 120 million are two countries that come immediately to mind. The changing climate will also leave its mark on decreasing biodiversity and existing ecosystems will have to adjust quickly. Longer growing seasons, for example, will make it easier for certain plants, animals, insects and fungi to thrive while other species will encounter unknown difficulties, causing migration to areas better suited to their original lifestyle. The expectation is that biodiversity will decrease rather than increase because long-established species that have evolved through thousands of millions of years will not be able to cope with the fast-changing new conditions.[65]

IPCC (International Panel on Climate Change)

The world community is bracing itself for the imminent climate changes by analysing several important factors. The IPCC of the United Nations is charged with bringing out an 'assessment report' every 5–7 years. The last report (no. 5) came out in 2014 and involved 800 scientists. The IPCC provides some research but mainly makes use of supplementary information provided by universities and research centres.[66] The IPCC report is the current standard in climate change research, and although its fifth report was shown to contain some mistakes, all the main conclusions were considered to be correct and mistakes were rectified. The IPCC's working method utilizes many checks and balances, with previous results serving as a basis for new conclusions. It maintains a sharp eye for conflicting reports and research practices in the hope of keeping dissent to a minimum when represented by leading specialist scientific authorities.

5.4 Social sustainability

Social sustainability is the least defined and the least understood of the different ways of approaching sustainability and sustainable development. Social sustainability has had considerably less attention in public dialogue than economic and environmental sustainability.

As mentioned in Section 5.2 the Brundtland Commission started with the definition of sustainable development from the environmental perspective but concluded that sustainability also has a strong and important social dimension. It found that human resource development in the form of poverty reduction, gender equity and wealth redistribution would be very crucial for formulating environmental strategies. Also the triple bottom line principles and many others prompted for attention to 'social sustainability'. Some speak of sustainable human development that can be seen as development that promotes the capabilities of people in the present without compromising the capabilities of future generations. In the human development paradigm, environment and natural resources should constitute a means of achieving better standards of living just as income represents a means of increasing social expenditure and, in the end, well-being.[67] There are several other approaches to and definitions found for social dimension of sustainability.

The first approach, which posits a triad of environmental sustainability, economic sustainability and social sustainability is the most widely accepted as a model for addressing sustainability. The concept of 'social sustainability' in this approach encompasses such topics as: social equity, liveability, health equity, community development, social capital, social support, human rights, labour rights, social responsibility, social justice, cultural competence, community resilience and human adaptation.

A second approach suggests that all of the domains of sustainability are social, including ecological, economic, political and cultural sustainability. These domains of social sustainability are all dependent upon the relationship between the social and the natural, with the 'ecological domain' defined as human embeddedness in the environment. In these terms, social sustainability encompasses all human activities. It is not just relevant to the focused intersection of economics, the environment and the social as in the Circles of Sustainability diagram (Figure 5.11).

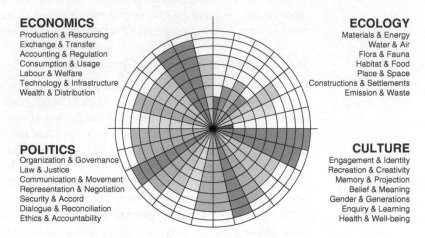

ECONOMICS
Production & Resourcing
Exchange & Transfer
Accounting & Regulation
Consumption & Usage
Labour & Welfare
Technology & Infrastructure
Wealth & Distribution

ECOLOGY
Materials & Energy
Water & Air
Flora & Fauna
Habitat & Food
Place & Space
Constructions & Settlements
Emission & Waste

POLITICS
Organization & Governance
Law & Justice
Communication & Movement
Representation & Negotiation
Security & Accord
Dialogue & Reconciliation
Ethics & Accountability

CULTURE
Engagement & Identity
Recreation & Creativity
Memory & Projection
Belief & Meaning
Gender & Generations
Enquiry & Learning
Health & Well-being

Figure 5.11 Circles of Sustainability[68]

A third approach divides the topic of sustainability into material sustainability, dealing with such material issues as the environment, air, water, food, fuel, housing, arable land, mineral resources etc., and social sustainability, dealing with non-material issues that affect the individual/family; these are society, politics/government, and economics/finance.[69]

A final, fourth, approach uses the following dimensions for social sustainability:[70]

- Equity – the community provides equitable opportunities and outcomes for all its members, particularly the poorest and most vulnerable members of the community.
- Diversity – the community promotes and encourages diversity.
- Interconnected/social cohesions – the community provides processes, systems and structures that promote connectedness within and outside the community at the formal, informal and institutional level.
- Quality of life – the community ensures that basic needs are met and fosters a good quality of life for all members at the individual, group and community level (e.g. health, housing, education, employment, safety).
- Democracy and governance – the community provides democratic processes and open and accountable governance structures.
- Maturity – the individual accepts the responsibility of consistent growth and improvement through broader social attributes (e.g. communication styles, behavioural patterns, indirect education and philosophical explorations).

The approaches to social sustainability differ but they all state that working on sustainable development only from the environmental perspective as sometimes is advocated will not achieve the sustainable development we need. Currently, the safe and just space framework developed by Oxfam is gaining increasing traction. It proposes that inclusive and sustainable development has a foundation (social justice) and a ceiling (ecological safety); human activity must confine itself within such a space. The planetary boundaries are the space's ceiling, while ten dimensions of social sustainability provide the space's foundations (health, water, income, education, resilience, voice, jobs, energy, social equity, gender equality).[71]

 5.5 Case Study: Biofuel's dilemma: Food or energy

Case prepared by Ankit Gaur

Biomass is a generic term used to describe all types of organic material that result from plant matter. Solar energy is stored in the form of chemical bonds in all organic matter. When these chemical bonds are broken by the process of digestion, combustion or decomposition, the chemical energy released is referred to as biomass energy. This has been one of the oldest sources of energy used by mankind and currently contributes 10%–14% of the world's total energy supply.[72]

Over the last 10 to 20 years, the rapid consumption of oil stocks and the ever-increasing demand for energy worldwide has increased the interest in renewable sources of energy such as biomass. Another reason why biomass as a source of energy is gaining interest all around the world is due to its easy availability in almost all countries around the world – in both rural and urban areas.

First-generation biofuels, which include ethanol and biodiesel, stem from biomass that is often edible. The production of first-generation biofuels is dependent largely on crops such as sugar cane and corn, although other feedstock such as whey, barley, potato waste etc. can also be used. Second-generation biofuels, unlike the limited raw material for first-generation biofuels, are produced from a large variety of feedstocks such as non-edible lignocellulose – plant dry matter. The final category of biomass is the third-generation biofuels. The main raw material for this is the algal biomass.[73] This type of biomass is dependent on the lipid content of algae, and species that have high lipid content (60%–70%) are usually used for biomass production. It is one of the cheapest sources for biomass production.[74]

Despite the benefits of using biomass as a source of energy, it has been associated with several criticisms as well – such as the food versus fuel debate. The world has seen a continuous increase in food prices over the last few decades. More than 30 nations across the world had food riots between 2008 and 2009. Although there are several reasons that have led to this, one of the most accepted reasons is that the main agricultural countries in the world, such as Brazil and the US, are converting large sections of their croplands into biofuel production.[75] The World Bank has estimated that about 100 million people could be pushed into poverty due to the competition between biofuel and food production. Even though it is often hard to prove that food prices rise (only) due to the increased production of biofuels, the increased food prices in 2007 to 2008 were analysed as such a situation.[76] However, there are some countries that have managed to maintain a balance between food and fuel and Brazil is one of them. Brazil is one of the world's largest producers and exporters of ethanol fuel in the world, and is considered to have one of the world's first sustainable biofuel economies. However, it is claimed that this is possible only in countries like Brazil due to their advanced agricultural technology and large investments in agro-industrial research and development, along with large availabilities of arable land. Over the last 37 years, Brazil's biofuel programme has been making use of the most efficient technology in the world for cultivating sugar cane; modern equipment and cheap, low grade sugar cane as feedstock, helping it sustain its economy and potentially set an example for the rest of the world.[77]

Case Study Questions

1. Apart from environmental benefits, suggest some other benefits of biomass energy.
2. Discuss the disadvantages of using biomass as a source of energy.
3. Provide examples of countries other than Brazil that have a sustainable economy dependent on biomass.
4. What considerations must a country keep in mind while converting a large amount of its energy requirements to biomass-derived energy?

5.6   Learning tools

5.6.1   Summary

- The industrial revolution after the Second World War created prosperity but caused many social and environmental impacts.
- Sustainable development is defined as: 'Development that meets the needs of the present without compromising the ability of future generations to meet their own needs.'
- Sustainable development is about the balance between people, planet and prosperity above the bottom line (triple P). Green growth is about investing in the environment to create growth and phasing out polluting industries.
- The planet has quantifiable ecological boundaries. Trespassing them means high risk of irreversible change. The use of large quantities of water, fossil fuels for energy and natural resources in our economy threatens boundaries such as loss of biodiversity and guarantees that we will run out of these resources.
- Climate change is caused by greenhouse gases like CO_2 and it seems that we will have to accept that the average temperature will rise at least 2 degrees and maybe even more. This means that areas with flood risks have to adapt to this situation and when they cannot they might have to move economic activities to safer areas.
- The percentage of energy produced by renewable sources is increasing very slowly worldwide.
- The number of species of mammals, birds, reptiles, amphibians and fish across the globe is, on average, about half the size it was 40 years ago.
- Producing biomass on agricultural land causes a dilemma concerning food production.
- Two countries account for a third of the world's total ecological footprint: China, at 19%, and the United States, with nearly 14%.
- The social aspects of sustainable development include such topics as: social equity, liveability, health equity, community development, social capital, social support, human rights, labour rights, social responsibility, social justice, cultural competence, community resilience and human adaptation.

5.6.2   Further reading

Elkington, J. (1997). *Cannibals with Forks: The Triple Bottom Line of Twenty-First Century Business.* Oxford: Capstone.

Organization for Economic Co-operation and Development. *Green Growth and Sustainable Development*. Retrieved from www.oecd.org/greengrowth/green-growth-key-documents.htm on 26 November 2015.

UN Water (2007). *World Water Day, 22nd March 2007. Coping with water scarcity: Challenge of the twenty-first century*. Retrieved from www.fao.org/nr/water/docs/escarcity.pdf on 26 November 2015.

World Commission on Environment and Development (1987). *Our Common Future* Oxford: Oxford University Press.

World Wide Fund for Nature (WWF) (2014). *Living Planet Report 2014*. Retrieved from http://wwf.panda.org/about_our_earth/all_publications/living_planet_report/on 26 November 2015.

5.6.3 Assignments

Assignment 5.1

Explain, using an example, the negative environmental and social impacts of the Industrial Revolution in the nineteenth century.

Assignment 5.2

Choose a country using a high percentage of renewable sources for its energy supply and explain why and how it achieved this high percentage.

Assignment 5.3

Discuss, with examples, to what extent sustainable development challenges can be addressed with technological change only.

Assignment 5.4

Discuss to what extent the Sustainable Development Goals can actually maintain global economic activity within the safe and just operating space for humankind.

5.6.4 Self-test questions

Self-test Questions

1. What planetary boundaries have been trespassed and what are the likely consequences?
2. Choose a sector of industry and explain what the balance between the three Ps above the bottom line means to it.
3. Why are water, energy and materials the most important resources for our economy?

(Continued)

4. What is eutrophication?
5. Define the difference between renewable and non-renewable resources.
6. Where are phosphates mainly used for?
7. What is the percentage of mobile phones that is being recycled?
8. Select an animal or plant that has disappeared from this planet and explain why this happened.
9. Why will we have to adapt to climate change?
10. Why is producing biomass for energy production causing a dilemma for food production?

GOVERNANCE OF SUSTAINABILITY

Overview and learning objectives

The Brundtland Report *Our Common Future* (See Chapter 5), commissioned and published by the UN, has become an important milestone for sustainable development.[1] The world community responded to a new challenge despite an overfull agenda dealing with poverty, war and the instability of world economies (see Chapters 1 and 2). Sustainability is largely related to the question of shortages. The situation is less severe if countries decide to stabilize population growth or take measures to trim consumption, but is this a realistic scenario? This chapter takes a close look at the governance of sustainability and how the market economy can contribute to the governance of sustainability. The question on the governance of sustainability was an important theme at the United Nations Conference on Sustainable Development (UNCSD) in Rio de Janeiro in 2012[2].

Section 6.1 of this chapter will explore developments in population growth, prosperity and technology. How have these factors influenced the environment and what policies and measures need to be taken to keep the damage to a minimum? Section 6.2 is devoted to interactions between the natural environment and the market economy. The market economy promotes welfare and many people assume that too much government interference is damaging because the market tends to regulate itself.[3] By taking a closer look though, we can see that this system has advantages and disadvantages. It certainly functions for the distribution of scarce supplies but it is not perfect and not all resources within the system are fairly priced. There are sizeable gaps, certainly when addressing the environment and the long term.[4] By studying the imperfections in the market economy we can discover to what extent Adam Smith's brainchild (see Chapter 2) can offer short- as well as long-term welfare solutions. Strong sustainability claims that you cannot get solutions for sustainability problems without changing the underlying economic market system that misuses the natural environment in an improper way.

Countless ways exist for governments to create long-term sustainable welfare but this is often tempered by the limited ambitions of the governments themselves.[5] Rational laws meant for the long term do not always get priority. Section 6.3 will look at the mechanisms and instruments that government uses to develop long-term policy.

> **Learning objectives**
>
> This chapter will enable students to:
>
> - Gain insight into the relevant factors that put stress on the environment.
> - Understand the gaps in the market economy and understand why this system may not always be the best option in the pursuit of long-term welfare.
>
> *(Continued)*

- Know and understand the instruments that the market economy has at its disposal to increase performance so that scarce materials remain available for short and long periods.
- Understand why society benefits from choosing long-term welfare solutions when the government has to deal with institutions that serve as countervailing powers.
- Comprehend the primary assumptions required to create a durable economy.

6.1   Factors influencing environment impacts

The 1968 bestseller *The Population Bomb* written by scientist Paul R. Ehrlich[6] sounded the alarm bells for impending environmental issues and their consequences for humanity. Ehrlich echoed nineteenth-century sociologist Malthus and warned about impending exhaustion of natural resources owing to unrestrained demographic and economic growth. He predicted a severe famine and mass starvation of humans in the 1970s and 1980s because of overpopulation. The book was sharply criticized by scientists not only for its alarmist views, but also the manner in which the research and conclusions were conducted.[7] Some of Ehrlich's theories were quickly unravelled as he failed to take into account innovations in agriculture, especially the 'green revolution' which occurred in the 1980s. India, for example, started using improved seeds, pesticides and fertilizers resulting in increased food production. Ehrlich's predictions of mass hunger were defused.[8] In a 2004 interview he admitted to several miscalculations but refused any further concessions concerning the population bomb.[9] He stated that since his book's original publication, world population had increased by 2.8 billion people compared to the 3.5 billion in 1968. He ended the interview with a rhetorical question for the interviewer: if these developments could not be better considered as a population explosion.

Ehrlich's formula

To further support his concern, Ehrlich developed a formula to indicate if worldwide environmental damage was increasing or decreasing. It reads: I = P x W x T.

I	=	Environmental impact
P	=	Population
W	=	Welfare per individual
T	=	Determining technique for environmental burden per welfare unit

The formula is appealing because of its simplicity but it remains a difficult task using it to ascertain environmental burden. When applying the formula, insight must be gained in the following trends:

- Population index (the index can be calculated by percentages of population growth).
- Index of environmental burden emanating from welfare (the welfare index is usually calculated on the percentage growth of GNP).
- Influence of technique on the index position (the role of clean or unclean technology in the production of consumer goods). The technique is relevant not only for different phases of production, but also for manufacture and waste.

Paul Ehrlich was pessimistic about these indexes. Improved health care led to population growth and production of goods for large numbers also increased. He predicted that welfare would increase, especially when coupled with industrial production.[10] Now that many countries have embraced the market economy and worldwide productivity has increased, there is growing pressure for clean technology and controlled population growth.

6.1.1 Population

Population growth is not generally considered to be a 'hot item' on the political agenda of many countries.[11, 12] The World Health Organization has pleaded for governments to pay more attention to family planning. There is a 40% chance that world population will be over ten billion people by the year 2100.[13] At the same time there is 85% chance that, in the same year, population growth will stabilize. The following paragraphs will examine the lively ongoing debate about family planning and population growth.

Population growth and prosperity

Sustainable growth is easier to achieve in smaller population concentrations because of the limits of arable land and the required space for housing and recreational development. Yet despite this, world population is set to grow in the coming decades.[14]

In 2014 growth percentage of the world population reached 1.16% annually, although when examined in a larger time frame (1965 for example when the rate was 2.04%) there has been a steady, general decrease.[15] The expected decrease in the next century will be largely due to personal choice with many city dwellers opting for smaller families and more and more people migrating to cities. In addition, increased welfare plays a role because the number of children per family decreases. This has led to a slow down and even a decrease in population growth.

We see that many governments do not generally take an active role in population control because by doing so they would be interfering in personal decision making for families or potential mothers. Western society, in particular, regards citizens' freedom as a central pillar. Looking closer at human rights, the emphasis is squarely on freedom of speech and self-determination. In some other countries the weight of the collective opinion is what counts.[16] During the last decades in China, for example, an ambitious policy has been in effect. The Chinese felt that poverty could best be combated by limiting family size.[17] Let's examine how China dealt with the issue.

Family planning in China

Forty years ago, China introduced stringent reforms for family planning. The changes were necessary in order to increase individual welfare. This Chinese family planning policy is known as 'late, long, few'. The families were advised to have fewer children by delaying the start of a family as long as possible and leaving considerable time between births. This programme was supported by the entire Chinese health service and had dramatic consequences. Between 1970 and 1979 average childbirth statistics decreased from 5.9 to 2.9. To decrease the numbers even further, the one-child policy was adopted in 1979 and by 1995 the birth rate had stabilized at 1.7 children per family (see Figure 6.1).[18]

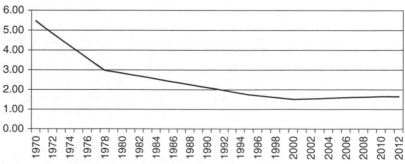

Figure 6.1   Fertility rate of women in China[19]

The measures taken by China represent a technocratic approach to the family planning problem.[20] People who violated the rules and had more children were forced to pay hefty fines and there were many unpleasant side effects such as increased abortions of female foetuses, because many families preferred a male heir. Individual rights were less important than results. China's family planning policy has supporters and detractors. The post-war West, placing increasing emphasis on human rights, is the strongest critic. Proponents of the one-child policy talk about poverty reduction which has been realized. Opponents take the same poor as a starting point and indicate that they are being deprived of their freedom to have more or fewer children.[21] The dilemma points out the different values that are played against each other. It is a problem that Amartya Sen, winner of the 1998 Nobel Prize for economics, has examined in depth in *Principles of Development as Freedom*. He states that eliminating poverty has a direct relation to freedom, because underprivileged members of society do not have free access to food and essential goods.[22] Governments that have human rights high on the agenda, but that are unable to offer the poor a chance to improve their economic lot, are just as guilty as governments with little or no respect for people's rights.

The Chinese authorities have stated that their family planning programme has been a success and point to the fact that 250 million fewer children were born between 1978 and 2000.[23] The World Bank expects the Chinese population to expand until 2030 but that it will not exceed 1.5 billion people.[24]

6.1.2   Prosperity

The degree of citizens' welfare in a country is often measured by the per capita GDP with the goal obviously being increased growth. Whether per capita GDP really does give a true picture of welfare remains a debatable subject. Economist Stiglitz is one of the main critics.[25] To present both sides of the argument the following section, including Box 6.1, will take a look at growth and its relation to prosperity, well-being and the environment.

Box 6.1   GDP[26]

GDP and prosperity and well-being

A country's GDP is calculated by adding up salaries, profits, leases and interest. GDP can increase when public health decreases, with a good example being the need for more public health employees to combat growing obesity. This translates directly to the need for more salaries to compensate insurance agents, physicians, nurses, and pharmaceutical research and development. Other projects such as restoration work due to vandalism and the clean up of tainted ground also raise GDP by providing extra work, but have nothing to do with increased well-being and welfare.

GDP and prosperity and well-being in the short or long term

A country can have a high GDP with relatively low prosperity at present because it has chosen to invest in the future. Investments in railways, glass fibre and solar panels increase GDP by providing employment opportunities, but the real welfare improvements will be measured in the coming decades because people will consume more and enjoy comfortable travelling, better communications and clean energy.

(Continued)

GDP and environmentally friendly prosperity and well-being

GDP is a reference for prosperity only and does not provide information about environmentally friendly consumption. This has to do with the type of products that people purchase. Two people with the same income can affect the environment in different ways. Spending €25 to see a ballet performance can theoretically have a positive environmental effect. Dancers and the public leave their homes for the performance, turn down the central heating and use public transport instead of cars and thus use less CO_2. In this case the environment benefits. But, if the same €25 is spent at the Formula One races, the environment will suffer. To get a clearer picture of the harmful effects of prosperity, it is necessary to look at spending patterns.

Economic growth and the environment

Zero growth[27]

Environmental protesters in the 1970s and 1980s saw unfettered economic growth, rather than population growth, as the main cause of environmental deterioration. They argued that there was a trade-off between growth and the environment. The more growth, the more pollution and the fewer non-renewable natural resources and fragile ecosystems left. Growth ought to be stopped if humankind was to survive. Dryzek (1997) calls these ideas 'survivalists'. The 'zero growth' economy was the goal of the most prominent survivalist institution: the Club of Rome. An international organization composed of academics, politicians and industrialists, The Club of Rome's (Meadows et al.'s) best-selling report *The Limits to Growth* (see Chapters 2 and 5)[28] addressed methodological criticisms pointed at Ehrlich's book *The Population Bomb*. The report used computer-generated projections to forecast that the pattern of economic growth and use of natural resources would cause humanity's extinction in 100 years. The spread of prosperity within the dominant capitalist model, fuelling unrestrained consumption and production, would lead to natural resources' exhaustion and contamination, incrementally limiting the capacity of ecosystems to support agricultural and industrial activity and resulting in famines and wars over natural resources. Eventually, the world's life support capacity would collapse as even air would become unsuitable to breathe.

Environmental problem solving and environmental Kuznets Curve[29]

Zero growth became a flagship claim of environmental activism in the 1970s. However, it made impossible to develop a common agenda with scientists, policy makers and industry stakeholders which strongly supported growth-orientated economic models and an alternative way to deal with environmental challenges. One of the models where growth is a possible scenario is termed 'environmental problem solving' (EPS) by John Dryzek.[30] EPS acknowledged the existence of trade-offs between economic growth and the environment but denied the need to forestall growth to prevent a hypothetical environmental catastrophe. EPS argues that *The Limits to Growth*, which is an important starting point for zero growth, systematically underestimates the occurrence of 'feedback mechanisms', by which increases in price will always result in a decrease in consumption, more efficient technologies and more efficient use of stocks.[31]

EPS supported a staged model of development, proposing an inverted U-shaped relationship between GDP growth and environmental deterioration. An increase in environmental degradation is an inevitable price to pay in the early stages of development, but there is turning point. After it, increases in GDP result in industrial efficiency, technological innovation and environmental awareness. The result is growing prevention and remediation of environmental problems (cleaning rivers, replanting forests, using treatment technologies and regulation) until environmental degradation disappears. There is no need to radically change business-as-usual approaches. Environmental problems are just short-term problems to be fixed in the long term, once development is assured and there are resources available to cover environmental costs.[32]

The empirical evidence supporting environmental Kuznets Curves (see Figure 6.2) was thoroughly analysed by Stern (2004). Stern concluded that the basis of environmental Kuznets Curves was flimsy econometrics. None of the empirical studies he scrutinized was econometrically robust enough to be conclusive. He also identified several theoretical flaws in econometric models advocating environmental Kuznets curves. Stern further observed that recent evidence shows that for most pollutants – critically, CO_2 – developed countries' emissions have continuously increased with economic growth, far beyond the turning point predicted by the environmental Kuznets Curve. At the same time, Stern proves that many developing countries have been growing without creating sharp environmental deterioration, sometimes reaching developed country standards with a very short time lag and sometimes performing better than some developed countries.[33]

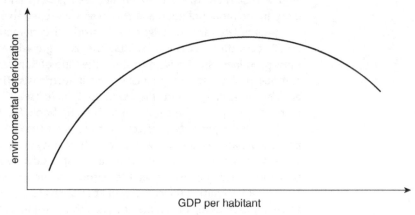

Figure 6.2   Kuznets Curve of environmental deterioration

Sustainability and growth

As we saw in Chapter 5, the conceptual stalemate between survivalists and problem solvers ended in 1987 when the Brundtland Report introduced the groundbreaking idea that growth is compatible with environmental protection through dematerialization of the economy, greener consumption and lifestyles, environmental technologies and eco-efficiency.

Dematerialization of the economy, also known as decoupling, is a process of separation of economic and social well-being from the use of physical resources. It can take three forms:

1. Efficiency: economic growth – as measured by GDP growth – may be separated from increase in material and energy throughput with new environmental technologies and eco-efficiency.
2. Sufficiency: material and energy throughput are decoupled from social well-being through lifestyle changes such as greener consumption, anti-consumption and austerity.

3. Equity: social well-being becomes decoupled from economic growth through changes in social norms and values – e.g. the 'Gift Economy'[34] (Haberl et al., 2004).[35]

In Europe the first form of dematerialization seems to be happening: resource productivity augmented by 26% from 2012 to 2013. Countries such as the Netherlands and Germany managed to increase GDP while reducing material consumption (Eurostat, 2015).[36] However, part of the success might be attributed to the decline of resource-intensive industries after the crisis, new patterns of trade and outsourcing of material-intensive processes. Overall, global progress towards dematerialization has been disappointingly slow and political traction has been lost.

A recent concept within sustainability, namely green growth, goes beyond decoupling and proposes a virtuous circle between economic growth and environmental protection. The concept is focused on investing in the protection of the natural environment as a driver for inclusive growth.

As a consequence, GDP growth has not usually been seen as a hindrance to sustainable development. However, the global recession has restored the thunder to more critical views. Critical green growth argues that investment in the green sector is not enough; some types of growth are inevitably linked to pollution and should be restricted. Critical green growth proposes a green GDP where activities that pollute or exhaust natural resources are no longer included. This perspective also argues that governments should actively help the market phase out polluting industries and focus on green industries in a process of creative green destruction.[37]

In turn, some environmental groups feel that the market economy is a failing system because of its influence on culture and identity and that it makes no tangible contribution to meaning and happiness. GDP is not an appropriate measurement of prosperity and well-being. Many of these arguments are reflected in Tim Jackson's influential book *Prosperity without Growth*.[38] The book argues that the economic crisis in 2008 signals the failure of growth-oriented market systems in the West. Western economies need to prepare for a process of de-growth. Prosperity without growth is not an ideal but a financial and ecological imperative.

Alternatives to GDP

Because higher GDP is not an end in itself, it has served as the motivation for scientists to look for alternatives and one of the most popular theories of recent times is the Happiness Index. The basic premise is that all government policy should have public contentment as its starting point. Another indicator gaining popularity is the Happy Planet Index from the New Economic Foundation.[39] Together, these new approaches have created fresh ideas to give better insight into human well-being and future-orientated goals for society.

Happiness Index[40]

Economist Richard Layard has studied the concept of happiness and has concluded that people's level of contentment is not necessarily dependent on GDP and personal income. His findings have opened the axioms of economy to discussion. Many economists assume that higher income is a good thing without ever having delved deeply into the subject.[41] The machinery of the market economy achieves desired results, but whether the results are useful has been insufficiently examined.

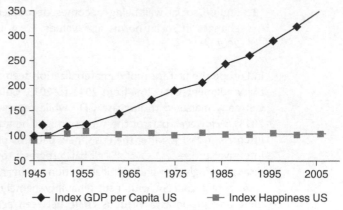

Figure 6.3   Income and happiness in the United States[42, 43]

Increased prosperity in high-income countries goes hand in hand with habituation. The initial euphoria of increased wealth quickly fades when one realizes that others are becoming wealthy as well. Research has proved that a lot of people are concerned with 'who has the most' and stands out from the rest.[44]

*'OK, if you can't see your way around a payrise then its only
fair that David Jones should turn in his company car'*

Figure 6.4   Feelings of fairness[45]

Layard's research demonstrated that in the West, the concept of happiness has hardly improved despite increased income. Happiness remains unchanged when other people enjoy similar income rises. In those countries, the Happiness Index is paradoxical (income paradox). An income raise for the people there is like a shot of whiskey, the happiness index keeps the same. It feels great for a while but it does not last long, especially when everyone else is being served at the bar.

The research is also reassuring. If society chooses for sustainable development while being fully aware of the extra costs involved, it does not necessarily imply a lesser degree of contentment. Happiness is not only the result of high income. Table 6.1 presents some results of Layard's research.

Table 6.1 Effects on happiness[46]

Contentment factors	Fall in happiness (points)
Family income decreases one-third	2
Divorced (rather than married)	5
Unemployed (rather than employed)	6
Subjective health down 1 point (on a 5-point scale)	6
Quality of government	5
'God is important in my life'. You say 'no' to this rather than 'yes'. (Also followers of a more rational philosophy as Buddhism are happier.)	3.5

The indicators for the happiness studies give insight into people's well-being. Layard's study demonstrated that decreased income has relatively little effect on happiness. A government striving for improved well-being will place more emphasis on job security even if it results in less than desirable income. It has also been shown that a concept of well-being is dependent on a feeling of trust and social capital[47] (see Chapter 4). Government can contribute to happiness by allowing everyone within society to make their own contribution but additional data showed that people are keenly aware about whether fellow citizens are sharing the burden.[48] It is important for people to develop identities which they can be proud of and at the same time enjoy security and the respect of others. A sense of pride can be stimulated and the will to stand out from the rest is a strong drive, but governments who emphasize this do not make people happier. Layard's research summarizes this with the question: 'How can we tame the rat race?'

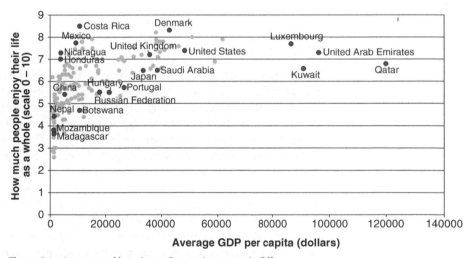

Figure 6.5 Income and happiness: Comparing countries[49, 50]

Results from Figure 6.5 show that a number of countries with a relatively low average income do fairly well on the contentment scale but also that none of the high-income countries have a low happiness score.

Happy Planet Index

The Happiness Index (HPI) has been criticized as a welfare indicator because it has not provided information about the environmental damage caused by individual citizens in their countries. An independent think tank, the New Economics Foundation, developed the 'Happy Planet Index' (HPI).[51] Using the variables 1. Human happiness, 2. Average life expectancy and 3. Ecological footprint (see Chapter 5), the aim of the index is to assign a single number to a country's attempts at providing a good life for its citizens without damaging the environment.

Table 6.2 Happiness Index[52] / Happy Planet Index[53] / GDP per resident[54]

	Happiness Index		Happy Planet Index		GDP per habitant	
	Range 30–100	Ranking	Range 16–76	Ranking	Range (Int $)	Ranking
The Netherlands	95	1	51	4	46,400	2
United States	91	2	31	7	53,000	1
Colombia	87	3	66	1	12,800	5
Indonesia	87	4	59	2	9,600	7
China	73	5	57	3	11,900	6
Iran	63	6	42	5	16,200	4
Uganda	63	7	30	8	1,700	8
Russia	41	8	35	6	24,300	3

Explanation: Colombia, Indonesia and China score fairly high on the Happy Planet Index (HPI) because they have a greater eco-efficiency than industrialized lands, especially when examining their ecological footprint. Columbia scores high because there is a relatively high happiness score and at the same time the ecological footprint and income level are acceptable. Low average life expectancy in Uganda has kept its HPI score very low. Life expectancy is highlighted for the HPI because the focus is on a long, happy life with minimal damage to the environment.

6.1.3 Technology

The Enlightenment of the seventeenth century changed culture and placed the 'idea of progress' at the centre of human thought.[55] Problems could be solved through the contributions of entrepreneurship and scientific research. With the age of progressive thinking, new fields of exploration came into being and the steam engine, electricity and combustion engine became parts of everyday life. The productivity increase and the new technology of the time helped to improve health and diminish hunger, thirst and cold. Besides this, technology has its own dynamic and is a power in itself which rapidly spreads. This is certainly true when technological innovation is seen to benefit groups of people in society.[56] Even in cases where initial results are problematic, the march of technology remains largely unstoppable.

The following paragraphs will look at the spread of technology as related to society and also those aspects of technology that have caused problems.

Spread of technology

Hans Jonas, ethics and technology philosopher, suggests that the spread of technology is unstoppable, even that which has problematic consequences. He calls it the compulsion for application.[57] An example of a problematic technological spread is the chemical composition of chlorofluorocarbons (CFCs). These substances were used widely in the 1980s as a cooling chemical for refrigerators and as a propellant for aerosol sprays. They entered the atmosphere and penetrated the ozone layer resulting in more ultra-violet

(UV) light reaching the earth's atmosphere, especially in Australia. It soon became clear that the increased UV rays were a major contributor to increased cases of skin cancer and the Australian government started an information campaign to inform its citizens how to best protect themselves.[58] The increased UV rays caused international concern and led to the signing of the Montreal Protocol in 1987. Sponsored by the UN, almost all of the world's countries agreed to sharply reduce CFC emissions. Former UN Secretary-General Kofi Annan saw the agreement as an example of how countries can work together in emergency situations.[59] It should be mentioned that alternatives to CFC were easy to find and today's refrigerators and sprays incorporate gases and propellants that have a far less severe effect.

The degree of technology spread determines the harmfulness

The degree of distribution is relevant when looking at problems, for example antibiotics. Many people owe their lives to these medicines and commerce has ensured that they are available at relatively affordable prices. Nonetheless these drugs have created an undesirable market dynamic. Their low price has meant antibiotics have been used in huge quantities for the cattle industry and have been even been directly added to enhance cattle feed. Adding antibiotics to animal feed has produced cheaper meat prices.[60] Such a policy would have had greater effect with a long-term view regulating the disbursement.

Future technology

A green economy needs clean technology and innovation in the supply chain.[61] It is important that worldwide measures are in place that give both business and government a role in this process.[62] Green economy has a strong focus on the creation of stable, balanced cycles that interact with other systems. Ensuring the *vitality* and *sources of raw materials* comes immediately to mind but the *damaging effects of waste products* is another important criteria. Some materials in (technical) waste products can be recycled for reuse and other (biological) types of waste can serve as nourishment for a natural system which keeps the ecosystem involved in balance. Cradle to Cradle products can play a particularly important contribution. For example, diapers are harmful to the environment in the waste phase, because they are not biodegradable. The Cradle to Cradle certified gDiaper is a disposable diaper, and its inserts are compostable and flushable.[63] A final thought on the role of technology concerns the *possibility of a calamity*. To determine the level of danger, an inventory of the risks involved must be made, and to do this, the serious consequences of the calamity must be ascertained plus the odds of the calamity actually occurring.

6.2 Environment and the market economy

The free market has had a positive effect on technology and welfare but has run parallel with increased environmental burdens.[64, 65] This has resulted in a greater desire for control from governing bodies in order to have tighter regulation on what and how much is produced. This does not imply that governments want to become 'back seat drivers' in the free market and have their say in supply and demand, but it has put the steering mechanism of the market on the defensive. The market will retain its importance as a regulatory mechanism, but for the transition to a sustainable economy it is important that government maintains an active role.[66]

6.2.1   Tragedy of the commons

The idea that the free market cannot be totally free has been highlighted in the story of the 'tragedy of the commons'.[67] This classic tale employs game theory. The main premise is that rational human behaviour depends on choice. The theory makes clear that long-term prosperity is lower when individuals decide on production levels for communal land or 'commons'. The tragedy of the commons describes how complete individual freedom for communal use of goods (products) leads to overexploitation. This excess is caused by the individual's quest for maximum profit while the costs involved to achieve this are shared by all others (individual profit maximization).

Box 6.2   The tragedy of the commons [68]

On a commonly shared pasture, cows belonging to several farmers graze peace-fully. Each farmer is hoping for maximum milk *quantity* from his herd and every farmer benefits by having their animals eat as much as possible even though this can have negative effects for the other farmers. An individual farmer can earn more by having an extra cow in the herd and the costs of overgrazing (less milk per cow) will be shared by all. Choosing the sensible, obvious economic option will lead to a serious form of overgrazing and limit maximum milk production. The moral of the story is that principles of the free market do not always apply and not all questions of division and sharing can be solved with one standard maxim. In such a scenario, government intervention is necessary.

The story of the tragedy of the commons, outlined in Box 6.2, easily translates to environmental issues. Nature, the seas and clean air are all common property. When no preservation controls are in place for individuals, business or countries, over-exploitation will surely be a consequence despite the fact that the market economy encourages individual businesses to produce as much as possible.

A good example would be CO_2 emissions and the resulting climate change. During the past centuries, citizens, business and government have paid hardly any compensation for the harmful effects caused by CO_2 gases.[69] To avoid a 'tragedy of the commons' situation, participants should pay for the use of communal goods. We can also steer behaviour of market participants by legislation or by making international treaties. The Kyoto Protocol (see Box 6.3) is a good example of latter.

Box 6.3   The climate treaty

UN members gathered in Rio de Janeiro in 1992 to look for a solution for CO_2 emissions. They hoped to avoid a 'tragedy of the commons' situation. The end result was the first international climate treaty known as the UNFCCC (United Nations Framework Convention on Climate Change) and it was signed and ratified by almost every country.[70]

The goal was to reduce predicted emission levels for the year 2000 back to the levels of 1990. Industrialized lands had a huge problem because their ecological footprint, due to higher CO_2 emissions, was larger. For emerging and developing countries the treaty had less urgent consequences. They felt that a smaller ecological

(Continued)

footprint was not realistic for them because the low GDP per habitant meant less damage caused to the environment. The Rio treaty was seen as too global and five years later a new one was produced with stricter guidelines. This treaty pinpointed targets for 2012 and was called the Kyoto Protocol. It offered more clarity for the percentage-wise reduction of greenhouse gases for different industrialized countries.[71] Germany, for example, is committed to a 28% reduction while Holland is reducing its footprint by 6% maximum. Although the Kyoto Protocol led to CO_2 legislation in many countries, it has not been a uniform success. Thus, for example, the US has never ratified the agreement and other countries failed to implement the decisions taken. In 2007, for example, a booming Spanish economy produced 53% higher emissions and the 2012 expectations were not very realistic. A new climate summit took place in Copenhagen in 2009. New agreements were made but not all the participating countries adopted the accord. The US, China and other large developing countries also approved the result but the contract is not legally binding and those countries who ignore the decisions will not incur any sanctions.[72]

6.2.2 Incomplete efficiency of the free market

If the market is to function as a problem solver for the division of shortages, it must be a total system and one that performs well. For the market economy, this is not the case. Many products are not fairly priced due to a multitude of reasons.[73] We will now take a look at some of the causes of unfair pricing. We will also clearly show why the market economy, with its flaws, does not work perfectly and why it cannot be considered a total system.

Let's look at three causes that offer a partial explanation of market inefficiency:

1. Common goods
2. Future shortages of goods
3. Goods with undesirable (damaging) effects.

Common goods[74]

Freely obtainable goods such as air and water and more unique items such as mined materials, coral reefs and rare animal species are often freely accessible but can also belong to an organization, a government, a business or private owners. These items are often poorly priced, with their 'uniqueness' not being appreciated. These goods often demand an under-market price because the 'random' owner is the only one with exclusive rights. Seen in this context, the market economy fails. A more effective solution would be to assign pricing of these goods to science which would then be able to determine the true higher price based on scarcity and singularity. This would force the market participants to implement better exploitation of the product. For mined materials, nature reserves etc. we see that the actual owners tend to calculate their price based on extraction costs only which leads to overexploitation because the price is lower than socially desired.

Future shortages of goods

Determining the price for products coming to the market rarely includes considerations for future shortages. This happens frequently in the mining industry especially for precious metals.[75] Its decision to increase or decrease production is dependent on short- and medium-term price expectations. In practice, available mined materials with low extraction costs are quickly put to use. Future shortages, especially after a 50-year period, have no role in the decision making.

Goods with undesired effects

The price of an item cannot be properly determined if stakeholders are not aware of potentially damaging side effects. Think only of the many people who purchased asbestos and paid premium prices while being totally unaware of its hazardous health effects. When society implements manufacturer-directed responsibility laws, more safe and approved goods with fair prices become available because the market will not tolerate faulty or health-damaging products. The same is true for goods that are damaging to the environment.

Externalities[76]

Externalities refers to underpriced goods or services, because the effect of production or consumption of goods and services imposes costs or benefits on others which are not reflected in the prices. Communities would never allow degeneration of a major coral reef (for example, the Great Barrier Reef, Australia), knowing full well the costs involved to generate a new one even though the 'know-how' is there. Decibel damage resulting from extreme noise caused during building projects is also a cost that can be passed on to the client. The extra money received by the contractor can theoretically be used to compensate neighbours who have suffered unbearable noise aggravation during construction. For this same reason, entrepreneurs do not calculate costs and ask low prices because they do not have to compensate all of the stakeholders. Third parties are a part of society who never demand payment. With unfair pricing evident in the market economy, it is up to the government to play a regulating role of putting a price tag on 'external costs'.

6.2.3 Government tools for market regulation

A smoothly running market economy relies on morality and on the way institutions function. The following section will cover institutions and the regulatory tools that government has at its disposal.[77, 78] These tools are here explained in brief:

1. **Ownership:** To limit access to common goods, such as a nature reserve, by assigning ownership rights to a foundation charged with maintenance and preservation.
2. **Financial incentives:** Just as in the market economy, the government uses financial incentives. In an attempt to influence supply and demand, the government can, for example, decide to count external costs by taxes and duties. Such a measure is considered a correction of the dysfunctional market economy.
3. **Market transparency:** By providing information about positive and negative characteristics of goods and services, the government can influence buying behaviour which helps to ensure that market participants take pragmatic and responsible decisions relating to supply and demand.
4. **Commandments and prohibitions:** Laws and regulations can define, for example, acceptable emission standards and they can allow or disapprove use of certain substances. They can also limit business freedom and exclude goods from the market.

The following paragraphs will look at different cases which aimed to regulate the free market. One or more of the previous four starting points are applied in these cases.

Ownership

With nature becoming a vulnerable commodity it is more important than ever that property rights for natural resources are in the hands of dedicated and competent governments and private organizations. There is an immediate pressure placed on developing countries when the need arises for more agricultural land or room for urban expansion. The rainforest and nature reserves are considered common land but who actually controls them is a diffuse subject. The original habitants of Brazil, for example, who have for centuries lived in and exploited these areas are in a head-to-head conflict with government with both groups claiming property rights.[79] When business has plans to develop pristine, unblemished land for construction, the battle for property rights begins. The government is often the winner in these disputes and quickly grants building permits to the developers. The government collects needed income for its coffers while ensuring economic growth, making it hard to put a halt to the deforestation of the Amazon. Property rights granted to Brazilian entrepreneurs have opened up the Amazon jungle to free exploitation which, in retrospect, is comparable to a similar policy carried out for the deforestation of Europe between the fifteenth and nineteenth centuries.[80]

Now that old-growth forest is becoming scarce in the twenty-first century, a worldwide consensus seems to agree that deforestation of the Amazon jungle is not a good thing. Some are also calling to limit Brazil from being the sole arbitrator in deforestation decisions. The Amazon can be seen as community property and belongs to the world. If this is carried further, it means that the world at large has the responsibility to regulate ownership. This can be effectively realized by the purchase and management of wooded areas by independent organizations who are dedicated to preserving these areas. Sufficient funding is often the key factor to their success.

Standards

To facilitate the greening of the economy, government develops product standards, either independently or working with others. These measures can be quickly passed into law, but sometimes waiting a while before putting the law into effect can be a smart move. The advantage of passing laws that are due to take effect at a later date gives companies more time to prepare for the impending changes as well as raising the standard. An example would be the way in which the auto industry is informed well beforehand about new guidelines for CO_2 emissions in the European Union that are due to be implemented at a later date.[81] The result is that companies during the phase of product development are more aware of legal product demands that will come into force in the future. To give a business more possibilities to adjust to a new situation, they are often granted several extra years to comply with the stringent norms.

Greening of the tax system

Many countries incorporate a tax system which is designed to generate income for the government. Some tax rules are designed to guide behaviour patterns of business and the private sector. The best known example is the duty put on cigarettes in an attempt to encourage people to quit smoking. Gasoline tax is also a method used by government to influence business and individuals. Many countries impose excise duties on diesel and petrol hoping to persuade car owners to choose a more economical vehicle.[82] This tax has a direct relation with externalities. Many other forms of taxation have no relation to costs for society. Personal income tax is a good example and is based on the ability to pay principle to the public treasury. No consideration is given to whether the taxpayer is putting an extra burden on society, and government is not trying to change behaviour.

If we note that one of government's goals is the creation of employment opportunities, then the idea of income tax seems irrational because labour would become more expensive. In some countries we see that the environmental movement is pleading for a revised tax system in order to create new jobs and have a more long-lasting effect on society.[83]

Scientific research has also shown that this could have a positive effect. 74% of the studies (Ekins et al., 2011)[84] claimed that a CO_2 emissions tax coupled with a simultaneous reduction in employers' social security contributions would be reflected in increased work opportunities. GDP prospects are also encouraging, with 54% of the studies pointing to a slightly higher percentage using an environmentally based strategy as compared to the present system.[85]

Binding of international measurements

Economic sustainability depends to a large extent on binding measures which apply at international levels. For efficient control of worldwide common goods, it is important that the general rules apply to everyone. The general validity of these rules offers a solution to the 'tragedy of the commons'. The importance of international treaties becomes paramount because desired environmental measures are not always easily realized. A clear example are the duties for aircraft fuel (kerosene). A country would not independently, on its own with no regard for others, put a tax on kerosene. This would lead to unfair competition between countries by making it attractive to refuel in places where no taxes are levied. Discussions about excise duties are starting to appear on the agenda of more international organizations including the European Parliament.[86] They admit that a common European excise tax should be implemented. The chance of this happening is increasing because the European Commission has produced a strategic White Paper with aims of making aircraft fuel emissions greener, but there are opponents who claim that a worldwide approach is the only viable one for solving the problem.[87] The European strategic White Paper should only be seen as a first step. Only when the US, China and other regional partnerships take similar initiatives will there be a possibility of introducing a kerosene tax for most parts of the world.

Artificial markets for externalities

An ideal market gives the possibility of the tennis match of supply and demand without government or third party interference. The price is established and reflects the scarcity of goods and services. The market is in essence the medium which allows efficient and effective allocation of resources but, as we have said earlier, there are many 'allocation' issues where government is required to lend a helping hand due to market imperfections.[88] For the more complex issues concerning resource allocation, the market is often unable to cope and government or other agencies must be able to offer supportive measures. Using the power of the law among other options, an effort is made to bring the allocation of sources to higher level. A good example of this would be Western governments that require companies to invest in cleaner production methods. These types of measures lead to better allocation of resources, because externalities are taken into account. However, they still exclude the optimization of scarce resources. When Western business invests in cleaner production techniques, a fair amount of resources are used up because the current advanced clean technology must be replaced by an even more advanced technology. The money could have better been spent in countries that are still working with outdated polluting technology. In cases like this the market can be an effective collaborator. Allowing trade in liabilities creates a new artificial market that gives possibilities for a better allocation of resources. Restrictive regulation to limit emissions in combination with an artificial market gives an improvement in the allocation of resources. An artificial market can be a good tool for situations that are described as the 'missing market'. This situation exists due to market imperfections, transaction costs or if government measures are enacted that influence allocation of resources.[89, 90]

Box 6.4   The carbon market

The idea of artificial markets has, in the meantime, been implemented. The CO_2 question has market of its own. This refers more to CO_2 emission trading (carbon market) and is a tool used by different countries that signed the Kyoto treaty to exchange CO_2 rights (carbon credits). Because the ecological footprint is strongest in Western countries, industry here must bear the liability for major reductions of CO_2 emissions. This involves significant investments, because it requires working with more advanced installations and producing relatively lower emissions per product unit. On the international carbon market, industry can buy emissions rights. The money paid for the emission rights is transferred to industry in non-Western countries with the return being that these countries must adhere to stricter emissions standards. It has meant that Russia, for example, with relatively little investment in emission reductions, has been able to replace old, outdated and polluting machinery and installations with more environmentally friendly alternatives. The emission trade has also made it easier for countries to fulfil the worldwide agreements for reduction of CO_2 gases.[91]

The creation of nonzero sum

Sustainability issues are largely related to the question of shortages and it appears at first glance to be a typical 'zero sum' problem (see Section 4.1.11). To avoid zero-sum situations it is important that stakeholders or countries cooperate.[92] Increasing prosperity and new systems are dependent on the creation of partnerships. Sometimes the government can play a role here. For instance the European Union could set up an information system for the transport sector, in order that transport companies gain insight into the goods being transported throughout Europe. Trucks can then be deployed more efficiently and this would result in less CO_2 emission. But there are many other points on the compass. New systems often profit from a 'borderless' approach. Realizing prosperity using environmental pre-conditions is definitely a challenge because it is actually a search for new synergy and addresses complex questions designed to convert 'zero sum' situations to 'nonzero sum' ones.

Box 6.5   The super grid

If the EU wants to achieve its goal of a 20% increase in renewable energy use by the year 2020, it can best focus on electricity. Long-term power consumption for the transport sector is more expensive because today's cars use advanced technology including electric and hybrid vehicles which demand a high quality built-in battery.[93]

(Continued)

A number of researchers are proposing that Europe would be best served in its long-term goals by implementing a new electricity network or super grid.[94] New improvements in cable technology have made it conceivable to produce 'equal power' between European and North African countries. An equal power network is desirable because less energy is wasted. The super grid has the possibility of exchanging power on a large scale. It would be possible to make an effective, smart use of power generated by Scottish wind farms, Norwegian water and sun energy from southern Europe and North Africa.

If electricity can be exchanged, countries can make use of each other's overcapacity. The system is viable because the production of wind and solar power fluctuates due to weather conditions. If more countries participate, the chances increase that some will have more power available than they actually need due to favourable weather conditions. This overproduction can be supplied to those countries with less optimal weather. If a large number of countries participate, the 'law of large numbers' comes into effect. This law makes it possible to make a statement about an 'average' as long as this average is based on a series of a large number of arbitrary incidents. The law refers to a phenomenon encountered in the world of statistics. For example, the daily amount of hours that the sun shines tends to approach a permanent value if the method of determining this is based on a large number of participants. If we take a large area like Europe, the areas where the sun does and does not shine are in fact separate events. Applying the law of large numbers, we can surmise that on a given day, the average number of hours with sun will deviate slightly from the yearly average because there is a low probability that Europe is completely cloudy or sunny.

If Europe invests in the super grid, countries will not have to invest in expensive overcapacity or storage methods. A new structure for equal power would involve a cost price of €46.50 per megawatt hour which is close to present levels.[95] Finally, a super grid network will stimulate many to invest further in sustainable energy because the excess power offers opportunities for export.

6.3   Environment as a government problem

Many different instruments can be used to create long-term sustainable prosperity and government can assist with a large range of possibilities concerning creating laws and giving financial stimulus in the right direction. Nonetheless the transition to a sustainable society remains a formidable challenge. Many governments struggle to implement good, rational legislation designed to be in place for 30–50 years.[96] A good example of this is European energy policy. Europe would be better served if it was less dependent on gas supplies from Russia and oil from the Middle East. With an ambitious energy policy, Europe could become less dependent on conventional fuel sources while at the same time increasing sustainability and creating jobs. We can ask ourselves why, in a modern society, professionals are incapable of making long-lasting welfare decisions. To put it more succinctly, why does a country choose one marshmallow for immediate consumption and not for legislation that will deliver two marshmallows for the future? It seems that governments also wrestle with the trade-off between instant and future welfare just as in the Marshmallow Experiment described in Chapter 4.

The question then becomes, how does government enact legislation for long-term prosperity? Part of the answer is that governments must employ independent institutions which are given enough leeway.[97] Good policy is effective if it is not too dependent on power changes within government. This has consequences for the set-up of the state in relation to its various branches and the different advisory bodies that government has to work with. Responsible legislation develops when proven knowledge in different policy areas has enough space to deal with meanings and opinions, with management being delegated to those who are most capable.[98] It is important that this power is assigned to individuals and organizations on the basis of knowledge, insight, track record and achievements.[99] Section 6.3 will examine the tools and assumptions that come into play for countries trying to create rational policy decisions with a view to long-term welfare. The challenge is the constitution of a green state, which actively invests in green sectors and enacts stringent regulation in non-green sectors. East Asian economies, notably South Korea, are pioneers in this aspect.[100]

6.3.1   Governance of well-being in the long term

Library shelves are bursting with books offering advice on how to set up a modern state and which form of government is best. Chapter 3 pointed out that parliamentary democracy and the decision making and policy that accompanies it is more often inclined to provide short-term solutions. In this section we will discuss several concepts with strong ties to rational and responsible decision making. These include meritocracy, technocracy and 'buttresses of society'.

Meritocracy

The concept of meritocracy implies that people are appointed to positions on the basis of their track record. It simply means that those involved with policy making are experienced professionals. Societies who are capable of applying these principles often meet with success. The principles of meritocracy can be applied to different subjects. Let's take Brazilian football as an example. Brazil's reputation as a football super power owes much to its national recruitment system.[101] Talented players from the slums get the opportunity to train to become professional players. In the West the realization of meritocracy within society began centuries ago. The market economy and professionalized education led to substantial improvements. In the nineteenth and twentieth centuries, in this area it was far ahead of Asia which was content with an antiquated system of hierarchy to maintain regulation. Although this hierarchical order had been in place for centuries, it was not truly able to provide for increased prosperity. As compared to the market economy where competition is institutionalized, the old hierarchy has little dynamic.[102]

With society now on the lookout for ways to increase sustainability, it has become evident that within the market economy meritocracy is not too bad, because companies have to perform well to survive. Nevertheless there is no steering for sustainable economic development. This is true for democracies as well. Politicians have a substantial part of the power and this system does not enhance meritocratic decision making. Meritocracy is often mentioned in the same breath as democracy but the relationship between the two is diffuse. Parliamentary democracy reflects the people's choice and the meaning of parliamentarians is not always based on solid research.[103]

Box 6.6   Hesitant fox makes better predictions[104]

The exact sciences are capable of making accurate predictions within feasible limits. We know for certain that the next total solar eclipse of the sun will occur on 7 October 2135.[105] Other predictions are more complex. No meteorologist would bet on the chance of heavy precipitation eight weeks hence. The atmosphere is too complex and many factors work with and against each other, making accuracy difficult to establish. Beta-scientists face the challenge through experimenting and developing models to see how different factors affect each other. This approach is popular in the field of social sciences and allows researchers to get a good grip on the reality of a situation. UCLA Anderson Forecast, for example, makes independent economic prognoses for the US which are considered scientifically sound. It does admit that long-term predictions have a tendency to be less accurate.

Research into the subject of predictability by economic and political experts, performed by Philip Tetlock, professor of Psychology at Berkeley, have been enlightening. Tetlock tested if experts make better predictions than average citizens or the unassuming computer, relying on data input.[106] The average scientist has no special advantage if asked to predict the future exchange rate of the euro. The same is true for predictions relating to political change. Trying to guess if the course of democracy in China will develop positively or negatively is typical and a question which has elicited many different published responses from the scientific community. It has been shown that for this type of question, an educated layman is just as capable of making a good prediction as the expert, although a hopeful footnote does apply.

Some experts were systematically better than others and Tetlock claims this is due to individual personalities. He divides the experts into three groups: the hesitant fox, the stubborn hedgehog and something in between. The hedgehog has strong opinions and is ideology orientated. The fox is completely opposite. This group takes bits and pieces of ideologies that they like. They have no qualms about changing their opinion and are not afraid to admit lack of knowledge in certain areas. The study proved that doubting foxes do better than stubborn hedgehogs in making predictions.

Society is thus well served by offering the doubting fox sufficient chances. Hesitant technocrats deserve a place next to strongly orientated ideological politicians. Government keeps this balanced by making room for these organizations to counter decisions influenced by headstrong ideology.

In most democracies there are solutions to increase the force of meritocracy. Many countries opt for a parliamentary democracy with a dual legislature consisting of a lower chamber (House of Representatives) and an upper chamber (Senate). After a new law is passed in the lower chamber it is sent on to the higher body for final approval. Its function is to re-examine proposed legislation from the House of Representatives, whose members are chosen by the general public.[107] Despite these precautions, many democratic systems still struggle with rational long-term decision making. Public discussion is often pointed directly at the quality of government legislation but this does not suggest that democracy should be discarded. The fact that power can be corruptive makes strong counter offensives imperative. The people's rebuttal is often voiced through the free press and elections held at regular intervals which can herald a change.

Technocracy

Technocracy is a form of government whereby policy is largely dependent on scientific and technical knowledge. Scientists, engineers, sociologists, economists and experienced professionals replace the politicians.[108] It is spearheaded by rational, effective planning and implementation of specific projects. It is result orientated and democratic decision making is seen as a hindrance. Technocratic governments create policy on the assumption that political ideology is destabilizing and their representatives are often experienced professionals without any ideological affiliations. Rest assured there are many critics. One of them was British author George Orwell. In his novel *Coming Up for Air* he stated that technocracy is a forerunner to totalitarianism.[109] It becomes an alienating process because the citizens don't have a voice and they become a small wheel in the system.

Buttresses of society

The struggle that continuously plagues parliamentary democracies in their attempt at effective long-term decision making emanates from the time when the voice of the people was allowed into the political process. It has become clear that although parliamentary democracy may not receive top marks for general performance, it remains a reasonably good system. The fact that the people can vote to change government has had a generally positive effect.[110] In addition the GDP of parliamentary democracies is on average higher than other regimes.

During the course of their existence, parliamentary democracies have taken measures to compensate inherent weaknesses in the political system. Modern, democratic societies have basic laws in place that cannot be changed without a two-thirds majority. These laws are often to be found in a country's constitution and guarantee among other things freedom of speech, privacy and fair treatment. Institutions have also been created to keep a check on government if mistakes are made or if they or not working effectively. For society to realize healthy development, government must be able to deal with (opposing) institutionalized countervailing power which can also be described as buttresses of society. In other words: to achieve a society based on culture and trust, distrust must be institutionalized. You can call it the dilemma of institutionalized distrust.[111]

A modern society is just as fragile as old cathedrals from the past and, like them, would collapse if supporting buttresses were not in place to keep it upright. Society can make use of several support (buttress) options. The independence of scientists is a buttress option with these elite members of society operating without government interference. Their eternal quest is for truth. Science as an institution is a system which initiates research under the watchful eye of other scientists. They are geared up for criticism and do not publish research findings until their research methods are proven acceptable. Other supports for society are the free media, non-governmental organizations (NGOs) and organized religion.

The idea of countervailing institutions is embedded in civil society. The elite are confronted with opposing truths and a legitimation of power, in political as well as economical spheres, remains a strong discussion point.[112] When developments in the market economy result in increased inequality, a point is reached when adjustments have to be made. It is not without reason that discussions are growing about retuning the economic system, which is the cause of the increasing inequality in the US.[113] Unfair and insufficient division of economic resources in society serves to create tension. Pluralism and democracy cannot exist if too much power is in the hands of one segment, including business. Pluralism, human rights, democracy and institutionalized opposition are all chips off the same block. With improved worldwide welfare and increasing pressure on the environment, a new form of institutionalized countervailing power is becoming necessary. In a pluralistic open society these initiatives sometimes start from the bottom up with Greenpeace and the World Wide Fund for Nature being good examples. They mobilize the public for protest and this often serves as the catalyst which moves government to place the problems on the agenda to see if the laws and their enforcement need to be improved. In addition to these independent organizations, there is a need for public bodies that have a more formalized method of buttressed support.

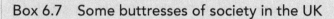

Box 6.7   Some buttresses of society in the UK

In the UK, organizations such as the Bank of England, the Statistics Authority and the Office for Budget Responsibility (OBR) come immediately to mind. These bodies have their own responsibilities relating to the institutionalizing of meritocracy. They do research into many different policy areas and inform government about the effects that can be expected from different sorts of legislation.

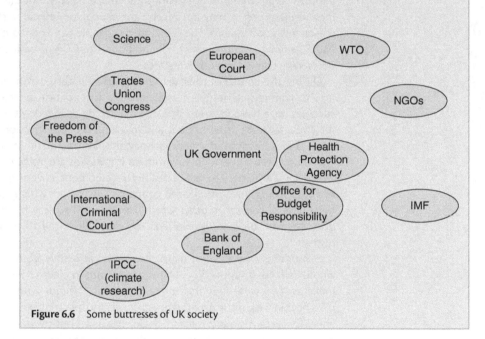

Figure 6.6   Some buttresses of UK society

International buttresses

In the last 50 years there has been a marked increase in international buttresses (support). More and more national policy is being developed within the framework of international agreements.[114] The number of countries who have chosen to relinquish part of their power is on the increase and they deal with the international rules set up by such organizations as the World Trade Organization (WTO), the International Monetary Fund (IMF) and the International Court of Justice.

Within the UN, the most important programmes for sustainable development are regulated by the United Nations Development Programme (UNDP) and the United Nations Environment Programme (UNEP). Founded in 1965, the UNDP is the elder of the two and coordinates programmes for developing countries.[115] This is accomplished via training, advice and material support for the war on poverty, HIV/AIDS, human rights and female emancipation. The UNEP was founded seven years later in 1972 to support environmental tasks and was involved from the beginning with the Intergovernmental Panel on Climate Change (IPCC), the study institute that looks at and reports on climate change every five to seven years.

6.3.2   Circular economy

Seven billion people in this world are in pursuit of welfare and a good quality of life and many are dedicated to leaving the planet in better shape than they found it.[116] Many politicians try their best and humanity must decide on the trade-offs between short- and long-term solutions. Is one marshmallow better for a quick fix or are two at a later date a wiser choice? Adam Smith's ideas on the institutionalizing of property rights and free trade led to a significant increase in productivity. New production technologies, globalized supply chains and decreased labour input are the result, but it is now becoming evident that the current set-up of the market economy is not sustainable. Today's system is a linear industrial economy. Within this model natural resources are mined or acquired with little regard for reuse or regeneration of the sources from which they were taken. The linear economy makes use of complex and international supply chains, is material and energy hungry and often does not take external costs into consideration. The universal target of the linear economy is today's consumer and future welfare is off the radar. The citizens of OECD countries consume yearly 120 kilos of packing material and 20 kilos for clothing and shoes, most of which is waste material.[117]

Despite these foreboding facts, little initiative has been taken to switch to what we now call a circular economy. The aim of this system is to create welfare for a future population without depleting the earth's natural resources. A circular economy is by definition an industrial one that in design and purpose ensures regeneration and recycling. Products are designed to be reused, recycled or taken apart for regeneration. In the circular economy roles are reversed: unlimited labour assumes a central role while materials and naturally supplied sources assume a subordinate position.[118]

Developing a circular economy is not easy. A tragedy of the commons element is part of the equation and worldwide cooperation is necessary. There are a lot of variables to consider when trying to balance a quality industrialized economy together with ecological systems. More can be produced locally but international business will also contribute to welfare. Legislation at national levels has limited influence. Many environmental problems can only be solved through international legislation. Institutionalizing of the circular economy depends on public opinion but also on those in charge. Laws must touch on people's feeling of justice when considering welfare for future generations. The esteem accorded to elected political leaders, resulting in public empathy and compassion for and involvement in the vision they have for present and future generations is also a factor. A sense of value must be inherent in any transition. Institutionalizing of the circular economy is about change and established interests will feel threatened.[119] This change does not happen automatically but it is encouraging to see that in society there are always people who identify with the future. This has been proven in the past. An example of this relates to the end of the slavery (see Box 6.8). Britain played an important role here, even though the country itself hadn't a direct interest in the abolition.

Box 6.8 Abolition of slavery

The Quakers, a seventeenth-century religious sect residing in Pennsylvania, were the first Western group to protest against slavery, as far back as 1688. A hundred years later, the cause was taken up by the independent Yorkshire member of British parliament William Wilberforce, who mobilized public opinion and became the major proponent for the abolition of slavery. There was huge public support for his plea and by 1792 the British government had received 519 petitions with 390,000 signatures.[120] This led to the elimination of slave trade in 1807 and in 1834 possession of slaves was forbidden for the entire British Commonwealth.

 6.4   Case Study: Forest management in Uttranchal, India

Case prepared by Ankit Gaur

Hardin's 'tragedy of the commons' began the debate surrounding management of common property resources. His ideas have been widely accepted to explain the degradation and exploitation of commonly held resources such as oceans, rivers, forests, and pastoral land. Two important characteristics make common property unique and difficult to manage. Firstly, its 'excludability' implies that the physical nature of the property is such that controlling and restricting access to the property is usually very expensive, and often impossible. Secondly, the 'subtractability' means that every user can reduce or subtract from the benefit of the resource for the other users.[121]

This case focuses on one such tragedy of the commons witnessed in the Kumaon region, in the northern Indian state of Uttranchal. Almost 70% of the land in Uttranchal is legally classified as 'forests'. Historically, this region has been known for its community forest management systems, including both formal government arrangements and unofficial community management.

Rural households are highly dependent on the forest and common land. They form the main source of livelihood for the people of this region, providing them with fodder and grazing for their livestock, fuel wood and manure for cooking and heating their homes, green manure for their agricultural land, timber, and leaf litter amongst other benefits. In the absence of this common resource, household incomes would fall significantly.[122]

The forests in the Kumaon region form an essential part of agriculture in the area. Also, several village communities purposely set fire to the pine forest floor every spring, in order to increase and improve the grass cover for their livestock. However, over time, extreme grazing by the livestock, felling of trees and out-of-control fires led to degradation of the forests and adversely affected the livelihood of the rural households. After witnessing this tragedy, several village communities decided to control and restrict the grazing of livestock and felling of trees for the greater good of the overall community. This initially caused problems for the village women, who had to travel longer distances to collect firewood; however, results started coming in within one year of the initiative.[123, 124]

One successful example of the efforts of the local community to manage its common forest resource was the village of Suyalgarh that had about 100 hectares of common forest land. Most of this previously healthy and dense forest cover had been degraded due to excessive grazing and lopping by the villagers. Realizing the

(Continued)

extent of the damage caused, the whole village community decided to put under restriction 70 hectares of the common while the remaining 30 hectares was still open for use by the villagers. Once the forest began to improve and yield grass, the grass was equally divided between all the villagers. The surplus grass was auctioned off to neighbouring villages. The cash that was collected from the sale of the surplus grass was saved in a village fund and used to buy communal goods for the entire village. In this case, timely intervention by the village community was successful in protecting their common resource.[125]

However, not all cases of common resource management have been successful within the Kumaon region. Several government institutions as well as not-for-profit organizations have attempted to reduce the degradation and improve the condition of common resources, but barriers in this process are low levels of education, poverty, and a lack of understanding and awareness amongst the local village people.

 Case Study Questions

1. Using the Uttranchal case study, clarify the concepts of excludability and subtractability.
2. Which of the government tools mentioned in Section 6.2.3 is best suited to combat degradation of the forests? Present your arguments.
3. Name concrete measures that can be taken by using the government tool(s) mentioned in the previous question.
4. What are the strong and weak points of the measures that you have suggested in question 3? Present your arguments.

6.5   Learning tools

6.5.1   Summary

- The environmental burden (I) is dependent on the factors of population (P), welfare per individual (W) and technique for environmental burden per welfare unit (T) and can be calculated using the formula $I = P \times W \times T$.
- An ambitious government family planning policy contains an ethical component because the authorities have influence over individual freedom of choice.
- Amartya Sens' 'freedom' concept touches many different areas. The expanded application of the term has meant that the Western understanding of the theory can also be seen from a different viewpoint. Freedom of speech and freedom of choice constitute a partial list. Freedom can also include, for example, the sense of freedom people feel when they have easier access to the job market, communal health care and education.
- The way in which GDP is calculated by adding up salaries, profits, leases and interest gives a false picture of prosperity because not all of the figures that make up the GDP make a contribution to welfare.
- Alternative indicators that give a picture of a country's success in implementing good policy for its citizens are called the Happiness Index and the Happy Planet Index.

(Continued)

- 'Critical green growth' and 'prosperity without growth' perspectives see the financial crisis as the inflection point in growth-orientated market economies. Critical green growth argues that investment in the environment creates economic growth but also emphasizes that polluting activities should be actively phased out.
- The story of the 'tragedy of the commons' makes clear that long-term prosperity is lower when individuals decide production levels for communal land or 'commons'.
- The market economy is not a good regulating mechanism for questions pertaining to scarcity (incorrect price forming) for the following scenarios: goods which are freely obtainable, common goods, future shortages of common goods, goods with undesirable effects.
- Solutions that contribute to a better functioning of a sustainable market economy are property rights, standards, greening of the tax system, binding of international measurements and creation of a market.
- Applying meritocracy to society contributes to the welfare and well-being of its citizens.
- Meritocracy implies that people are appointed to positions on the basis of their track record.
- For society to profit from healthy development, government must be able to deal with (opposing) counterforces which can be described as the buttresses of society.
- In a linear economy resources are removed from the earth for production and consumption without consideration for reuse or active regeneration of the sources from which they were obtained.
- In a circular economy, products are designed for easy reuse, salvage, renovation and recycling, with the understanding that a large portion of the material comes from end-of-life products and the reusability is the basis for economic growth.

6.5.2   Further reading

Heller, M. A. (1998). The tragedy of the anticommons: Property in the transition from Marx to markets. *Harvard Law Review, 111*(3), 621–688.

Jackson, T. (2009). *Prosperity without Growth.* New York, NY: Routledge.

Layard, R. (2005). *Happiness: Lessons from a New Science.* London: Penguin Press.

Vázquez-Brust, D., Smith, A. & Sarkis, J. (2014). Managing the transition to critical green growth: The green growth state. *Futures, 64,* 123–148.

6.5.3   Assignments

 Assignment 6.1: The formula of Ehrlich

a) Determine, on the basis of research you can find on 'Google Scholar', how indexes, contained in part of the 'environmental burden' formula by author Paul R. Ehrlich, will develop in the next 30 years.

b) Do you think that Western countries who are faced with an ageing and sometimes decreasing population should create a revised migration policy which would make it easier for citizens from other continents to settle in these countries for a certain period of time? Present and defend your arguments.

Assignment 6.2: Economic activities and external costs

a) Describe an important economic activity for the country where you study that is coupled with substantial external costs for stakeholders. Research the effects of this economic activity and show how much money is involved.

b) Indicate which instruments the government can use to stimulate sufficient business investment, so that companies involved in an economic activity invest sufficiently to lower external costs for the stakeholders.

c) Indicate if the measures you have suggested form a threat to established interests. Present your arguments.

Assignment 6.3: Happy Planet Index

Provide an economically responsible package of measures the government could use to obtain a higher rating on the Happy Planet Index. Defend your position.

6.5.4 Self-test questions

Self-test Questions

China's population policy
- Describe the main points of China's population policy over the last 40 years.
- On which freedom principle discussed in *Principles of Development as Freedom* (Amartya Sens) did China base its policy? (Present your arguments.)
- Which of the freedom principles have basically been ignored by the Chinese? (Present your arguments.)

GDP
- Give a definition of GDP.
- Can a country's GDP per habitant increase without an improvement in prosperity and well-being? (Present your arguments using examples.)
- Can a government take measures to increase short-term GDP with a view to long-term prosperity even though short-term prosperity results in a decrease or stabilization? (Argue your case using examples.)

External costs
- Elaborate on the expression 'a market economy fails when pursuing sustainable development because "external costs" are not included'.
- Provide and describe a solution to compensate for these failings.

Meritocracy
- Describe the principles of meritocracy.
- Describe the concepts of 'buttresses of society' and 'countervailing power institutions' and discuss the differences and similarities between the two.
- Provide two examples of buttresses of society.
- Indicate a 'buttress' in your country that ensures 'institutionalized meritocracy' in the field of environment. (Clarify your answer.)

(Continued)

Tragedy of the commons

- Describe in detail the 'tragedy of the commons' story.
- Is the tragedy of the commons a support to allow the market to function without necessary government intervention? (Present your arguments.)

Government to regulate the market economy

- Indicate which four categories of government measures exist in order to regulate the market economy.
- How can market transparency contribute to the regulation of the market economy?

7
GLOBALIZATION

Overview and learning objectives

Contact between business and people from different countries has witnessed an explosive growth in the last 50 years. When Marshall McLuhan metaphorically used the term Global Village in 1959, few realized how prophetic his phrase would become.[1] People are communicating in a scale never seen before with trade, investment, multinational corporations, political cooperation, migration, tourism, and cultural and scientific exchanges all playing a strong part. For many, these are indicators of a fundamental transformation happening in the world economy in which national cultures, economies and borders are dissolving. A new term, **globalization**, was coined in the 1960s by American and French writers to explain what was perceived as an incipient new phenomenon. In 1961 the world 'globalize' entered the dictionary.[2] During the 1990s the use of the term took off dramatically, capturing people's imagination. In 1992 alone, 200 books about globalization were published. By the end of the decade globalization had found expression in all major languages in the world and became one of the most talked about concepts of the twentieth century.[3]

Nowadays, the term is the buzzword of our age but is growing dangerously close to becoming a cliché: a fashionable 'big idea' that seems to explain everything from global markets to the Internet to terrorism and the success of JK Rowling books. The word globalization is widely used but its meaning has become confused. The problem is that different people use it in different ways. Many use it wrongly or redundantly to refer to another concept, a case in point being the anti-globalization movement, which is actually against the international political project promoting free markets, more accurately described by the term liberalism (or neo-liberalism). As a consequence, after thousands of books and years of debate, globalization still remains controversial.

Debates around globalization include:

- What is globalization and to what extent do we live in a globalized economy?
- Is what we call globalization a novel condition?
- What are the causes of globalization?
- Can globalization be controlled or it is inevitable?
- Will globalization result in the disappearance of national states?
- What are the impacts of globalization?

This chapter provides an overview of the globalization debate, basic definitions and trends. One of the key issues is the lack of consensus in a definition. Adding to the multiplicity of definitions (each author seems to have their own) many of them are vague or overlap with other concepts. Since we cannot discuss the existence, causes and consequences of globalization without a clear definition, this chapter will start with a review of definitions of globalization and the related concept of globality. This is followed by a review of debates around the novelty of the term and the existence of globalization as a new phenomenon. Finally we will look at the causes of globalization, while its consequences will be discussed in Chapter 8.

Learning objectives

This chapter will enable the student to:

- Understand definitions of globalization and their differences from redundant concepts.
- Identify the key features and theories of globalization.
- Understand the structural forces promoting globalization processes.
- Understand the roles of the International Monetary Fund, World Trade Organization and World Bank.

7.1 Definitions

7.1.1 Globalization, economic globalization and globality

Globalization can best be described as a continuing process of integration between different economies, cultures and societies, participating in a worldwide network driven by business, supranational institutions (i.e. the World Trade Organization) and radically expanded communication and transport capabilities.

This working definition contains the main dimensions of globalization. First, globalization is political, technological and cultural, as well as economic. Second, its outcome is increased integration as opposed to just openness of borders and free flows of capital and goods. Third, it is a historical process, 'the result of human innovation and technological progress, it has been influenced above all by developments in systems of communication, dating back only to the late 1960s' (Dicken, 2014).[4]

In turn, economic globalization refers to the increasing *integration of economies* around the world, through qualitative transformation and increase of cross-border flows of goods and services (trade), capital, knowledge and people.[5]

Trade: Integration of economies through trade is a shallow form of integration, since companies can reduce or halt exports to a foreign country at their will. What is important is not the volume but the composition of international trade. Analysing what countries export and import and who are their trading partners may identify patterns of interdependence.[6] Trade in commodities creates limited interdependence. China imports soy from Argentina, but can easily switch to other producers since soybeans from Argentina do not differ from soybeans from Brazil or India.

Capital movements: Capital flows are official flows of 'aid' or development assistance or private investments such as FDI (foreign direct investment), portfolio investment and bank credit.[7]

Portfolio investment and bank credit are flows of capital that can be stopped at short notice As in the case of trade, these types of capital movements are associated with shallow integration (internationalization). It only takes a phone call for portfolio investments and bonds to be liquidated.

On the other hand, **FDI** is a type of capital movement that represents a deeper degree of integration between the investor and the economy taking the investment. When a country receives FDI (inwards FDI) the investment goes into the acquisition of existing physical goods (land, a factory) or the creation of new physical goods (building a factory). Withdrawing FDI from a country is a much slower process than withdrawing portfolio investment.[8]

Spread of knowledge and technology: The dissemination of knowledge and technology favours deeper forms of integration through convergence on the use of ideas, inventions and standards. FDI and the spread of technology are closely related. Not only does FDI bring expansion of capital stocks in a country, it also brings about technical innovation of production methods, management techniques and economic policies.[9]

Movement of people: Tourism and short business travels are flows of people associated with shallow integration between countries. Deep integration is associated with increases in the quantity, diversity (how many different countries) and length of long-term work assignments (expatriates, diplomatic staff, migrants). Migrants are people that move to other countries for good, mostly to find better employment opportunities but also for political or family reasons. Migrations influence convergence of global wages (see Box 7.1).[10]

Box 7.1 Migrations influence convergence of global wages

Let's analyse the dynamics between countries A and B where A has higher wages than B. A will attract migrant workers from B. This increase in the supply of labour in A will move the supply curve to the left and market equilibrium will lead to cheaper wages. On the other hand, companies from Country A will be attracted to produce in B taking advantage of cheaper labour. As companies move to B, the demand curve for labour moves to the right and market equilibrium will lead to higher wages. At the same time, less demand for labour in Country A will further drive wages down, leading some migrants to return to B, where wages are now better. This cycle continues until wages in both countries are equal.

Nowadays, migration occurs mainly between developing countries but the increasing flow of migrants to advanced economies is likely to provide a means through which global wages converge. International migration has enormous implications for growth and welfare in both origin and destination countries. An important benefit to developing countries is the receipt of remittances or transfers from income earned by overseas emigrants. World Bank data estimates developing countries' remittance receipts at $516 billion in 2015, more than three times the amount recorded by the UN in 2004, when remittances totalled $160 billion –already exceeding development aid from all sources by 60%.[11]

Scholte (2010) conceptualizes globalization as a series of processes leading to globality. In turn, globality is a condition or final state, defined by Scholte as the spread of transplanetary connections with a supraterritorial quality (2010). In other words, globality is an economic order that is not based on the nation state and is not defined by the boundaries of national territories. Scholte identifies many manifestations of globality. Examples include global currencies (such as the US dollar, euro and yen that are used anywhere on earth at the same time), global financial markets (stock markets in New York, London, Tokyo, Beijing and Singapore enable transactions 24/7), global regulation on trade through the World Trade Organization, global products, supply chains, marketing strategies and so on. However, Scholte also argues that globalization does not eliminate territoriality, the dependence on physical places. All manifestations of globality are dependent on territorial spaces and borders.[12]

7.1.2   Competing concepts: Internationalization, liberalization, universalization

Scholte strives for conceptual clarity. In doing so, he emphasizes the need to differentiate globalization from 'redundant concepts' such as liberalization, westernization, universalization and internationalization. He argues that both critics and supporters of globalization tend to use 'redundant definitions' of globalization that fail to capture what is unique about globalization. Redundant definitions cover some other concept. He identifies four trends in the global economy that are wrongly considered the same as globalization: neoliberalism, universalization, westernization and internationalization. Scholte also differentiates globalization (the trend) from globality (the condition).[13]

(Neo)liberalization: This is a process of elimination of state-imposed barriers – such as tariffs, capital controls and visas – to flows of products and resources (capital, labour, knowledge) across national borders. The end result of a neoliberalized world would be an open, borderless economy organized as a single free global market. Neoliberalism aims to reduce the level of intervention of national governments in the economy. Therefore in addition to removal of barriers to flows of resources, it promotes policies such as privatizations and 'hollowing out' of states, reducing state budgets and spending. The expansion of free markets across national borders has been discussed for years without using the term globalization. Defining globalization as neoliberalism makes the concept of globalization redundant.[14]

Universalization: This is a process of dissemination, homogenization and convergence of ideas, practices and standards across national barriers. In a universalized economy the same institutions, products and standards will be used worldwide. We may still have national markets but selling the same products at similar prices is done following similar procedures and standards.

Westernization: This is a particular type of universalization which leads to worldwide convergence of economic activities into the Western model of political economy (rationalism, capitalism, trias politica, individualism).

Internationalization: Internationalization refers to the extension of economic activities across national boundaries. The geographical scope of economic activity is expanded through quantitative changes in patterns of exchanges between countries (more trade, more tourism). There is increased integration of nation state economies into world market relations but such integration is superficial: the principal entities are still national economies. Hirst and Thompson (2002) identify three elements driving internationalization processes: multinationals; reduction of barriers to exchanges of products, knowledge and capital between national markets; and international agreements, endorsed by nation states, regulating such exchanges through local regulation.[15]

Box 7.2   Transnationals and multinationals

Hirst and Thompson differentiate between transnationals and multinationals. Transnationals are associated with globalization. Multinationals are the result of internationalization.

Multinationals are defined by Hirst and Thompson as companies that operate in many countries but are strongly connected with, and dependent on, their country of origin. Hirst and Thompson argue there is little that is global about multinationals. Everything they do in foreign markets is influenced by their country of origin. Multinationals are cross-border extensions of their country of origin. This can be

(Continued)

seen in terms of the nationality of their decision makers in foreign subsidiaries, origin of capital and major markets (i.e. American multinationals tend to have a majority of American managers in key positions in their subsidiaries and most shareholders are American, while the majority of sales and profits tend to come from the US).

Transnationals will be genuinely footloose capital, with international management and without specific national identification, willing to relocate their activities anywhere in the world to obtain the best returns. Hirst and Thompson also discuss differences between global markets and international markets and between global regulation and international regulation of economic activity. In a truly global market, we will have just one aggregated demand curve and one aggregated supply curve defining market equilibrium. Therefore the same product (for example an HTC One mobile phone) will have exactly the same price everywhere in the world. In a situation of truly global governance, we will have one global regulator deciding on taxes, interest rates and regulation, while also empowered to take action to penalize economic offenders regardless of the country where they are based.[16]

Globalization involves both quantitative and qualitative change. Geographical scope of economic activity is expanded while simultaneously there is increasingly deep integration of national economies. For instance, it is not just about more international trade but also about changes in the nature and patterns of trade.[17] In a truly globalized world economy, national economies would be subsumed and rearticulated into the global system by transterritorial processes such as global supply chains. The consequence of a truly global economy for multinational companies is that multinationals would transform into transnational companies.[18]

7.1.3   The globalization debate: Radicals, sceptics and the pragmatic perspective

There are three main positions regarding the existence of globalized economy. The radical view, the sceptic view and the pragmatic or transformationalist view. Radicals such as Ohmae and Giddens argue that empirical evidence, such as increased international trade, openness of markets and international flows of capital are evidence of a globalized, borderless economy.[19, 20] Neither Hirst and Thompson nor Scholte nor Dicken fully agree with this view. Hirst and Thompson represent the sceptics' view. They argue that increased international trade and international flows of capital do not imply the economy is globalized. On the contrary, increased trade and flows of capital can be taken as evidence of an internationalized economy.

Hirst and Thompson's conclusion is that evidence mostly supports internationalization rather than globalization and they further use statistical data to argue that the economy was more open and integrated in Victorian times than today.[21]

Authors such as Jones (1996) use historical perspectives to arrive at a similar conclusion. The world economy has always had cycles of expansion and contraction, each cycle driven by a new type of technological development. The expansion phase is characterized by an increase of openness and transaction across borders; while in the contraction phase, world economies resort to protectionism and limit flows across borders. Therefore, a second argument used by sceptics is that globalization is just a fancy new name for the expansive phase of the world economy.[22] A third argument is that globalization is just a rhetoric tool used to frame the 'free-market' neoliberal project as natural and inevitable. Neoliberals argue that globalization happens because markets regulate themselves to reduce their imperfections.[23]

Dicken and Scholte represent the pragmatic position – they agree that we do not have a globalized economy but they both observe patterns that suggest the economy is moving from internationalization towards globalization. Dicken points out that the world economy is not so much more open now than 100 years ago, but qualitatively different and increasingly interconnected in rather different ways than before. Such qualitative change is not captured in aggregated data of the kind used by sceptics. Qualitative changes include intra-industry and intra-firm trade and dramatic changes in the operation of financial markets. Dicken concludes that we have a globalizing economy where four types of processes co-exist: localizing processes, internationalizing processes, globalizing processes and regionalizing processes.[24] Dicken and Scholte disagree with Hirst and Thompson's view of the economy as increasingly internationalized. They think that although internationalization processes are still strong, on the whole the world is globalizing more and more; however, globalization is geographically uneven with some countries globalizing faster than others. Even in a globalizing world, economic activities are geographically localized. Different regional, country, provincial and local conditions influence global processes, giving territorial embeddedness to the economy (Dicken, 2014).[25]

7.2   Increase of globalization?

The rise of activities beyond national borders owes much to business and trade as well as homo economicus's eternal quest for profit. Human nature encourages us to expand our horizons and remain on the lookout for improvement. Cross-border flows of people, goods and capital in the form of internationalization has always been part of society, and has gone into high gear during several periods in history which can be seen as antecedents of contemporary globalization. Held, McGrew, Goldblatt and Perraton (2009) argue that globalization – defined as global interconnectedness – is a discontinuous historical process with three distinctive periods characterized by great unevenness, shifts and reversals.[26]

Early modern globalization extended from 1500 to circa 1850. The period is known as the 'Rise of the West'. Vasco da Gama's fifteenth-century maritime voyage to India led to an increase in international trade with distant lands. In the nineteenth century, the invention of the telegraph and steamships had similar effects. Increase in the speed of interconnectedness launched modern globalization which was characterized by Western military and political expansion. Things came to an abrupt halt in 1929 with the stock market crash in New York and it took more than 20 years before international economic exchanges peaked again, this time in the shape of contemporary globalization: a new pattern of interdependencies and deeper integration due to the role played by new sociological and technical innovations.

In the views of Held et al., contemporary globalization is characterized by:

1. The unprecedented extensity of global networks (involving almost all countries in the world after the end of the Cold War).
2. The increasing regularity and permanence of global networks, which go beyond occasional cross-border connections.
3. Accelerated velocity of global interactions and diffusion of ideas.

4. Deep enmeshment of the global and the local, with the consequence that 'the impact of distant events is magnified and even the most local development may come to have enormous global consequences' (Held et al., 2009).[27]

What are the drivers of contemporary economic globalization? Although academics still debate the causes of globalization (and indeed, as we saw before, its existence), there is some consensus that economic globalization has been brought about by a combination of interrelated processes creating global interconnectedness, through facilitation of action at distance and integration of economic activities regardless of territorial boundaries.[28] We can broadly classify such processes into a) technological and economic processes leading to an enormous reduction in costs and time needed for transportation and communication and b) political, economic and cultural processes leading to the breaking down of artificial barriers to the flows of trade, capital and to a lesser extent knowledge (still protected by property rights law) and people (still restricted by immigration policies).[29, 30]

Specific developments which have been alleged to speed up the globalization process (acceleration of globalization) are:

1. Acceptance of the market economy.
2. Removal of restrictions to international trade and capital transfers.
3. Innovations in logistics, transport and communications.
4. Increased regional cooperation.
5. International developments in areas of peace and security.

However, the literature proposing these five factors is undermined by its limited or generic understanding of what globalization really means. For instance, authors defending removal of restrictions to trade and capital transfers tend to use the word globalization when they actually talking about neoliberalization (recall the discussion about globalization and competing concepts in 7.1.2). Therefore it is debatable to what extent such developments actually contribute to processes of globalization. It becomes necessary to bring some conceptual clarity in terms of causality between each of these developments and globalization.[31]

7.2.1 Acceptance of the market economy

What is important to emphasize to add clarity to the debates is that neoliberal capitalism is not the only type of capitalism. Hall and Soskice (2001) identify two main models of the capitalist economy: the liberal market economies (e.g. US, UK) and the coordinated market economies (e.g. Germany, Japan). The difference between the two is grounded in one basic dimension: coordination. In liberal market economies the main coordinating mechanism is the market, favouring investment in transferable assets. In coordinated market economies the main coordinating mechanism is 'strategic', non-market coordination (for instance state intervention or agreements between companies) favouring investment in specific assets. In practice, world economies use a mix of both.[32]

From 1944 until the 1980s, the dominant macroeconomic school was Keynesian economics. The Keynesian model is based on selective use of non-market coordination mechanisms when market mechanisms are not working well. Keynes argued that the 1930s world depression was caused by market failure to create enough aggregate demand and adjust the economy quickly to full employment. Therefore non-market mechanisms, specifically, state policies aiming to create aggregated demand, were needed. Such mechanisms included increasing government expenditure, lowering taxes or interest rates, and increasing the amount of money supply with more currency emission (in other words allowing inflation to stimulate consumption). They were meant to be activated only when markets worked badly to prevent economic downturns. Once full employment was restored government intervention was no longer needed and governments could allow markets to return to the driver's seat.[33]

Keynesian economics neither advocates protectionism nor total substitution of market coordination. Indeed Keynes's ideas were closer to the liberal market model than they were to the coordinated market model. Non-market mechanisms are used selectively, only when markets are working badly. However, many countries, particularly in Latin America and Africa, misused Keynesian ideas to justify over-reliance on state spending, protectionism and inefficient state-owned companies. Competitiveness and efficiency suffered while inflation and public debt escalated until their economies collapsed in the 1970s when a drastic increase in oil prices lead to global depression.[34]

By the 1980s, neoliberal ideas replaced Keynesian policies in the US and UK. Neoliberals argued that states' failures were worse than market failures and therefore states should be stripped of means to interfere with markets. This was called market liberalization and consisted primarily of three processes: deregulation (including removal of capital control and trade barriers), privatization of state-owned companies and functions (e.g. health provision), and restrictions in state spending and use of monetary policy (austerity, high interest rates, zero inflation).[35]

The rise of neoliberal capitalism policies in the US and UK cascaded neoliberal reform across the world when capitalism became the world's dominant economic paradigm with the fall of communism in Russia and its allies. More than one-third of the world's population was presented with new economic realities. In Eastern Europe, for example, more than 400 million people embraced economic reforms with a minimum of violence. The trend continued in developing countries such as Mozambique and Vietnam who took measures to improve conditions for business and trade based on free-market principles. A prime example is the liberal reforms introduced in the 1990s by India, the world's largest democracy with a population of almost 900 million. The era of protectionism came to an end and the market as an economic indicator was accepted.[36]

Box 7.3   China's liberalization policy

The largest country to accept economic transformation was China with the government taking the first steps towards a liberalization policy in the late 1970s. However, China did not move into a neoliberal capitalist economy but a hybrid of planned and market economy.[37] The emphasis was on productivity. The Communist Party, which had ruled since 1949, was able to provide sufficient manpower but productivity remained low, largely due to a lack of motivation. To combat this, China took significant measures using a step-by-step approach. Income and rewards became more dependent on productivity, and a pricing system was introduced in the 1980s with the price of certain items being determined by local communes and business. In the agriculture sector, one of China's most crucial areas, families were given more freedom to pursue their own interests. The 'collective farming system' was shifted to the 'household responsibility system'. Business gained more freedom to choose their own markets and more opportunities to attract investment capital.[38] These measures helped to largely eliminate China's food shortages by the end of the 1980s. State businesses also entered the market but the government had to bail them out if they didn't make a profit. In the 1990s further business privatization took place and the government took an important step by setting up special economic zones.[39] Shanghai and other coastal cities received permission to develop products for export.

Despite initial impetus and strong support of institutions such as the International Monetary Fund the neoliberal ideal of a borderless market with minimal state intervention remains utopian. Governments charged with overseeing the transformation process to neoliberal capitalist market economies often had to face difficult decisions which affected their own position. Negotiating for positions of power and dealing with pressure groups were tiresome and not easy. Transformation to the market economy also demands budget discipline in order to attract foreign capital. It can also lead to a reduction in social services with the poor being the most affected when concerned with government provisions for education, health care and food subsidies[40]. In addition, a succession of global crises confirmed the failure of the free market economy to prevent cycles of boom and bust.[41]

A closer examination of evidence reveals mixed openness in the current economy. Trade and capital liberalization have increased but regulation and state controls have not disappeared. Although most direct barriers to imports, such as tariffs, have been removed, more subtle red tape (bureaucratic obstacles) and political controls remain strong. In the wake of deep economic crisis and social unrest, many countries abandoned neoliberal policies reverting to non-market coordination mechanisms such as capital controls. Russia and Argentina experienced a process of rapid neoliberalization that ended up in a hollowing out of their economies leading to major crisis and default on foreign debt in both countries (Russia in 1997, Argentina in 2001). After that both countries settled for a market economy protected by subsidies and with high levels of government interference.[42] In Russia former communist elites controlled privatized companies. Internal farm lobby and state businesses who were not capable of dealing with foreign competition maintained important restrictions to trade and repatriation of profits. In Argentina privatized companies such as Repsol YPF (oil) and Aerolíneas Argentinas (airline) were expropriated and returned to state ownership.[43] In turn, China never abandoned state controls on the type and quantity of capital inflows. Despite pressures from the World Trade Organization strong barriers are still in place for banking and insurance products. In addition, the direction of China's economy is centrally planned and tightly controlled and foreign companies are required to hire local managers for key positions. The largest Chinese companies are all state-owned enterprises and local authorities have strong levels of involvement with economic activity in their territories.[44] Most countries refrained from taking the transformation process too far and those who went further (as did Argentina) were rewarded with a catastrophic financial crisis in the first decade of the twenty-first century. The global recession that started in 2008 halted further expansion of neoliberalization processes and heralded a return of the state to the driver's seat, although clear-cut protectionism is no longer a viable option.[45] Increased cases of dumping were reported after 2008, although less than during the 2001 crisis. In addition, protectionist measures did not escalate. World Trade Organization chairman Pascal Lamy was upbeat when he stated: 'We have had a few slippages here and there, much less than was expected'.[46]

It is debatable to what extent enhanced acceptance of free-market neoliberal policies increases globalization. Reduction of trade and capital barriers and the hollowing out of the state obviously contribute to a more neoliberalized economy, but they are not necessarily driving globalizing processes towards qualitative change and deeper integration. The effects of neoliberal policy in internationalization are mixed. On the one hand, the importance of states as regulatory actors decreases, on the other hand the scope and quantity of cross-border flows is increased.[47] To understand if acceptance of free markets increases globalization we need to look more closely at what types of international trade and capital investment are the main results of free markets.

7.2.2   Removal of restrictions to international trade and capital transfers

In Section 7.2.1 we mentioned that free-market mechanisms favour investment in transferable assets (those that can be exchanged at short notice without loss of value). Investment in transferable assets (such as buying products from another country or transferal of capital to a foreign bank account) is a shallow form of economic integration, which can be easily reverted. Therefore open market mechanisms on their own are more likely to favour increased economic internationalization (the process of simple extension of economic activities across national borders) than globalization (the process of deep integration and interdependence of economies). Removal of trade restrictions increase international trade, but an increase in international trade is not evidence of globalization. Quantitative changes in traditional patterns of international trade are evidence of internationalization (Dicken, 2014).[48]

To decide on whether free trade is also driving globalization in addition to internationalization, we need information about increases in volumes of types of trade associated with deeper levels of economic integration across country borders, such as intra-firm cross-border trade or trade within global production networks. Intra-firm trade refers to trade of products between subsidiaries of a same company located in different countries. Intra-firm trade is based on non-market coordination mechanisms such as the headquarters' strategy. Dicken (2014) argues that intra-firm trade is one of the drivers of globalization. In turn, trade within global production networks is driven by large manufacturers or retailers which set up production networks through arrangements with producers in exporting countries.[49] Whether this type of trade is associated or not with globalization depends on the type of relationships between the principal firms and their subcontractors. It is not associated with globalization when contracting is short term, motivated by the principal's need to save costs, and the principal does not provide components, design specification or technical support. On the other hand, globalization is driven by increases in the volume of long-term contracts creating interdependences between firms. For instance, when contracts are motivated by complementarities or the need for specialist services or when the principal provides materials, components, design, machinery or funds in exchange for exclusivity agreements.

Similarly, removal of capital restrictions increases international flows of capital but increase in cross-border capital flows is not per se an indicator of globalization. Capital flows can be divided into portfolio investment (e.g. bonds, loans) and FDI. FDI implies control over a specific asset which cannot be liquidated at short notice without risking loss in value[50] (for instance, when a multinational company sets up a foreign subsidiary or acquires majority ownership in an existing company). Increase in portfolio investment only means shallow integration of economies and indicates internationalization. On the other hand, increase in FDI is commonly associated with increased globalization. Hirst and Thompson argue that only FDI that is conducted by transnational companies (recall the difference between transnational and multinational) should be considered evidence of globalization.[51] In turn, Dicken looks at what types of FDI are likely to create lasting interdependencies between the subsidiary and headquarters.[52] Lasting interdependencies will be lower in vertical/factor-seeking FDIs that focus on natural resources extraction or use the country as an export platform by exploiting cheap labour advantages. In these cases the company will abandon the country once the resource or cost advantages are exhausted. The performance of the subsidiary does not depend on the host country's welfare (indeed, if the country's economy is doing badly, the subsidiary might even benefit from lower production costs). This type of FDI is a deeper form of internationalization than trade, but not yet globalization. On the other hand, market-seeking FDI results in long-term interdependencies. The economic performance of the subsidiary will depend on volume of sales in the host country's market. As a consequence the subsidiary's survival will be tied to growth of its host country's market. If the host country's economy is doing badly, demand for the subsidiary products will drop. Therefore, horizontal/market-seeking FDI is one of the main drivers of globalization processes.

A final aspect to be analysed is the relationship between FDI and trade. FDI can increase trade if the subsidiary needs to import many raw material or parts and/or if the subsidiary's main purpose is to export to other countries rather than serving the local market. Thus, factor-seeking FDI and exports/imports are complementary. The more factor-seeking FDI, the more exports. China is a case in point, with several quantitative studies finding causal links (Beugelsdijk et al., 2013).[53] Therefore removal of trade barriers has a double effect as a driver of internationalization processes.

On the other hand market-seeking FDI and trade are substitutes. Therefore the less restrictions to trade in a country, the less FDI is attracted. Foreign companies can simply export their products instead of setting a subsidiary to enter the market. Since market-seeking FDI = globalization, this implies that the more the trade barriers the deeper integration and globalization. This may seem counter-intuitive but let's see an example. In the 1970s and 1980s the volume of Japanese cars exported to the US grew steadily until the US government introduced quotas to restrict imports. In order to sustain their share of sales in the American market, Japanese companies set up manufacturing subsidiaries in the US. Market-seeking FDI was driven by the desire to bypass quotas restricting exports.[54]

7.2.3   Innovations in technology

There is widespread consensus that technology is a major driver of the globalization of economic activity. 'Space shrinking' logistics, computer and communication technologies had a major impact on globalization making transport and especially communications easier and less expensive.[55] New innovations in the field of communications has made it possible to develop new concepts that have had a profound effect on society's wealth as a whole. In developing countries this has led to the concept of 'capacity building' which refers to a country's possibility of improving its own welfare and well-being.[56] Cheap communication technology has allowed creation of global system for mobile communication (GSM) networks in Africa. These new services are beneficial to the business community and have a positive effect on transaction costs. These costs are defined as those which are necessary to operate in the market to do the actual transactions. These costs are higher for companies as they have to do with things like a bureaucratic government, corruption and poor infrastructure. In developing countries, these costs tend to be high.

We will now take a look at technology's influence on logistics, communications and capacity building.

Communications technology

The Internet and the mobile telephone have played a significant role in globalization with internet communications skyrocketing in the last decade. Blueprints for important projects can instantly be sent to all corners of the globe while maintaining quality control from home. The technology has also led to major price reductions. Between 1930 and 2010 prices for telephone calls between the US and the UK decreased by 99.9%.[57, 58] For many companies, international phone bills are hardly an issue anymore.

In Africa, cheaper mobile phone rates accounted for a 650% increase in subscribers between 2003 and 2008.[59]

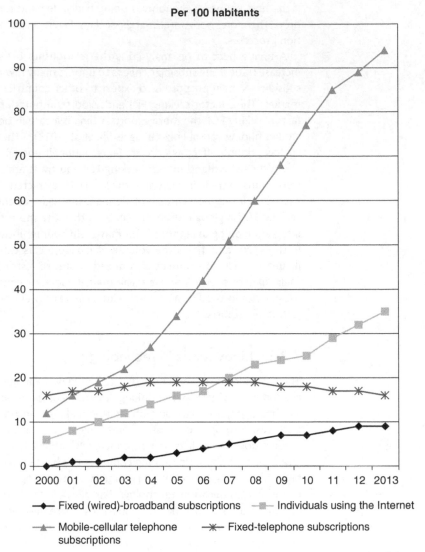

Figure 7.1   Global Information and Communication Technology development, 2000–2013[60, 61]

Outsourcing

Cheaper and better communications has also been responsible for 'outsourcing' of services, with the West setting up IT centres in India as the best-known example but many developing countries have followed suit. A good IT job in India pays $5000 to $9000 per year.[62] Compared with European counterparts, a saving of 85%. Indian software exports rose from $997 million in 1997 to $23.2 billion in 2007. By 2010 the Indian software and related supporting industries accounted for over two billion jobs, with call centres, data storage and financial administration contributing strongly to these numbers.[63]

This success is largely due to the characteristics of the services being offered. Low transaction costs have stimulated international software business with the import tax for Indian-made software in the US and Europe being 0%.[64] There are no transportation fees and many services can be handled online. IT jobs are also labour intensive and ideal for countries on a lower salary scale.

Logistics

In 1966 the first cargo ship from the Sea-Land company docked at Rotterdam harbour with a load of 266 containers. Eight cranes were necessary to offload them onto the quay.[65] Containers were nothing new but this was the first time a ship had been specially built to handle such a huge volume. This, and continued innovation, led to a 60%–70% decrease in international transport shipping costs compared with the 1930s. Air freight has been even more appealing. Corrected for inflation, air transport costs per ton were 90% cheaper in 2004 as compared with 1955.[66]

Cost development in the transport sector

In 2010, it cost €1850 to send a large 40-foot sea container ($67m^3$) from Shanghai to Rotterdam. Goods like textile products can be transported for a very low price: a full container of T-shirts would be about 5 cents apiece in transport costs.

The average air-freight price per ton/km is around 20 eurocents.[67] Using this example, 500 grams of green beans sent from Egypt would cost 30 cents to send while a 300 gram bouquet of roses from Kenya, 3000 kilometres further south, would cost 37 cents.

Technology and capacity building

In developing countries, capacity building was usually administered by the government and NGOs (non-governmental organizations) such as Oxfam, Novib, Doctors without Borders, and UN international aid groups. Today the business community is contributing more to capacity building which has given citizens of developing lands more opportunities to influence their own welfare and well-being. Telcel, for example, has contributed 'capacity services' to the health care industry. In Mozambique, via a mobile app, health workers can now ascertain dosage and types of medicine to be used for patients.[68] This has been a great benefit for rural doctors and nurses in supporting their diagnoses, prescribed medicines and treatment methods.

The possibility of settling financial transactions has also grown. Before the advent of mobile phones, banks in Africa were not terribly popular but the technology of mobile banking gave an acceleration of payments through the banking system. Cooperation between banks and mobile communications companies has led to great improvement with new infrastructure. In 2002 Telcel introduced mobile banking in Zambia under the name Celpay. By 2009 it was working together with six large Zambian banks and accounted for monthly payment transfers of $25 million or 2.4% of Zambia's GNP.[69]

7.2.4 Regional partnerships

The past 20 years have seen increased partnerships between neighbouring countries and not only in the field of trade.[70] One of the first steps towards expanded partnership was the concept of customs union. Countries with common borders maintained the same policy for the import and export of goods outside of the region. Other areas where regional cooperation can provide benefits are:

1. Free traffic for people and services.
2. Monetary policy for establishing a stable exchange rate or common currency.
3. Coordination of national laws in areas of security, labour laws, energy, migration and taxes.

Examples of regional or reciprocal partnerships are the European Union, the African Union, MERCOSUR (common market area in South America including Argentina, Brazil, Uruguay, Paraguay and Bolivia), NAFTA (North American Free Trade Agreement including Canada, Mexico and US) and APEC (Asia Pacific Economic Cooperation, a forum promoting free trade between 21 member countries surrounding the Pacific Rim) with each having agreements to suit their individual needs.

The first step towards partnership is often economic and suggests that regional partnerships will have positive influence on decision making at international levels. Because of this the World Trade Organization has benefited from being able to deal with regional partners searching for a common goal. This is especially evident when similar products are presented to the world market. Instead of fierce competition between individual producers, a unified block approach has made negotiations much more palatable for both parties.[71] This has also been good for larger regional blocks who have been able to present more balanced and convincing arguments after first negotiating with competitors on the opposite side of the fence.

7.2.5   International developments for peace and security

Box 7.4   Territorial conflict

Peace and security for individual countries and their neighbours has had influence on globalization. Between 1996 and 2005 there were fewer reported armed conflicts than at any time in the previous five decennia.[72] Countries are learning the advantages of cooperation and the idea of territorial claims is slowly becoming an outdated concept. Since the Second World War none of the great powers has made any significant territorial demands.[73]

The end of the Cold War

The fall of communism signalled the end of the Cold War. An important milestone in this process was the 1987 INF (Intermediate-Range Nuclear Forces) treaty which was signed by both the US and the former Soviet Union. Central to the agreement was the unilateral decrease in long-range continental missiles and easier decision making for the five permanent members of the UN Security Council (Russia, US, China, France and England).[74]

The CNN effect

After studying conflicts in Rwanda, East Timor, Haiti and Bosnia, researcher Panajoti concluded that the scale of the conflict and human abuses are not necessarily criteria for foreign intervention. Media attention and especially the 'CNN effect' had the most influence. The visual images help countries to decide if limited or strong action is required.[75]

The International Criminal Court and International Court of Justice

In 2002, judicial history was made in The Hague with the establishing of the International Criminal Court (ICC). After years of negotiation there was finally enough worldwide support for a permanent body to prosecute perpetrators of genocide, war crimes and crimes against humanity. ICC is directly involved with peace and security and works with all countries who are allied to it.[76] In 2015 there were 123 countries who accepted the court's jurisdiction with two notable exceptions.[77] Russia and the US have signed the statutes but they have yet to be ratified. The court has an entirely different mandate than the International Court of Justice, also situated in The Hague and founded directly after the Second World War. Countries appeal to this court to resolve disputes with other countries. It often concerns border conflicts, differences of interpretation and disagreements of an environmental nature.

The degree to which these topics have helped to diminish conflicts is a research field that fascinates many scientists and organizations. There is no simple answer but the fact remains that armed conflicts and accompanying mortality rates have decreased significantly in the last 20 years.[78] During 1989 to 2008 the average number of yearly war-related mortalities was 66% lower than for the period 1949 to 1988.[79] Between 1989 and 2008, the yearly average was 130,000 compared to 300,000 in the previous 40 years. Mortality rates in war zones are still declining and it may be cautiously concluded that globalization has played an influential role in lowering the statistics.

7.3   Global economic governance: Supranational public institutions

The function of supranational public institutions is to help set the rules to make globalization work. They provide governance (systems of accountability, distribution of welfare and responsibility) of the global economy. They focus on issues where collective action is desirable or even necessary.[80] Collective action is desirable when markets by themselves do not result in efficient outcomes (market failures, See Chapter 2). Externalities and public goods are typical market failures. When there are externalities (when the action of individuals have effects on others for which they are neither paid nor compensated), the markets typically will result in the overproduction of some goods and the underproduction of some others. In other cases the markets will be unreliable in producing goods that are public in nature (like lighting in the streets). The government has an important role in promoting economic stability by correcting markets' imperfections at the national level. Globalization has meant that there is an increasing recognition of arenas where externalities and impacts can take on global dimensions:

- Global political security: local wars, unless contained, can draw into conflagrations.
- Global financial stability: economic downturn in a country can lead to slowdowns elsewhere, poverty and inequality.
- Global trade: restrictions in one country can affect other countries' economies, global environmental issues and global health issues.

The recognition of these arenas has been paralleled by the creation of global institutions to manage such impacts and assure 'global governance'; these are termed international intergovernmental institutions.[81]

The three main institutions governing economic globalization are the International Monetary Fund (IMF), the World Bank and the World Trade Organization (WTO). These three institutions are known as the Bretton Woods Institutions because they originated during the Second World War as a result of the UN Monetary and Financial Conference at Bretton Woods, New Hampshire (US) in 1944. The conference was a concerted effort to set up global institutions to save the world from future economic depressions. The IMF would address the difficult task of ensuring global economic stability and governing international financial relations while the World Bank would finance the rebuilding of Europe after the Second World War and alleviate poverty in European colonies. A third international economic institution called to govern international trade relations was encouraged by the Bretton Woods agreement, but it was not until 1995 that the WTO was created. Bretton Woods participants saw the Second World War as the result of 1930s global economic crisis. The so-called great depression was capitalism's most severe crisis and led to unprecedented increases in unemployment with up to one in four people unemployed in the US.[82]

British economist John Maynard Keynes explained the crisis as the result of global market coordination failures. He proposed that markets often did not work well. They could result in massive unemployment and might fail to make needed funds available to countries to help them restore their economies. He also argued that lack of aggregate demands explained economic downturns. Keynes prescribed non-market mechanisms, namely the intervention of governments, to stimulate aggregate demand. Two main instruments were proposed: monetary and fiscal policy. When monetary policy was ineffective, governments could apply fiscal policies: cutting taxes or increasing expenditures.[83]

7.3.1 Keynes's 'leaky bucket' model of aggregated demand

Aggregate demand is when expected disposable income determines consumption. The income–expenditure model finds its equilibrium in the way a leaky bucket does (see Figure 7.2): inflow must equal outflow. Economic stability (equilibrium of aggregate demand and aggregate production) is achieved when saving + taxes = investment + government spending. Investment and government spending have multiplier effects on aggregate demand.

A multiplier effect always occurs when there is an injection of capital in the economy. The money spent by somebody becomes someone else's income. Increase in income enables more spending, which creates additional income, and so on.[84] The implication is that government must take an active role in an economy to maintain economic stability.

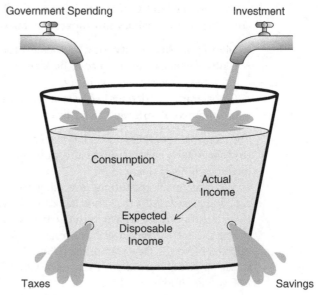

Figure 7.2 Keynes's model

Keynes was a key participant in the Bretton Woods conference and his ideas influenced the IMF's original conception. Keynes's main points were:

- To save capitalism from cycles of growth and depression (boom and bust), it has to be redesigned to account for global interactions and compensate distributive failures. Such a redesign should create institutions promoting international financial cooperation.
- The aim of global financial systems was to take away the threat of economic blackmail from individual nations that resulted in the Second World War.[85]
- International financial cooperation was needed to correct global market imperfections leading to depression, unemployment and war. Therefore a robust financial global financial system ought to be created to:
  - Orchestrate financial cooperation between nation states.
  - Correct market failures to generate aggregated demand.
  - Achieve global financial stability.

7.3.2   International Monetary Fund

The IMF is the central player in the global financial system. The IMF is the central institution of the international monetary system – the system of international payments and exchange rates among national currencies that enables business to take place between countries. The original IMF started in 1944 with 37 members. New states steadily increased membership but this was not an automatic process. In the 1960s and 70s the IMF provided services primarily for countries with market economies and by 1975 there were 125 member states excluding most communist lands who had a different set of rules for dealing with financial crises. This was reflected in a lower level of monetary stability with limited international transactions and capital flow. This changed in the 1980s, and by 1995 178 countries had joined. The increase in membership continued and by 2014 almost all of the world's countries were participants.[86]

The IMF's statutory purposes include promoting the balanced expansion of world trade, the stability of exchange rates, the avoidance of competitive currency devaluations, and the orderly correction of a country's balance of payments problems. Its function is to prevent crises in the system by encouraging countries to adopt sound economic policies; it also provides low-rate loans (lender of last resort) to assist member countries in economic difficulties.[87]

However, it does impose strict conditions on the countries to which it lends money. These may include a requirement that the country's government remove any barriers to free trade, including tariffs and quotas and subsidies to any sector of industry, including farm-support subsidies.

Balance of payment support

A shortage of international currency can occur if a country has weak exports or has to pay back large foreign loans. This is a very undesirable situation and leads to lack of confidence from lenders and the chance of the economy plummeting into a negative spiral. Welfare comes grinding to a halt especially in developing countries where those people with little or no income are hardest hit by the policies of organizations like the IMF who, in an attempt to regulate finances, impose reductions on food subsidies for the general public. International implications, leading to crisis when large bank loans are not repaid on time, become headline news. In such cases the IMF plays a helping hand in extending new credits called bail-outs.[88]

> ## Box 7.5 Thailand
>
> The 1990s were halcyon days for the economy of Thailand. In 1990 more than $10.9 billion in investment capital poured into the country and six years later it had risen to $18.2 billion. Things changed rapidly in 1997 when the market became more critical and foreign investors and banks began demanding their money back.[89] Thailand was essentially bankrupt and it was partially caused by the panic reactions of creditors.
>
> The IMF does not easily offer free money to countries with financial problems and its terms are stringent. This policy has been criticized because governments are expected to get their domestic affairs under control as soon as possible and this causes a decrease in welfare with the poor suffering the most.[90]

Monitoring national governments

Credit facilities for qualifying countries are not the only product in the IMF's portfolio. They also strengthen stability through monitoring and experience. The IMF has assisted many countries in establishing a sound monetary policy by intervening at an early stage in questions of balanced fiscal policy and realistically attainable goals. The IMF's experience is documented in publications which are made available to candidate countries whether requested or not. The early identification of financial imbalance means that steps can be taken to correct the impending problem. International monetary stability is meant to be the result of the preventive and monitoring arm of the IMF.[91]

The last 20 years have seen increased global financial instability despite IMF intervention. Is the IMF no longer able to fulfil its role owing to changes in the world economy? Stiglitz argues that the problem is not that the IMF has not changed. Indeed, the IMF has changed dramatically and such changes have shaped world economies. It was originally created out of the belief that markets behave badly and coordinated intervention was required to put pressure on countries to implement policies expanding aggregated demand (expansionary policy). By 1980 it had morphed into a champion of free-market fundamentalism, providing last resort loans only when a country commits to apply contractionary policies reducing aggregated demand, such as cuts in public expenditure and increases in taxes and interest rates.[92] Chapter 8 will look at the consequences of this ideological shift.

7.3.3 World Bank

The second Bretton Woods Institution is the World Bank. The World Bank has the mission of seeking global poverty reduction and the improvement of living standards. It is made up of two development institutions – the International Bank for Reconstruction and Development (IBRD) and the International Development Association (IDA) – owned by 184 member countries. It also has three affiliates: the Multilateral Investment Guarantee Agency (MIGA), the International Finance Corporation (IFC) and the International Centre for Settlement of Investment Disputes (ICSID).[93]

The IBRD provides low-interest loans to middle income and creditworthy poor countries, while IDA focuses on interest-free credit and grants for the poorest countries in the world. Developing countries are provided funding for education, health, infrastructure, communications and many other purposes.[94]

Poverty trap

Credit facilities from the World Bank are especially attractive to developing countries because of their modest-to-low interest rates. This allows them to avoid borrowing elsewhere and helps them to avoid the 'poverty trap'. These are self-reinforcing mechanisms which cause poverty to persist. Lack of money makes it difficult to find the way to the top. Poverty seems inevitable. Countries normally unable to borrow because of low incomes and weak saving and investing policies can become eligible for World Bank loans to be used for investment. Local banks receive funds from the Bank with the provision that the money must be lent to small- and medium-sized business. These types of businesses often have a hard time finding money in the capital markets and the World Bank loans create conditions to improve themselves and the economy.[95] In 2014 the World Bank lent out capital amounting to $290 billion.[96]

Box 7.6   A cement factory in Burundi is an interesting investment

Cement is an expensive item in Burundi. It is imported from Dar es Salaam in Tanzania but the most important raw material, limestone, is easily found locally. The situation will only change when investors are ready to part with $31 million. This huge amount is necessary because cement produced in small quantities causes price escalation and 100,000 tons per year is considered the minimum capacity. This is no problem for Burundi as it has a large internal market and any surplus can be easily sold to neighbouring countries bordering on Lake Tanzania. The lake also provides inexpensive water transport and cement should be a wonderful export product for Burundi with a high return prognosis and investments being recouped after three years. Theoretically this project would have a higher yield than similar ones based in Europe and could be of interest to two European producers, Heidelberg Cement in Germany and the French company Lafarge. Both firms supply building materials and are already active in East Africa. Acquisition of a subordinated loan from the World Bank can help one of the companies to take the investment risk knowing that it will not be forced to use 100% of its own investment capital.

Case based on the feasibility study 'Small scale production of Portland cement in Burundi' by Patrick Ndizeye.[97]

Cheap money for the World Bank

The World Bank enjoys Triple-A status which simply means that it can borrow money from the financial markets at favourable rates. This status is the bank's reciprocation (trust) for governments of industrialized countries who have taken bona fide loans. Triple-A status has allowed the World Bank to not only offer loans at favourable rates, but to also make a profit on its lending activities since 1994.[98]

7.3.4   World Trade Organization

The Bretton Woods agreement called for an international organization to govern international trade relations. Policies by which countries raised tariffs to maintain their own economies but at the expense of their neighbours' were regarded as spreading the Great Depression. An international institution was required to prevent recurrence and encourage the free flow of goods and services. However, fulfilling the aims of Bretton Woods' participants took 50 years, and finally led to the creation of the WTO.[99]

The theoretical foundation for free trade is the principle of comparative advantage (Ricardo, 1817).[100] Simply put, the principle of comparative advantage says that countries prosper first by taking advantage of their assets in order to concentrate on what they can relatively produce best, and then by trading these products for products that other countries produce better (see Chapter 2 for details).[101]

The International Trade Organization charter was agreed at the UN Conference on Trade and Employment in Havana in March 1948 but was blocked by the US Senate. Instead, the General Agreement on Tariffs and Trade started and its first round succeeded in lowering tariffs of 45,000 products involving 23 countries but a consensus accord was difficult to achieve.[102] The Uruguay Round was a trade negotiation lasting from September 1986 to April 1994 which transformed the General Agreement on Tariffs and Trade into the World Trade Organization. 153 countries, involving 97% of world trade, belong to the WTO (Figure 7.3 shows how its membership has grown) which oversees a large number of agreements defining the 'rules of trade' between its member states.[103] Facilitating trade between countries is at the core of the WTO's philosophy.[104] A 'non-discrimination' clause, better known as 'most favoured nation status' plays an important role. It means that a country cannot negotiate a deal with attractive business advantages unless these advantages apply to all other countries. A uniform policy must be adhered to, even if more appealing options exist. An exception to this is the forming of a trade block that in essence functions as a new country. This applies, for example, to the European Union (EU). The EU is, together, a large free-trade zone and any individual trade obstacles with non-member states apply to all EU partners. Another exception to the rule is trade with developing countries. Under certain circumstances, more favourable conditions can be granted to developing countries for a limited period of time, especially if the measures are seen to improve economic growth.

Box 7.7   Trade barriers

Governments and public authorities who take steps to make imported goods and services less competitive than those locally produced do this by using trade barriers distinguishing between tariff and non-tariff barriers.[105]

Tariff barriers are the taxes levied on goods and services imported from abroad and can be viewed as a transparent form of trade barrier. Dependent on the level of the tariff, goods from foreign exporters are offered at higher prices.

Non-tariff trade barriers constitute several different forms. A number of these have immediate impact on pricing exemplified by currency devaluation, export subsidies or subsidies for local businesses so that they can be more competitive. Other non-tariff options that governments can use are import quotas and countervailing duties.[106]

In addition to these measures which are primarily implemented to protect local enterprises or support their export policies, there are government measures which function as trade barriers; however, those measures do not aim to discourage import. For example, customs procedures.[107] Companies that export abroad will always be faced with customs issues. These procedural issues are legitimate and

(Continued)

governments have the right to keep track of incoming and outgoing goods. However, if the procedures are unnecessary and or inefficient, they can also be construed as illegal and those exporters who feel that they are victims of complex bureaucratic import practices (procedural barriers) can take their case to the WTO.[108]

Businesses who are involved in international trading must also deal with technical standards that can apply to different countries and regions. Government again has the right to demand that imports meet a desired standard of safety and quality. Importing countries can and do make demands for product quality control, especially if the product presents a danger to public health. These so-called technical barriers are also perfectly legitimate as long as they are not improperly used. The EU, for example, blocked imports of genetically manipulated food for many years. In 2003 the US, Canada and Argentina lodged a complaint with the WTO. In 2006 it was decided that the EU had acted unfairly which led to talks and a new agreement being implemented in 2009.[109]

Increased WTO membership

Discussions with aspiring member countries are taking place at the time of writing and stress the importance of decreased import duties, freedom of the internal market and protection of 'intellectual property'. The WTO does not impose rules itself. It provides a forum to conduct trade negotiations and makes sure that its agreements are not disregarded. At the WTO each country has a single vote but decisions are traditionally by consensus. The WTO has two basic functions: it is a forum for discussion and negotiation of new and existing trade rules, and it is a trade dispute settlement body (DSB).[110]

The DSB decides on trade disagreements between member countries. Once it has made a decision, i.e. whether the complaint was right or wrong, the DSB may request the 'losing' party to align its trade laws or policies with the WTO agreements. There is no 'punishment' or restitution. The losing member will be given a 'reasonable period of time' to satisfy the WTO request.[111] If the losing member does not change its policies within the 'reasonable period of time', the DSB may authorize the winning party to adopt retaliatory trade measures to trigger action on the losing party, but this is unusual. Generally WTO members 'willingly' implement DSB decisions in time.[112]

Since the Uruguay round, the WTO also monitors international infringements of trade-related intellectual property rights (TRIPS). WTO membership implies an obligation of member states to sanction and enforce national regulation protecting the property rights of foreign companies. A country's failure to protect another country's IPR can be denounced by the affected country to the DSB. If the DSB decides that TRIPS were infringed, the offended country is authorised to apply trade sanctions to the offending country.[113]

Of course, when a losing country brings its laws etc. into conformity it may choose how to do so. It may not necessarily make the changes that the winning party would prefer. TRIPS placed WTO at the centre of protests by anti-globalization protesters who claim that TRIPS only favour powerful patent holders at the expense of customers and poor people. As we will see in Chapter 8, during the 2000s The Doha Round of trade negotiations attempted, unsuccessfully, to redress some of the balance towards developing countries' interests.[114]

Box 7.8   WTO principles

The trading system should be:

- Without discrimination – a country should not discriminate between its trading partners (giving them equally 'most favoured nation' or MFN status); and it should not discriminate between its own and foreign products, services or nationals (giving them 'national treatment').
- Freer – barriers coming down through negotiation.
- Predictable – foreign companies, investors and governments should be confident that trade barriers (including tariff and non-tariff barriers) should not be raised arbitrarily; tariff rates and market-opening commitments are 'bound' in the WTO.
- More competitive – discouraging 'unfair' practices such as export subsidies and dumping products at below cost to gain market share.
- More beneficial for less-developed countries – giving them more time to adjust, greater flexibility and special privileges.

Source: http://www.wto.org/english/thewto_e/whatis_e/tif_e/fact2_e.htm[115]

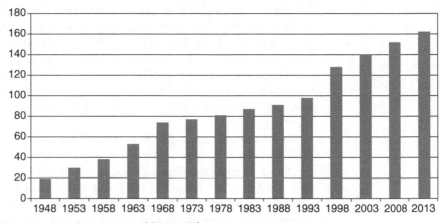

Figure 7.3   Member countries of the WTO[116]

 7.4   Case Study: Which is the most transnational company?

Remember from Section 7.1.2 that one of the differences between internationalization and globalization is that internationalization is driven by multinational companies while globalization is driven by transnational companies. The question is, how can we measure a firm's degree of internationalization and transnationalization? Grazia Ietto-Gillies (1998)[117] identifies two main conceptual frameworks that have been proposed to measure the degree of internationalization and discusses to what extent they truly measure internationalization and how they can be adapted to measure transnationalization.

The United Nations Conference on Trade and Development (UNCTAD 1995) proposed a transnationality index (TNI) based on the extent of foreign location of activities. The index is the sum of three components: percentage of foreign assets over total assets (AI), percentage of foreign sales over total sales (SI) and percentage of foreign employees over total employees (EI). The higher the value of this index,

(Continued)

the less dependent the company is on its home country resources. The firm with highest percentage of foreign assets was Seagram Co Ltd, with 97.2%. The highest SI was the Swiss pharmaceutical Roche Holding AG whose foreign sales represent 98.2% of total sales. In terms of foreign employees the highest index was again showcased by Seagram (97.3%), which also exhibits the highest TNI (again 97.3%). A strength of TNI is that it captures both the supply and demand side of cross-border activities.

Globalization researchers did point out important conceptual weaknesses in this index, showing how companies with high values could be neither truly internationalized nor transnational. Sullivan (1996) proposed an alternative index: the network spread index (NSI).[118] The NSI examines the geographical spread of economic activities by taking into account the number of countries where a multinational has operations. The more countries where a company operates, the more the cultural context of each host country needs to be understood. This leads to the development of a global mindset within the company. The index is simply the number of countries where the company operates, divided by the total number of countries in the world where the company can potentially have a subsidiary (this is the total number of countries minus one, to discount the home country). The company with the highest network spread is Shell, which, with an NSI of 62%, has subsidiaries in 109 countries (whereas Seagram 'only' has subsidiaries in 35). As an indicator of internationalization, this is a very good index, but as an indicator of transnationalization it misses some of TNI's strengths.

Ietto-Gillies proposed a practical solution, a combination of both indexes, termed the Transnational Activity Spread Index (TASi), where the NSI is used as weight for the components of the transnationality index. TASi accounts for both spread of activities and extent of dependence on home country resources. TASi = asset spread + sales spread + employment spread:

$$TASi = TNS \times AI (ASi) + TNS \times EI (ESi) + TNS \times SIi (SSi)$$

Applying this index to the top 100 multinationals in 1998, Ietto-Gillies found the 'most globalized company' in the world: Nestle SA, the Swiss food giant. Nestle's TASi is 50.3% (as opposed to Seagram's 19.1% and Shell's 40.8%). Nestle has subsidiaries in 94 countries, its percentage of foreign assets is 90.9%, foreign sales account for 66% of total sales, but foreign employment is only 53%. Therefore, the most 'transnational company' is still quite dependent on supply-side home country resources. The second highest TASi (45.3%) is for Swedish energy firm Abb (Asia Brown Bovery), which has less spread (84 countries) but does not depend on home resources from supply or demand side (AI = 96%, SI = 97.5%,[119] EI = 94.7%).

 Case Study Questions

1. What do you think were the weaknesses of TNI pointed out by Sullivan?
2. Do you think TASi is a fair indicator of transnationalization?
3. How would you measure 'regionalization'?
4. How would you improve the TASi index?
5. Group task: Visit the corporate pages of Nestle, Abb and Apple. Calculate their TASi today and look further at the spread of nationalities in Nestle's, Apple's and Abb's corporate board and management board. Which company do you think is now closer to being truly transnational?

7.5   Learning tools 🔧

7.5.1   Summary

- Talk of globalization started in the 1980s but there is still controversy about its existence. This chapter argued that a clear definition of what globalization is and what debates take place around the concept is crucial to advance knowledge and policy.
- Three main views were outlined:
  - Radicals, who see globalization as a new and irreversible phenomenon (Giddens; Ohmae).
  - Sceptics, who see it as largely a myth, resulting from hype, conceptual confusion and misread evidence (Hirst & Thompson; Jones).
  - Finally, pragmatists (Scholte, Dicken) talk about ongoing processes of qualitative change towards deeper economic integration (a globalizing economy) that co-exist with quantitative processes, simply extending economic transactions beyond borders (an internationalizing economy).

- Scholte proposes that globalization is a trend towards globality (a condition), still in its early stages. Clear understanding of differences between globalization and other trends in the world economy is crucial. Globalization (transplanetary and supraterritorial processes of integration) is different from: internationalization, neoliberalism (an ideology), universalization, westernization. In particular, discerning differences between neoliberalism and globalization are key to understanding if alleged negative impacts of globalization are not in fact the result of neoliberalism.
- The chapter analyses the main drivers of globalization, concluding that free market acceptance and technology promote a mix of globalization and internationalization processes, with trade liberalization favouring internationalization whereas liberalization of foreign direct investment favours globalization. Processes of regional cooperation lead to increased regionalization of the world economy.
- The final part of the chapter focused on supranational institutions governing globalization. As Dicken notes, international economic systems are increasingly integrated and interdependent and so, therefore, is the international political system.
- The supranational institutions are at the centre of a 'web of interdependencies'. Nation states are now not the only or perhaps most important seat of power. All supranational institutions are of great importance. We focused on the Bretton Woods institutions (global financial system): the International Monetary Fund, the World Bank and the World Trade Organization. They fulfil the role of assuring governance of the global economy across nations.

7.5.2   Further reading

Dicken, P. (2014). *Global Shift: Mapping the Changing Contours of the World Economy* (pp. 537–547). London: Paul Chapman. See, in particular, chapters about the role of states in globalization.

Hill, C. W. L. (2014). The international monetary system. In *International Business. Competing in the Global Marketplace.* Boston: McGraw-Hill.

Hirst, P. & Thompson, G. (2002). Introduction: Globalization – a necessary myth? In
P. Hirst & G. Thompson, *Globalization in Question* (pp. 2–12). Cambridge: Polity Press.
Scholte, J. A. (2007). Defining globalization. In J. A. Scholte, *Globalization: A Critical
Introduction* (pp. 22–41). London: Palgrave.

7.5.3 Assignments

 Assignment 7.1

Is the world economy becoming more globalized, more internationalized, more
westernized or more neoliberal? Discuss with evidence.
Key authors: Hirst and Thompson, Scholte, Dicken.

 Assignment 7.2

Discuss the extent of transnationalization of the 100 largest firms in today's world
economy.

 Assignment 7.3

Analyse to what extent the Bretton Woods institutions are enough to provide global
economic governance. *Note: This is not a discussion on the successes and failures of
Bretton Woods. The question requires you to discuss to what extent these institutions
(created in 1994) are able to provide a system of economic governance in the current
globalizing economy and post-normal state.*

7.5.4 Self-test questions

 Self-test Questions

1. Describe differences between a radical's view, a sceptic's view and a pragmatic
   view.
2. Describe differences between neoliberalism, internationalization, westernization and globalization.
3. What forms of trade indicate deeper economic integration and can be used as
   evidence of a globalizing economy?
4. What forms of foreign investment are associated with internationalization and
   what forms with globalization?
5. What is the CNN effect?
6. What are the roles of the Bretton Woods institutions?

THE IMPACT OF GLOBALIZATION ON SUSTAINABLE DEVELOPMENT

Overview and learning objectives

Lloyd, in his 2009 work *What on Earth Happened* invokes the prophecies of three great thinkers of the past who believed humankind was doomed: Marx, Malthus and Darwin. Marx questioned the long-term survival of capitalism. He believed capitalism was a necessary historical phase which would be one day altogether replaced by a fairer society. According to Marx, capitalism is unstable and doomed to suffer increasingly severe cycles of 'boom' and 'bust', until inevitably collapsing amidst spiralling inequality, unemployment and social unrest. In turn, Malthus acknowledged that human life expectancy and quality of life have been extended by economic growth and science but warned that resulting rising levels of human population and consumption will put unsustainable pressure on natural resources, and predicted that eventually nature would take revenge in the form of 'sickly seasons, epidemic, pestilence and plague and gigantic inevitable famine' (Malthus, cited in Lloyd, 2009)[1]. Finally, Darwin prophesied that humankind will follow the same fate of extinction as any other natural species. Individual instinct and self-interest will lead to overuse of resources and the destruction of natural systems needed to support life.

Lloyd's argument is that globalization can prove these authors wrong, if it is governed in a way that promotes collaboration and reduces inequality in the distribution of resources. Globalization has already contributed to economic growth, poverty reduction and environmental improvements through international agreements to curb pollution and cap emissions.[2]

There is potential for globalization to be a force for positive change. To what extent such potential has been unleashed is debatable. Indeed, writers such as Naomi Klein and Lorraine Hertz see globalization as a negative force that exacerbates the flaws of current socio-economic systems, disseminating worldwide unsustainable consumption and production patterns, while increasing inequality results from expanding market fundamentalism and egotistical disregard for others.[3] Grassroots movements such as Occupy Wall Street and the anti-globalization protesters campaigning against G8 and World Trade Organization meetings promote this view. However, as we have seen in Chapter 7, Stiglitz and Scholte argue that the cause of the problems highlighted by these movements is not globalization but neoliberalism.[4] Debates are still ongoing.

There are two ways to analyse to what extent globalization is a force for positive change. One is to identify patterns of changes in the economy, society and environment since the economy started globalizing. The challenge is to define what period should be considered as the dominance of globalization and how to separate the effects of globalization from other economic phenomena. We are mindful that in addition to globalization (deep integration) there is internationalization (shallow integration) and economic neoliberalization (push for free markets). The second part of this chapter attempts to conceptualize how these phenomena have influenced inequality and financial crisis, a growing concern for the global economy and the potential undoing of capitalism.

A second way to look at outcomes of globalization is to evaluate the impact of two main actors in globalization processes: global institutions and multinational enterprises. The following sections take a closer look at the impact of these major players' decisions in the last few decades. It will be argued that the shift of supranational organizations from global governance to neoliberal championship underlies the current state of affairs in terms of inequalities. In this regard we will also examine the impact of foreign direct investment (FDI). We argue that, very simply put, FDI + global institutions = globalization. Therefore, understanding the impacts of FDI is key to understanding whether globalization is a force for good. We will discuss views for and against FDI and see to what extent FDI has positive impacts on the economy of the host; particularly when the host is a developing country. Indeed, the poorer the country the more need of FDI but also the more risk of negative impacts. Combining both levels of analysis should provide a snapshot of winners and losers in the global economy.

Learning objectives

This chapter will enable students to:

- Develop understanding of debates regarding the positive and negative impacts of supranational institutions: the International Monetary Fund (IMF), the World Bank and the World Trade Organization (WTO).
- Develop understanding of debates regarding the impact of multinational companies in host countries.
- Understand current trends in terms of economic growth, well-being and inequality.
- Develop awareness of debates regarding the causes of inequality and global financial crisis.
- Develop critical awareness of the need to differentiate impacts of globalization, internationalization and neoliberalism.

8.1   The impact of economic supranational organizations

Stiglitz (2002) argues that Bretton Woods institutions were created to correct the imperfections of market capitalism that had been painfully exposed by increased internationalization of economies during the first half of the twentieth century.[5] Shallow integration of economies through international trade had resulted in competitive devaluations and the deployment of restrictions to trade as political blackmail. Therefore, a deeper form of global economic relationship was needed to prevent global political instability. This type of economic relationship should integrate economic systems and create interdependencies between national systems through institutions providing global governance.[6] In other words, the world needed more globalization and less internationalization. The result of this need was the Bretton Woods institutions: the first globalization institutions. Their goal was to provide governance of capital flows (IMF), trade (WTO) and inequalities in the distribution of welfare (World Bank). This section will examine to what extent they have succeeded in their goals.

8.1.1   The impact of the IMF

In Chapter 7, we explained that the IMF was originally created out of the belief that markets behave badly and coordinated intervention was required to put pressure on countries to implement policies expanding aggregated demand. When needed the IMF would provide loans to countries facing an economic downturn and thus unable to stimulate demand with their own resources.

The IMF also policed a global system of fixed exchange rates, the so-called Bretton Woods System (BWS). In the Bretton Woods System all countries fixed the values of their currency in terms of gold. The system signalled a global commitment not to use devaluation as a competitive weapon. However, as international mobility of capital increased, BWS became increasingly threatened by speculators. In 1973 the system collapsed due to speculative pressure on the dollar which followed an increase in US inflation and balance-of-payments deficit. In the aftermath of the collapse, the IMF switched to a system of flexible or floating exchange rates.[7]

Stiglitz argues that the abandonment of the fixed exchange system was unavoidable. Fixed exchange rates were a transition measure needed to stabilize the global economy after the Second World War. Once this objective was met the fixed exchange system should have been abandoned. Institutional inertia and political pressure from the US government had allowed the system to overstay its welcome. The problem was that amidst the debacle of the fixed exchange system, the IMF also abandoned all its foundational Keynesian objectives. Instead, it became a champion of neoliberalism 'promoting free markets with ideological fervor' (Stiglitz, 2002).[8] The IMF disbursed last resort loans only when a country had committed to apply contractionary policies reducing aggregated demand, such as austerity (e.g. cuts in public social spending) and increases in taxes and interest rates. As Stiglitz comments, Keynes would be turning in his grave if he were able to see what had become of its creation.[9]

Neoliberals in the IMF believed in what is known as the Solow hypothesis, proposed in 1956 by growth theorist Solow: austerity is needed to encourage savings, and savings are a pre-condition for growth. Keynes disagreed with Solow and proposed a counter-hypothesis: savings are a consequence of growth. Government and customers must spend first to stimulate growth, even if that creates indebtment. As the economy grows there are bigger amounts of income available for saving and repaying debts. Recent statistical analysis in developing countries suggests that Keynes was right and the IMF was wrong: austerity and savings are not a pre-condition for growth.[10]

8.1.2   The Washington Consensus

The 'Washington Consensus' is a term coined by Williamson to describe an informal agreement between the World Bank, the IMF and the US Treasury to promote neoliberal policy and – at least for its critics – market fundamentalism globally. The Washington Consensus endorsed a bundle of 'one-size-fits-all' policies considered as the solution for economic problems elsewhere.[11] In developing countries, the Washington Consensus promoted structural reforms including liberalization of capital flows, interest rates and trade, fiscal austerity, tax reform, inflation control, competitive exchange rates, protection of property rights, deregulation (particularly in employment, banking and foreign investment), and privatizations.[12] Countries taking either the IMF's bail-outs or the World Bank's development and structural loans would have to agree with conditions requiring the implementation of Washington Consensus policies.[13] As mentioned before, most Washington Consensus policies were designed in the 1980s as a response to the 1980 Latin American Debt Crisis when governmental budgets and deficits spiralled and were accompanied by loose monetary policies leading to hyperinflation. Washington Consensus policies aimed to correct the problems of inflation and debt created by governments that were spending beyond their means and protecting inefficient local industries (either through state ownership or restriction of imports).[14]

Box 8.1   The Washington Consensus commandments[15]

- Sustained growth is not possible with hyperinflation.
- Countries cannot persistently run on large deficits.
- Trade liberalization leads to efficiency gains and helps customers to stop paying high prices to inefficient private firms.
- Trade liberalization further promotes efficiency as new jobs are created when inefficient growths are destroyed.
- Governments should focus on public services rather than running enterprises that would perform better in the private sector.
- Developing countries must keep interest rates high and currencies pegged to a strong currency (i.e. dollar) to attract investors.
- Developing countries must focus on the efficient production and export of commodities to obtain trade surplus.

Figure 8.1   The three pillars of the Washington Consensus

Washington Consensus policies succeeded to tame spiralling debt and inflation in Latin America and became one-size-fits-all policies; unfortunately they were applied in countries with very different conditions from Latin America.[16] Despite some success stories (i.e. Chile), Peet (2008) argues that the results of the Washington Consensus's disregard for contextual variety have been disastrous, leading, for instance, to stagnating growth and rises in unemployment in many African and Asian countries.[17]

Stiglitz highlights that claims of success in Latin America (for instance in controlling hyperinflation in Argentina) overlooked long-term consequences for financial stability and equality. Washington Consensus policies contributed to global financial instability by making both developed and developing countries vulnerable to changes in foreign investors' sentiment.[18]

According to Rich (1996) Washington Consensus policies lead not only to deepening of pockets of poverty around the globe but also to environmental damage. Poor countries' need to sustain growth with increases in commodity exports resulted in unsustainable agrarian production and the replacing of forests with crops. In turn, increases in the global supply of commodities lead to a reduction in prices. As a consequence, developing countries needed to export increasingly larger volumes of commodities to compensate for falling prices, while over-exploitation reduced the quality of soil, further increasing pressure on the natural environment.[19]

Peet and Stiglitz provide a litany of examples of countries where Washington Consensus policies failed to promote economic growth and increased inequality. Peet adds that indeed countries with sustained growth both in the 1970s and 1980s (e.g. Korea and Taiwan) and in the 1990s and early 2000s (e.g. Poland, India and China) were those that did not strictly apply the Washington Consensus prescriptions and followed their own model of market economy.[20]

The reasons behind Washington Consensus failures are not only related to the disregard of differences between countries and historical periods, but also problems of implementation and overtly ideological blindness to potential market failures.[21] The pace and manner in which privatization and liberalization was pursued imposed huge costs in countries ill-equipped to incur them. Inappropriate regulatory frameworks, lack of competition and corruption meant that privatizations failed to provide more efficient services in many developing countries. Privatizations also contributed to unemployment: numerous redundancies resulted from new owners' cost-cutting programmes.[22]

Market liberalization led to destruction of local banks and foreign control of financial systems, thus restricting the access of small entrepreneurs to capital (small enterprises traditionally rely on local banking). Weakly regulated financial industries promoted risky behaviour and bubbles which made economies volatile while pegged currency made the countries easy targets for speculators. Ultimately fast market liberalization created financial crises, such as the East Asia Crisis.[23]

In turn, fast trade liberalization destroyed local industry, creating unemployment. As economies contracted, fiscal austerity was the only option left to government still needing to pay its debt to the IMF and other creditors. Fiscal austerity resulted in cuts in social services and the public service workforce. In a context of contracted economies and decreasing income from exports these measures further reduced aggregated demand. Cuts in social services increased vulnerability of the poorest sectors of society. Cuts in state employment in a context of receding industrial activity deepened recession.[24]

The excessive focus on inflation led to high interest rates and high exchange rates, reducing aggregate demand and creating more unemployment but not growth. Indeed, Stiglitz argues that Washington Consensus policies are not only one of the main causes of financial crisis in the last three decades, but also a factor increasing external debt, poverty and inequality in developing countries. In many of the poorest countries helped by the IMF, the application of conditionalities resulted in unmanageable levels of debt, and countries relying on IMF's bail-outs to be able to pay the interest of such debts.[25]

From 1994 to 2001 environmental and social consequences of the Washington Consensus became prominent in political and academic debates, while the world economy experienced a wave of financial crisis that the IMF seemed impotent to predict and control. In several cases – notably Argentina – the country affected by crisis had been systematically praised by the IMF for its commitment to Washington Consensus policies.[10]

As criticisms mounted, the institutions behind the Washington Consensus felt their legitimacy threatened. Although fundamental principles remained unchanged, Washington Consensus policies were adjusted to reduce social impacts, new initiatives were introduced specifically targeted to help poorest countries and more attention was given to context. Peet calls the resulting policies the augmented and benevolent consensus.[27]

8.1.3   The augmented and benevolent Washington Consensus

From 1996 to 2001 Washington Consensus reforms focused on solving the ever-increasing debt of poor countries. A flagship initiative of the new, more socially aware Washington Consensus was to forgive poorest countries' debts (debt relief) under the Heavily Indebted Poor Countries (HIPC) Initiative: The HIPC Initiative was launched in 1996 by the IMF and the World Bank. The explicit aim was to ensure that no poor country was burdened with a debt it couldn't manage. 'Since then, the international financial community, including multilateral organizations and governments, have worked together to reduce to sustainable levels the external debt burdens of the most heavily indebted poor countries' (IMF, 2015).

However, such largesse was not exempt of conditions: 'to be eligible for the initiative countries must have established a track record of reform and sound policies through IMF- and World Bank supported programs' (IMF, 2013).[28] In other words, to be eligible, countries should follow Washington Consensus conditionalities, which arguably created part of the 'unsustainable level of debt' (Peet 2008). For Peet, the HIPC amounts to economic blackmail forcing the poorest countries to stick to policies clearly detrimental to their progress prospects.[29] Stiglitz (2002) narrates how the IMF and World Bank withdrew support to Ethiopia when its government dared to propose an alternative economic plan, despite such a plan being designed and supported by leading international economists.[30]

From 1996 to 2001, the 'augmented Washington Consensus' gradually revised its 'one-size-fits-all' approach. It maintained previous neoliberal policies but acknowledged that capital account opening needed to be 'prudent'. It promoted environmental awareness, corporate governance, anti-corruption and the creation of social safety nets to protect the poor from the effects of unemployment caused by privatization and the disappearance of local industry.[31]

After Argentina, a country with a track record of reform through IMF-supported programmes, collapsed dramatically in 2001, even augmented Washington Consensus policies became unsustainable. Amidst growing claims that perhaps the IMF and World Bank had become obsolete, the Washington Consensus reinvented itself as the ideology behind a market-led international monetary system with a 'human face'.[32] For the first time in its history, the IMF acknowledged 'mistakes' and attempted to be seen as more receptive to the need of different policy approaches for low-income countries. 'The Fund realized that the institutional prerequisites for successful liberalization of international capital flows were more daunting than it had previously thought' (IMF, 2015).[33]

The term 'benevolent consensus' is used by Peet to describe the post-2002 neoliberal agenda with more flexible conditionalities and a focus on poverty elimination, debt relief and external aid to achieve the Millennium Development Goals, following Jeffrey Sachs's book *The End of Poverty*. The rationale is that markets do not work in poor countries because these countries are stuck in 'poverty traps'. When countries have very low levels of capital, small increments in capital do no yield high returns, therefore since it does not pay to invest, entrepreneurs do not save and the economy remains poor and low in capital. External capital injection (aid, FDI) is needed to move the economy to a level of capital where financial markets work and it does pay to invest.[34]

The benevolent consensus's most visible instrument is the Multilateral Debt Relief Initiative (MDRI) launched in 2005. The MDRI provides 100% relief on eligible debt from the IMF and the World Bank to a number of low-income countries. The initiative was aimed to help progress in United Nations' Millennium Development Goals (MDGs), which focused on halving poverty by 2015 (a target that was achieved by 2014).

Two groups of countries were eligible. The first group comprised all the countries that participated in the HIPC Initiative. The second group included all those countries with per capita income below $380 and outstanding debt to the IMF in 2004. To qualify for debt relief, the IMF required that countries were up to date in the repayment of principal and interests of IMF debt. Countries were also required to provide evidence of satisfactory performance in: sound macroeconomic policies; poverty reduction strategy implemented; and efficient management of public expenditure which does not lead to further debt. In other words, debt relief was still tied up to conditionalities which were not substantially different from those in the Washington Consensus. Therefore, Peet considers both augmented and benevolent consensus fundamentally flawed owing to its economics and ethical foundations promoting a 'laundry list' approach to reform, unrestricted open markets, foreign investment and privatization as tools to fight poverty.[35]

Rodrik (2006) points out that continued aid has not extricated African countries with open markets from poverty, while Vietnam – a country with a hybrid economy – took off in the 1980s despite a dearth of Western aid.[36]

Despite criticisms, the revamped Washington Consensus has been resilient and convinced the international community to give the IMF more resources and attributions. In 2006, the IMF was given a surveillance role over trade imbalances. In 2010, IMF country members increased by three times the Fund's lending capacity, which went up from $250 billion to $750 billion.

However, as proved by the Fund's reaction to the Greek crisis, neoliberal policy is still IMF's ideological bastion. In 2013, Greece faced a combination of unemployment, growing debt and recession uncannily resembling Argentina in 2001. However, the IMF basically recommended the same economic package that had failed to prevent crisis in Latin America: bail-outs, austerity and other contractionary measures. Despite some reforms there has been little structural change in the Washington Consensus.[37]

Another aspect where the IMF is still reluctant to change is in terms of decision-making structure. Poor countries and transition economies, which are the main recipients of IMF loans, have little say about loans and the conditions attached to them. Decision making is dominated by the richest Western countries, Japan and Saudi Arabia. Each member country has a number of votes proportional to its economic contribution to the fund. The US alone has 17% of votes. After the US, UK, France, Germany, Japan, Italy and Saudi Arabia are the main contributors with shares of votes between 3% to 16%. Together these seven countries held more than 50% of votes. Requests from China, India, Brazil, Russia and Korea to increase their share have led to some changes but have not altered the dominance of Western economies.

Even if the IMF addresses all its criticisms, a fundamental dilemma will constrain its ability to ensure global financial stability: moral hazard (see Box 8.2). The solution to moral hazard requires a new global financial architecture promoting collective responsibility and action through international political agreement to exert restraint in risky financial behaviour. At the moment, such agreement remains in the realm of political fantasy.

> ## Box 8.2   The International Monetary Fund's dilemma
>
> The key role of the IMF in providing bail-outs (loans of the last resort) creates a dilemma. Countries receiving emergency loans are in essence rewarded for irresponsible debt policies which creates a moral hazard. In economics, moral hazard is a situation where an economic actor (i.e. a firm or a country) will have a tendency to take risks because the costs that could result will not be felt by the actor. Since the IMF is there to provide bail-outs, governments and credit institutions feel less responsible. They know the IMF is willing to help therefore countries and firms have an incentive to make risky investments and take on excessive debt.

8.1.4   The impact of the World Bank

There is consensus on the early success of World Bank projects. From 1949 to 1968 the World Bank supported the reconstruction of Europe, devastated by the Second World War. Once its mission in Europe reached completion, from 1968 to 1981 the World Bank reinvented itself, taking on the crucial mission of elimination of global poverty. During this period World Bank policies were focused on how markets failed in developing countries and redirected at the improvement of markets and compensation for their failures through developmental loans. The World Bank played a major role in improving well-being in the least-developed countries. AIDS has been controlled in several African nations thanks to World Bank-funded projects. World Bank loans eradicated endemic diseases such as river blindness in Africa. They also provided capital to build basic infrastructure for growth such as roads, hospitals, schools and hydroelectric centrals, otherwise inaccessible. Indeed, life expectancy and Human Development Index improved in most countries receiving World Bank assistance.[38] However, in many cases where the World Bank claims success, such as in East Asian countries' miraculous growth from 1960 to 1990, credit must be given to the impact of Keynesian government strategies, with the World Bank playing a supporting role.

From 1980 onwards the World Bank accompanied the ideological shift advocated by the IMF. The IMF and World Bank believed that governments of developing countries were inefficient and hampered by corruption. Interventionist policies, cronyism and bloated government budgets (subsidized via indebtedness and monetary emissions) were the cause of the economic problems of developing countries. Solutions could be readily provided by free markets and constraints in government discretion (with the IMF and World Bank monitoring how the government applies standard neoliberal policy promoted by the IMF).[39] The bank started to require application of Washington Consensus policies as a condition for loans while providing loans to help implementation of structural adjustment programmes aimed to liberalize developing countries' economies.[40] Developed countries also pressured the World Bank to lend more and increase its portfolio of works. This resulted in risky and ill-advised loans as World Bank staff felt coerced to give positive appraisal of projects they thought inadequate. A World Bank project monitoring report (1992) stated that only 17% of staff believed in the quality of the projects approved.[41]

8.1.5   World Bank criticisms

A key criticism of World Bank policies is related to the repayment of loans given by the organization. The World Bank does not charge interest to the least-developed countries. However, once a loan contract is signed, countries have to pay a loan maintenance fee of 0.75% per year, even if the country does not receive the money because it fails to satisfy loan conditions. Conditions required by the World Bank prior to disbursing the first instalment of a loan take in average up to two years to be satisfied and generally include local legislation approving the loan, creation of autarchic entities to manage the project funded by the loan and structural adjustment measures in line with Washington Consensus policies. This includes privatizations, reduction in social spending and focus on export of commodities. In addition, repayment of loans must be done in the currency lent, often dollars to which developing countries have limited access.[42] If a country stops satisfying conditionalities after a loan has been granted, the World Bank can discontinue disbursements. However, Kilby (2009) identified a distinct political bias in the enforcement of conditionalities. Using panel data on structural adjustment loans disbursements between 1984 and 2005, Kilby demonstrated that continuity of disbursements is less dependent on achievement of conditionalities in countries aligned with the US (using UN voting as an indicator of alignment with the US).[43]

Two further aspects coalesced to make repayment problematic. First, structural adjustment conditions had typically resulted in devaluation of the currency, but still loans had to be repaid in dollars. Second, a large part of the loans went back to developed countries. Contractors were always from developed countries and sent back home profits, payment of indirect costs, foreign staff and licensing fees. The World Bank had a register of contractors qualified to execute works funded by the World Bank. The aim of this register was to ensure that contractors had the experience and financial clout required to undertake large and complex infrastructure projects. However, the practical consequence was that only large multinationals were eligible. Local firms in developing countries could only participate as minority partners in alliance with a foreign firm. In addition, a large proportion of direct cost was import of machinery. In many cases even the workforce was foreign. Rich (1994) observes that flows of capital from the least-developed countries to developed countries was on average more than 70% of the money lent. Still, developing countries had to repay the loans.[44]

A final criticism refers to the design of projects. The Bank encouraged projects which are seen as environmentally and socially damaging for little obvious benefit. For instance, Brazil and Indonesia received loans to implement in-mass relocation of urban slum dwellers to rainforest areas. This resulted in alienation of the newcomers, massive deforestation and destruction of the sustainable community lifestyle of indigenous people. In Paraguay and Thailand, loans were given to fund gigantic dams in community forests obliterating traditional irrigation systems.[45] In the 1980s and 1990s, the World Bank also granted loans to authoritarian regimes such as Chile, Paraguay and Romania's dictatorships, or countries with appalling human rights track records such as South Africa with its apartheid regime. In 1992 a World Bank internal report showed that many projects designed and supported by the World Bank, where inappropriate for the context and which had failed to achieve results, had increased the debt of the receiving countries.[46] Therefore authors such as Peet[47] and Stiglitz[48] claim the World Bank played a central role in exacerbating debt problem in developing nations during the 1980s and 1990s. Since then, the Bank has much improved internal quality controls but problems remain. In 2011 the World Bank acknowledged 70% failure of its ICT (information and communication technology) projects targeted at the underserved and the poor.[49]

In the last two decades the World Bank has shifted its economic mantra to the promotion of good governance, environmental sustainability and entrepreneurship as pre-requisites for well-being and poverty elimination. Clear efforts have been made to integrate local views in the development of policies and projects.[50] Peet (2008) argues that the World Bank is the Bretton Woods institution that has changed the most and more deeply in response to criticisms. It is now much more transparent, committed to environmental causes and ideologically more developmental and more distant from neoliberal approaches than the IMF. However, the World Bank still shares the same decision-making structure as the IMF, where Western countries have dominance. Ultimately, the World Bank is a bank, and as such accountable to its shareholders.[51]

Therefore, perhaps it is time to consider to what extent a bank is the best type of organizational form to be leading global efforts against poverty, and how it can be made more accountable and receptive to its 'customers', the governments receiving loans. Competition might be a way forward, as we will see in the case study closing this chapter.

8.1.6   The impact of the World Trade Organization

The WTO was created in 1994 as the extension of GATT (General Agreement on Tariffs and Trade), finally fulfilling the objectives of the Bretton Woods conference in 1944. As we saw in Chapter 7, the youngest member of the Bretton Woods organizations is also the most successful. However, it became almost immediately a major target of protest over globalization during WTO meetings in Seattle. Protesters presented the WTO as the symbol of global inequalities and emphasized the two-faced nature of developed countries' neoliberal policy.[52] The WTO was accused of unfair bias toward multinationals and developed countries. Indeed such biases are notable in WTO policy towards agricultural and service subsidies, decision making and property rights.

Developed countries' protectionism in agriculture and services

Developing countries were pushed into free trade by the WTO but protectionist agricultural policies are still tolerated in wealthy countries. Developed countries have long resisted the inclusion of agricultural goods in multilateral trade agreements under GATT authority. Europe, Japan and the US still keep their markets closed to the agricultural products of developing countries, typically subsidizing their farmers which makes competition impossible. While tariffs on manufactured goods have decreased from 50% in 1944 to 3% in 2014, the agricultural sector remains the most protected in the world.[53] This scenario clearly affects developing countries which tend to have a competitive advantage in agriculture. In 2014, for instance, Argentina presented two complaints to WTO demanding the removal of subsidies in US and Spain but neither prospered. Developed countries also oppose further liberalization of service sectors in which the developing countries have developed strengths. As a case in point, operation in the US of Mexico's telecommunications giant Telecom is restricted.

Decision making

Decision making in and related to the WTO has faced much criticism as well. While membership is voluntary, not joining practically places the recalcitrant nation under embargo. The non-discrimination principle requires that any concession or commitment be accorded to all members. Therefore, membership implies blanket acceptance of WTO rules. In negotiations of rules the approach is the single undertaking: nothing is agreed until everything is agreed.[54] New rules are a package deal: take it or leave it. Supporters see this as a fair and transparent system. Critics point out that this creates an international system of forced economic rules which discourage change and experimentation. In addition, some member states have adopted WTO treaties undemocratically or – allegedly – to the detriment of their citizens.[55]

Decision making is democratic. Although each country has one vote, in practice voting never occurs. The WTO operates by consensus and one objection is enough to block decisions. Thus, the WTO has by far the most transparent and equalitarian decision making between Bretton Woods institutions. However, the 'big three' members – the US, the European Union and Japan – have been accused of using the WTO to exert undue influence over less powerful member states. Poorer countries also lack resources to hire experts to decipher WTO complex rules and attend deliberations. Nevertheless, Since China joined the WTO, developing countries have been supported by a powerful ally.[56]

Free versus fair trade

The agreement on trade-related aspects of Intellectual Property Rights (TRIPS) is the WTO's commitment to protect intellectual property worldwide. It states that WTO member countries should enact and enforce regulation protecting the property rights and patents of foreign companies. Critics argued that TRIPS put the interest of multinationals over users and affect the welfare of developing countries by raising the prices of medicines, agricultural products and technology.[57] Peet contends that TRIPS were the result of multinational lobby to make WTO act as de facto enforcer of property rights under the guise of 'fair trade'. The argument is that it is 'unfair' that some countries are allowed to reduce the cost of their exports by using (without paying for it) knowledge generated by other countries' investment in research and development.

Box 8.3   The WTO, the Washington Consensus and environmental protection

The Hecksher–Ohlin trade theory suggests that developing countries should specialize in the production of goods intensively using factors that developing countries are abundantly endowed with: labour and natural resources. In turn, developed countries should specialize in human capital and manufactured capital-intensive activities. These specializations would lead to reduction of environmental degradation in developed countries and increases in environmental degradation in middle-income countries. Environmental regulation in developed countries might further shift polluting activities towards developing countries. The solution to this problem generated by free trade is widespread enforcement of similar regulation standards for developed and developing countries. Evidence suggests that developing countries can successfully grow with stringent standards.[58]

Interestingly, the WTO does not promote stringent standards worldwide, nor does it apply the fairness principle when it comes to environmental regulations. Firms in countries with low environmental standards have an unfair cost advantage over competitors with more stringent environmental regulations. However, the WTO has consistently ruled against unilateral attempts to ban imports on environmental grounds. For instance both Malaysia and Mexico won complaints against the US when it attempted to forbid imports of shrimps fished without turtle-excluding nets and imports of tuna from countries without dolphin protection fishing practices.[59]

(Continued)

The widespread destruction of natural forest coverage in the planet (one of the most threatened planetary boundaries) has been another unintended consequence of the WTO push for free international trade in conjunction with Washington Consensus policies. Structural adjustment programmes forced developing countries to increase the export of commodities and natural resources to achieve balance of trade payment.[60]

However, the increase in global supply led to a fall in commodity prices. Therefore poor countries needed to produce more in order to compensate for loss of revenue caused by lower export prices. Falling commodity prices were matched by overconsumption of natural resources' products in developed countries, thus increasing waste. Overproduction in developing countries resulted in more land used to expand agricultural and mining activities at the expense of natural forests. Air pollution was increased by the burning of forests to extend crops, water bodies were contaminated by uncontrolled use of fertilizers and land degraded by overexploitation.[61] As noted by the United Nations Development Programme in 1999:

> Rapidly expanded trade can result in serious environmental degradation when complementary environmental policies are not in place. Pollution of air, water and soil and unrestrained natural resource exploitation grow to levels that jeopardize the viability of the economic activities they support. Trade thereby becomes unsustainable as the potential for future trade is significantly reduced.[62]

Opponents such as Stiglitz argued that TRIPS raise the prices of all products requiring know-how and technology in poor countries, for instance patented seeds, copyrighted textbooks, patented software and medicines (see Box 8.4). It is therefore an impediment to development, as the speed of progress and innovation is slowed down by increases in the price of knowledge due to TRIPS; making it harder for companies in poor countries to learn from the products and processes of companies in advanced countries.[63]

Box 8.4   TRIPS and the pharmaceutical industry

Legrain (2003) argued that in a world that is anything but uniform, enforcing uniform intellectual property standards is inappropriate because it fails to acknowledge differences between stages of development and access to knowledge production. TRIPS disproportionately affect countries in the early stages of development which have not had the chance to develop their own technologies. As a case in point, in 2001 39 pharmaceutical companies presented a complaint against South Africa, trying to prevent this country passing a law allowing the government to distribute a locally produced low-cost generic HIV treatment which could have saved thousands of lives. The companies argued that the law would undermine the firms' ability to recover the investment made to develop anti-HIV drugs (the complaint was later withdrawn after a global media backlash following a campaign championed by Oxfam). If uniform standards are applied everywhere, the right to life may be subordinated to property rights when these block access to life-saving medicines or seeds in countries haunted by epidemics and famine. Countries

(Continued)

should be able to set their own standards that match local conditions and take a staged approach towards protection of foreign property rights.[64]

Moreover, TRIPS provided an avenue to formalize bio-piracy, the exploitation of developing countries' biodiversity and traditional knowledge by foreign actors. Multinationals – particularly in food and pharmaceuticals – patented traditional medicines and plants used by indigenous people, then claiming property rights on the products developed.[65]

Finally, it's not only developing countries that are affected by TRIPS. Customers in developed countries are also underhanded because enforcing intellectual property creates a temporary monopoly. Therefore property rights reduces competition which means higher prices for consumers everywhere.

TRIPS' criticisms can be encapsulated into three main aspects:

1. Inequality: failure to acknowledge inequalities in income and wealth between countries.
2. Development: prevention of free knowledge diffusion.
3. Competition: tampering with competitiveness and enforced unfair monopolistic advantages.

However, despite criticisms there is a powerful argument in favour of intellectual property rights (IPR). They are needed to encourage innovation. Innovation is a force for development but research and development of new products is very expensive. Sometimes research is paid by the government or philanthropists such Bill and Melinda Gates. However, it is usually profit-oriented companies that take the lion's share in the development of new products and technology. Imagine a pharmaceutical company that has been researching and testing a new medicament for years. It needs to recover its investment with profits from the sales of the drug once it is approved by government agencies. However, without IPR, a competitor can easily copy the product's formula and sell a generic medicament at cut price, since it did not need to recover research costs. Therefore, without the window that IPR give companies to recover their costs, there will be no incentive to innovate. Thus, 'IPR are a "necessary evil". TRIPS try to strike a balance between the need to encourage invention and the desire to spread the benefits of inventions as widely as possible' (Legrain, 2003).[66] This need to achieve a balance between encouraging innovation and spreading its benefits mirrors the need to find a balance between the needs of least-developed, developing and developed countries. This is a challenging task that the WTO bravely attempted during the Doha Round.

The Doha Round

In response to criticisms to agricultural and property rights shortcomings, the WTO opened a new round of trade negotiations in Doha in 2004. The Doha Round aimed to minimize agricultural subsidies and also to implement changes in TRIPS in consonance with developing countries' concerns. A historic consensus seemed to be achieved with the Doha Declaration which explicitly recognized that inequalities in income and wealth should be taken into account: least-developed WTO members do not need to apply patents and data protection rules until 1 January 2016.[67]

Other proposed changes in TRIPS included exceptions to the TRIPS regime in situations of national emergency. Each country determines if a national emergency or circumstance of extreme urgency exists. Parameters are provided on what the WTO regards as an emergency. In particular, it is recognized that HIV/AIDS is an emergency and special flexibility is accorded to it under TRIPS rules.

The Doha Declaration also reduced the market exclusion power of pharmaceutical patent holders in order to minimize efforts of patent holders to persuade or prevent governments from taking advantage of TRIPS agreement flexibilities. Under the original TRIPS a company could deny a country the patent to produce a medicine locally ('in-country patent') and still block efforts to produce or import generic medicines from other countries. In other cases, companies may have in-country patents only for private firms but refuse to give them to governments. They could also set out different prices for the same patent in different countries, using threat of higher prices to obtain prefer-ential treatment from governments.

Under the Doha Declaration, if a medicine is not under patent 'in country', there is no patent barrier to producing locally or importing. On the other hand, if a medicine is under patent 'in country', then government may issue a 'government use' authoriza-tion or 'compulsory licence'. If the patent is deemed too expensive, the government can authorize 'parallel importation', buying the medicine from the country where it is pro-duced at the lowest price. Governments can also negotiate voluntary restrictions, where firms agree to reduce the prices of their medicines in the country in an emergency.[68]

However, a fundamental criticism of TRIPS remained. The WTO should not be the organization in charge of enforcing property rights. Indeed, as argued by Legrain,[69] TRIPS can be seen as a double violation of WTO's reason to be. The Doha Declaration reaffirms that WTO member countries are mandated to enact and enforce regulation protecting the property rights and patents of foreign companies. A country violating TRIPS is hit with WTO authorized trade sanctions by a country whose companies' patents are not being upheld. The WTO's reason to be is all about freeing trade. It is not about 'fair trade'. Property rights create barriers to trade (companies can – for instance – deny licences to potential competitors in countries able to produce and export at lower prices) and TRIPS themselves are enforced with trade sanctions in the form of trade barriers.[70]

As of 2015, implementation of the Doha TRIPS declaration is in deadlock. Although new rules in TRIPS are consensual, developed and developing countries cannot achieve consensus in other elements of the Doha agenda. Developed countries resist reductions in agricultural subsidies while developing countries repel moves towards environmental regulation standards. Caught in the middle, poor countries are deprived of the benefits of agreements on TRIPS. The much-praised single undertaking approach of WTO (noth-ing is agreed until everything is agreed) has proved a stumbling block in helping the poorest countries.[71]

The gap in supranational governance: Regulating foreign investment

We have mentioned before that (as broad simplification) the difference between global-ization and internationalization can be sketched in terms of international trade and port-folio investment representing internationalization, and foreign direct investment (FDI) representing globalization. In previous sections we have glimpsed some impacts of free trade (internationalization) in sustainable development. The verdict is still pending but the evidence seems to highlight that free trade does increase growth, but also inequality and environmental deterioration, as countries with natural resources are forced to overex-ploit them when focusing on their 'competitive advantage' as exporters of commodities.

The WTO, we have seen, has done little to correct this situation, and indeed has blocked efforts to negotiate worldwide environmental and labour standards. The impacts of FDI, on the other hand, are less clear. FDI has always been more controversial than trade. It is only very recently accepted in a majority of countries and there is no supranational organization regulating foreign direct investment. The WTO's efforts in the 1990s to negotiate an agreement eliminating restrictions to FDI were thwarted by a developing countries lobby led by Malaysia and India.[72]

A second attempt to negotiate a 'free FDI' agreement in 2000 was frustrated by the US withdrawing from the agreement in protest at the many exceptions included in it. Similarly, the US and UK successfully lobbied against attempts to create a fourth Bretton Woods institution in charge of regulating excesses of multinational corporations and setting standards for good practice. The argument was that voluntary action and corporate social responsibility were a better course of action than restrictive universal rules.[73]

Detractors of FDI are not convinced by voluntary action. They think that in the absence of a supranational organization constraining the excesses of profit-driven multinationals, the governments of developing countries should have discretion to restrict or plainly forbid FDI. Otherwise, loss of sovereignty will be caused by the dependence on foreign firms. Once an economy becomes dependent on FDI, government attempts to regulate eventual excesses of FDI can be blackmailed by companies threatening to leave the country. As a result, host developing countries could be used as 'pollution havens' where dirty manufacturing activities can be carried on without costly environmental regulations.[74] In turn, unemployment will increase as local industry is competed away by foreign firms. A truncation effect may also happen if the economy as a whole does not develop because the best resources available in the country (e.g. local investors providing capital, qualified labour, land with good accessibility, technology) are seized by foreign investment in a particular industry. This is known as 'Dutch Disease' (Box 8.5).

Box 8.5   Dutch Disease

It was in Holland during the 1960s that truncation effects were first described. The discovery of large gas fields in Groningen attracted a great number of foreign mining companies, which lured qualified workers with generous salaries that manufacturing industries could not afford. Mining companies' need for new technologies and local suppliers led to more and more scientists, entrepreneurs and investors gravitating towards the mining sector. At the same time, the boom in gas exports increased revenues in Holland and the country's currency strengthened compared to its trading partners. Products manufactured in Holland became less competitive to export while imported products became more affordable to Dutch costumers. Demand for Dutch manufacturing declined internally and externally. Manufacturing sales dropped but the costs of production kept increasing as the mining sector's appetite for labour continued to mount (gas exports remained strong during the 1960s, since the global economy was expanding). As a consequence, the expansion of mining was mirrored by a collapse in the productivity of the manufacturing industries.[75]

This process of de-industrialization was called Dutch Disease by *The Economist*.[76] It should be emphasized that truncation effects are neither exclusive to foreign mining investment (in many countries truncation has been triggered by booms in foreign investment in industries other than mining) nor unavoidable.[77] Davies (1995) found no statistical support for the hypothesis that mining FDI will lead to Dutch Disease. He pointed out that truncation can be avoided if governments regulate foreign investment and use the increase in revenues to improve competitiveness in ailing industries.[78]

Supporters (e.g. IMF) believe that FDI is positive and should not be restricted in any way. They emphasize four advantages. First, injection of new capital into an ailing economy, for example, when Volvo bought the heavily indebted construction branch of Samsung in Korea; or when Ford opened automotive manufacturing facilities in Spain. Second, demonstration effects: local companies will learn best practice and new technologies from foreign companies. Third, FDI means that products previously imported are now made in the country, thus reducing imports and potentially increasing exports. An example is Toyota's opening of subsidiaries in the US which minimized car imports from Japan. Fourth, environmental halo: foreign companies bring advanced environmental standards and 'cascade' them in their supply chains.[79]

Pragmatists acknowledge that FDI can have both positive and negative impacts. FDI can expand or exploit national economies, foster or distort economic development, create jobs or destroy them, spread new technology or pre-empt its wider use. Therefore countries should encourage FDI but actively intervene to minimize the occurrence of negativities. Dicken (2011) frames FDI as a dynamic of conflict and collaboration between transnational corporations and national states. He assumes that states and multinational companies (MNCs) need each other, but acknowledges that the fundamental goals of the states and MNCs differ on important terms: MNCs aim to maximize profits and shareholders' value while the states aim to maximize growth of gross domestic product (GDP) and people's well-being.[80]

The extent of the benefits a country can obtain from FDI depends on its bargaining abilities and power. Less powerful countries are unlikely to be able to guarantee FDI outcomes will improve well-being. They rely on the responsibility of foreign firms to self-regulate. This will demand new solutions and new thinking to guarantee sustainable, improved welfare and well-being for future generations. The major players who will contribute to these ends are governments, international organizations and business and they will be charged with finding new solutions and dealing with multiple interests.

A cat-and-mouse game will rear its head because tensions will arise in an attempt to avoid zero sum situations, the pay-off between long and short term. History is a never-ending metamorphosis. Millions of words are being written about today's economic issues and the coming decades will demonstrate if countries, international organizations, business and the private sector have taken prudent decisions to ensure that their present dreams come to fruition. Prudent decisions are based on rationality and evidence rather than ideology. Clear understanding of mechanisms linking globalization and internationalization with consequences to well-being is needed. The second part of this chapter will look at competing theories and empirical evidence unveiling existing patterns and mapping the challenges ahead.

8.2 Consequences of globalization

In Chapter 7 we described different developments that have helped to speed up the globalization process. It's time to take a closer look at the impacts of these developments. What are reasonable expectations for welfare growth and what direction is it taking? Will the world's poor countries' productivity and welfare continue to increase? We will be looking at the consequences of welfare and globalization, keeping in mind that not all influences have been positive. Inequality is a key concern. In China, for example, increasing disparity in income is becoming evident between city dwellers and countryside residents. Globalization has also had an effect on culture and relations between countries. Humanity is being confronted with new questions. When people examine manifestos of political parties it seems as though globalization is not high on the priority list. World welfare has lower priority than national questions. In developed countries, immigration, environment, citizens' rights, social cohesion and sustainable development are currently hot items.

This section will look at the changes globalization has brought for humans as members of contemporary society.

8.2.1   Globalization and people's well-being

Communication technology, less stringent trade barriers, better organized economies and regional and world partnerships have ushered in a new era in world history, though not always in a positive context. New laws and policies often receive a lukewarm reception. Globalization has consequences for people's well-being. Increased dependency between countries may lead to less war and more welfare but dissatisfaction remains. The environment is under pressure and new society demands high flexibility and individualism. There are significant challenges arising from increased integration between national economies, cultures and people. Communication failures and information asymmetries or ambiguities lead to cultural misunderstandings, problems in reconciling conflicting value patterns and trade-offs between individual and collective interests. There is a dizzyingly complex array of issues that contemporary society has to deal with.[81] The well-known German philosopher Sloterdijk argues that rational mental health can only be obtained when people in a culture, sub-culture or community are not continuously confronted with having to choose in existential matters between right and wrong. These confrontations increase when individuals have to deal with multiple value patterns.[82] People prosper when they are part of a community (sphere) that exists when a group of people jointly participate in activities transcending several generations. Sloterdijk asserts that globalization has increased the (specialized) choices of smaller project spheres which has led to people being less content because they are no longer able to experience the 'community' or big picture. It is difficult to create a closed and comfortable world vision in a globalized world which is based on constructs like the true religion or Marxist ideology. People are more conscious than ever that the world has become a multi-polar space. People tend to subconsciously see their immediate situation as a small project.[83] Because we are all involved with different projects throughout our lives, more flexibility is required to deal with changing sets of standards and values. This leads to discomfort (hypothetically) because it makes it difficult to feel at ease. The attempt to reach commonality is a long shot because others in our direct vicinity are also involved in their own form of multi-tasking. Politicians, lawyers and other upholders of justice cease to be pillars of support and external spheres continue to force their way in. This leads to a further erosion of inner peace; more choices are available but it is impossible to link them together.

Cultural relativism also results from globalization and means that people deal differently today with cultural dilemmas. If we take Sloterdijk at his word, globalization will, in due course, eliminate the reassuring feeling of belonging to a community. People will feel less secure despite the many improvements in modern life. The shrinking world and the glut of contradictory information has meant that the concept of community membership has changed forever. In conclusion Sloterdijk states that the entire concept of 'community' has come under pressure and is critical about the creation of a worldwide commonality.[84]

Now that a majority of countries have embraced market economy and are working more closely together to address global challenges, we can cautiously conclude that certain ideals relating to well-being and reduction of poverty are becoming reality. This doesn't apply to everyone but a look at the statistics gives room for optimism. After colonialism, two world wars and a Cold War, government policies in different countries are starting to resemble each other more and more as shown by the increasing amount of new members for the IMF and the WTO. The reciprocal dependence on neighbouring lands is on the increase, which has led to a new sense of competitive spirit.[85, 86] There are no guarantees for continued success. International transport, for example, could suffer if taxes on CO_2 emissions are increased, but on the positive side, recent social and technology innovations seem poised for further expansion. Effective government, the market economy, international business agreements and pure know-how in areas of food production, mass production, hygiene and health care continue to evolve. There will be continued pressure on environmental issues but improved welfare will probably remain the dominant issue.

On the other hand, inequalities are on the rise, both between rich and poor countries and between rich and poor citizens within countries. Is inequality the result of globalization? The next section will discuss theory and evidence.

8.2.2   The age of inequality

Evidence collected by the World Bank during the period 1981–2010 shows that inequality within countries has sharply increased. On the other hand, inequalities between countries have decreased. Arguably, the latter is to great extent the result of rapid growth in East Asian countries.[87] Developing countries such as China, Korea and Singapore are the new economic titans, thus leading to income convergence between countries traditionally classified as developed and developing. However, striking patterns of inequality emerge once we discount the 'new winners': the handful of developing countries that have made impressive progress. What is left is a core of extremely poor countries that benefited substantially less than winners (old and new) from the expansion of global economy and are now being substantially more affected by the current recession.

The Kuznets Curve

Joseph Stiglitz has long been arguing that unfettered globalization and economic growth are major drivers of inequality both between countries and within countries.[88] On the other hand, neoliberal economists are convinced that inequality is just a phase in the development process, a short term consequence of improved welfare in developing countries. They use what is known as the Kuznets Curve or convergence theory to support their beliefs. Simon Kuznets was an American economist that noticed an inverted U-shaped relationship between economic growth and income differential (difference between the income of the richest 25% of population and the poorest 25% of population) in the period between 1940 and 1950. The U-shaped form of the curve was taken to mean that growth increases until there is a turning point when the distribution of the benefits of economic growth become more egalitarian and eventually all sectors of society benefit equally (convergence).[89]

During early stages of growth, the differences in income between rich and poor increase. The reason is that growing economic activity generally concentrates in cities. While urban populations become richer, lack of opportunities in the countryside creates a flow of rural migrants that settle around cities in slums lacking basic welfare infrastructure. Deprived of choice, these migrants take whatever low wages are offered.

However, in time, as economic growth rises and consumption increases, more capital is injected into the economy. With increased demand for labour to satisfy new consumption patterns, wages rise elsewhere. More employment is created in farms and mining sites in the countryside; while the worst problems of urban slums are addressed. This spillover effect means that after a certain point (the turning point in the Kuznets Curve), differences in income start to be reduced.[90]

Applying this theory to interpret current patterns, the explanation for the rise in global within-country inequality is simply the fact that many world economies have been going through the early stages of development. However, since 1995, within-country inequalities have been rapidly rising in countries such as the US, UK, France and Germany which have long passed the early stages in economic growth. According to Kuznets' theory, these countries should have had decreasing inequality, but there is no turning point in sight. Therefore, the relevance of Kuznets' hypothesis in the contemporary global context has become increasingly contested.[91]

Globalization and inequality

One explanation for the growth of inequality in rich countries is that globalization has led to fragmentation of production. Companies organize global supply chains and locate their activities elsewhere in the world looking for cheapest resources. Since low-skilled labour is cheaper and abundant in developing countries, multinationals shift to these countries labour-intensive activities requiring limited skills. Less demand for low-skilled labour leads to unemployment and flexibilities in wages affecting the poorest sectors in developed countries. Even if companies based on developed countries do not relocate or outsource production, inflows of migrants (legal or otherwise) will increase the supply of low-skilled labour. Therefore wages fall, particularly in countries with flexible labour laws allowing short-term contracts and limiting the influence of trade unions. On the other hand, relocation of low-skilled activities leads to skills upgrading in developed countries. Managing fragmented production requires specific skills and demand for high-skilled labour increases as headquarters focus on logistics, research and development, organizational innovation and portfolio management. Thus, inequality widens as increases in wages for high-skilled jobs are matched by decreases in wages for low-skilled jobs.[92]

We will see in the next section another explanation that attempts to elucidate why Kuznets' predictions are no longer supported by evidence. In order to do so, we will first introduce the Long Waves Theory of growth.

Long Waves Theory and inequality

The Austrian School of Economics offers an alternative explanation for growing inequality: The Long Waves Theory of capitalism. This theory proposes that economic growth is not linear. It follows waves: cycles of growth with an inverted U-shape where a period of rising growth is inevitably followed by a declining phase or recession. These waves, usually known as Kondratiev waves or K-waves (named after the Russian economist who proposed its existence) are associated with the expansion, maturity and decline phases of a new technology. Schumpeter combined his own entrepreneurship theories with Kondratiev's ideas. Technology acts as a gale of creative destruction, triggering entrepreneurial opportunities, and new forms of economic organization and competition, which in turn result in social and industrial change (Schumpeter, 1934).[93] Globally, there have been five such waves since the Industrial Revolution. Each of these waves or cycles last more or less 50 years. The global recession that started in 2008 might have been the turning point signalling the beginning of the recessive phase in the last wave.[94]

In terms of inequality, each K-wave can be seen as triggering a new upwards cycle in the Kuznets Curve. The new technology demands new types of skills and renders old skills obsolete, thus generating new patterns of employment and wealth. Moreover, the impacts of technological innovation are biased against low-skilled workers. These are generally less apt to adapt and develop new skills and are also the majority in manufacturing sectors, where the pace of technological change is higher than in service sectors.

Internationalization and inequality within countries

So far we have looked at globalization processes and inequality. Now we move to analyse how internationalization may influence inequality. In this regard, a conceptual milestone is Wolfgang Stolper and Paul Samuelson's Theorem (1954). The theorem conceptualizes inequality between countries as the result of international trade: in a two-factor world (i.e. capital and labour) international trade will increase the real income of one factor of production at the expense of reduction in the other factor's real income. For instance, international trade will increase the real income of capital at the expense of labour.

Box 8.6   Applying the Stolper–Samuelson Theorem

If we have two final goods (software and cattle) and two factors of production (high-skilled labour and low-skilled labour), a decrease in the price of a final good (i.e. cattle) decreases the reward for the factor used intensively in the production of such a good (low-skilled labour) and increases the reward for the other factor (high-skilled labour). Let's assume poor Country A has a protected economy with a) an incipient software industry depending on high-skilled labour; and b) a traditional cattle-raising industry that uses a great deal of low-skilled labour, but also needs high-skilled labour (for instance, to research disease-resistant cross-breeds). If A opens its economy to imports from a Country B, with competitive advantage on software, prices for software will plummet in A. As a consequence, rewards for high-skilled labour will be reduced elsewhere in A; not only in the software industry, but also in the cattle industry.

The Stolper–Samuelson Theorem predicts the outcome of liberalization of trade between two countries B – developed – and A – developing – as follows. When the developing Country A moves from protected trade to open trade, the prices of goods using high-skilled labour fall. Therefore, reward for high-skilled labour declines, but the majority of low-skilled workers benefit. Thus, international trade reduces inequality within poor countries. On the other hand, when Country B (advantaged in high-skilled labour) opens its economy to imports from A (advantaged in low-skilled labour), there will be a decrease in prices of goods using low-skilled labour in B, thus reducing the reward for low-skilled workers elsewhere in the country. Thus, international trade increases inequality within developed countries.

Inequality between countries

The combination of Long Waves Theory with the Stolper–Samuelson Theorem can be used to theorize how growing internationalization and marketization of the economy reinforces differences between poor and rich countries. Each K-wave is associated with a particular geographical region or 'leader' that specializes in the new dominant technology and develops competitive advantage through high-skilled labour for such technology. In a free-market global economy, leader countries will initially benefit more from the new technology than latecomers. However, latecomers with strong institutions in education and research will have developed 'adaptive capabilities'. Adaptive capabilities allow latecomers to speed up learning and catch up with first movers very fast. These capabilities enabled countries such as Taiwan to imitate and upgrade imported technologies, therefore benefiting from catching up with technological change introduced by leaders.[95]

The poorest countries in the world, lacking skilled labour and adaptive capabilities, are initially benefited by falling rewards for low-skilled labour in technologically focused countries, but in the end they are always losers in each new wave of technological change. Imports of the new technology will decrease rewards for high-skilled labour and increase the reward of low-skilled labour, as the country specializes in providing commodities to satisfy demand from a growing economy. As the majority of the low-skilled population benefits, poor countries' economy grows. However, dependence on low-skilled labour creates less long-term value and hinders these countries' chances to become an 'origin country', thus locking poor countries in a pattern of exploitation of dwindling natural resources and cheap labour.

Quantitative evidence seems to support the theory presented above: free trade (or internationalization) tends to increase inequalities between poor and rich countries.[96] On the other hand, there is also an agreement that globalization and fragmentation of production tends to increase within-country inequality.[97] In this case, globalization may increase market failures to allocate a fair value to low-skilled labour. The conclusion seems to be that, in a market economy without corrective mechanisms and state regulation (i.e. neoliberalism), internationalization – international trade – will increase differences between countries while globalization (FDI, global supply chains) will increase differences within countries.

However, this conclusion was shattered in 2014 by an unlikely global bestseller from French economist Thomas Piketty. Neither internationalization nor globalization are the root of inequality, says Piketty, but capitalism itself: the more 'perfect' the market, the more unequal it is, regardless of its degree of internationalization or globalization.

Capitalism and inequality

Piketty's book *Capital in the Twenty-First Century* analyses economic patterns since the beginning of capitalism and provides comprehensive evidence showing that capitalism has always increased inequality. Indeed, he argues, the period of relative decrease in inequality from 1950 to 1980 was an exception caused by the egalitarian devastation brought about by two global wars and a major recession in the 1930s. Such devastation not only caused private wealth to shrink drastically, it also triggered the rise of the welfare state, modelled on US president F. D. Roosevelt's New Deal coalition between trade union movements and the Democratic party.

The welfare state implemented Keynesian policies which aimed to share the benefits of post-war productivity with workers and less-advantaged sectors of society. According to Piketty, as the welfare state retreated and free-market neoliberalism progressed, capitalism's key inequality relationship re-emerged with a vengeance. Such a key inequality relationship is very simple to explain: in perfect markets the rate of return on capital raises above the rate of growth of the economy.[98]

In other words, wealth always grows much faster than economic output. Workers and the poor sectors of the population only benefit from increases in economic output (wage increases and more government resources to invest in welfare). All increase in wealth over economic output is captured by the rich owners of capital. The more concentrated capital becomes, the more unequal the distribution of personal income as, in simpler terms, wealth attracts more wealth.[99]

Piketty further argues that inequality has been steadily rising since 1980 but hasn't yet peaked. Indeed, as more countries complete the transitions to market economies, inequality will escalate to levels unseen in modern history.[100] Despite a spat of controversy with names such as Microsoft founder Bill Gates[101] and the *Financial Times*'s chief economist, Chris Giles, challenging Piketty's conclusions and data collection methods, there is widespread agreement that Piketty's methods are as robust as possible considering the data available.[102, 103] The conclusions stand out: as argued by Marx more than two centuries ago, capitalism has caused rampant inequality. Piketty's finding directly contradicts Kuznets' hypothesis, which in Piketty's view was only valid in the post-war decades because the high level of redistributive state intervention controlled capitalism's bias towards inequality.[104]

So, capitalism created inequality, but is that inevitable? A pattern happened in the past, but that does not necessarily mean that it will be repeated in the future. Piketty agrees, saying that inequality can be corrected in the future with heavy taxes on capital. However, this will require a politically unfeasible international agreement to apply a substantial universal tax on wealth in every country. Otherwise, in a globalized economy, capital will fly away from countries with heavy taxes to low-tax paradises.

More crucially, the question we may ask is whether inequality is necessarily such a bad thing. As long as those in the lower levels of society are out of poverty and have sufficient means to make a living, why should it be important that the richest 1% of the world captures 90% of growth in wealth? Indeed, isn't inequality a drive for individual progress and achievement? Those who have less are motivated to work harder or innovate to reach the standards of those who have more. Such social mobility dynamics keep society going, and as Bill Gates argues in his blog, many of the mega-rich of today are the sons and daughters of poor families.[105]

Piketty has two counter-arguments. First, many of today's new mega-rich entrepreneurs were raised in a world dominated by welfare state policies that gave relief to their poor families. Moreover, welfare states capped the power of incumbent mega-rich, thus giving way to new entrepreneurs.[106] The second counter-argument relates to the extent of inequality. A gradient of wealth between more and less favoured is desirable since it creates social mobility. However, as argued vehemently by Joseph Stiglitz in *The Price of Inequality*, the current level of inequalities within most countries will lead to social polarization and the fracture of social cohesion.[107]

When social cohesion is fractured there is no working together towards common objectives, consequences range from apathy, disinterest and demoralization to an increase in criminal activities, violence and terrorism.[108] Democracy and freedom are impossible when just a few monopolize wealth and power to influence policy.[109] Social and political instability will without doubt affect prospects for growth.[110] Ignoring the consequences of inequalities within a country is myopic.[111]

In turn, inequalities between countries will prevent balanced governance of globalization. Inequalities undermine trust, a precondition for international agreements based on collective action.[112] Lloyd (2009) points out that unsustainable economic inequality between countries was a trigger for global wars. Inequality fuels resentment between countries and within societies. It drives economic migration and global terrorism.[113]

Can we make globalization work towards global justice?

Is globalization exacerbating the inequalities created by capitalism as argued by the anti-globalization movement?[114] Stiglitz argues that the problem is not globalization (transplanetary integration) but internationalization (free trade) paired with neoliberalism (weak state). Indeed, Stiglitz is convinced that is possible to have a capitalist system without excessive inequality, but such system is not neoliberal but Keynesian.[115] Piketty agrees with this; he points out how Keynesian redistributive policies effectively reduced inequality in many countries and still underlie Scandinavian and East Asian economic models.[116]

As we mentioned before, Piketty thinks that the world needs international agreements to set standards on higher taxes for the mega-rich (see for instance the Tobin tax). Stiglitz thinks we need more globalization, but a type of globalization that is inclusive, with global governance that re-enacts the dream of Bretton Woods: a new world of countries working together to address the challenges of humankind.[117]

8.2.3   Globalization and financial crisis

We described in Chapter 2 how crises can be caused by weaknesses in the domestic financial sector (solvency hypothesis) or by self-fulfilling prophecies (liquidity hypothesis). In the former hypothesis, institutions are overcapitalized owing to bubbles, and their market value is much higher than it should be given their actual incomes. In the latter hypothesis, investors lose confidence in the ability of the financial sector to repay them. This triggers a run to withdraw funds from the system. Short-term shortages of capital to satisfy mounting requests of investors lead to institutions being forced to sell their assets at short notice. Eventually, financial institutions cannot work if leakages of savings continue; they then become unable to repay. In practice, most crises are a result of a combination of both causes, which mutually reinforce each other in 'vicious circles'.

Capital account liberalization increases both liquidity and solvency problems. Capital account liberalization is risky because it makes countries vulnerable to changes in investors' sentiment, affecting liquidity (particularly in countries without strong banks and mature stock markets). 1996's Asian crisis, 1998's Russian crisis and 2001's Argentinian crisis were all triggered by capital account liberalization. Unsustainable high levels of foreign debt resulted from unchecked capital inflows. Countries were forced into contractionary policies, such as cuts in social spending, to keep up with debt obligations. The catastrophic US sub-prime crisis was also influenced by capital account liberalization. 'Toxic debt' was sold to foreign investors through collateral debt obligations (CDO) and other financial instruments. High levels of foreign debt fuelled the sub-prime market bubble.[118]

Capital foreign capital flows are pro-cyclical. They flow out of a country in a recession, when the country needs them, and flow in during a boom, exacerbating inflationary pressure or overvaluation of currency. Pro-cyclicality means that capital liberalization is a boomerang leading to looming crisis. Therefore, capital account controls are needed to prevent excess of capital during booms and massive flights during busts.[119]

What is the relation of globalization to capital flows? First, globalization increases opportunities for portfolio capital mobility, as investors can operate 24 hours a day, 7 days a week in stock markets in New York, London, Tokyo or Shanghai. Second, global integration in procedures and transplanetary connectivity in the financial industry (one of the few truly global industries) means that transactions can be implemented in real time across the world, with only seconds of delay once the decision to move capital has been made. Therefore, decisions taken in a country can spread almost immediately over the world, without margin for political interference or negotiation. Think how different the case is for a company that wants to withdraw foreign direct investment, which is a more lengthy process.

Third, the Washington Consensus (IMF, World Bank, US Treasury) pushed capital account liberalization policies worldwide; even in countries with high savings rates and little need for foreign capital, such as Korea. We have seen already how risky capital account liberalization policies are.

Box 8.7   The IMF and three decades of crisis

The IMF made serious mistakes in its initial response to the East Asian crisis in 1996, when it advised against capital controls (first round of mistakes) and later recommended contractionary policies triggering recessive effects (second round of mistakes).[120]

In Russia the IMF pushed fast privatization, liberalization and austerity measures without proper governance structures in place to deal with their consequences in terms of employment and inequality. The IMF provided bail-outs, even when it was clear they stimulated moral hazards. High levels of corruption meant that the funds provided by the IMF were misused; often directly transferred to foreign accounts. The Russian crisis of 1997 ensued, and the country devalued its currency and defaulted in its foreign debt.

A very similar pattern of IMF mistakes in structural adjustment policies ended up with the Argentinian crisis in 2001, even when Argentina had been lavishly praised by the IMF only months ago. Scalded, the IMF acknowledged mistakes.

However, changes are slow. In the build up to the sub-prime crisis, the US Treasury promoted the same type of capital account liberalization policy advocated by the IMF[121] in East Asia, Russia and Argentina, again with catastrophic results. Yet again, Stiglitz notes that IMF intervention during the Greek crisis in 2013 is underpinned by the same ideological fixation on structural adjustment and recessive policies applied in Argentina.

However, IMF's failures tend to have much exposure than its successes. When the IMF has got it right, there has been no crisis and therefore no headlines. Its role of lender of last resort – moral hazard aside – has been fundamental to boost confidence and avoid a crisis in ailing economies. The consensus against IMF owes a lot to Joseph Stiglitz's powerful characterization of the IMF as the villain; a villain that created economic crisis with the betrayal of its Keynesian mission. However, corrupt (or simply misguided) governments and irresponsible companies are also to blame for crises. In 2002, Benjamin Friedman wrote that Stiglitz made the best possible case against the IMF. He also asked if somebody would take the challenge of 'writing the best possible book laying out the other side of the argument' but such a book is still elusive.[122, 123]

Although anti-globalization movements associate the Washington Consensus with globalization, we have seen that it should be more accurately associated with neoliberalism. If global institutions had applied a different type of policy, crises could have been avoided. Therefore, crises are not always an inevitable consequence of globalization. They could be prevented with a less ideological stance on capital control and taxes on capital flows and wealth: implement them when needed, as recommended by neo-Keynesians.

However, globalization also contributes to dissemination of crises due to a) supply chain, financial and trade linkages and interdependencies; b) contagion effects in investor behaviour. Globalizing world economies are becoming increasingly integrated and interdependent through trade and supply chains. Crisis in one country cascades down to its trade partners, whereas the problems of multinationals affect foreign companies involved in the multinational supply chain. Fernando Solanas's award-winning movie on the Argentinian crisis, 'A Social Genocide', illustrates how multinationals, particularly banks, can increase a country's level of foreign debt as subsidiaries receive loans from their headquarters. High levels of foreign debt make a country vulnerable to speculative attacks.

Contagion effects refer to the withdrawal of foreign capital from countries that are perceived by foreign investors as likely to be affected by a financial crisis in another country. In some cases such a perception has a real basis (for example when economies are closely integrated through trade or supply chains or when countries share a similar economic model). In other cases, the loss of confidence in a country is merely based on geographical proximity to a country in crisis. Contagion effects created a capital withdrawal domino effect in Asian economies after the start of the crisis in Thailand. Eventually contagion also affected Russia as investors exited from all 'emerging markets'. In the sub-prime, contagion effects made the crisis global. Since toxic debt (debt which could not be repaid to banks by its debtors) was hidden in CDOs (collateralized debt obligations, see Section 2.7), the credibility of the whole global financial system was affected since it was impossible to assert the extent of toxic debt acquired by foreign institutions.

From these aspects, it transpires that globalization increases the vulnerability to financial crisis in those countries more dependent on highly mobile foreign capital – countries with high levels of debt in foreign currency and poorly developed local financial markets – and in countries that make themselves targets for speculators with fixed exchange rates combined with capital account liberalization, as it was the case in Argentina.

 ### 8.3   Case Study: The World Bank faces competition

For many years the World Bank and the IMF were the only organizations providing loans at taxes below market levels for countries in distress, or without interest to poorest countries. Nowadays, poor countries have more options for obtaining loans. Brazil, China and India have established their own developmental banks and are making significant inroads in Africa, Asia and Latin America. Their interest rates are sometimes higher than World Bank rates but they recommend a different developmental model without Washington Consensus neoliberal conditionalities. The Chinese Developmental Bank (CDB), which is bigger than the World Bank, with assets over U\$350 billion, recommends the hybrid socialist market Chinese model,[124] the so-called Beijing Model (BM), a Chinese development model which advocates for state regulation, prudence in market openness and political neutrality in foreign markets.[125] The Brazilian Development Bank (BNDES)[126] champions neo-Keynesian development policies and industrial policies which share the emphasis on institutions rather than markets, promoted by Stiglitz's new structuralism economics.[127] Brazil and China are the driving forces behind two new multilateral banks challenging World Bank dominance and reflecting the growing power of developing economies: the New Development Bank, funded by BRIC countries (Brazil, Russia, India, China), and the Chinese-led Asian Infrastructure Development Bank (AIDB).[128] Ironically, a globalized market with a variety of ideological offers might be the Washington Consensus's undoing as the following examples suggest

(Continued)

Ghana has recently discovered offshore oil and gas fields. The state-owned Ghanaian oil company approached the World Bank asking for resources to build a platform for extraction and pipelines to transport the gas. However, after several months of negotiations, Ghana decided to use Chinese funding instead. The reasons given by the president were that negotiations with the World Bank had been tiresome and too time-consuming, requiring conditions 'detached' from the political reality of Ghana. The pipeline is already in construction, under an agreement by which Ghana will repay most of the $3 billion loan with gas (a fixed % of volume produced) rather than currency. Some of the 'tiresome' conditions required by the World Bank, but not by China, were an environmental impact assessment and a public consultation with the indigenous tribes that will have their lands expropriated to build the pipeline.[129]

The Brazilian Development Bank, on the other hand, is funding monumental construction projects in neighbours Bolivia and Argentina. The viability of some of these projects is dubious, but the Brazilian bank does not question whether the project is really needed as far as the borrowers employ Brazilian construction companies and import Brazilian products.[130] Brazil also provides funds for Mozambique to buy Brazilian first-generation biofuel technology using maize or sugar cane as a raw material.[131] The World Bank would be more cautious since first-generation biofuel production, as we saw in Chapter 3, represents a threat to food security in poor countries such as Mozambique.

The risk of this new wave of funding is that developmental loans will become a race to the bottom, where developmental banks compete with each other on the basis of offering less stringent environmental and human rights conditions (as the World Bank was criticized for doing before its current 'governance' approach).[132] However, both Brazil and China have insisted that the New Development Bank will endeavour to follow and upgrade World Bank best practice on environmental, labour and procurement standards.[133]

Case Study Questions

1. How do Chinese and Brazilian developmental loans differ from World Bank loans?
2. How can competition between developmental banks affect sustainable development?
3. Does globalization play a role in this case?

8.4   Learning tools

8.4.1   Summary

- This chapter looked at the positive and negative impacts of globalization. It differentiated conceptually between consequences of globalization and consequences of internationalization and liberalization. More empirical data is needed to arrive at conclusions. Evidence shows that inequality has been growing faster than growth for the last three decades. In particular a sharp increase of inequality

(Continued)

has occurred within developed countries and between developing and developed countries.

- The causes and long-term impacts of inequality are controversial. Kuznets sees inequality as a temporary consequence of development, while Stopler and Samuelson see it as the permanent consequence of international trade. In a market economy without corrective mechanisms and state regulation (i.e. neoliberalism) an increase in internationalization – international trade – will increase differences between countries while an increase in globalization (foreign direct investment, global supply chains) will increase differences between the more and less advantaged within a country. The losers are the poorest countries and poorest people in developed countries.

- Globalization increases the vulnerability to financial crisis in those countries more dependent on highly mobile foreign capital – those with high levels of debt in foreign currency and poorly developed local financial markets – and in countries that make themselves targets for speculators with fixed exchange rates combined with capital account liberalization.

- The solutions to inequality and financial instability are the same: inclusive globalization, a type of economic relationship integrating economic systems worldwide; and creating interdependencies between national political systems through supranational institutions providing global governance. The supranational institutions are at the centre of a 'web of interdependencies'. The nation state is now not the only or perhaps the most important seat of power. All supranational institutions are of great importance but the chapter focuses on the Bretton Woods institutions defining the global financial system: the International Monetary Fund (IMF), World Bank and World Trade Organization (WTO).

- All three institutions are controversial. Some of the questions raised by their detractors are: is there still a reason for the existence of some supranational institutions? Have they all been efficient in their missions? The chapter argues that there is a pressing need for their existence. They fulfil the role of assuring governance of global economy across nations.

- However, growing inequality, resilient extreme poverty and recurrent financial instability cast doubt on their efficiency. Bretton Woods failures are in no minor part due to the substitution of rationality for ideology through the so-called Washington Consensus. Neither is the defence of the market the mission of the IMF (it is to assure financial stability); nor is championing structural adjustment the mission of World Bank; nor is the defence of property rights the mission of WTO.

8.4.2 Further reading

Dicken, P. (2014). *Global Shift: Mapping the Changing Contours of the World Economy* (pp. 537–547). London: Paul Chapman. See, in particular, chapters about the impacts of FDI in home and host economies and in the natural environment.

Peet, R. (2008). *The Geography of Power: The Making of Global Economic Policy*. Oxford: Oxford University Press.

Rodrik, D. (2006). Goodbye Washington Consensus, hello Washington confusion? *Journal of Economic Literature, 44*, 973–987.

Stiglitz, J. (2002). *Globalization and its Discontents*. London: Penguin.

Stiglitz, J. (2012). *The Price of Inequality: How Today's Divided Society Endangers Our Future*. London: Penguin.

8.4.3   Assignments

 Assignment 8.1

Globalization has meant that a number of problems confronting society can only be solved in a global context. Today's supranational organizations are not sufficiently set up to handle these problems. Name two policy areas where your country's interests would be served by developing improved international administrative powers. Present and defend your arguments.

Suggest two administrative areas that could remain the matter of an individual country. Present and defend your arguments.

 Assignment 2.2

In the last five years, Tanzania, Angola, USA and Canada have achieved contrasting levels of economic growth and inequality. Discuss the arguments that could help to explain the difference in these four countries. Make use of the theories and arguments presented in this and previous chapters.

 Assignment 8.3

Discuss to what extent the Bretton Woods institutions have been responsive to criticisms and have changed in the last two decades. Analyse each institution separately, explaining what aspects have been reformed or not, why and how.

8.4.4   Self-test questions

 Self-test Questions

1. Explain why inequality is a problem.
2. Explain the Stopler–Samuelson Theorem.
3. What is the Kuznets Curve? Is it relevant in a globalized economy?
4. Outline three criticisms of each Bretton Woods organization.
5. Describe differences between the Washington Consensus, augmented consensus and benevolent consensus.
6. Discuss the pros and cons of FDI.
7. Explain the consequences of globalization in a financial crisis.
8. Why is pro-cyclicality a risk?

PART III

BUSINESS IMPLICATIONS OF 'GLOBALIZATION' AND SUSTAINABILITY

9

INNOVATIONS IN GLOBAL SUPPLY NETWORKS

Overview and learning objectives

Globalization created very complex worldwide industrial supply chains and networks for production and distribution of materials and products all over the world. This chapter tries to explain how the dynamics of supply and network management occur in practice. It also explains that within the context of corporate social responsibility (CSR, Chapter 10) companies are increasingly being held responsible for the societal (social and environmental) impacts during the whole life cycle of products and in their international supply chains and networks.

For assessing the environmental and social impacts of products during the life cycle, tools are used to determine the most important aspects and the most relevant phases so strategies for improvements can be developed. Life cycle assessment (LCA) methodologies and the principles of Cradle to Cradle are explained. How the results of these assessments are being used in new cooperation's in supply networks and for the development of new business models is described and illustrated with examples. The fashion/clothing industry is used to illustrate the development of new, more sustainable strategies and activities in its supply network. Because innovations towards more sustainable supply networks do not only occur in big mainstream networks, sectors and companies using grassroots innovations are also examined in this chapter.

Learning objectives

This chapter will enable the student to:

- Understand the impact of globalization on worldwide international cooperation between businesses.
- Understand the basic principles of and the dynamics in international supply chain and industrial network management.
- Know that companies are increasingly being held responsible for the social and environmental impacts in the whole supply chain.
- Know how resources and materials are managed in supply chains and why and how recycling of these resources and materials is increasing.
- Understand the environmental impacts of products during their life cycle and the principle of life cycle assessment (LCA).

(Continued)

● Understand the Cradle to Cradle principle and have insight into the consequences of the introduction of this principle.
● Know what a circular economy is, versus a linear economy, and how new business models are being developed for integration of sustainability in supply chains and networks.
● Know why and how grassroots innovations take place for the development of more sustainable supply networks.
● Understand how these developments take place in the fashion/clothing sector.

9.1   Increasing international business activity

In previous chapters a number of macro developments were discussed that have led to intensified international business traffic and globalization. Among other things, we stated that many countries with low productivity have found easy and practical ways to increase growth. Policies aimed at stimulating business activity have proven effective and a feeling of optimism exists in many emerging and developing economies. The number of countries with an economic growth of more than 5% is creating a dynamic in society. Business people and investors are attracted to the new opportunities and develop fresh initiatives. These initiatives put added pressure on the environment and more companies are confronted with sustainability issues. A second noticeable trend is the decrease in scale of those enterprises aspiring to international operations. It is expected that more and more small businesses will expand to an international level. The new communications technology gives them better outsourcing possibilities and puts them in a better position to enter international trade.

Globalization's increase has meant that division of labour is becoming a continuing process. The 'stand-alone' factory that purchases its raw materials and afterwards produces all parts relating to the final product is becoming a thing of the past. Suppliers of materials, machines and special parts will base their operations on cooperation with others, and global material sourcing will increase rather than decrease. The Internet and expanded intercontinental transport possibilities has meant that actual production location is becoming less important. Nonetheless, cost will continue to play an important role, certainly in future situations where energy issues are at stake. This is certainly the case if 'external costs' of transport are included in the service or product being provided and will have a slow-down effect on the internationalization of business activity. This is, however, an important field that has a stimulating effect on international trade. Whether this happens or not will strongly depend on the type of activity.

To determine if business activities are location linked, they are divided into the following categories:[1]

● Source-linked business activities.
● Market-linked business activities.
● Footloose business activities.

A business is source linked if raw materials are required that are cumbersome, large in volume, or perishable. Brick factories, for example, are usually located close to a river where clay can be easily obtained and cotton and fruit producers are often to be found in areas that are close to where the products are harvested.

Business activities such as health care, restaurants and sales are market linked because these services are directly related to the customer. The sale of less complex items and services can often be done by telephone or the Internet but these are also partially market linked because they must be delivered quickly. Language and culture also play a role in sales and transport costs so can sometimes be included as well. Soft drink companies, but also brick producers, are usually to be found in close proximity to their customer base to avoid excessive transport fees. See Box 9.1 for more on transport costs.

Box 9.1   Transport between two continents

Transport costs can be the determining factor in trade between two continents. Air freight fees, in particular, are high. This means that lightweight products with a relatively high worth are often transported by air. There are examples, however, of cheaper goods which also depend on air transport. A good example of this are roses produced in Kenya. Air transport costs for one bouquet of roses are about 10% of the consumer retail price. This low figure can only be realized with regularly scheduled flights and a minimum cargo. For example, there are weekly flights with fully laden aircraft, packed with flowers, taking place between Amsterdam's Schiphol airport and the Kenyan airport located close to the flower growers. In addition, transaction costs must not be forgotten and these include management hours and chauffeur hours which are linked to government red tape, plus the fact that the country's infrastructure remains a problem. By contrast, to send a container 7000 km from the American city of Baltimore to Holland costs only €1500, while expenses incurred to send the same container 6000 km to Lima, Peru rises to €4000.[2]

In addition to source-linked business activity we also have footloose activities. These can include client contact, language and culture, transport costs and client-related product specifications, all of which have a less important function. A prime example of this are mass producers who have very limited production plants which supply the whole world. The Internet has created an increase of footloose activities. Customer-orientated software for American and European companies can be developed as far away as India. Business administration is often outsourced to countries where low incomes are the norm. The same trend is taking place for numerous call centres. In India alone, there are call centres with more than 10,000 employees to cover the North American and British markets. Quality is improved by providing language courses for employees to use 'British English', as the locally spoken English can be difficult to understand.

9.2   Products, materials and resources

9.2.1   Materials management

The goal of materials management is to provide an unbroken chain of resources for the manufacturing of products. The materials department is charged with releasing materials to a supply base, ensuring that the materials are delivered on time to the company using the correct carrier. Materials are generally measured by accomplishing on-time delivery to the customer, on-time delivery from the supply base, attaining a freight budget, inventory shrink management, and inventory accuracy. The materials department is also charged with the responsibility of managing new launches. In some companies materials management is charged with the procurement of materials by establishing and managing a supply base. In other companies the procurement and management of the supply base is the responsibility of a separate purchasing department. The purchasing department is then responsible for the purchased price variances from the supply base. In large companies with multitudes of customer changes to the final product over the course of a year, there might be a separate logistics department that is responsible for all new acquisition launches and customer changes. This logistics department ensures that the launch materials are procured for production and then transfers the responsibility to the plant materials management.

The major challenge that materials managers face is maintaining a consistent flow of materials for production. There are many factors that inhibit the accuracy of inventory, which results in production shortages, premium freight, and often inventory adjustments. The major issues that all materials managers face are incorrect bills of materials, inaccurate cycle counts, unreported scrap, shipping errors, receiving errors, and production reporting errors. Materials managers have striven to determine how to manage these issues in the business sectors of manufacturing since the beginning of the industrial revolution.

9.2.2   Scarcity of resources and the need for recycling

Up until now, material management was described as a method to move materials forward in the supply network, often called forward logistics. As mentioned in Chapter 5 many natural resources are becoming more and more difficult to extract from the earth or from ecosystems. Water, phosphate, cotton and other resources were mentioned as examples. At the same time the demand for many of these materials is increasing worldwide. This means that the prices go up and the question arises about how these materials could be recycled.

Companies looking for eco-efficiency start realizing that in addition to their product, the systems relating to its manufacture are becoming equally important. The environmental impacts of a product can be decreased by recycling the materials when the company controls the cycles. This includes not only production, distribution and purchase of the product but also includes the final link – the waste phase, when the product is no longer in use. Companies play an important role in this process. They know their products and if these can be disposed of and returned in a proper manner, companies can assist in the improvement of eco-effectiveness. This is due to the know-how they have concerning the materials used in production. Generally speaking, they also have more possibilities of incorporating the used building blocks into new goods. Even the environmental impacts of harmful or damaging materials can be reduced drastically if they circulate sufficiently within a long-lasting cycle.

In Chapter 5 the technical aspects for recycling were mentioned. To get the materials back, the field of material management should be increased and the waste phase of the life cycle of products is becoming part of material management strategies. The question is how to get back the materials that have been used in the products so they can be used for making new products. This means that the supply chain is being redesigned and these changes are being recognized as one of the important 'drivers' for change towards the implementation of CSR in business. Closing the loop[3] needs the opposite approach from traditional forward logistics and is covered by the field of reverse logistics (see Figure 9.1).[4]

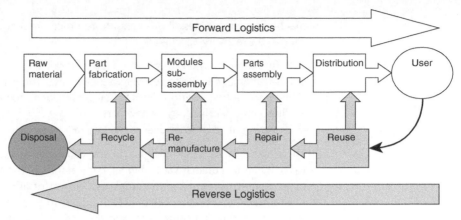

Figure 9.1 The close relationship between the supply chain and reverse logistics[5]

Reverse logistics stands for all operations related to the reuse of products and materials. It is 'the process of moving goods from their typical final destination for the purpose of capturing value, or proper disposal. Remanufacturing and refurbishing activities also may be included in the definition of reverse logistics'[6] Growing green concerns and advancement of green supply chain management concepts and practices make it all the more relevant. The reverse logistics process includes the management and the sale of surplus as well as returned equipment and machines from the hardware leasing business. Normally, logistics deal with events that bring the product towards the customer. In the case of reverse logistics, the resource goes at least one step back in the supply chain. For instance, goods move from the customer to the distributor or to the manufacturer.

When a manufacturer's product normally moves through the supply chain network, it is to reach the distributor or customer. Any process or management after the sale of the product involves reverse logistics. If the product was defective, the customer would return it. The manufacturing firm would then have to organize shipping of the defective product, testing the product, dismantling, repairing, recycling or disposing of the product. The defective product would travel in reverse through the supply chain network in order to retain any use. Because transport is rather cheap and the companies want to unburden the customer, more and more reverse logistics are increasingly being developed as part of new business models for the circular economy (see Box 9.2, and Sections 9.5.3 and 9.5.4).

Box 9.2   Reverse logistics at IBM

IBM is a leading manufacturer of IT machines and services. Annually, the company is responsible for several ten thousand tonnes of reverse goods flows worldwide in several categories.[7]

The first category is used machines. Used products mainly come from the business market. The sources of used product returns are returns of leased products, trade-in offers and environmental take-back programmes in which any used products are taken back by IBM if customers want to get rid of them. Generally, the used

(Continued)

machines from business customers are returned through a national distribution centre. The recovery options are:

- Refurbishment, when considered eligible for reselling.
- Dismantling, in order to recover valuable parts. The parts enter the spare parts network, but another option is to sell generic parts to external parties. Dismantling is cheaper than buying new parts.
- Recycling, in order to recover secondary raw materials.

The return flow of used machines in the consumer market is not collected individually, but in a branch-wide manner. For instance, in the Netherlands, IBM is part of a system organized by the Dutch association of information and technology producers. Municipalities collect used products from different manufacturers, ship them to recycling subcontractors and the costs are divided among the members, corresponding with the amount of products in the return flow.

IBM and GEODIS, a supply chain operator, collaborate on the reverse logistics of IBM's 'end-of-lease' personal computers.[8] The customer collection of the personal computers throughout Europe is organized by GEODIS and the computers are brought to GEODIS's Asset Recovery Centre in which, for example, computers are tested, repaired and dismantled. The key success factors of the management of the reverse goods flow are:

- Responsibility and control over end-to-end process.
- Hybridstrategy: both efficient and responsive.
- Quality of rework.
- Flexibility in capacity.
- Dedicated division for reverse logistics.
- Clear disposition trees.
- Process visibility.

The second category is unused machines. The unused products also mainly come from the business market. The return flow of unused products exists because of retailers, who can return parts of their unsold stock against refunding, and customers, who have the right to cancel their order. By taking into account the technically new condition of unused products, IBM's priority is to resell them. Reselling unused products is highly time-critical due to the short product life cycles. Therefore, another option is to provide input to production processes by disassembling the unused products. The last option is letting the unused products go through the same circuit as used products by parts dismantling or recycling.

The last category is rotable spare parts. The spare parts serve to support IBM's service activities. The spare parts stock consist both of good parts and repaired parts. As a result, keeping parts instead of buying them creates a closed loop that reduces procurement costs. In addition, dismantled used products are a source of spare parts. Although this alternative is considered cheap, the downside is that it is uncertain which components the used products contain as it is possible that brokers or customers rearranged the settings. Quality is considered as another problem. In this case, dismantling is again a cheap option yet in order to confirm and guarantee the quality of spare parts of used products, expensive examination is necessary.

IBM has established Global Asset Recovery Services (GARS). GARS is mainly concerned with the allocation of globally returned products to reuse options on a product, part and material level, which results in an annual financial benefit of several hundred million US$.

9.3 Assessment of product life cycles

9.3.1 Environmental aspects of products

The insight is increasing that the environmental aspects of products should be evaluated looking at the whole life cycle of the product (see Figure 9.2).[9] Every life cycle starts with the mining of the materials. After the extraction of the materials from the earth (material extraction phase) they are processed and used for manufacturing products (manufacturing phase) that are used by consumers (user phase) and after use end up in landfill, incinerator or are recycled (end-of-life phase). The environmental aspects can be very different in these phases and improving aspects in one phase often causes increase of environmental impacts in another phase.

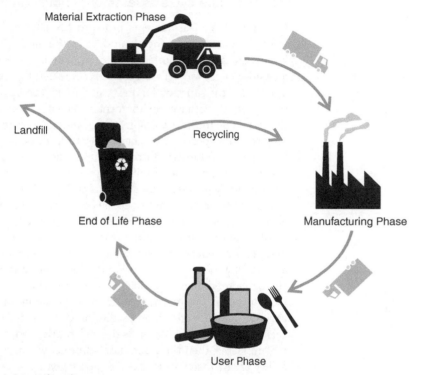

Figure 9.2 Life cycle stages

Therefore improving the environmental performance of products should evaluate all environmental aspects during all these phases and the improvements should focus on optimization of the whole life cycle and not only one phase. Eighteen environmental aspects are used for the evaluation and they are categorized into three groups of environmental impacts concerning human health, ecosystems and resources. This methodology for aggregating the environmental aspects in categories to develop environmental indicators for products is called ReCiPe[10].

9.3.2 Life cycle assessment (LCA)

The concept of life cycle assessment was introduced in the 1980s and is an instrument used to determine the environmental impacts of a product during its whole life cycle. The analysis looks at items during the entire life cycle including scarcity of raw materials and their extraction plus the accompanying environmental impacts. Transport, production methods, harmful emissions and waste disposal come under scrutiny, as well as environmental consequences during the product's active life and disposal phase. The LCA now has accepted standards set up by the ISO (International Standards Organization). The first prerequisite for any LCA research is to determine the scope of the study. This can be very complicated especially in situations when a manufacturer purchases raw materials in different countries. Difficulties can increase if the manufacturer is dealing with multiple distribution links and different target groups who use the product in varying ways. By limiting the scope of the LCA it becomes easier to achieve results and also leaves room for criticism because the study does not include all of the variables (see Box 9.3).

Box 9.3   Life cycle assessment choice of criteria

Objective LCA measurements prove to be difficult. Complications occur if, for example, a company brings a product to the market using clean technology but it ends up causing pollution when it is put to use. It is possible that LCA can have a positive effect for 'light users' when compared to competitive goods. This is the opposite of the situation for 'heavy users' who can be better off buying a competitor's product because environmental benefits during the product's lifetime are deemed to be more important. LCA remains difficult to work with but in fact is the only tool that provides insight into a product's positive or negative environmental impacts. To further illustrate this, serious discussions took place in the 1990s concerning the benefits of milk being sold in cartons or returnable glass bottles. The dairy industry preferred using cartons and said that the LCA of returnable deposit bottles made no difference since the bottle was made of glass, thus requiring more energy to produce. Furthermore, cleaning the bottles involved abrasive soaps and extra transport was necessary to bring the empty bottles back to the factory. LCA findings are dependent on assumptions that are made on the intensity of reuse and the distances to be covered in order to bring the product to the consumer. Furthermore, different variables have to be compared which, in the end, remain incomparable. This means that normative opinion forming plays a role. The LCA assigns a value for the wood used to produce the milk carton as well as the sand, calcium and soda used to make the milk bottle. If we assume that a raw material is replenish able, then the wood-based product will have the advantage. If the availability of raw materials is taken as a point of departure then the glass bottle can achieve a high score because sand, calcium and soda are not scarce items.

Extensive research was done in the 1980s and 1990s into LCA carton packaging because many milk producers had abandoned the glass bottle. Tetra Pak is a worldwide leading food packaging company. It was criticized by environmental groups because of the environmental impacts of carton packaging. This was a good reason for them to initiate an LCA study and change to an active environmental policy. The results of research done in the areas of bottle versus carton show a more effective environmental result through the use of cartons instead of glass.[11]

LCA analysis can give a complete picture of a product's environmental impacts and proves to be a good instrument for comparing two similar items because all aspects are being considered.[12] Central databases come into play and provide information on the environmental impacts of different raw materials. LCA is a useful tool for governmental and certifying organizations who create policy to determine which products are most suitable for certain eco labels.

Despite this, it is not always necessary to perform the analysis. Tropical hardwood coming from replanted forests (FSC certificate) can, without LCA, be compared with uncertificated hardwood.

ISO 14040:2006[13] describes the principles and framework for life cycle assessment (LCA) including: definition of the goal and scope of the LCA, the life cycle inventory analysis (LCI) phase, the life cycle impact assessment (LCIA) phase, the life cycle interpretation phase, reporting and critical review of the LCA, limitations of the LCA, the relationship between the LCA phases, and conditions for use of value choices and optional elements (see Figure 9.3). The inventory phase makes an inventory for all the stages of the life cycle of all the resources used and of all the emissions to the air, water, soil and in waste production. The impact assessment phase assesses all the environmental impacts caused by the use of resources and the emissions and the waste production.

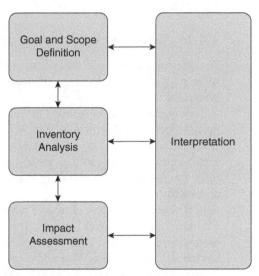

Figure 9.3   Life cycle assessment according to ISO 14040[14]

ISO 14040:2006 covers LCA studies and life cycle inventory (LCI) studies. It does not describe the LCA technique in detail, nor does it specify methodologies for the individual phases of the LCA. In the market many LCA software programs have been developed and are offered to companies for conducting LCAs for their products.[15]

9.3.3   Social assessment of a product life cycle

Product life cycle analysis has not only been used for environmental aspects but also for social life cycle analysis,[16] which has been applied for some decades to determine the social aspects in the supply network and prioritize them towards a strategy and selective activities.

Social impact is the effect of a product on three stakeholder groups: workers, consumers and local communities. These stakeholder groups are correlated with the different life cycle stages of the product: sourcing, manufacturing, use phase and end-of-life.

Unlike other methods, product social impact assessment looks at the product level instead of the corporate level. The method identifies points of excellence, improvement opportunities and social hotspots throughout the life cycle of a product, and does not just focus on the supply chain and managing risks. The development of this method is an important step towards establishing a standard for social impact assessment.

Product social impact assessment is designed to address three main objectives:

- Make positive and negative impacts of products measurable and visible.
- Support decision making and communication at product level.
- Contribute to overall sustainability assessment.

The method is described in the *Handbook for Product Social Impact Assessment*[17] and was developed by the Roundtable for Product Social Metrics, a collaboration of 12 multi-industry market-leading companies.

9.4   Sustainability in supply chains and industrial networks

9.4.1   Supply network dynamics

To understand how the implementation of sustainability in supply chains and networks takes place, first the dynamics of these chains and networks in general need to be understood.

Supply chains are, in reality, not linear chains but complex networks with many linkages between the different actors within the network. The process of globalization has strengthened this characteristic. As a result, the relations between the different actors have become extremely complex and diverse. Through the networks, lines can be drawn, symbolizing the chains, but these lines can change radically and swiftly.

In this book the supply chain and network approaches are integrated and, therefore, the term 'supply network' is used. Theories about supply network management are mainly developed from logistics as the basic discipline, but have become a more interdisciplinary field of study. Three different approaches for analyzing the management of industrial supply networks are found: the technological/economical approach, the inter-organizational approach, and the complex systems approach.

The *technological/economical* approach represents the rational way of thinking and focuses on using materials, information, money and other resources to manage the supply chain processes in an effective way. The approach is based on the engineering and economic perspective[18] and the resource-based view,[19] and focuses on improving the effectiveness of the material, information and financial flows through the supply networks. This approach uses engineering and economic tools like life cycle analysis and transaction cost analysis. The strategies and activities are chosen based on the results of these rational analyses and are frequently managed top-down through the supply network.

Inter-organizational approaches focus on the relation between actors (organizations and individuals) in the supply network and the way they cooperate with, stimulate and influence each other. They can be seen from a network perspective or a more social/cultural perspective where the supply network is seen as being a social system with normative and interpretive schemes.

The *complex system* approach defines a supply network as a complex advanced system. This approach states that we should recognize supply networks as complex adaptive systems (CAS), and proposes that many supply networks emerge rather than being a result of purposeful design by a singular entity. To become a successful network the emergent patterns should be managed by freedom and stimulation (positive feed-back) while, in reality, supply chain management literature emphasizes mostly negative feedback.[20] This approach not only asserts that the supply chain is a complex network, but also emphasizes the difficulty of managing it.

Traditionally, technological/economical approaches have dominated the literature on supply chain dynamics. Later on, the literature has expanded to include inter-organizational approaches. While the technological/economical approaches remain, they now seem to have become part of a wider inter-organizational management context. The complex system approach gives little insight into managing supply networks, seems to be too complex and is now hardly found in theory and practice.

9.4.2 Managing the dynamics

In all (except CAS) approaches, the question remains about who is managing the dynamics in the supply network. In the literature, the so-called 'focal' company in the centre of the chain or network[21] is seen as the most important actor in this process. The focal company is the company that influences the whole supply network because of its position and related power position. In the literature, this 'focal' company is sometimes called the 'leading' firm[22] or 'focal' firm.[23] A single 'focal' company cannot easily be distinguished and 'multiple' focal companies can be found in the supply network. This makes analyzing the dynamics more complex because the interaction between the 'multiple' focal companies will have a large influence on the dynamics found in their supply network as a whole. Their individual strategies can strengthen a specific development but they can also conflict with and frustrate each other's strategies.

A well-known theory for understanding supply network dynamics is the industrial network approach. This theory defines three relevant components: resources, activities and actors. An industrial network is defined as: 'All of the actors within one industrial sector, or between related industrial sectors, which can (potentially) cooperate to add value for the consumer'.[24] It seems that the supply chain structure is highly influenced by the resource structure. Therefore, how resources are controlled is a criterion for selection and also determines the relevant actors and their activities. These activities are the commercial, technical and administrative functions of individual firms. In the network, these activities from the different firms are linked together. The performance of the network depends upon the quality of each activity and the links between them. The third industrial network component (actors) can be organizations or individuals.

9.4.3 Supply network responsibility

Companies are part of a supply network and have organizations supporting the incoming and outgoing goods and services. They are often criticized for not taking sufficient responsibility for affairs that can occur in other parts of the supply network. A main premise is never to do business with organizations that exhibit irresponsible behaviour and this can apply to employers who underpay their employees or cause big environmental impacts, as well as customers that do not dispose of the product properly or exhibit unprofessional conduct. The principle of responsibility that an organization has for the links in early stages of the supply network is called 'up-stream' responsibility while responsibility for those links occurring later on are referred to as 'down-stream' responsibility.[25]

Box 9.4   The Centre for Research on Multinational Corporations[26]

The Centre for Research on Multinational Corporations (SOMO) is an independent, not-for-profit international research and network organization working on social, ecological and economic issues related to sustainable development. Since 1973, the organization investigates multinational corporations and the consequences of their activities for people and the environment around the world. By conducting independent research, SOMO builds knowledge about companies and sustainability issues in the global economy. In order to disseminate this knowledge, SOMO coordinates networks such as OECD Watch, Good Electronics and the CSR Platform. In addition, SOMO also trains and advises civil society organizations in research and advocacy. It is seen as a critical stakeholder for the worldwide activities of multinationals and many NGOs use the results of its work.

Determining factors for supply network responsibility

Assuming responsibility for companies in the supply network has a direct link to CSR because, in general, business cannot be held liable for people and organizations in the early or later stages of manufacture. There is, however, a moral appeal for supply network responsibility. Doing business with criminals or untrustworthy characters is not viewed as honourable dealings. The consumer however, does have significant power as well as NGOs, journalists, religious organizations whose influence can lead to the exposure of corrupt practices.

In addition to the ambition and moral integrity of the organization there are other important factors which influence supply network responsibility:

1. **Dominance**[27]
   - Corporations with a dominant market position often have a key position in the supply network. Many people are convinced that this position brings with it increased obligations because larger companies have an easier time of bringing innovation to the supply network which will affect people and the planet.
2. **Production complexity and diversity**
   - Companies with a product that requires a large array of raw materials and parts supplied by many different manufacturers in the production line cannot provide a smooth uniformity and must set limits on its supply network responsibility. Take, for example, the Western auto industry which receives raw materials and parts from many different purveyors.
   - Companies that rely on a single or limited amount of raw materials have an easier time influencing links in the production network. In addition, these businesses are also vulnerable to public opinion, with coffee producers and plantations being a good example.
3. **Mainstream and niche markets**
   - Enterprises operating in a mainstream market must keep in mind that by applying CSR principles, behavioural changes must be realized for large groups of suppliers, clients and consumers.
   - Smaller operations can use CSR to get distinctive power and make use of a niche market strategy.

The multinational and supply network responsibility

Corporate social responsibility (CSR) is an important element for multinationals in developing reputation management concerning their supply network responsibility and is often based on a defensive strategy. This is certainly true in the case of relatively simple production networks where multinationals can develop a CSR policy for their procurement. In the case of these simple production lines, multinationals often develop a CSR strategy based on procurement. Multinationals like Nike (see Box 9.5) and D.E. Master Blenders 1753[28] (previously the Dutch coffee company Douwe Egberts and part of Sara Lee) deal mainly with only one type of supplier (Chinese gym shoe suppliers and South American coffee farmers) and have developed a procurement policy that is based on improving working and environmental conditions in the preliminary production stages. Companies like these often come under scrutiny because the consumer has a stereotypical image of factory workers making gym shoes and peasants harvesting coffee beans. This means that multinationals often have to deal with action groups who investigate the working conditions of suppliers and later confront the consumer with ethical questions. Many multinationals operating in simple production-line situations have chosen an active CSR approach. This policy puts little financial pressure on the multinationals because labour costs for the suppliers' employees make up a relatively small part of the total cost price.

Box 9.5   Nike[29]

Nike experienced hard times in 1998. The sport shoe manufacturer, known worldwide for its excellent price/quality relation, was faced with increasing competition. The brand name emphasized its quality only, without differentiating for worldwide markets. In the booming Asian economy, Nike applied the same market strategy as it was using in Europe and North America. Public opinion in Western countries also became more critical and it was taken to task by the international press because of the abominable working conditions and low salaries which were prevalent in its factories. Nike began to get image problems and public opinion opposed more and more their suppliers which were seen as 'sweatshop' slave traders, and exploiters in the workplace. Nike realized that they had to change their ways and developed a 'code of conduct'. All of their suppliers were required to improve working conditions and it became evident that this was an attainable goal within a business–economic strategy. Factory labour costs in the shoe factory were less than 5% of the shop retail price. Nike realized that a 10%–20% increase in labour costs (improvements) could have a positive effect on profits. Based on a 1% increase in the retail price or some percentage of extra sale, net profits remained the same even if labour (production) costs increased by 20%.

9.5   Innovations towards sustainability[30]

9.5.1   Introduction

A specific approach concerning the implementation of sustainability in supply networks was known as 'integral chain management' which was defined as supply chain management, taking environmental and social issues into account. Based on a literature review[31] in Germany three 'integral chain management' schools were defined: material and information flow school; strategy and cooperation school; and regional industrial network school. The regional industrial network school does not examine global supply networks, but focuses on regional networks from the perspectives of different industrial actors. Even though they are an integral part of the definition, the social aspects were excluded from the 'integral chain management' practices. The implementation of sustainability in chains and networks seemed to focus mainly on the environmental aspects.[32] Some[33] used life cycle assessment methods for selecting management priorities on environmental aspects and others[34] discussed the upgrading of environmental management systems from 'site level' to 'supply-chain level'.

In the literature, the term green supply chain management (GSCM)[35] replaced integral chain management, which indicated environmental aspects were indeed dominating social aspects. The word 'greening' is used as a synonym for 'environment'. A great deal of research has been published on 'green' practices and why 'greening' takes place. Less documented is how the process of 'greening' occurs related to the different aspects and characteristics of the specific chain. Articles published in the 1990s on integral chain management and green supply chain management were mainly found in environmental journals.[36] The environmental researchers (often biologists, chemists, engineers etc.) were mostly focused on a rational technological approach. Only recently the logistic, operations management and supply chain management research groups have started publishing more about the implementation of sustainability in supply networks.[37] Also in this discipline the focus was primarily on the environmental aspects and the rational/technological approach we have seen from the environmentalists. Together with the change in society from an environmental management approach towards a wider corporate social responsibility approach, social aspects have increasingly become the focus of attention.[38]

The process of globalization of industrial supply networks resulted in many developing countries becoming the production site for developed countries. Besides their responsibilities for their environmental impacts (planet), the societal values (people) entered the public debate on corporate social responsibility. Child labour, working/labour conditions[39] human rights and poverty are now addressed by management throughout the whole supply network. Research on how management is addressing these social aspects in supply networks has been conducted more recently and has been published in social and ethical journals.[40] From this ethical perspective, the research conducted follows the inter-organizational approach and focuses mainly on the implementation of codes of conduct, guidelines and conventions. Publications in operations management journals attempt to show how attention to social aspects in purchasing and logistic processes influence supply chain relations. Empirical findings show that increased involvement by purchasing managers in socially responsible activities can lead to improved trust in and commitment to suppliers.[41] Although it appears that the social aspects within the wider context of CSR and the supply networks have received attention only recently in the literature, such research is actually not new.

Besides the attention paid to environmental (planet) and social (people) aspects in the supply networks, the 'prosperity' aspects, the third element of sustainability, are also getting more and more interest. Not because these aspects are new, but because they are now becoming part of a wider corporate social responsibility/sustainability approach.

'Fair trade' initiatives are well-known for their focus on paying a fair price to the producer at the beginning of a supply network. From this perspective, these initiatives have already for many decades paid attention to economic development, community development and reduction of poverty by business through supply networks. Fair trade initiatives started with food products (coffee, bananas, etc.) but they are now expanding towards textile/clothes and other products. Pressure to integrate environmental and other social aspects into fair trade initiatives is increasing because of the demands from stakeholders for integral CSR policies.

9.5.2 Cradle to Cradle (C2C)

Another 'driver' for change towards the implementation of CSR in business, besides the reverse logistics mentioned in Section 9.2, is the Cradle to Cradle Principle. In 2002 a German environmental chemist, Michael Braungart, together with an American architect, William McDonough, wrote a book and started a movement called 'Cradle to Cradle'.[42] They stated that waste doesn't exist and that waste equals food. The three basic principles are closing the material circles, using renewable energy and creating diversity. They distinguish the biological or natural loop for the materials that are biodegradable and the technical loop for the materials that are recyclable (see Figure 9.4). They state that products should be designed and produced in such a way that after use 100% of their parts or materials *can* go back into one of the circles. Their approach was at first looked at very critically. But in contrast with what often environmental groups state, that production and consumption should be reduced to protect the environment, their message was a positive environmental strategy. They said that production and consumption have no limits as long as the systems are based on the principles. In the last ten years many companies joined their movement and now hundreds of products have been certified according to the international Cradle to Cradle standards by the Cradle to Cradle Products Innovation Institute.[43] The criteria used for certification are material health, material reutilization, renewable energy, water stewardship and social fairness, and certification can be achieved at five levels: basic, bronze, silver, gold and platinum. Material health is one of the most difficult criteria to be met because very detailed proof is needed that the materials in the product do not contain any hazardous substances. Information to prove that is sometimes hard to find and if materials show to be hazardous they are often very difficult to replace with less hazardous substances. Gold and platinum levels demand organizational criteria as well as technical criteria for water, materials and energy related to the product. These criteria demand take-back and recycling systems for the products (reverse logistics).

The Cradle to Cradle philosophy assumes that in product development, materials are used that belong to a specific cycle and that these cycles must not be abused[44]. It differentiates between technical building blocks such as metal and plastic as opposed to biological building blocks which include wood, vegetal materials, water and soil. This second category implies that during product development the product is not intended to be recycled after consumer use. Recycling is frowned upon because the materials lose their original value and this is referred to as 'downcycling'.[45] It becomes the designer's challenge to incorporate biological and technical building blocks that are later replenished in the cycle after the product has been used.

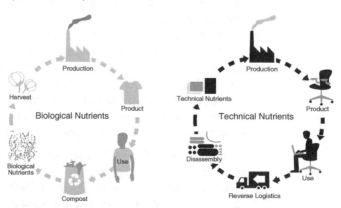

Figure 9.4 The biological and the technical cycle[46]

The Cradle to Cradle concept is based on eco-effectiveness and simply means that industry is geared to social values, safety and low costs, and aims to strengthen the position of natural sources instead of implementing a damage control approach. The term eco-effectiveness is used together with eco-efficiency. This last term refers to production methods whereby companies try to limit the damage to nature as much as possible. When implementing the Cradle to Cradle principles no limitations to economic growth would occur anymore and this is seen as the main reason for the success of Cradle to Cradle in businesses.

The dismantling or decomposition phase must be reckoned with in the product's original development. The term 'ecological intelligence' applies here and supports the use of materials that are abundantly available or obtainable in a responsible way. Another demand is that during the production process, product use and product disposal, elements must interact naturally with other natural systems. Cradle to Cradle emphasizes that its position is markedly different from those taken by earlier generations designing products which caused less environmental impact because the focus is on improving nature instead of providing damage control. An example of a Cradle to Cradle product is the disposable diaper made by gDiaper which is entirely decomposed within 53 days.

Box 9.6   Cradle to Cradle in the Desso Group[47]

The Desso Group is a leading world supplier of high quality carpets for commercial use, for the hospitality, maritime and airline sectors and for consumers.

Desso has become a pioneer in Cradle to Cradle development. One of its main objectives was that 75% of its products would have a Cradle to Cradle certificate before 2010 with all of its products conforming to this standard by 2020. Desso incorporates biological and technical cycles. Carpets currently available but not biologically decomposable are returned and completely recycled and the company has developed its own international return system for this purpose. For further product development Desso plans to make use of natural colour materials plus Cradle to Cradle principles for production combined with green energy as well. Suppliers are also expected to comply with demands set up by Cradle to Cradle. The steps that Desso took in 2010 are the result of earlier developments. In 1999 it began an active waste recycling policy and has achieved environmental certification since 2003.

Assessments of products according to the Cradle to Cradle Certified Product Standard[48] are performed by a qualified independent organization trained by the Cradle to Cradle Products Innovation Institute.[49] Every two years, manufacturers must demonstrate good faith efforts to improve their products in order to have their products recertified. All Cradle to Cradle certified products are registered at the publicly available website of the Cradle to Cradle Products Innovation Institute.[50]

Cradle to Cradle has attracted some major criticism[51] from experts in the field of sustainability, because it does not comply with all conditions for a sustainable society. The main criticisms can be summarized as follows:

- Energy: Cradle to Cradle does not provide a solution to our energy problem. The paradigm is focused on materials.
- Industrial ecology: the basis of Cradle to Cradle is industrial ecology, which is basically connecting industrial material flows with each other. This is something we have been trying for years and which until now has not been easy.

- Society: Cradle to Cradle products have to be kept in their material flows, while currently consumers just throw away their waste, of which a large part ends up in a landfill or in an incinerator. This will require a paradigm shift at the consumer side, which is easier said than done.
- Consumption: Cradle to Cradle is the first sustainability theory which is pro-consumption. The idea that consumption can limitlessly grow is not true and a dangerous signal to consumers and industry.
- Material cycles: Cradle to Cradle is based on the premise of endless material recycling, which is theoretically impossible; all materials disperse (the quality goes down) over time, which brings us back to using virgin material again.
- Transport: material flow management requires a lot of transport, which costs a lot of energy.
- Developing countries: Cradle to Cradle in general does not focus on social sustainability in developing countries, which is an essential part of sustainability.

9.5.3   Principles of the circular economy

The circular economy is a generic term for an industrial economy that is, by design or intention, restorative and in which material flows are of two types: biological nutrients, designed to re-enter the biosphere safely, and technical nutrients, which are designed to circulate at high quality without entering the biosphere. The circular economy is grounded in the study of feedback (non-linear) systems.[52]

The Ellen MacArthur Foundation was formed in 2010 to inspire a generation to rethink, redesign and build a positive future. The Foundation believes that the circular economy provides a coherent framework for systems-level redesign and as such offers us an opportunity to harness innovation and creativity to enable a positive, restorative economy. The Foundation published three *Circular Economy Reports* that can be downloaded for free from its website.[53] The purpose of the reports is to make the case for a faster adoption of circular business models, quantify their economic benefits and lay out pathways for action. The reports conclude that considerable environmental savings are possible. For instance, the UK economy could save up to $1.1 billion (€850 million) annually and could reduce yearly greenhouse gas emissions by up to 7.4 million tons by keeping food waste out of British landfills. The resource intensity of the current industrial model presents economic and environmental risks. Many companies and governments are actively exploring the opportunities of efficiency and new forms of energy, but less thought has been given to systematically designing out material leakage and disposal in the first place. This, the reports say, is where the case for a circular economy begins.

Over the past several decades, the concept of a circular economy that emulates natural systems has attracted the attention of thought leaders in fields from material science to industrial ecology. At its core, a circular economy aims to 'design out' waste. Products are designed for disassembly and reuse – in their entirety, or on a material/component level – whilst being supported by a shift towards licensing 'performance' over selling 'products'. Though circular business models have been explored in niche markets, the *Circular Economy Reports* argue that market conditions and tighter environmental standards are now combining to give the framework its full, large-scale potential. To seize the technical and financial opportunity, both the corporate sector and government must drive change and create an environment more conducive to circular product offerings. These reports were created to trigger debate. They conclude by summarizing possible steps forward for businesses, governments and researchers eager to help push the circular economy into the mainstream.

9.5.4   New business models for sustainability

More and more experts state that the existing business models will not be able to integrate sustainability towards a circular economy and that new business models will have to be developed (see Box 9.7 for an example). Many new business models are being distinguished even though some commentators doubt if they are all as new as they pretend to be.

In 2012 a first study on new business models for sustainability[54] showed seven characteristics that they should display:

- Creating multiple value.
- Cooperative collaboration. Entrepreneurship will become the art of the new collaboration.
- Money is not the only means of exchange. Time, energy, or care could also be deployed as exchangeable assets.
- The economy is focused on needs and utilization.
- Owning production means is no longer essential. It might be a lot more important to have access to it.
- Expressing long-term commitment.
- Contributing to a circular and sharing economy.

Box 9.7   New business model: 'Lease a jeans' becomes 'cotton lease'

To illustrate new business models for sustainability the medium-sized fashion company 'MUD Jeans' in the Netherlands can be seen a very good example. It designs and sells modern fashion products like jeans, shirts and sweaters. It has a very strong sustainability ambition and related policy. It uses only organic cotton and other natural materials in its products. Recycling the cotton used in its products would reduce the environmental impact of the cotton life cycle even more drastically. But how do you get the used jeans and other products back after they have been used?

MUD Jeans initiated the fashion concept 'lease a jeans'. The concept represented a new consuming philosophy, one that is about using instead of owning. The jeans could be leased as well as bought. The user could send them back after they had been used. All returned materials would then be recycled and used for new fashion items. Recycling reduces the amount of waste, water and consumption of raw materials drastically.

Using a lease concept in the consumer market for fashion/clothes was very innovative and MUD Jeans was the first fashion company in the world that introduced it. The business model corresponds with one of the characteristics that was found in the first study on new business models for sustainability: 'Not owning the products but paying for the services/use of the products'.[55] The company started this new business model in January 2013 and the first jeans came back from users during 2014. MUD Jeans developed a sweater made from the jeans that came back and these sweaters can also be leased or bought. The company also offers the possibility of buying the used jeans second-hand, giving the buyer information about the first user. MUD Jeans took a great risk and didn't know if this business model would bring success in the long term for its business. Unfortunately, two years later it had to change its lease a jeans concept into a cotton lease concept. This was due to financial problems with taxes and the banks who didn't seem to be ready yet for this new business model in the consumer market!

(Continued)

MUD JEANS
COTTON LEASE

Figure 9.5   Cotton lease of MUD Jeans[56]

MUD Jeans does not offer lease contracts any more for its fashion products but does still take back the products for recycling.

From its website:[57]

'Cotton lease'

'Our story starts with sustainable denim fabrics that we make into well-designed jeans. All-time essentials that are designed with a circular mindset. The jeans are bought, but the cotton is leased. While the jeans are yours, we retain ownership of the raw materials. Not wearing your jeans anymore? Send them back! They hold valuable materials that we like to reuse. Your old jeans are transformed into unique vintage denim or may be recycled into a sweater or other product. You will be rewarded!'

The results of the 2012 study show that more and more new business models are being developed, in different sectors, for different products and at different levels.[58] But they stay up till now in the niche and are not found in the mainstream markets. Private and local initiatives together with many SMEs seem to be ready to increase the use of these new business models drastically but two hurdles should be taken away to make this really happen.

The first hurdle is caused by the government(s). Many financial (tax) and legal systems mean the transition to new business models is difficult or even impossible, as was illustrated with the 'lease a jeans' business model. The government could reduce this hurdle by developing more progressive circular green tax legislation.

The second hurdle is the fact that a paradigm shift is needed; many actors are waiting and they do not dare to act. The arguments used for waiting are that time is needed for the next generation of new technologies, that stimulating measures are not ready yet and that it simply is not the right moment and the risks are too high:

The barrier is in our head. My vision is that we can only be successful by making a radical change. I compare it sometimes with learning how to fly. We are standing on a cliff and we should jump. That feeling gets close to the situation we are in now; change our thinking and acting radical. (John Elkington)[59]

9.5.5   Grassroots innovations[60]

Grassroots innovations are defined as community-led solutions for sustainability. Grassroots innovation movements (GIMs) can be regarded as initiators or advocates of alternative pathways of innovation. Sometimes these movements engage with more established science, technology and innovation (STI) institutions and development agencies in pursuit of their goals.

Three international well-known examples of GIMs are: the Social Technologies Network in Brazil, the Honey Bee Network and the People's Science Movement – both in India.

The cases show that the innovation processes do not follow a clear path and more research is needed to understand these processes creating new alternative pathways towards sustainable development. This search for new innovative solutions is very similar to the development of new business models for sustainability as described in Section 9.5.4.

9.6   Case Study: Sustainable innovations in the supply network of the fashion/clothing industry

The supply network of the fashion/clothing industry consists of the eight phases as shown in Figure 9.6.

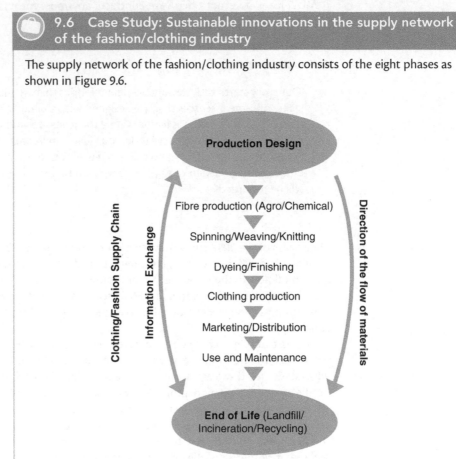

Figure 9.6   Supply chain clothing

The products are designed in the offices of the big fashion companies in Europe or the US. Choices are made about the design, models, colours and the materials to be used in producing the products. The fibre will be produced as an agricultural product from fields like cotton, one of the most-used natural fibres. Or it will be harvested from other natural systems (hemp, bamboo etc.) or from animals (wool, silk etc.). A high percentage of the fibres used are so-called artificial or plastic fibres made from oil.

(Continued)

The fibres are spun at industrial scale to make yarns from different thicknesses and strengths. Often the fibres are mixed to make the yarn stronger and more elastic/flexible depending on the function. The yarns are used to make the fabrics (or garments) by weaving or knitting. To give the fabrics nice colours and improve some of the quality criteria many chemicals are used in the dyeing and finishing process. The ready-made fabrics are then cut based on the designs and put together in the clothing production phase. The clothes are then transported, often from Asia, to other parts of the world by ship and sold in the shops of the brands. After the clothes have been used they often end up in a landfill or incinerator. A small part is collected separately and is reused/recycled.

The fashion/clothing industry is more and more recognizing the social and environmental impacts of its activities in each phase of supply, production, distribution and disposal, and it increasingly develops CSR strategies and policies for its supply network. It is held responsible for the bad working conditions in low-wage countries, mainly in Asia. In 2013, an eight-storey factory building collapsed in Bangladesh, killing more than 1100 people. As a result, public pressure about working conditions became even stronger.[61] That is why many companies now join programmes such as the Business Social Compliance Initiative (BSCI)[62] and the Fair Wear Foundation (FWF)[63] or use certification schemes as the SA8000.[64] Joining these programmes or using the certification schemes means that relations in the supply networks change so control over the conditions can be improved. Often the amount of suppliers is reduced and the chains are shortened by removing intermediate traders out of the network.

From an environmental perspective the use of pesticides for the production of cotton and the chemicals used for dyeing and finishing the garments are seen as the main environmental impacts besides the enormous amount of waste produced by used clothes that are thrown away by consumers. Companies are developing environmental programmes and management systems (ISO 14001) in which they introduce organic cotton (cotton produced without pesticides)[65] and waste water treatment technology for the water polluted with textile chemicals, and they are increasingly starting recycling programmes[66] for used clothes. To get the used clothes back for recycling they use new business models in their supply network, like the lease concept of MUD Jeans, or they give a reduction to the consumer on a new product when bringing back a used fashion product.

 Case Study Questions

1. What are the most important social and environmental impacts of the fashion/clothing supply network?
2. How did the accident in 2013 in Bangladesh change the CSR strategies of the fashion sector?
3. What are the differences between the BSCI, FWF and SA8000 programme certifications?
4. Which take-back systems do fashion companies use to get back used clothes for recycling?

9.7   Learning tools 🔧

9.7.1   Summary

- International business is becoming less location dependent.
- In supply networks, besides forward logistics, the importance of the development of reverse logistics is increasing.
- Life cycle assessment determines the environmental impacts of all the phases of the life cycle of a product.
- Product social impact assessment assesses the phases of the life cycle of a product for its social impacts.
- Supply 'chains' do not really exist. They look more like complex industrial networks.
- Companies are increasingly being held responsible for the social and environmental impacts of their supply network, upstream and downstream.
- Cradle to Cradle is a principle that brings back materials into the technical or biological cycle using only renewable energy sources.
- The circular economy is an industrial economy that is restorative and in which material flows back into the biosphere safely or circulates at high quality without entering the biosphere.
- The two main hurdles for the development of new business models for sustainability are the financial (tax)–legal systems and the necessary paradigm shift.
- Grassroots innovations are defined as community-led solutions for sustainability.
- The fashion/clothing industry is reducing the environmental and social impacts in its supply networks by shortening the supply network, reducing the amount of suppliers and starting to take back old clothes for recycling.

9.7.2   Further reading

Braungart, M. & McDonough, W. (2002). *Remaking the Way We Make Things.* New York, NY: North Point Press.

Collado-Ruiz, D. & Ostad-Ahmad-Ghorabi, H. (2010). Comparing LCA results out of competing products: Developing reference ranges from a product family approach. *Journal of Cleaner Production, 18*(4), 355–364.

Cramer, J. (2006). *Corporate Social Responsibility and Globalization: An Action Plan for Business.* Austin, TX: Greenleaf Publishing.

Ellen MacArthur Foundation (2012). *Towards the Circular Economy: An Economic and Business Rationale for an Accelerated Transition.* Retrieved from www .ellenmacarthurfoundation.org/publications/towards-the-circular-economy-vol-1-an-economic-and-business-rationale-for-an-accelerated-transition on 20 November 2015.

Hawks, K. (2006). What is reverse logistics? *Reverse Logistics Magazine,* Winter/Spring.

Heijungs, R., Guinée, J. B., Huppes, G., Lankreijer, R. M., Udo de Haes, H. A., Wegener Sleeswijk, A., Ansems, A. M. M., Eggels, P. G., Duin, R. van & Goede, H. P. de (1992). *Environmental Life Cycle Assessment of Products: Guide and Backgrounds.* Leiden, The Netherlands: CML.

Jonker, J. (2012). New business models: An explorative study of changing transactions creating multiple value(s) (Working Paper). School of Management, Radboud University Nijmegen, the Netherlands.

Kumar, S. & Putnam, V. (2008). Cradle to cradle: Reverse logistics strategies and opportunities across three industry sectors. *International Journal of Production Economics, 115*(2), 305–315.

Smith, A. (2014, 1 July). When grassroots innovation movements encounter mainstream institutions. Academic papers, GIHCP (Historical and Comparative Perspectives).

9.7.3   Assignments

 Assignment 9.1

Go to the website of a company that is producing a Cradle to Cradle product. Describe the product and how it is brought back into the biological or technical cycle.

 Assignment 9.2

Search for an example of a new business model for sustainability and explain which of the seven characteristics mentioned in this chapter is dominant in it.

 Assignment 9.3

Search for information about the Honey Bee Network and explain why it is a typical grassroots innovation.

9.7.4   Self-test questions

 Self-test Questions

1. What are supply chains and industrial networks?
2. What is a focal company?
3. What is a life cycle assessment of a product?
4. What is the basic principle of Cradle to Cradle?
5. What are characteristics of new business models for sustainability?
6. What are grassroots innovations?
7. What is a circular economy?
8. What happened in 2013 in a textile company in Bangladesh? Who is to blame for the disaster?

10

CORPORATE SOCIAL RESPONSIBILITY

Overview and learning objectives

Previous chapters have dealt with globalization and increased prosperity and their influence on the environment. The world is interconnected as never before and mutual differences between countries are getting smaller. More countries are becoming affiliated with organizations like the International Monetary Fund (IMF) and the World Trade Organization (WTO) who demand that governments have their house in order in the areas of finance, trade and trademark recognition. Today, national government legislation is not always determined within its own borders and the Internet and news media follow developments at close range. We get instant feedback if government is doing an irresponsible job and if it is not working hard enough to improve prosperity and well-being for the people. Citizens and national and international governments are also often vocal critics of business which has led to action and reaction from both sides. Businesses are more aware of their surroundings in a broad sense and many enterprises now incorporate a pro-active policy towards people and the earth.

This chapter will examine the motives behind the decisions of more and more businesses to follow the principles of corporate social responsibility (CSR) and will include different themes and concepts that are associated with it. We will also discuss values and standards, emphasizing how business sees itself in relation to customers, investors, employees and different groups in society.

Learning objectives

This chapter will enable the student to:

- Know and understand the historical development of the principles of CSR.
- Understand the motives for the development of CSR.
- Have insight into the different labels, guidelines, standards and schemes used in relation to CSR.
- Have knowledge and insight into the guideline for global reporting – the Global Reporting Initiative.
- Understand the relevant factors for the implementation of CSR.
- Have insight into criticism concerning the principles of CSR.

10.1 Corporate social responsibility in the twentieth century

At the beginning of the twentieth century, electronics giant Philips developed a vision of an employee policy which was geared to social issues. The reason for this was the success of its light bulb with its new tungsten filament. By 1929 20,000 people were reporting for work. This large number of employees made Philips vulnerable to labour conflicts; good social legislation would benefit the company as a whole.[1] Among other things, this led to a housing policy for Philips employees which was far ahead of its time. In 1910 'Philips Village' was built, taking into consideration living conditions for the new modern factory employee and was based on a total living concept. A modern house, vegetable garden, sport facilities, music clubs, public baths and a bread factory were all included. The trend continued in succeeding years with the best-known housing project being 'Drents Dorp' in Eindhoven, a building project with 1000 houses for workers who had been recruited from the Dutch province of Drenthe in another part of the country. Philips based its personnel policy on the concept of 'enlightened self-interest' (see Box 10.1) and felt that investing in a visionary housing programme would reap rewards. The offer of a comfortable dwelling made it possible to search for motivated and disciplined workers in other parts of the country.[2] Previously, most employers tried to keep wages as low as possible. A more active personnel policy, where business was prepared to invest in its employees, was a truly visionary concept for its time.

Box 10.1   Enlightened self-interest

The expression 'enlightened self-interest' is a term that is used when sustainable behaviour is based on self-interest and it plays a central role in the article 'The Welfare State is not in danger' by sociologist Wim van Oorschot. He claims that the generous contributions paid by the Dutch into their social system is motivated by personal self-interest and is not done for altruistic reasons. People know that a time will come when they will have to make use of its services and many people have family, friends and acquaintances who are already making use of it. The social security system makes it possible for people to receive aid without depleting personal financial reserves or calling on others for financial support.

Study of the manner in which enterprises invested in schooling, productivity and sales techniques began to take definable form in the last century and the term 'business studies' was coined. Work division within the production line was looked at seriously and the role of direct stakeholders as suppliers and competition was analysed. It wasn't until the end of the 1980s that business realized the importance of the involvement of indirect stakeholders as action groups.[3] Protesters denouncing environmental and social problems created by firms were less radical than in previous decades, and therefore appealed to a larger audience. At the same time business leaders became more conscious of their responsibilities. This resulted in many companies taking a new direction to develop strategies to serve the broad public interest.

10.2   Motives for corporate social responsibility

Multinational companies, together with medium and small enterprises, supply society with goods, services and employment opportunities. They are appreciated because of the initiatives they take in risky situations but despite this, society often has ambivalent feelings towards the business world. This happens when business leaders are perceived to be using their operations for increased personal benefit. We admire clever people who are able to combine capital and labour but not at any cost.

A company helps itself by having society's best interests in mind. A strategy focused on a good deal between itself and the public, without fully considering the role of other involved parties, is a risky business even if the law is strictly obeyed. It means that business benefits from having an inventory of strong allies in society so that businesses can aim their strategy at finding their own comfortable niche. Let's examine three concepts which are relevant to this approach: licence to operate, stakeholders and self-regulation.

10.2.1   Licence to operate

In the 1990s public opinion turned against oil giant Shell's decision to purposely sink a storage tank (Brent Spar) in the ocean (see Box 10.2). Shell thought it had acted responsibly but the public thought otherwise. The confrontation with society forced Shell to change direction. It found that it had to take broad public support more seriously, especially when it concerned an issue that could be exposed to public debate. The new policy that Shell introduced became known as 'licence to operate' and is a classic tale. Today it has become common terminology in management circles.[4]

Box 10.2   Brent Spar[5, 6]

In the 1980s Shell stored North Sea oil in a floating storage tank known as the Brent Spar. The tank was located in the sea to the north of Scotland at a depth of more than 100 metres. By the 1990s most oil was being piped through to land storage facilities and the huge steel tank had outlived its usefulness. Shell intended to dismantle the colossus in a responsible way but problems arose because of the deep water location and the impracticality of towing it to an arbitrary harbour. After looking for other alternatives, the company concluded that most of the tank could best be dismantled in the ocean. The remaining bits could then be towed to deeper waters and sunk. It seemed like a good solution. Disassembly on shore had environmental consequences but sinking 14,500 tons of steel in the ocean was a clean operation. The amount of accumulated silt remaining in the tank would be limited to 100 tons and it seemed to be a good risk. Shell opted for this policy and asked permission from the British and Scottish authorities to 'sink' the tank. Permission was granted quickly and other European countries were informed of the decision but lodged no protest.

When the sinking was about to begin, environmental group Greenpeace arrived and said that it was irresponsible to use the ocean as a dumping ground. Shell ignored the protest and relied on its reputation and prestige. Greenpeace volunteers and a German television crew gained access to the Brent Spar to take samples of the unprocessed silt and showed that it was much more than the 100 tons Shell had claimed. Public opinion turned against the company and everyone felt that Shell was trying to dump chemical waste while everyone looked the other way. Greenpeace sought publicity, which was quick in coming. It pleaded for consumers to boycott Shell products and claimed that 14,500 tons of 'poisonous' silt had been dumped. The protest succeeded, especially in Germany. Protestors damaged petrol stations and two were pelted with Molotov cocktails. The government even got involved and Germany, Denmark, Sweden and Holland now objected to the sinking of Brent Spar, whereas before they had taken little notice.

(Continued)

Shell realized that it was fighting a losing battle and former board chairman Cor Herkstroter announced that the Brent Spar would be towed to a remote Norwegian fjord for dismantling. It was a short-lived victory for Greenpeace. Even before a research team from Norway (Det Norske Veritas) boarded the Brent Spar, it was forced to admit that the levels of tainted oil and contaminated silt were less than claimed. It may have been a pyrrhic victory for Greenpeace but the pill was just as bitter for Shell. It had complied with all formal procedures and intended to limit environmental damage, but in the end Shell's image was heavily damaged.

The Brent Spar affair makes it clear that in business, being right is not always an advantage. Despite rational, methodical research, the most practical solution was not effective. A company's existence is not only dependent on customers and direct stakeholders such as financiers, governments and trade unions. Enterprise has to deal with society. The lesson learned from Brent Spar is that good relations with society are an essential element of business strategy. Without relations based on mutual trust, a company is vulnerable and can end up being a football between protest groups and public opinion. It is important for business to recognize the different roles of the citizen and the consumer.[7] The consumer is looking for 'value for money'. Citizens' concerns are directly related to society, safety, environment and a comfortable living situation. The citizen's disappointment and outrage does not have the same meaning for the consumer. The gasoline purchased at Shell pumps is appreciated by the consumer because it gives him or her freedom and mobility but has a different connotation for citizens. They are confronted with the downside of the oil business and via the media get daily information about damaging CO_2 emissions and the behaviour of oil companies operating in vulnerable natural environments. It's no wonder that people cast a critical eye at business. And citizens certainly have good reasons for demanding more sustainability. Another group of stakeholders that entrepreneurs now deal with are those who have a direct relation with companies through contracts, money or legislation. They are called direct stakeholders.[8]

For a business it means that it is involved with three groups of stakeholders which are coupled with three types of licences:[9]

- **Licence to sell** (consumer-value orientated)

  Consumers give authorization for a company to manufacture an item so long as it conforms to certain standards. This is dependent on the consumer. Sometimes only the price, technical quality and product safety are considered, but at other times the consumer places demands on production methods. This can include elimination of animal testing during product development, or ecology and employee labour conditions for the company itself or other enterprises connected to the production chain.

- **Licence to produce** (authorization from direct stakeholders)

  An enterprise is via legislation, voting rights of financial backers and contracts, directly allied to stakeholders consisting of employees, government and owners. The continued existence of the business is directly dependent on the authorization of these parties.

- **Licence to operate**[10] (goodwill of society)

  Licence to operate is authorization from society. Businesses seek society's approval to carry out their main operations; society grants the enterprise the space and recognition – a licence to operate – when social expectations are peacefully met to a satisfactory degree. The licence to operate is difficult to pin down because it is based on public opinion (society) and is often given conditionally. Business, in its own element, can be addressed on its sustainability efforts and be called upon to answer questions from non-governmental organizations, citizens and consumers. Social dialogue becomes an important interactive element for a licence to operate.

10.2.2   Stakeholders

Stakeholders theory holds firms responsible for delivering benefits to all their stakeholders rather than only shareholders and customers, defining stakeholders as 'the individuals and constituencies that contribute, either voluntarily or involuntarily, to firms' wealth-creation capabilities, and that are therefore its potential beneficiaries and/or bearers' (Post et al., 2002).[11] Strategy is not only determined by analysis of consumer habits, new technology, new materials and competition, but also includes consideration of the media, local residents and protest groups.

Stakeholder management is more than determining the opportunities and risks involved in creating a business strategy that takes different stakeholders into account. Stakeholder management implies an established relationship with these other involved groups. Dialogue with other partners results in a dynamic process of integration of stakeholders' concerns within corporate practices and strategies. When everyone's wishes and interests are clear, it is hard to pursue a one-sided approach. Dialogue has as a goal, the pursuit of the right course of action and stakeholders' management is dependent on a broad input of information to determine strategy and, at the same time, cement relations between the involved groups. However, firms have limited resources while stakeholders often have competing claims. Thus, companies need to develop a system to decide whose interests are given priority. Companies with a purely strategic vision of stakeholder management will only take on board the interest of the most powerful stakeholders – those with the ability to affect the firms' licences to operate – and ignore other claims. This is a short-sighted strategy because changes in the political environment may shift relations of power and leave the company in a difficult position (see Box 10.3). Mitchel et al. (1997) argued that companies should take into account the salience of stakeholders' claims. Salience includes power (ability to affect the company) but also legitimacy of claims (to what extent the stakeholder is affected by the company and has a moral or legal basis for the claim) and urgency of claims (magnitude of damage caused by the delay in addressing the claims).[12]

Box 10.3   The consequences of poor stakeholder management: Orica Chemicals and Meridian Gold[13]

The well-documented case of Orica Chemicals in Botany Bay, Australia, is an example of how tardy stakeholder management has adverse results for the firm. Orica produced toxic waste for four decades without reaching an agreement on how to dispose of it. When the firm settled in Botany Bay, the local community was in a vulnerable position, unable to perceive the risk due to lack of information. However, in the 1980s the local residents were empowered by new legislation which required the consent of communities in projects which involve environmental risk.

(Continued)

Additionally, the community's perception of the risks had been growing while its human and social capital strengthened by public participation and social networks. Orica, on the other hand, had made no policy changes; it did not improve its systems of stakeholder integration, rather it continued taking decisions based solely on its own criteria and that of technical consultants. In 1990, Orica presented a project for a new waste treatment plant requiring community approval. The firm's incapability of detecting and acting on the community's environmental concerns gave rise to civil unrest which culminated in the government's rejection of the proposal, obliging the firm to opt for the much more costly (and environmentally controversial) measure of exporting its toxic waste to a European site.

Poor stakeholder management had far more adverse consequences for British mining company Meridian Gold in the Argentinian Patagonia locality of Esquel. Meridian Gold had the support of the government but it had neither the strategies nor the willingness to manage other stakeholders or to adapt its practices to address the community's concerns about the use of cyanide in the company's new mining project. Unfortunately for the firm, it confronted a community that was well organized and educated, with high social and human capital built around a local economy based on activities other than mining (agriculture, tourism, services). The community organized a coalition of stakeholders against mining: journalists, educators, legislators, church authorities, opinion leaders and other industry representatives. The government was forced to call a plebiscite asking whether the community wanted the mine. 80% voted against. In the end not only had the firm to abandon the project – with an estimated loss of $500 million – but also the use of cyanide in mining was legally prohibited in the region.

10.2.3   Business regulates itself

Businesses have a strong influence on the economy. The world became very aware of this in 2007. The decision by a number of American banks to make mortgage brokers' bonuses dependent on the number of houses sold led to money being lent to buyers with relatively low incomes. The risks involved in this type of loan were neatly covered by selling the risks to other banks worldwide. The results of this policy became clear when the US housing market cooled off. The resale of the loan risks to other banks led to a scenario where everyone was in the dark about who was holding the bad debt and this led to a complete breakdown of inter-bank trust. Worldwide capital transfers stopped and resulted in a recession which we now know as the credit crisis (2008). It is hard to point the finger of responsibility at any one person or institution. The banks were legally regulated and, in fact, hardly any rules were violated. The government could have chosen to enforce stricter banking regulations but this comes with a price tag. To begin with, bureaucracy within society would increase and government and society always pay close attention when ethical and social involvement are part of intrinsic thinking within business. To avoid more legislation, government stimulates businesses to put CSR on their agendas (see 10.2.4.). Also the academic world here makes a contribution. It ensures that businesses are kept informed about research into ethics, sustainable behaviour, long-term strategy and the effect of these elements on their profits.

Free market economy and noblesse oblige

'The actions of powerful people have more impact and affect more people than those without power'.[14] This quotation is the idea behind the concept of *'noblesse oblige'* or 'mandatory nobility'. It basically serves to make the use of power legitimate with the condition that the rulers are required to demonstrate moral fortitude. This can equally be applied to multinationals and companies producing important technologies and we can ask whether these powerful organizations can be expected to take sufficient responsibility for their actions.[15] We can also ask if society benefits by having more control over large multinationals as compared to other businesses. If society is willing to trust the premise of *noblesse oblige*, extra regulation is not required. However, misguided *noblesse oblige* can result in multinationals' cover-up of their competitors' misdeeds. For instance, against community protests and scientific evidence, mining giant Xstrata publicly supported use of cyanide to refine gold in Argentina, despite the fact that the company did not apply this controversial technique in its own Alumbrera mining site.[16]

Box 10.4   Glyphosate

New pesticides and genetically altered crops have contributed significantly to the green revolution. Due to these new techniques, farming output is higher and there is more food for the world market. The bigger chemical and seed producers have also played a role which began in the 1980s.[17] Companies such as Monsanto and Bayer produced new products, among which was a total pesticide with the active chemical ingredient glyphosate. The product was produced under the commercial names of Roundup, Basta and Finale. It is a potent weedkiller and decomposes easily but there is a disadvantage. It can only be used in combination with modified crops because these crops have been implanted with a pesticide resistant gene. Farmers have switched to using the seeds and pesticides offered by the big multinationals. From 1997 until 2007 for example, the share of genetically modified soybeans grew from 5% to 70%.[18] We can safely assume that these specialized products have had a positive influence on world food supplies but nonetheless pro and con discussions continue. Proponents, especially scientists, say that the modified crops pose no real danger and the new pesticides have made a positive contribution to the environment. Opponents, from the other camp of the scientific community, feel that there are too many unknown effects that have not been brought into perspective. Critics seem to be gaining the upper hand. Several components of the popular pesticide do not decompose well and legislation is becoming necessary. Several European countries are now creating new legal requirements.

The actions of chemical concerns Monsanto and Bayer in Box 10.4 can be easily explained if we consider the forces in the market economy. Glyphosate in combination with modified crops accounted for strong sales and farmers were enthusiastic about increased productivity. In addition the use of these products seemed to be good for the environment. The producers and official controlling bodies researched the issue and came to the conclusion that the products could be sold with a minimum of restrictions. Despite this, questions have been raised. The free-market economy puts pressure on businesses hoping that they will make responsible decisions. Companies like Monsanto are betting on different horses at the same time. On the one hand it is in their interests to have strong sales. On the other hand they strive for a low risk factor to protect their reputation. They know they must work with government and society to analyse risks and have a responsible technology policy and this creates a dilemma for business.

10.2.4   Government emphasizes values

The law and its application is an important instrument in determining how business functions and is based on clearly defined rules and standards. The regulation of acceptable corporate behaviour via the law does not always work positively and business has to deal with bureaucracy and coercion. This is why it is important for government to involve business with values and starting points that have been used to implement rules and standards. We call these value instruments and they allude to the active role government must play in spreading the principles of society that enjoy widespread consensus such as honesty, solidarity, thrift and involvement. Generally speaking, values have an emotional connotation and are, more than laws, meant for people (and business) to involve them in a search for solutions to society's problems. It is not by chance that governments place corporate social responsibility on the agenda next to law and application.

What multinational cooperative behaviour ideally should be remains an issue for society. It is naïve for governments to rely only on a 'licence to operate' and on stimulating CSR. *Noblesse oblige* is not an issue here. Government is required to introduce additional legislation to allow corporations to enter another new power field. More than ever before, business must be increasingly aware of society's interests. The present power field, which concerns itself only with profit potential from technology, has undesirable consequences. Sufficient solutions are available. For example, government can require a corporation to set up a fund that can only be used when it has been proven that within a determined period the technology has been properly implemented. It is also the government's responsibility to develop good legislation for businesses desiring to bring useful, but not entirely harmless, products to the market.

10.3   Definitions and guidelines for corporate social responsibility

In Europe, business practice and its accompanying aspects are referred to as corporate social responsibility (CSR).

CSR is defined by the European Commission as 'the responsibility of enterprises for their impacts on society'.[19] The Commission encourages that enterprises 'should have in place a process to integrate social, environmental, ethical human rights and consumer concerns into their business operations and core strategy in close collaboration with their stakeholders'.

This definition implies that the company itself has chosen responsible business practices beyond legislation (voluntarily) and is generally understood as the concept of corporate citizenship. It is about social and environmental concerns integrated in (and not besides) all business operations including the ones that are outsourced in the supply network. The interaction with the stakeholders asks for an active dialogue, the scope should be long term (definition of sustainable development) and the policy, activities and results should be transparent (reporting). The interaction with stakeholders means that there is no standard recipe for the 'right' CSR activities. A CSR strategy is contingent on both the type of organization and its stakeholders' needs. However, there are similarities in practices within the same geographical context. European CSR is more influenced by regulation than CSR in the US. African and Latin American CSR have a much stronger developmental and philanthropic orientation than European and North American CSR.

Despite the variety of strategies, Crane, Matten and Spence (2013) identify six core characteristics of CSR, relating these to different definitions and perspectives of CSR such as geographical context and organizational type.

1. **Voluntary**
   KFC, McDonald's, Pizza Hut, Pret A Manger and McDonald's agreeing in 2011 to introduce calorie labelling.

2. **Internalizing or managing externalities** (see Chapter 6 for a definition of externalities)
   Corporation of Australia's carbon footprint mapping on eggs and protein sources.

3. **Multiple stakeholder orientation**
   CSR Asia's definition of CSR expands focus beyond shareholders to include other groups.

4. **Alignment of social and economic responsibilities**
   General Electric's definition of CSR which aligns enlightened self-interest with social and economic responsibilities.

5. **Practices and values**
   Business Social Responsibility (BSR) definition of CSR[20] which highlights philosophy or values underpinning practices.

6. **Beyond philanthropy**
   CSR International states that CSR needs to become the new DNA of business.

10.3.1   International Guideline for Corporate Social Responsibility

The Organization for Economic Cooperation and Development (OECD) was one of the first organizations to formulate CSR guidelines for multinationals as early as 1976. The guidelines gave international companies a framework to implement responsible business practices, and they were used by these organizations to develop socially responsible policy. It took until 2010 before the International Guideline for Corporate Social Responsibility was published by the International Standard Organization, the ISO 26000.[21] The International Organization for Standardization began developing this international guideline in 2005. Developed by stakeholders from industry, government, labour, consumers, non-governmental organizations and others it was the first time in history that the majority of the members in the ISO working groups were from developing countries. In the past a lot of criticism was heard from the developing countries that ISO working groups were dominated by the Western European countries. The aim was that ISO 26000 should become the worldwide guideline for CSR and should put an end to all the different definitions used for CSR. The ISO 26000 guideline is voluntary, and includes no specific requirements; therefore it is not a certification standard but a guideline. The working group stated very clearly that the guideline was not ready and suitable (yet) for certification. It promised to follow the implementation, and national organizations for standardization register the companies that use the ISO 26000 with a self-declaration.[22] So the guideline defines CSR in an international context and focuses on seven subjects, based on two fundamental principles and elements for integrating CSR throughout an organization. Figure 10.1 shows the relation between these factors in a schematic overview.

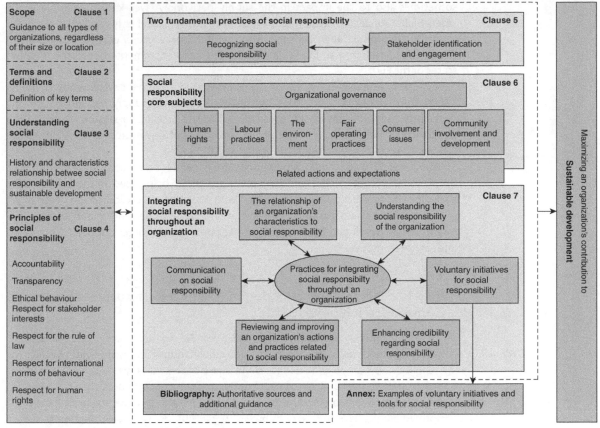

Figure 10.1   Schematic overview of ISO 26000[23]

10.3.2   CSR performance ladder

Based on the ISO 26000, AA1000 (accountability) and the Global Reporting Initiative, a CSR performance standard was developed in the Netherlands.[24] This standard can be certified at five levels and uses 33 CSR indicators. It was developed by consultant agencies and certification bodies and offered in the market in 2010 shortly after the publication of the ISO 26000. This performance standard is against the wishes of the ISO 26000 working group but the group could not stop it coming onto the market. At the time of writing nearly 200 companies are certified for this standard, mainly in the Netherlands and Belgium but they are expanding to other countries.[25]

10.3.3   Various CSR-related guidelines, standards, initiatives and programmes

In addition to the CSR guideline ISO 26000 and the CSR performance ladder, many different tools are available for corporations to carry out their business operations with increased attention to people and the planet. Different labels, standards, guidelines, initiatives and guidelines are being offered in the market and can be applied depending on a company's goals. They could be categorized into: environmental versus social; product-related versus organizational; general versus sector specific.

Many national and international environmental (or eco-) labels exist for products and services. They are related to the environmental impact of the product in use and sometimes also to the impact in the supply network. A well-known example is the 'energy label' for cars, houses, washing machines etc. This label only focuses on the 'user' phase of the product and only the environmental aspect 'use of energy'. The European Union (EU) developed an EU-Ecolabel scheme that is implemented in all the member states of the EU.[26]

At organizational level the use of environmental management systems based on ISO 14000 is increasing very much in international operating supply networks.[27] For the social aspects, guidelines or standards related to the product or service are not in use but for controlling working conditions in companies at organizational level, the standard Social Accountability SA8000 is being used.[28]

The guidelines and standards mentioned are general for all sectors and organizations but in some sectors specific guidelines or standards are being used. In the leisure sector a specific standard has been developed for hotels, restaurants etc. called the Green Key.[29]

Besides these standards and guidelines many programmes and initiatives have frequently been developed by sector organizations and sometimes supported by NGOs and/or governments.

Box 10.5   Fair Wear Foundation (FWF) versus Business Social Compliance Initiative (BSCI)

The Multi-Stakeholder Initiative (MSI) Fair Wear Foundation was set up to improve working conditions in the clothing, shoe and handbag industries and the NGO Clean Clothes Campaign (CCC) is on the board of this initiative. In general it works with companies who bring to the market brand-name products that have been produced in low-income countries. Within the production line, makers of known clothing brands have to deal with buyers' organizations, agents, production ateliers and their sub-contractors. Transparency within the chain is very low. Clothing brands that take steps to improve working conditions are confronted with more obstacles. The Fair Wear Foundation does not issue certificates of approval. Clothing manufacturers who choose to be allied to the Foundation are interested in improving labour conditions for their suppliers but not based on demanding criteria. The Fair Wear Foundation is a verification organization and can be seen as a support organization to help business improve working conditions in a production line. The businesses do not have to automatically refuse to work with suppliers where working conditions are at a minimum. However, the suppliers are paid a visit in the local production areas and an audit report is made to summarize working conditions. This audit gives the brand-name producers a tool to enter into dialogue with the supplier to determine what steps are necessary to improve employment conditions.

You can find information about 'business efforts' on the FWF website. In this way the consumer can see the attempts being made by a company to improve production conditions. Companies working together with FWF are generally not permitted to display the FWF label on their wares. This is only allowed for exceptionally well-performing enterprises who can verify their improvements. Clothing manufacturers are thus limited in their attempts to get publicity for improved working conditions.

There are other options available than Fair Wear to obtain approval on the theme of corporate social responsibility. An example is the European Business Social Compliance Initiative (BSCI).[30] This is not a multi-stakeholder initiative but a business initiative and is not developed only for the fashion/clothing sector but more in general for the retail sector. In this initiative, NGOs are not on the board of the organization.

10.3.4   CSR reporting

Many large companies in addition to yearly financial reports for stockholders and potential investors also produce an annual social responsibility report. In Europe, some of the biggest enterprises are required to do this.[31] Companies do have considerable freedom in writing these reports because legislation is practically non-existent. Despite this, it is evident that most large companies strive for a certain level of CSR reporting and make much use of guidelines set up by the Global Reporting Initiative (GRI).

Since 1999, GRI has provided an integral Sustainability Reporting Framework[32] that is widely used around the world. The framework is based on the Sustainability Reporting Guidelines which focus on credibility, consistency and comparability. The framework has in 15 years become the worldwide standard in sustainability reporting.

The GRI works with different gradients of reporting and enterprises can use extended or less expansive forms. Participants also have the option of having their reports examined by independent accountants or the GRI itself and these choices can be seen on their website. This helps stakeholders to ascertain the quality of the reporting. The GRI system has led to a feeling of legitimacy being attached to the yearly social report of big multinationals.

Two important premises that the GRI uses for reviewing an annual report are relevance and quality. The relevance of the information is determined on the basis of the company's activities, and if it is of value to the stakeholders. This means that companies have a degree of freedom concerning the report's content. When they produce their report, businesses have to ascertain the important issues for stakeholders and provide thorough coverage. The criteria are especially important for large organizations with diverse activities. Companies can be taken to task if the report includes insignificant items that do not seem to present any pressing problems.

The criteria used by the GRI to enforce content (relevance) are the following:

- Materiality is associated with the impact of a theme, taking into consideration the economic range of the activity and its impact on environment and social territory. It is expected that all information is complete and trustworthy.
- Stakeholder inclusiveness is determined on the basis of their influence on themes and indicators for which information has been provided.

In addition to content, information is also evaluated for quality. GRI guidelines are that they should be:

- Trustworthy: Facts provided in the information can be verified.
- Clarity: Stakeholders should be able to understand the information.
- Balance: The report should include relevant information for all concerned stakeholders with mention of positive and negative elements to create a well-balanced overall view.
- Comparability: The information should be directed at the stakeholders to allow them to make easier comparisons with reports from previous years and similar enterprises.
- Accuracy: The report must be up to date and presented in detail.
- Timely: The information must be made available in a reasonable period of time.

Although not a competitor with GRI, government is also involved in the area of 'annual public reports'.[33] There are not many demands regarding publication obligations and serious attention is not devoted to the report's content. Brazil, Denmark, France and South Africa are pioneers in sustainability reporting practice and policy. They share their experience with the rest of the world and contribute to making corporate sustainability reporting standard practice. The minister for foreign affairs for the government of Denmark commented in 2012: 'Governments can play a crucial role in driving sustainability practices and disclosure at a national level'. Similarly, in South Africa companies listed on the Johannesburg Stock Exchange are required to produce a report integrating their financial and sustainability performance. In Denmark, the legal requirement for the largest companies to report is having positive effects – increasing Danish companies' international reputation and creating value for the companies and their stakeholders. These positive outcomes have in turn motivated more companies to address their corporate social responsibility standards and to report on their sustainability performance.

10.4   Implementation of a CSR strategy

Long-term development is essential for determining an organization's strategy and includes localizing profits from diverse business units, analysis of product/market combinations and determining where money should be invested to realize future revenues.[34] However, not every large company embraces future-orientated strategy. This can be illustrated with the case of Toyota and General Motors (GM). At the end of the 1990s, Toyota began experimenting with a hybrid car while GM was convinced that its future would be defined by gas-guzzling SUVs (Sports Utility Vehicles). It was not until 2009 that GM finally started thinking about sustainability after encountering serious financial problems in the previous year. Banking on previous success is probably the best explanation for GM's difficulties but there were many indicators that should have caused the company to sit up and think hard. To mention a few: the increasing Asian thirst for oil, the speculation about diminishing oil reserves, and the numerous world conferences looking for a way to diminish CO_2 emissions. It is irrational when business retains an outdated strategy that is not directed towards the future. GM's decision to produce larger, less-fuel-efficient American cars was a risk and it failed to anticipate a world with more expensive fuel and increased attention to CO_2 emissions. Many companies admit that CSR contributes to the development of a CSR-orientated business strategy. CSR thinking creates an open mind and companies who focus on short-term profits only are 'narrow minded'. When a CSR approach is used to develop new business strategy, it leads to questions from society receiving a deeper analysis. It allows companies to develop their own personal vision towards the public and allows them more insight into developments in society. Poverty issues, social isolation and environment offer good opportunities for companies to develop new products and services but CSR has to be well applied if it is to contribute to profits. If earnings remain the primary objective, CSR policy has to conform to several preconditions. Meta research culled from 52 earlier studies concluded that there is a light positive correlation between profits and CSR but that the relationship is weak.[35] It is important that CSR is centrally directed and companies must concentrate on CSR tactics directly aimed at attaining a competitive advantage.[36, 37] There is much professional information available explaining ways in which CSR can be applied to core business to create this advantage. A direct competitive advantage can be achieved, for example, by analysing the possibilities in the supply chain. CSR can provide another vision for development of purchasing, reorganization, or innovative marketing concepts which can improve the overall functioning of the enterprise. The challenge is to find a comprehensive approach and to do this requires not only professional tools to solve problems, but the company itself must formulate the premises that it deems important to change itself into a CSR-orientated operation. Some critical success factors[38] that should be considered for any business implementing CSR are:

- Choose a clear mission.
- Develop a community.
- Look for cooperation.
- Be transparent.
- Be authentic.

10.4.1 Choosing a mission

Organizations consolidate their energy by having missions that encourage people participation. This is 'work that works' and implies that people enjoy doing meaningful work.

Carpet manufacturer Desso (see Box 9.6) has chosen sustainability as one of its core values and has set up concrete goals to strengthen its policy. In 2020 it hopes to make use of 100% recyclable energy and its primary materials will be supplied from either sustainable or reusable sources.[39] Its carpeting will be produced safely and with a clear difference between biological and technical materials to make biodegrading and recycling possible according to the Cradle to Cradle principles.

Companies aspiring to higher goals can be inspirational. It is important for employees to recognize that their company practices what it preaches. There is little to be gained by having an admirable set of values which only exists on paper and going on to say that the use of CSR initiatives is higher when the values are translated into strategy, capital investing decisions, and personnel policy. Work cooperation improves when people are receptive to ideas and opportunities, and they tend to take better decisions when the company's values are shared by the majority of its employees.

10.4.2 The community model

On the basis of the content of Chapter 4, it can be said that in general, people's well-being improves when sufficient possibilities are offered to exhibit social behaviour. This has implications for an organization trying to establish itself. Setting up a business which employs people involves social and competitive elements. The community model is pitted against the hierarchical model with its cumbersome procedures and work protocol, the so-called machine bureaucracy. Studies have showed that 71% of employees in these large- and medium-sized companies have little involvement with their work.[40] In a large hierarchical organization a good, involved work ethic is hard to create. The loyal hard-working employee is barely appreciated and apathy and dissatisfaction increase in the long term. Company managers wishing to apply the community model to their business have to consider which vision they have about their own employees. If staff are seen purely as a resource, it is doubtful if the community model concept can be put into practice. For employees to feel part of the community is dependent on whether the community is sufficiently in tune with their values.[41] It has been demonstrated that a personnel policy based solely on human resource management limits the possibilities for companies embracing corporate social responsibility.[42] Human resource management places too much emphasis on employee skills which results in too little attention to the values that employees are motivated by.[43] Research articles destined for management literature indicate that the foundations of human resource management have limitations and more attention can be paid to 'workers' values'. This theme is called human value management.

One of the key words applying to the concept of human value management is 'talent' and this assumes that employees want to exploit their own abilities.[44] This creates a challenge for organizations to offer surroundings where employees' talents can be developed and this is an interactive process. To achieve this, the companies' values must be attuned to the individual or (potential) employee but the reverse is also true. Workers can identify with a company whose appearance exudes passion, pleasure and satisfaction. The relationship involves more than receiving a salary for services provided.

In addition to further exploration of human value management we will look at the concepts of scientific management and human resource management. All three of these can be used to set up an organization. Two important criteria that complement these ideas are efficiency and effectivity. Business processes should be set up efficiently with an optimal mix of people and equipment but this does not mean that setting up a business must always focus on the efficient and effective set-up of the workflow. Motivating and keeping employees, development of knowledge and business culture must all be included. In setting up a company you can make use of different management concepts.

The three management concepts to be discussed are:

- Scientific management.
- Human resource management.
- Human value management.

Scientific management

Taylorism is a term that is used to describe a systematic approach to labour division designed to cut costs. It is named after Frederick Taylor who as far back as 1900 had applied a scientific approach for work organization in companies which later became known as scientific management. This resulted in many companies entering the start-up phase with a relatively high level of work division which emphasized clarity of tasks and speciality fields plus clear decision-making procedures (see Box 10.6). This approach made a large contribution to productivity, although today other points of departure are used to raise production goals.

Box 10.6   T Ford

The early twentieth century was the dawn of the automobile industry. Innovative businessmen built their own factories and produced handcrafted cars destined to become collector's items. Holland also produced automobiles with well-known classic names as Spijker, Van Altena, and Aerts. However, there was a low production rate with high expenses.

Around the same time, American businessman Henry Ford also began making cars using the principle of 'scientific management'. The set-up of the production plant was simple but effective. Each employee was trained to produce and install a limited number of components. Through efficiency and keeping high standards, productivity increased enormously. Production costs for Ford's cars decreased to under $300. By applying principles of scientific management, his cars became affordable for a large population with more than 15 million Model T Fords being produced and sold between 1908 and 1927. An effective and efficient system of chassis spray painting also became part of factory operations and Henry Ford's legendary quote has not been forgotten: 'You can get a Model T in any colour, as long as it's black.'

Taylorism and scientific management had its heyday at the beginning of the twentieth century and thrived until the Second World War. In the 1960s and 70s it became clear that the philosophy had limitations for the contemporary world. Companies still adhering to Taylorism were considered mediocre and out of touch for their 'total concepts' approaches. It led, in many cases, to management conflicts and the creation of invisible walls between employees working in different divisions. The companies looked good on paper with well thought-out decisions relating to production. An important failing was that these organizations were not often able to react quickly to constantly changing surroundings which led to a sense of alienation. Task division, based on the rationality of homo economicus, led to individual employees having a weak or no sense of commitment to the company's objectives. It became clear that organization design has more to it than efficiency and effectiveness of the labour division. Today, the ideas behind Taylorism are used to a limited degree.

Human resource management

Post-Taylorism organization principles give more attention to the central position of people.[45] One approach of the 1980s which is still well known is 'human resource management' (HRM). This school of thought is based on viewing people as capital for business rather than cost factors. Companies spent more attention on education, motivation and career development. Many Dutch businesses have an employee policy based on 'connect, motivate and keep'. Continued learning opportunities for personnel and more involvement in the company are major premises of HRM. Investing in your people, with every employee in the right place with well-monitored plans leads to maximum involvement. In this context HRM does not have a factual relationship with CSR. Maximum profits remain the company's main goal. To give the people perspective of CSR a bit more substance, an extra step must be taken. This can be done by applying the vision of the human value management (HVM) approach.[46] That is why the HVM approach is seen as one of the important 'drivers' for the implementation of CSR in business.

This HVM approach becomes a substantial part of a CSR policy because employees will only participate in the company's network when they are actually in a position to implement social and societal values. Meaning becomes essential for many people. When it is possible, via your work, to support others or to assist in providing solutions that contribute to a better future, people are much more prepared to be involved in the company's activities. The value synchronization between human beings and the organization is an important starting point. The concept of 'work for money' assumes a secondary position. The 'boss–employee hierarchy' is exchanged for a 'network relation' with the company offering satisfaction and fulfilment in the workplace. The individual's response in making a commitment to the company reflects the desire to give additional meaning to his/her lifestyle. Work satisfaction, shared values between employer and employee, passion and identity are potent stimuli that can be used as a basis for business concepts.

Organizations embracing HVM ideals feel that worker happiness and fulfilment form an excellent base to operate in society and markets. The company must take the lead in placing social values at its core so that employees believe unequivocally in their goals. It goes without saying that HVM demands a well thought-out business strategy. For many businesses it becomes the search to find a synthesis between market orientation and personnel management. Developing such a strategy requires renewal and innovation but when HVM succeeds with integration into a market-orientated society, a competitive edge can quickly be established. It also gives the possibility of attracting the most qualified people to organizations. Fine-tuning of this concept also implies the element of synergy. Values formed between workers and the company are often the same values attached to the operation by customers. Of course, there are the necessary preconditions and certain cost levels must be achieved but HVM has a lot to offer, especially because with it, motivation and worker self-management increases (see Box 10.7). The influence of HVM on employees' needs should not be underestimated.

For HVM to succeed, personnel policy should form an important part of any strategic thinking. HVM has different premises than HRM. Table 10.1 clarifies the different points of departure.[47]

Table 10.1   Human resources management and human value management as a dichotomy[48]

Human Resources Management	Human Value Management
• The organization is a closed system. • The employees are the business capital. • HRM assumes an instrumental approach. • The organization is risk orientated and reacts to changes in surroundings. • HRM strives for consistent policy to create equilibrium between strategy and employee commitment.	• The organization is an open system. • Companies and employees are social partners reacting to each other. • Businesses practice corporate social responsibility and are market orientated. • Values form the core of operations. • Values are seen as 'social capital' and make it possible to attract talented people. • Employee policy is based on stakeholder management in combination with identity forming and social engagement.

Box 10.7   Helping Hands home care

The public health care system in the UK National Health Service (NHS) has been facing criticism over the past few years, highlighting the need to bring in more private players to health care and make it more beneficial for the general public. One of the problems of the NHS was the extensive and overly managed teams and slow bureaucratic systems which led to dissatisfaction and low motivation levels amongst the staff. The NHS has recognized this problem and the number of managers within the system has been steadily declining in the last four years before the time of writing. The management costs have also dropped over this period of time.

As an alternative to the public health care systems, the private health care sector in the UK is growing. Helping Hands was formed in 1989 with the aim of providing quality care to people in the comfort of their own homes. It was set up as a family business and it believes that it is 'small enough to care but big enough to cope'. Its priority lies in satisfying the needs of its customers in a dignified and respectful way by providing companionship along with medical care. Over the last 25 years, Helping Hands has spread across England and Wales and provides care services in more than 30 areas with over 900 carers. It provides live-in care as well as hourly and night visits to its patients based on their needs and requests.

One distinctive aspect of Helping Hands is the approach of human value management (HVM). As an organization, Helping Hands follows the values of its employees, whose focus is to provide the best medical and personal care to its customers. This approach of the company shows the belief it has in the values of its employees and helps in further motivating them, which in turn brings success to the company.

(Continued)

Helping Hands tries to pair its carers with the customers, the employees have been given the freedom to use their skills in the most appropriate way and perform their responsibility in line with the values they consider important. The supervisors of Helping Hands pride themselves in having warm, loving and enthusiastic carers to help their patients live a comfortable and independent life. The carers not only provide medical assistance but also help the patients with personal tasks such as getting dressed and shopping, or even just talk to them. Since it is a family-run business, the management, bureaucratic hurdles and hierarchy are minimal and are not a burden on the employees. The carers are therefore free to focus all their energies on fulfilling all the needs of their patients with the values they consider central. A research study conducted in the UK by the Cabinet Office showed that medical and health care practitioners in the UK are in the top 10 of most satisfied employees[49]. Within the Helping Hands community, the job satisfaction for the nurses and carers arises from the fact that not only are they helping those in need to live a better and more comfortable life, but also that the environment and the motivation that is provided to them by the organization, where there is reduced bureaucratic systems, helps them to focus more on their values and jobs and waste minimal time handling unnecessary bureaucratic systems.

Case questions:

1. Explain why Helping Hands is an example of a community model.
2. What might be a risk for this approach when the organization becomes larger?
3. Why is this approach not only less bureaucratic but also cheaper?
4. Which organizational values would be chosen by Helping Hands if employee values are considered the principal point of departure?

10.4.3 Cooperation

Many organizations see themselves as a unique entity, a sort of black box with incoming and outgoing goods. The relation with suppliers, distributors and the customer remains one dimensional. The exchanges are concerned with the 'money path' and the 'goods and services path' and are commonly referred to as a 'conventional relation' using the principles of 'homo economicus'. Hollender and Breen[50] claim that more options are available for organizations to give better form to their relationships with the outside world. A relation based on cooperation has more to do with dimensions and different variations that can apply. For example, the quality of relationships can be defined by obvious nature aspects such as esteem and empathy. A company can ask customers to participate in new product testing or can ask suppliers for suggestions concerning innovation and parts development. It can even extend to a concept that makes use of volunteers' assistance in production without incurring extra costs. The open source computer operating system Linux is a good example. It makes use of the exploratory urge and social behaviour of volunteers who spend hours of unpaid time working on the solutions for software problems (see Box 10.8 for another example of cooperation strategy). In South Africa, this concept of cooperation is known as Ubuntu and simply means that people need each other to thrive.[51] This idea is important for businesses because it opens their eyes and gives more sophisticated options for setting up their operations.

> ### Box 10.8   British Petroleum in India[52]
>
> A successful example of cooperation strategy to deliver responsible practices is the alliance established by British Petroleum (BP) with three microcredit companies in India for the distribution of a portable oven which uses both liquid fuel and biomass. The innovative device responded to a need of poor communities to switch to biomass in economic scarcity, while avoiding toxic fumes release. BP introduced environmental and hygiene and security standards as non-negotiable requirements for partnership, while at the same time providing the necessary training to their local colleagues through a partnership with community NGOs. The microcredit companies, on the other hand, once empowered by training, maximized their ability to bring into the partnership their knowledge of local needs and resources, in turn enabling BP to design suitable solutions and make the product available to isolated rural communities. The oven was a fast-selling product and brought BP not only profit margins but its community and policy makers goodwill, which is still strong in India despite the fall of BP's reputation elsewhere in the world after the catastrophic Deep Horizon spillage in the Gulf of Mexico.

10.4.4   Transparency

Are businesses in a vulnerable position if they are transparent about their activities? This question is especially relevant for CSR-orientated enterprises because they are set up on the pretention of healthy contributions for people and the planet even if it is likely that things will go wrong and enthusiastic ambitions and goals turn out to be impractical. The question can be asked about whether openness can be considered a contributing factor, but also if a closed shop attitude makes a business vulnerable, because setbacks are often brought to public attention in a negative light. Transparency and CSR should go hand in hand. Companies intrinsically motivated to conduct business in a socially responsible context profit from this approach.

> ### Box 10.9   Timberland dispenses with its sedate CSR yearly report[53]
>
> Companies who focus on transparency force themselves to be ahead of the game. Transparency creates ambition. This has been the approach of shoemaker Timberland which employs 6000 people. It has scrapped its annual CSR report in favour of a quarterly report with clearly stated output indicators. To communicate information about a number of products, Timberland uses the 'Green Index Tag' which resembles the labels to be found on many food products. It offers the customer information in a nutshell about the eco-effects of its product. The CEO believes this direct information is necessary to confront customers with the urgency of the environmental problem. He goes on to say that Timberland is a business which is part of a worldwide community and no effort should be spared in the effort to realize positive transformations.

For business management, internal transparency from within is a tool for better performance. Transparent communication from business to stakeholders contributes to a mutual feeling of trust, but transparency can also be stressful. Many people are keenly aware of to whom you should, or should not, expose your vulnerability. For openness a trust relation is necessary. But openness has precisely a trust relation as a consequence. To manage transparency, companies must keep in mind that they are in a complex area when developing policy. Certain messages are absorbed by the media and others arouse controversy. To control this, in the hope of being less vulnerable, the idea of information continuity is important. Trust occurs when stakeholders are honestly informed about aspects of a company's progress and are able to take stock of the development at various intervals. Relations with those involved are strengthened because narrative ethics and intention ethics come into play (see Chapter 4). Regular communication between enterprise and stakeholders creates a healthy dialogue. Presenting target indicators and improvement projects on a regular basis is a verification of a company's good intentions.

10.4.5   Authenticity

A company is stated to be *authentic* if its external and internal aspects correspond to each other. This refers to image vs. reality. The authentic enterprise presents a recognizable identity. It sets up the values by which it plans to operate plus the mission it wants to fulfil, and strives to ensure that these elements are firmly anchored in all sectors of its operations. Think of authenticity as a company's outward image corresponding with its inner DNA (see Box 10.10 for an example). The concept of authenticity has similarities with the concept of 'identity' as used in psychology. The definition of identity in psychological terms is described as 'the more or less complete picture that a person has of themselves which, in general, corresponds to the way he/she is seen by others'.[54] In professional psychology, identity is often associated with identity forming and an important condition for success in this area is to a large extent dependent on surroundings. A person is proud of his or her identity if it conforms to positive surrounding values and if he or she can identify with these in a natural manner. Good identity forming allows people to be themselves without confusion about their roles.[55] In business, identity and identity forming make partial use of these same mechanisms.

Many companies struggle with the issue of whether or not their outside and inside should correspond with each other and if adjustments need to be made to either side. It seems that often the quest for short-term profits weighs heavily against environment, integrity and well-being questions which receive less attention. Companies are not eager to admit their neglect of these subjects to the outside world and sometimes try to present a picture that is prettier than reality. A company's authenticity can become liable for legal proceedings.

Box 10.10   Douwe Egberts

The question of identity forming plagued the Dutch company Douwe Egberts for several decades. At the end of the twentieth century, protest groups accused it of being irresponsible because it chose to distance itself from supply chain responsibility. The protesters claimed that Douwe Egberts did nothing to improve the coffee price for small growers. At first, the company reacted defensively and claimed that it would not be able to compete with other coffee producers if it had to purchase coffee at a higher price on the world market. In addition, a fixed price for small producers was not considered an option because these growers would not have any stimulus to improve their productivity. Despite pressure from society, Douwe

(Continued)

Egberts did its best to retain its old identity but was finally forced to make some changes in the twenty-first century. In 2004 it agreed to purchase part of its coffee beans using the responsible coffee standard Utz Kapeh (later called Utz Certified[56]). The power of the certification meant that working conditions for the growers on the coffee plantations had to improve. The company chose a pragmatic approach. During successive years the purchase of Utz Kapeh coffee increased and led to the majority of coffee coming from certified sources. This was a clear sign that Douwe Egberts was changing its identity, with its external communications (outside) and internal structure (inside) changing simultaneously. In the end, despite internal and external changes, Douwe Egberts' authenticity remained more or less the same.

The concept of *reputation management* is used in conjunction with CSR, but is part of a bigger picture. CSR policy supports reputation, but there are other influencing factors as well. Especially for large corporations, CSR has become a part of reputation management. Other aspects related to this are:

- Emotional attractiveness
- Products and services
- Finances
- Work climate
- Vision and leadership.[57]

Reputation management is important for companies because building a good reputation can determine its success even though this is to some degree very fragile. A good reputation that has been built up through many years can go down quite rapidly if there are negative incidents. For multinationals it is important to have a risk analysis in order to see which part of its operations are most vulnerable to reputation damage. It is also possible that a CSR policy can make a company vulnerable, especially if it becomes greedy for publicity. For this reason many international companies are reluctant for their CSR policy to be seen in the limelight, but there are enough examples of the opposite situation occurring. Several oil companies have been accused by the NGO Corpwatch of 'greenwashing'.[58] Greenwashing is a sort of window dressing which can seem very attractive, but it can cause reputation loss of the company.

10.5 Limitations of corporate social responsibility[59]

Many authors agree that the practical contribution of voluntary business initiatives to reduce the most pressing contemporary social and environmental challenges such as poverty and climate change has been so far limited and has only worked in particular circumstances. CSR has furnished a good deal of charity in poor countries but it concentrates in communities surrounding a multinational. CSR strategies have failed to develop solutions that can be scaled up to address societal challenges. Very few companies develop CSR practices using their own unique resources and know-how. An underlying problem is the reactive approach of most CSR strategies. In the search for social legitimacy, the stronger the pressure, the stronger the answer, which leads companies to leave the control of their CSR agenda in the hands of stakeholders such as NGOs that do not understand the companies' potential capacities. Furthermore, there is no guarantee that the problems claimed by the more vehement stakeholders are the most important ones.

The focus on corporate reputation and business case entails the risk of having a never-ending exercise of public relations with minimum value for society and scarce benefit for business. Many companies engage in what is called decoupling. On the one hand, the firm publicly endorses CSR and environmentally friendly practices. On the other hand, is business as usual in its operational practices. Indeed, adoption of ISO 26000 is often used to signal responsibility to external stakeholders while the company actually does as little as possible. It is a way of lobbying to deflect threats of more regulation or consumer protest.

10.5.1 Critical CSR

To address these criticisms, an increasing number of authors are working on the development of a critical CSR research agenda. As a case in point, 'the enabling environment view of CSR'[60] stresses the need for a greater focus on poverty and more integration of community participation, corporate willingness and governmental regulation. However, despite growing recognition that any effective long-term solution to the problem of poverty must also provide solutions to the problems of environmental degradation and depletion of natural resources, environmental issues do not yet play a central role in 'enabling environment CSR'. Many limitations of CSR could be addressed with a good distribution of resources across different types of responsibilities and more stakeholders' engagement with the design of CSR practices. These themes are the core of our final section.

10.5.2 Corporate social responsibility orientation (CSRO)

CSRO is the extent to which companies privilege particular types of responsibilities over others when making social investments. Archibald Carrol identified four main types of corporate responsibilities: economic (responsibility to be profitable), legal (responsibility to obey the law), ethical (responsibility to act in accordance with social norms, values and moral principles) and philanthropic (responsibility to be a good citizen).

All four responsibilities must be embedded in corporate behaviour and must be fulfilled at all times. They are the components of CSR strategy.[61] Many criticisms of CSR are the result of companies failing to fulfil all these types of responsibility or failing to identify the best allocation of resources across components when budgets are limited or trade-offs between components cannot be avoided.

Carroll proposed a pyramid of which economic responsibilities are the foundation, followed by legal, ethical, and philanthropic or discretionary at the top (see Figure 10.2 for an adapted version). The first two are fundamental, required responsibilities. A firm cannot exist if they are not fulfilled. Being profitable also means paying taxes which are used by governments to improve welfare. Ethical responsibilities are expected by society, they are the basis of social licence and needed for firms' long term survival. All three can be encapsulated by the principle 'do no harm'. Finally, philanthropic responsibilities are about 'doing good'. They are the most visible and key for firms' reputation. They should embody each firm's values and identity.[62]

All components *must* be fulfilled at all times. This is a distributional model, not a sequential one. For each dollar spent, 40% must go to economic responsibilities, 30% to legal, 20% to ethical and 10% to philanthropic responsibilities. Empirical studies ratify the pyramid's usefulness in a Western context. However, it does not work well in poor countries where rule of law is weak and government failure means that being profitable does not benefit communities since taxes are not efficiently used. In poor countries basic economic responsibilities include creating employment and even infrastructure, while philanthropic responsibilities are much more important that legal (see Figure 10.3). Another problem is the explicit lack of recognition of environmental responsibilities as an independent component.[63]

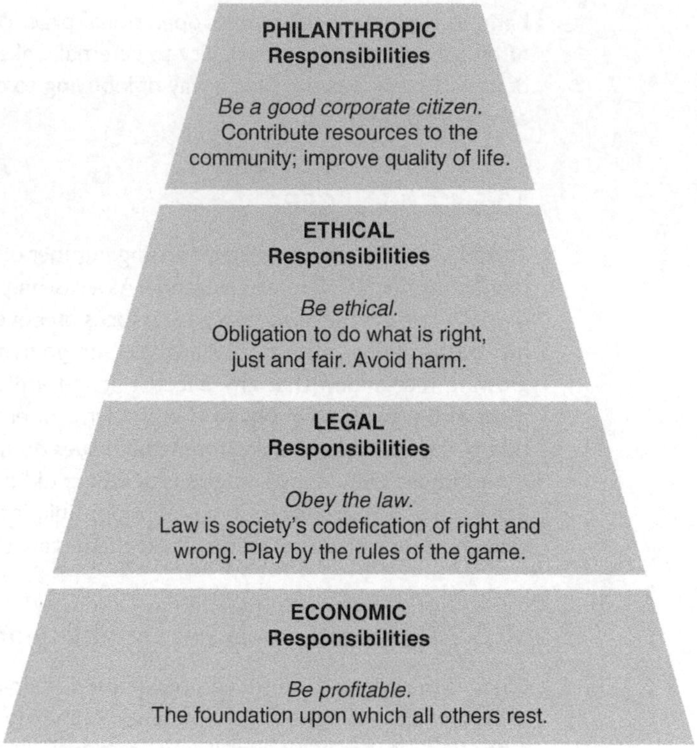

PHILANTHROPIC Responsibilities

Be a good corporate citizen.
Contribute resources to the community; improve quality of life.

ETHICAL Responsibilities

Be ethical.
Obligation to do what is right, just and fair. Avoid harm.

LEGAL Responsibilities

Obey the law.
Law is society's codefication of right and wrong. Play by the rules of the game.

ECONOMIC Responsibilities

Be profitable.
The foundation upon which all others rest.

Figure 10.2 Western CSRO (adapted from Carroll)[64]

LEGAL Responsibilities
Obey law.

ETHICAL Responsibilities
Be Ethical and Virtuous.

ENVIRONMENTAL Responsibilities
Protect the Natural Environment.

HUMANITARIAN (PHILANTROPIC) Responsibilities
Do Good to Communities.

ECONOMIC AND DEVELOPMENTAL Responsibilities
Be profitable and contribute to economic development.

Figure 10.3 Critical CSRO in less-developed countries (adapted from Yakovleva and Vázquez-Brust)[65]

10.6   Case Study: CSR in the mining industry

Case prepared by Ankit Gaur

The emergence of CSR as an important concept within the mining industry developed because the main benefit that used to be provided by these corporations to the local community was employment. However, over the last few decades due to technological advancements, most of the mining sector has become mechanized and the requirement for unskilled labour has reduced. Therefore, as the local communities are no longer receiving any direct benefit from the corporations, they are opposing their projects more frequently. This has led to the increase in CSR policies to meet the needs of the local communities affected by the projects.[66]

The CSR policies followed by the mining companies are often considered by many to be merely compensations for the social and environmental costs associated with the business. The pressures associated with such business include environmental concerns, increased housing and food prices, influx of migrants leading to pressure on health services, prostitution and gambling amongst others. As a result of these, the CSR policies developed by most mining companies include investment in infrastructure such as roads, schools, homes, better drainage etc. and also health care, better sanitation facilities, and information on family planning and HIV amongst others. Apart from the social concerns, the increased knowledge and acceptance of environmental damage caused by mining operations has led to an increase in environmental development-related CSR policies such as afforestation programmes, setting up plants for cleaning local water sources, wildlife rehabilitation programmes etc.

Often, mining companies collaborate with local NGOs to develop and work on their CSR policies. NGOs such as Save the Children and Care collaborate with mining companies to help maintain a check on their activities.[67] For example ActionAid Zambia along with some other local NGOs have been opposing the extensive land acquisitions by Canadian Mining firm FQM and have highlighted the plight of the local farmers that have been inadequately compensated.[68]

'Green mining' or 'greenwashing'

CSR policies are often only considered a PR strategy put in place by the large corporations to take advantage of the local communities and their resources.[69] Mining companies have realized that the disruptions caused to their operations if the local communities are unhappy can result in a delay in projects and also cause large amounts of financial losses. As a result of this, it is in their best interest to keep their stakeholders happy.[70] Things have been changing for the better and CSR strategies are no longer only to benefit the organization but also have a positive impact on local communities.

Mining organizations operating in the Copperbelt area in Zambia have set up several CSR programmes to support the local communities in the area such as creating toilet facilities, setting up a specialized eye care centre for diabetes patients and starting a centre for skills development in collaboration with various trades training institutes. Mining multinational Barrick Gold has initiated projects in agriculture, health, education and women's financial security and savings. The CSR managers at the Lubambe copper mines started a resettlement project which will look into resettling families that have been affected by the mining activities of the firm. A large number of Canadian mining organizations have also set up several good CSR projects in the Copperbelt area. These include building schools and mobile laboratories, and providing free books, uniforms and stationery to students.[71]

Case Study Questions

1. Elaborate on the ways that mining companies can compensate for the environmental damage caused by their operations.
2. Explain the various levels of regulation that are offered by local communities, NGOs and governments in controlling the activities of large mining corporations.
3. Suggest methods in which CSR policies can be used by organizations solely for their own benefit.
4. Explain how good CSR practices by mining companies in Zambia have influenced the country's economy and overall welfare.

10.7   Learning tools

10.7.1   Summary

- Businesses need three licences to operate: a licence to sell (market), a licence to produce (government) and a licence to operate (society).
- Corporate social responsibility (CSR) implies that companies work voluntarily on the integration of the concern for environmental and social aspects into their daily operations in interaction with their stakeholders. Voluntarily means they are not forced by governments using policies and legislation.
- CSR includes all the subjects that are part of the definition of sustainable development.
- ISO 26000 is the international guideline for CSR published in 2010.
- For the successful implementation of CSR a strong vision, new business models, cooperation in the supply chain, transparency and a strong identity are very important.
- CSR orientation 'pyramids' are useful tools to guide companies in their allocation of resources. Companies must fulfil five types of responsibilities at all times: economic, legal, ethical, environmental and philanthropic.
- Companies that pretend to implement CSR are being accused of 'greenwashing' or 'window dressing'. Critical CSR argues that companies need to engage a range of stakeholders when designing CSR strategies.

10.7.2   Further reading

Burgos-Jimenez, J., Vázquez-Brust, D. & Plaza-Ubeda, J. (2011). Adaptability, entrepreneurship and stakeholder integration: Scenarios and strategies for environment and vulnerability. *Journal of Environmental Protection,* 2(10), 1375–1387.

European Commission Brussels (2011). *Opinion of the European Economic and Social Committee on the 'Communication from the Commission to the European Parliament, the Council, the European Economic and Social Committee and the Committee of the Regions – A renewed EU strategy 2011–14 for Corporate Social Responsibility'.* COM (2011) 681 final.

Freeman, R. E. (1984). *Strategic Management: A Stakeholder Approach.* Cambridge: Cambridge University Press.

Moratis, L. & Cochius, T. (2011, May). *ISO 26000: The Business Guide to the New Standard on Social Responsibility*. Greenleaf Publishing.

Reed, R. (2012, February). The CSR Performance Ladder Certification Standards. *The Executive Times*, 13–15.

Schoemaker, M., Nijhof, A. & Jonker, J. (2006). Human value management: The influence of the contemporary developments of corporate social responsibility and social capital on HRM. *Management Revue, 17*(4), 448–465.

Zerk, J. A. (2006). *Multinationals and Corporate Social Responsibility: Limitations and Opportunities in International Law*. Cambridge: Cambridge University Press.

10.7.3   Assignments

 Assignment 10.1

Go to the website of BSCI and select a company that participates in this initiative. Determine why it participates and what actions it has implemented as a member of this initiative.

 Assignment 10.2

Choose a multinational company and analyse why and how it has implemented CSR in its business. Use different sources of information for your work.

 Assignment 10.3

Select a sustainability report of a company. Analyse if the content is following the GRI guidelines and if they are being completely honest or are just using the report for public relations.

10.7.4   Self-test questions

 Self-test Questions

1.   Which three licences does a company need to be successful in society?
2.   What are the core characteristics of CSR?
3.   Why should the definitions of CSR stakeholders and not the CEO decide which societal aspects are important for a specific company?
4.   Why is ISO 26000 not a standard but a guideline?
5.   What is the difference between human resource management and human value management?
6.   What is the aim of the Global Reporting Initiative (GRI)?
7.   Why is cooperation in supply networks a very important factor for improving societal aspects?
8.   What are the limitations of and the criticisms about CSR?
9.   What is 'greenwashing'?

11

GLOBALIZATION AND STRATEGY DEVELOPMENT

Overview and learning objectives

The mobile phone has created the possibility for billions of people to get connected worldwide. Globalization is having an impact on everyone and attracting us to consumer markets. Everything from looking for a job to setting up electricity and water bills, purchasing insurance or buying a prepaid mobile is now not only a normal activity for the West but is rapidly affecting the developing countries as well with their combined population base of five billion people (Asia, Latin America and Africa).[1] In many of these countries more people in rural areas are connecting with the cities and changing modes of production and consumption.[2] Fewer farmers now adhere to the old-fashioned subsistence farming where they harvested crops primarily for their own consumption without giving much thought to creating a market surplus.[3] People were not able to purchase or consume much, output was low and natural resources were kept largely intact. In this subsistence economy a light ecological footprint also forms part of the general picture but now that these people are participating in the market economy, worldwide pressure on our natural resources is increasing significantly.

This fast connection is being aided by a number of new technologies being brought to the market that can be applied to rural residents in developing lands. Mobile phones, small-scale solar energy installations and bio fuel will be the harbingers of change to the countryside. The investment required to spread these technologies can be provided by private companies. Governments' role as 'investor' will decrease because investments in rural areas will no longer be dependent on setting up cable connections for electricity and telephone services. Power points for single households can now be realized on a small scale.[4] The new term 'off-grid technology' has come into being and implies that business and the private sector can embrace the new technologies without always relying on government support.[5] For mobile phones and data networks, capital investment in digital transmitter masts by private entrepreneurs is sufficient to set up operations.

Sustainable development has in principle become essential for everyone. Innovations in the supply chain, the economy of sharing, new materials and network organizations will be part of the solution to bring a circular economy within reach. Companies hoping to be part of this future should have taking care of the environment and worldwide prosperity as core beliefs.[6] Enterprises who are geared up for these challenges of the twenty-first century are confronted with enormous potential. See Figure 11.1 for an overview of breakthrough technologies across history.

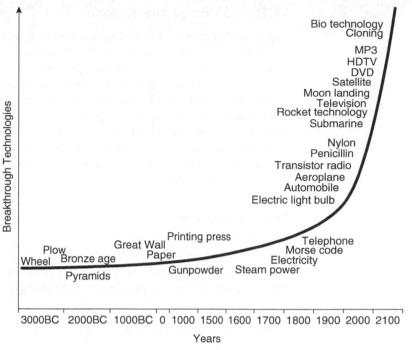

Figure 11.1 Breakthrough technologies

This chapter will focus on globalization, sustainability and the challenges that businesses face in the twenty-first century. Section 11.1 will examine the changes taking place in emerging economies and developing countries. In these countries businesses make up part of an international network and use new strategies. Section 11.2 will look closely at these strategies and the methods and instruments used to develop new business. The concept of 'CSR strategy' plays a pivotal role in this process.[7] What steps do businesses take to introduce new strategies using new technologies and business models, so that they are able to contribute to a solution for problems which we currently face?

Learning objectives

This chapter will enable the student to:

- Understand how globalization is increasingly becoming the working terrain for small and medium enterprises (SMEs) and social entrepreneurship.
- Understand why business has good reason to focus on markets with low individual purchasing power.
- Gain insight into the external drivers for developing an innovative CSR strategy.
- Learn to apply models for developing innovative business strategies.

11.1 Business opportunities for new economies

The opportunity to increase welfare in countries with low productivity is large if transaction costs are kept under reasonable control. The know-how for making good products efficiently is readily available on the Internet and globalization makes it easy to find suitable business partners. This section will look at developments in emerging and developing countries.

11.1.1   SMEs go international

The global integration of economic environments and ICT has created new frontiers for business to operate internationally.[8] Online communication has made it simple to start business activities on other continents. International big business has now made room for international SMEs (small and medium enterprises). New markets, co-partnership, outsourcing and purchasing now occur in different parts of the world and the word multinational no longer applies to large companies exclusively. We have even seen that private individuals have formed businesses as alternatives to development aid. The Internet offers a plethora of small-scale alternatives for entrepreneurs. Let's examine the significance of this using the concepts of micro multinationals and 'social entrepreneurship'.

Micro multinationals

Micro multinationals are companies with a maximum of 250 employees with branches spread out over several continents. We see many examples of this in the agricultural sector. Using an example of rose farmers in Box 11.1 we will look at the micro multinational and the situations it encounters when working on different continents.

Box 11.1   Rose growers

Dutch rose growers consider Kenya an ideal location for their product. The country is close to the equator and has excellent weather with 12-hour sun-drenched days the norm.[9] There are few temperature changes during the year and in the mountainous areas daily temperatures vary between 18˚C–28˚C. At the moment the surface area of the Dutch rose growers in Kenya is the same as back home in Holland.[10] Even the life cycle analysis is reasonably opportune, despite the fact that the flowers are sold on the Dutch market. The CO_2 emissions produced in bringing a Kenyan rose to the Dutch market are more favourable than producing it locally.[11] This is because the lighting and heating necessities of Dutch greenhouses cause more harmful emissions, at least in cases where older and outdated heating techniques are used.

Important aspects that play a role when business decides to manufacture a product in a developing country are: political stability, culture and infrastructure.[12] Starting business abroad demands detailed preparation and a real understanding of the complexity of implementation.[13] It often takes years before production, material supply and distribution are properly and efficiently aligned. Considering this, the following criteria are imperative for smaller companies starting a new business or production abroad.

- The company deals often with weaker countries and a new culture. The new situation requires that a business strategy must be developed on a broader scale. The micro business is operating in unknown waters. The education levels of professionals and workers demand a new management style. It is even conceivable that new facilities must be implemented for health care because of inadequate hospital services for workers. Management will also be confronted with questions about corruption, bureaucracy and ecology.
- The scale size of the site is often a critical success factor. In many developing countries, businesses are self-contained. They have an extensive technical staff with facilities such as transmission towers and power plants. These facilities are important because infrastructure in these lands is not highly developed. Many companies have,

for example, their own source of energy. The scale size has special relevance for international transport and production must have sufficient scope. In addition, unfamiliar management habits must be dealt with and attention paid to building up relations. Increased turnaround time for projects become the case if there is a complicated question.

- The development of international law so that long-term expenses can be calculated for taxes and duties. Clear policy must be drawn up for future international development concerning duties on kerosene, for example, so that international air transport also contributes its share to the external costs involved in CO_2 emissions.[14]
- When setting up operations in a less industrialized country, companies will be directly involved with the learning curve. The calculation of production costs must also take into consideration that the cost per product will be much higher in the initial phase as compared to later periods because efficient work habits are not always in place in new companies (see Figure 11.2). This means that it is imperative that enterprises have a sufficient financial buffer to cover extra expenses in the early stages.

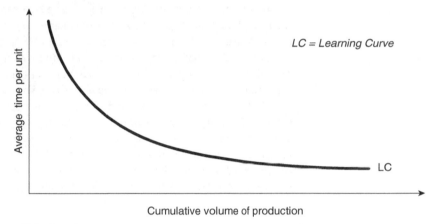

Figure 11.2   Learning curve

Social entrepreneurship

A part of international business activities are developed through initiatives that are born out of ideals. This can be neatly described as 'social entrepreneurship' or 'social venture entrepreneurship'. This type of venture differs from conventional definitions because it is aimed at social improvement with economic yields and profits assuming a secondary role. Health care, culture, environment and combating poverty come under this category. The company's 'success' is evaluated on the basis of goals attained to improve society. Social entrepreneurship is different from charity. Social entrepreneurs remain responsible for producing good returns. They are directly involved in any estimation errors related to attempts to provide increased value and remain focused on efficiency and effectiveness.[15]

A relatively large number of social entrepreneurs who start their own businesses are confronted with limited investment capital. The existence of these companies is largely dependent on the skills of the founder and whether he/she is capable of building a network. The lack of capital is offset with time and means that a number of years can pass before a reasonable turnover can be achieved. These operations are often founded on dreams coupled with passion and entrepreneurship.[16] Network building and profit perspectives are often satisfactory but generally occur over a longer period of time than originally conceived.

> ### Box 11.2   MAMA DIOP[17]
>
> When Dutch Fred van Hessen visited the Gambia in 2004, he noticed that the Gambian people were unable to make any profit from the abundant fruit harvests, especially mangoes. In 2006 he began a business called MAMA DIOP to build hybrid solar fruit dryers. These machines would hopefully contribute to a reduction in poverty in West Africa by allowing women to have a source of income. Initial experiments with small-scale drying units led to the conclusion that export quality products could not be produced in this manner. Working together with engineer Jan Kluiver, they spent several years developing a semi-industrial fruit dryer that could turn 1000 kilos of fresh fruit into 60 kilos–80 kilos of dried fruit on a daily basis.
>
> The development of the solar fruit dryer relied on 'custom-made technology' that can best be described as 'sophisticated low tech': only 4% of all required energy is electrical, but the drying process is controlled by digital measuring and regulating technology. During the day the warm air required to dry the mangoes, bananas, papayas, tomatoes, peanuts etc. is collected in a heat module that also functions as the roof of the building. At the same time heat from the sun is also stored in water tanks so that the drying process can continue to a second phase in the evening. In 2011–2012 a small prototype model was built which was capable of processing 150 kilos of fresh fruit per day. Test results are very encouraging with higher than expected capacity and an excellent quality of dried mangoes.
>
> In 2013 van Hessen went searching for investment capital. He needed in excess of €100,000 for a larger dryer with sufficient capacity in order to turn a profit. Potential investors were invited to witness the drying process technology in person. In 2014 van Hessen's luck changed. An investor from the Gambia was convinced of the dryers' potential and provided the necessary cash to start production in 2015.[18] Nine years after MAMA DIOP was set up, the profit element is finally on the horizon.

11.1.2   Principles for the Bottom of the Pyramid

The four billion poor with a maximum yearly income of $1500 constitutes a huge potential market despite the low purchasing power per individual.[19] This group forms the 'Bottom of the Pyramid' (see Figure 11.3) and remains largely neglected because business produces goods aimed at higher income targets. With his book *The Fortune at the Bottom of the Pyramid*, management guru C. K. Prahalad (1941–2010) discusses strategic possibilities for accessing this market. The idea behind it is the development of Bottom of the Pyramid Products (BoP products) designed for workers earning between $1 and $5 a day to allow them some participation in society.[20] Mobile phones, medicine, building materials, credit and basic articles such as soap and clean water are necessary to support their existence. Clean clothing and being able to communicate by telephone has meant, for example, that people have more possibilities to participate in the workforce. A comfortable house and access to medicines also provide marked improvements.

> If we stop thinking of the poor as victims or as a burden and start recognizing them as resilient and creative entrepreneurs and value conscious consumers, a whole new world of opportunity will open up. (C. K. Prahalad, 2006, p. 1)[21]

With this quote the author is pleading for a new approach to the poor. This well-known academic has inspired multinationals to rethink their business models and the markets they are trying to reach. Essential innovation forms the foundation. In the same way that Henry Ford was able to produce his Model T automobile for average incomes at the beginning of the twentieth century by switching from handmade to factory production lines, businesses must be on the lookout for new paths and sales innovations. Stuart Hart has referred to this as the 'great leap downward', in other words the idea of offering products and services to people on the lowest rung of society.[22]

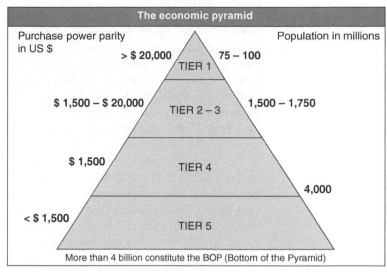

Figure 11.3   The Bottom of the Pyramid[23]

Businesses whose innovations succeed, and whose products and services are made available to people with the lowest incomes, have a substantial competitive edge. Prahalad's challenge was taken up by many enterprises who were already looking at the bottom of the pyramid possibilities as compared to consumer markets targeting Western buyers.

Prahalad targeted the four billion people living under the poverty line. Achieving scale size and innovation directed towards structural reduction of production costs are important elements in his theory. This approach has led to new business initiatives worldwide. A good example of this is Jaipur Foot.[24] They manufacture affordable prostheses for poor people who have lost a limb. The average cost is around $45, an amount that many families are able to scrape together. The cost in India is significantly lower than a prosthesis in the US where $12,000 would be considered a normal selling price. Among other things, Jaipur Foot manufactures artificial limbs made of rubber. This makes it possible to walk without losing balance on uneven surfaces; these are present in many poor Indian towns and villages. In addition the company has insisted that the artificial limbs must be easy to produce. This is important because in the area where the limbs are manufactured, there is a shortage of skilled labour.[25]

To realize the 'leap downward' Prahalad formulated various principles to make products available for the lowest income group. For more insight into entering a market with four billion people, we provide a summary.[26]

Nine principles for Bottom of the Pyramid production

1. **Create the capacity to consume (price achievement)**
    The structural determination of a good price is the result of innovation and an important criterion is whether or not the company is able to achieve significant change in the price–quality relation. Creating purchasing power for the lowest earners can also be achieved by creating new methods of payment. Savings options should be set up to accept small deposits.

    For example, manufacturers of relatively expensive lighting systems using solar storage could begin with a collective savings system where all participants deposit small amounts at regular intervals before the lamps are made available. Every time enough money is saved, a new lamp is delivered to one customer. The duration of the savings system remains intact until everyone has received a lamp.

2. **Innovation: Hybrid**

   Low-income markets are not waiting anxiously for products that are cheap replicas of Western counterparts. It is essential that anyone involved in developing BoP products makes use of advanced technology, research and new product concepts. Multinational Unilever has developed specific marketing and product strategies tailored to developing countries. A good example of this is the iodine content added to food. In most industrialized lands, iodized salt is purposely added to many food products. By doing this, the industry is contributing to children's health because lack of iodine inhibits physical development and can lead to a higher percentage of people with learning difficulties. In India, 70 million children suffer from a lack of this substance in their diet and it constitutes a grave danger for public health. The problem is that adding iodine to food in tropical climates, especially in India, is far less effective. Storage of iodized salt in warm warehouses, transport in sweltering heat and unhealthy cooking methods means that the effect of the added iodine has been neutralized before it can be consumed. Unilever has come up with a new technology to provide a molecular form of iodine in capsules. This can be used as a food additive to salt in tropical countries and it remains much more stable and decomposes at a slower rate.

3. **Scale of operations**

   It is a challenge to create wide-ranging initiatives for a market consisting of four billion people. Multinationals are among the few organizations with sufficient 'clout' to address these demands. Prahalad uses the term 'scalable' to transform smaller NGO initiatives into large-scale international efforts. With a private investment of only €1000, it is now possible to realize a sustainable energy project benefiting an entire village in a developing land. These initiatives are often small scale with the overhead being used to finance the venture. The overhead costs are not passed on to the consumer. A multinational, obviously, cannot function in this manner. It strives to develop commercial activities and keep variable and permanent expenses at a low ebb. In this type of situation 'economy of scale' (see Figure 11.4) is applied to the overhead, the research and the machinery, so that low per capita operating expenses can be achieved.

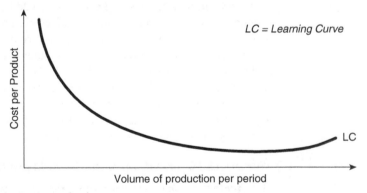

Figure 11.4   Economy of scale

4. **Sustainable development**

   Realizing turnover and production in an expansive Bottom of the Pyramid market with four billion consumers does not take place in the same way as in developed countries. Environment plays an important role in this market. Many products used in industrialized countries are eco-inefficient and eco-ineffective. I think, for example, of Western sanitary systems that rely on large amounts of water being pumped through a water closet cistern. Such products are totally unfeasible for poor, densely populated countries with a structural water shortage.

5. **Functionality**

   Successful entrance into the markets of developing countries depends on the attention that has been paid to clients' needs because these are very different than Western demands. Houses, shops and infrastructure come immediately to mind, not to forget culture. What does it mean, for example, if a product is used in the context of an extended family as compared to a 'European' nuclear family of three people?

6. **Supply chain innovation**

   Innovations in the production process or supply chain make it possible to realize considerable cost reductions that are necessary to reach low income markets (see also Chapter 9). The role of ICT can be paramount in such situations with a good example being the ITC Group, an Indian company specializing in farm exports. They developed a new trading system which eliminated middlemen and offered better contact between the company and the farmers themselves by setting up a computer system in small Indian villages to contact the local growers directly. This allowed them to maintain a product inventory which was adjusted to improve transport efficiency. This meant that the locally produced products could be directly transported to the factory.

7. **Making better use of uneducated employees**

   Communications technology has opened up possibilities to employ people with little or no education. The health services in Peru use mobile phones to support provincial health care workers in making a good diagnosis. Using photographs of diseases in different stages, the employees were better able to determine the extent of the illness they encountered in the countryside.

8. **Schooling and client empowerment**

   Many poverty prevention projects incorporate elements of schooling and empowerment and this has been taken up by multinationals hoping to access this market. Unilever, for example, chose to work together with local NGOs when it introduced a new disinfectant soap to the market which was designed to improve public health and cut back cases of diarrhoea which remains a leading cause of child mortality in developing countries. The programme encouraged school-aged children to wash their hands with the new soap. Demonstrations using ultraviolet light allowed the children to see 'first-hand' the thousands of bacteria that remained on their hands when they only washed with water. It led to the children being the best ambassadors in their own families for improving hygiene and sanitary conditions at home.

9. **Integral approach**

   Success in the BoP market depends on the development of new concepts. To reach the lowest income markets requires an integral approach to the target group. Economy of scale and new technologies are not in themselves sufficient to obtain a low cost price. Consideration must be taken for the world's poor to improve their own situations themselves without external aid.

11.1.3   Discussions on the Bottom of the Pyramid

The Bottom of the Pyramid approach gives businesses necessary tools to contribute to society and reach the poorest segments with profit and reduction of poverty being equal goals. It can create new nonzero sum scenarios but the disadvantages of BoP should not be overlooked. With their limited funds the poor can often only afford to make a one-off expenditure. If products are not very useful or if they have inferior quality they do not contribute to a reduction in poverty. Multifunctional poor quality digital watches, glitzy jewellery and other useless gadgets may help to create a feeling of identity but offer no tangible or fundamental improvements for the target group. Andrew Crabtree has stated that overestimates of the indulgences and potential purchasing power of the poor can lead to the creation of artificial needs.[27] Companies who 'pretend' to design their products for the BoP have a responsibility. Prahalad goes on to say that the government's role should also be considered and any Bottom of the Pyramid solutions should not be a half-hearted effort. The private sector cannot compensate for the failure of the state. In a discussion about the slums of Mumbai in India, Prahalad stated that the government should assume responsibility for providing fresh water to the poor.[28] Government plays a prominent role in matters of health, sanitation and education for the underprivileged. Enterprise can certainly fulfil some tasks but in a market economy 'economic responsibility' remains the domain of business and the government is held responsible if the market fails.[29]

11.2   Development of an innovative CSR strategy

The increased pressure on the environment, plus improved welfare coupled with an ever-growing world population has meant that the global search continues for solutions regarding waste disposal, dangerous emissions and the increasing need for raw materials. It is becoming clear that business has to be a major player in these fields and it is time for a new era of 'creative destruction'.[30] Creative destruction and outdated technologies have to be replaced by new, sustainable ones.

Developing a new enterprise with 'disruptive' (positive) connotations is a complex creative process. In addition to new technology it includes redefinition of markets, change in the organization and the creation of new innovations in the supply chains. Section 11.2 will discuss models used to develop business strategy based on abandonment of outdated ideas.

11.2.1   Beyond Greening

For businesses hoping to benefit from the new developments on the horizon, it will be imperative that they make fundamental choices to implement strategy. To support the case of 'creative destruction', Stuart Hart uses the term 'Beyond Greening'.[31] He differentiates between companies following stepwise innovation and those pursuing untrodden paths which could lead to breakthrough innovations.

The definitions used are:

- Greening: businesses that pursue stepwise innovation for better environmental results.
- Beyond greening: businesses that apply creative destruction in the hope of achieving a major breakthrough.

Many companies adhering to the greening theory take existing frameworks as a point of departure.[32] Larger companies in particular have chosen stepwise innovations and previously unheard of agenda topics such as decreased emissions, refuse disposal, increased use of environmentally friendly items and sparing use of energy and raw materials.[33] With good management, risk control and small steps forward, market developments can be monitored at close range. Focusing on trying to improve one's position in an existing market can have a prohibitive effect on an innovative CSR strategy. New developments encounter obstacles because of people's 'fear of the new' and reluctance to give up longstanding positions. Companies that wish to participate in new developments must realize that 'creative destruction' is part of the process. Any beyond greening strategy needs room to experiment and results are rarely achieved in the short term. Also, formulated innovation goals must not be excessively SMART (specific, measurable, attainable, relevant and time-bound). Breakthroughs require new search methods, opposing points of view, discussions and finding a link between logical and illogical components to serve as new points of departure.

Summarizing,[34] it can be concluded that 'strategies for greening' focus on the existing products, processes, suppliers, customers and shareholders while 'strategies for beyond greening' focus more on new developments related to technologies, markets, partners, needs and stakeholders. And not only the focus differs but also the features prove to be different. 'Strategies for greening' follow rational paths and will work stepwise towards continuous improvements while 'strategies for beyond greening' restructure processes using creative destruction in an interruptive way.

An example for a 'strategy for greening' could be the development of a responsible environmental programme while an example for a 'strategy for beyond greening' could be the innovation of a revolutionary biotechnology. See Box 11.3.

Box 11.3   Changes in strategy: DSM

Within the last 50 years, Dutch chemical giant DSM (Dutch State Mines) has undergone two radical changes of strategy.[35] It began operations in 1902 with the aim of exploiting underground coal reserves in the Netherlands. In the 1960s DSM had to change its tactics. Expensive labour and difficult to reach coal reserves were the reason that DSM's costs were higher than other world competitors. An earlier policy to enter the bulk chemical market now received top priority and the company spared no effort to become a major supplier of petrochemicals and other synthetic materials. During this time income from production of synthetic materials rose by a factor of 14. A second change of direction occurred at the end of the 1980s. DSM transformed itself from a provider of bulk chemicals into a supplier of specialty chemicals and life science. It purchased businesses with a proven track record in biotechnology, pharmaceuticals and high-quality materials. The transformation was visible at the DSM plant site.[36] Large chemical factories were torn down to make way for many different smaller operations. In 2008 it had a turnover of €9 billion with a net profit of €900 million. All of its activities were directed at the triple bottom line and in that same year DSM won prizes for its contributions to people and planet.

11.2.2   Drivers for CSR business and manufacturing

Technological developments deserve their fair share of credit as external factors that influence business and manufacturing strategy but global and workforce trends also form part of the picture as well as new legislation.[37, 38] It is important that companies see new trends as 'drivers' for strategic changes and that these are properly evaluated on their merits. Think only of internet technology that has revolutionized the concept of the supply chain for many different operations. Amazon.com has changed our book purchasing habits and most people today go online when booking hotel accommodation.[39]

When discussing CSR, social values (people) and sustainability (planet) are important themes. This book has emphasized five so-called 'drivers' that can give a starting point for a new CSR strategy. These are: Cradle to Cradle, redesign of the supply chain, Bottom of the Pyramid, human value approach and sharing (see Figure 11.5).

In the field of sustainability, Cradle to Cradle and redesigning the supply chain are paramount. Use of biodegradable materials, recycling of technical materials, reverse logistics and chain responsibility are a few of the areas where these concepts are applied. Material technology offers opportunities by redesigning the product and its supply chain while information technology proves its worth by adding new features to the links in the supply chain and eliminating links that are less effective to further enhance strategies for closing the material loops towards a circular economy.

By contrast, drivers that support CSR in the realm of social values are the Bottom of the Pyramid and the human value approach. For markets to prosper in countries where individuals have little buying power, disruptive innovation leading to new business models or other production concepts is often put into place. Drivers from other areas can also work together. A new Bottom of the Pyramid strategy can, for example, only succeed through application of information technology and redesign of the supply chain. The same applies to the human value approach which can often be a good partner for intelligent automation of planning and administration. When this works, employee motivation and job satisfaction can be rekindled. A good example would be the field of home care where many organizations are faced with a high overhead. Employees lack motivation because of bureaucratic red tape which prevents them from doing the jobs they were hired for. By working with self-directed teams, nursing staff can make use of planning software, apps, SMS and scanning devices which gives them more influence over their administrative tasks and creates more time for patient care.[40]

A fairly recent upcoming driver is the concept of sharing as a potential for new business.[41] Contemporary examples of this development would include Airbnb (sharing living space) Zipcar (shared car hire) Wikipedia (shared information) YouTube (shared videos) and Napster (free sharing of digital music and films). A sharing and collaborative consumption movement seems to be turning the old paradigm of the consumer-orientated society on its head, certainly when applied to the philosophy 'you are what you own'. A new catchphrase could be 'you are what you access'.[42] The following paragraphs will discuss sharing and how it is affecting new business.

Figure 11.5   Drivers for CSR business and manufacturing concepts

The word 'mothering' and the phrase 'pooling and allocation of household resources' provide opportunities for a typology for sharing.[43] Mothering is associated with 'non-reciprocal pro-social behaviour' and closely allied with the nature characteristic empathy; behaviour that is manifest when actions are spontaneous and less dependent on ratio.[44] If sharing does not have to do with 'mothering' then we arrive at the grounds of reciprocal exchange. More diffuse forms can be recognized, but reciprocity can also be very concrete. If there is a diffuse form of reciprocal exchange a transaction takes place, but mostly it is not expressed as such and the return favour is not been explicitly discussed. For example, if you ask someone to keep the door open because you would like to bring a tray with cups of tea to another room it is generally expected that you will say thank you and only give a smile. Although the ownership of an item or items is not always specified, there is a kind of bill involved in the transaction, but there are no agreements and in particular the contra-performance is not defined (e.g. a smile).

This 'imaginary' bill is not necessarily a pronounced agreement, but may also be more diffuse. Reciprocal exchange can take place between two parties, but can also be applied to a specific group or humanity in general. It is expected that this general concept of giving is duly rewarded. In this way sharing is linked to the cultural values hospitality and cordiality. This type of sharing goes without saying for friendship and family ties but is also valid for internet contacts, in public and in the workplace where people connect virtually or physically. New is that the concept of sharing as a 'driver' is now increasingly being applied within the economic domain (see Figure 11.6). This type of sharing embraces values that can be directly linked to the terrain of 'homo economicus' with an example being an exchange of scarce materials which imply a cash settlement. Items such as renting, the second-hand products market and all other economic transactions belong in this category. This type of sharing is about calculated self-interest and performance and compensation are specifically identified.

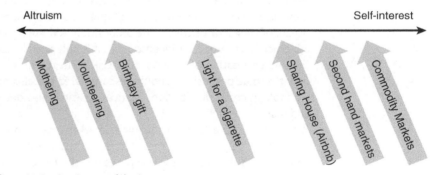

Figure 11.6   Continuum of sharing

Just as with the other drivers, the 'sharing' concept is easily combinable. Communications technology has used it extensively and there are numerous success stories. One of the best known is Etsy, a business community where small businesses come into contact with their clients but also with other small business entrepreneurs. Mutual sharing of information and communication technology paves the way for new business models that put citizens in the dual role of consumer and producer. This has resulted in the vocabulary of standard economic ideas such as business to business (B2B) and business to consumer (B2C) being expanded to include consumer to consumer (C2C) and consumer to business (C2B).[45] A textbook model of C2C is Wikipedia where citizens are consumers as well as producers. With the exception of a small team of professionals to monitor the software, it is primarily a volunteer force that provides the online diction-ary's content. Expanding this idea even further, the governments of a number of West-ern countries including Germany have given citizens the chance to become green energy suppliers. Companies, but also citizens who produce renewable energy, have the right to supply power to the grid.

11.2.3   Developing innovative business strategies

Section 11.2.3 will look at three methods for developing a new strategy which can be used for 'beyond greening'. The first of these will concentrate on how companies can develop a distinctive value proposition. This theory focuses on new marketing concepts that stand out from the competition. Up next will be Stuart Hart's 'expansion of scope' theory. Hart's method provides an intensive step-by-step plan in the search for new business strategy. Finally, in the last section, we will examine Osterwalder's 'Business Model Canvas'. This instrument serves as a template to help form an integral thought process about all relevant aspects of a new enterprise.

Distinctive value proposition

For enterprises embracing the principles of 'Beyond Greening' theory, it is worthwhile to examine whether the product or service can be offered under a distinctive value propo-sition. One of the methods offering a new take on the subject is described in the book *Blue Ocean Strategy* by Chan Kim and Renee Maubrogne.[46] They state that many compa-nies are mercilessly pitted against each other in an attempt to outdo their competitors which has little effect in the end. Without creativity, a slight percentage-wise improve-ment in market share is the best that can be expected. To obtain more creativity, they use the metaphor of the difference between the blue and red ocean. Companies that are fierce competitors swim in the red ocean and do everything possible to obtain a larger share of an unchanging market. To avoid the sharks (competition) in the red ocean, they have developed instruments that make it possible to create or navigate to the blue ocean, offering a distinctive value proposition. Although a distinctive value proposition is a crucial factor for a business strategy, it is only one element of the whole package for the implementation of an innovative CSR strategy.[47] To set up a business strategy not only the value proposition should be considered but also the strategies concerning the technology, costs, distribution, finances, research and development, and organization and management.[48]

In order to give form to this niche market where no other company is operating, values must be pinpointed that exist in the red ocean. After determining these values and the roles they currently occupy, essential questions must be posed to ascertain if possibilities exist to escape. Also, within the sector, it is important to explore values that can be important for customers, but have yet to be named or discovered.

Key questions central to redefining the value proposition and creating a blue ocean strategy are:[49]

1. Which values must be weakened or diluted to a lower level than branch standards?
2. Which obvious branch values have to be eliminated?
3. Which values need to be strengthened to levels higher than branch standards?
4. Which values (that the branch has never offered) must be created?

It is the challenge for Blue Ocean advocates to create new links between the needs of the target group and solutions offered by unfamiliar sectors that have been successfully applied elsewhere.

The case study in Box 11.4 is about Zipcar. The 'economic responsibility' (see Chapter 10) of their business plan can be defended through use of the 'Blue Ocean' theory and the drivers sharing and ICT.

Box 11.4   Zipcar[50]

Case prepared by Ankit Gaur

Traditional car rental companies are facing stiff competition from companies that have adopted a completely new outlook in the rental industry. Most major European countries recorded a negative growth of market value in the car rental sector for 2012. In contrast to this, the car sharing sector is expecting a 600% growth to reach US$6 billion by 2020. The two main factors that traditional car rental services lack are, firstly, the relative ease of finding a car close by and, secondly, the price. While traditional car rentals are more expensive, Zipcar was the first to introduce the concept of hourly hire rates making it cheaper and thus more attractive to the customers.[51]

Zipcar is the world's largest car sharing and car club service and was established more than a decade ago in the US and has now spread to several countries around the globe including Canada, UK, Spain and Austria with over 850,000 members and 10,000 cars. One of the main values of the company is the easy availability of the cars for the customers. It provides its members with 24/7 access to several thousands of cars located in several cities around the world. In London alone, Zipcar has around 1500 locations from where the cars can be picked up or dropped. These areas are conveniently located near train stations and bus stops to increase ease of access. Another key value of its operations is self-management by the clients. Cars can be located easily using the Zipcar App on mobile phones; they can be booked either online or by telephone and picked up from the closest Zipcar bay area. Using a Zipcar takes away the hassle associated with owning a car such as fuel, taxes, cleaning and insurance while still providing all the benefits of having a car whenever and wherever one requires it. Zipcar reports that around 4.6 million Londoners are within ten minutes' walking distance of a Zipcar. A Zipcar member saves £3162 per year, or £264 per month, compared to owning their own vehicle. The company prides itself in protecting the environment by trying to reduce the carbon footprint we leave behind. It aims to reduce the total number of cars that are on the road and claims that 33% of members have reduced the number of cars owned by their household since joining Zipcar.[52]

Like traditional car rental companies, Zipcar has its own set of values that it adheres to. It is these values that help Zipcar stand apart from the traditional car rental companies and that are also responsible for its success in this sector.

Table 11.1 gives an indication of the value proposition of Zipcar in comparison to the value proposition of other standard rental agencies on a scale of 0 to 5 (0 = Least important and 5 = Most important).

For the customer self-management, digital processing, locations in the city and the environment are important values. Less relevant are the 'price' and 'type of car' because the customer chooses the possibility of having a car at all times in many places. Also, service is less important because the customer operates autonomously.

(Continued)

Table 11.1   Value proposition of Zipcar and standard rental agencies

Value Proposition	Location	Service	Price	Different Cars	Environment	Processing	Self management
Standard rental agencies	2	4	4	4	3	2	0
Zipcar	5	3	2	2	5	4	5

Creating a new business model with a distinctive value proposition is obviously not for the faint hearted and requires letting go of previously held market beliefs. Thinking should not be influenced by habitual client behaviour patterns and the accompanying market segments that have existed within the sector. An open mind is also important for analysing customer needs so that the new market is clearly definable. Changing surroundings can also be influential. Zipcar owes much of its success to increased city parking chaos. Self-management, care for the environment and a club feeling are also values that mix well with individualism and offer the chance for freedom without worries.

Stuart Hart's expansion of scope[53]

Stuart Hart views the market economy as part of the problem, but also as part of the solution. On the one hand, unbridled growth, on the other hand strong dynamics and an enormous potential for innovation. He feels that the strength of innovation in particular is the way to a sustainable economy and gives pride of place to modern enterprises. They are the vital organs in our society and must be given the room to search for solutions benefiting the entire world. Stuart Hart has proposed a stepwise plan to give form to future-orientated business strategy. The method is called 'expansion of scope' and it helps managers and developers expand their horizons and control the risks involved.

Expansion of scope depends on three stages:

1. Transactive links
2. Renewed research fields
3. Incubation.

The first two stages are directly related to expansion. The incubation period is necessary for consolidation.

Transactive links

Many business models are based on a one-dimensional approach involving direct exchange between producer and client. We provide you with a desired product or service and you pay for it. For the commercialization of a breakthrough innovation, it is often necessary to abandon trodden paths. This means that it is important to realize that innovation transcends the product itself and in addition to product innovations, improvements must also be made to the supply chain. Think, for example, of a waste return system, but also of other innovations that can only be implemented through cooperation between different sections of the supply chain; what Stuart Hart calls new 'transactive links'. Hart suggests that alternative relations with stakeholders or new functions that can enhance existing relations are drivers for breakthrough innovations. Car manufacturers, for example, have no contacts with health care, environmental and insurance services, but they do share a common interest, namely the drivers' well-being. Hart calls these 'fringe stakeholders', meaning that marginal contact with the target group exists, but in fact they belong to a completely different circuit. These organizations often possess good networks and could fulfil an additional role. For businesses on the lookout for breakthrough innovations it can be a good approach to analyse the possibilities of working together with these parties using new transactive links.

Renewed research fields

Imagination is an important part of any breakthrough innovation. Managers are asked to create and produce new non-existent combinations. A steel producer, for example, must look for new innovation in the synthetics branch. Relations can be created with stakeholders in other areas who do not necessarily share your line of thinking. It is probable, for example, that the fishing industry and Greenpeace could learn something from each other just as banks can often learn more from bad debtors than faithful clients. Breakthrough innovations depend on browsing and snooping around in unknown territory. For this reason the American concern DuPont appointed an international consulting panel to develop a robust strategy for biotechnology (see Box 11.5).

Box 11.5   Bacteria make a web as good as a spider's[54]

DuPont's new material 'spider silk' is as strong as steel but weighs nothing and is biologically decomposable. It has the possibility of competing with super strong high-tech fibres like Kevlar and Twaron.[55] It is now made in laboratories using bacteria (and not spiders). Scientists have been working since the 1990s to reproduce the spokes in a spider's web but the spider farm never came into being because 'milking' a spider is not an easy thing to do. Furthermore, spiders tend to eat each other. The conventional alternative would involve using genetically manipulated animals, bacteria or plants to produce the crucial web enzyme but this met with little success until South Korean biotechnologist Sang Yup Lee and his team became involved. The problem has now been solved and Lee was able to artificially create the well-known bacteria Escherichia Coli in the lab and was the first to produce threads resembling the strength of an actual spider web. Lee's threads have a tensile strength of 500 Megapascal (MPa) as compared to the spiders' 740–1200 MPa.

To broaden research into scope expansion involves not only imagination, but also the combination of different techniques for new products/markets and the realization of transactive links.

Hart and Sharma[56] determined an outline for scope expansion containing the goal and a procedure as the main elements.

The goal should be to stimulate managers to search for business concepts that are diametrically opposed to current practices. In such a way that the powers of imagination and new ideas can be harnessed to create new goods and services.

And *the procedure* should contain the following three activities:

- Defining the research fields making use of societal and renewed technical domains such as climate change, social inequality and human rights, and engage new stakeholders for the enterprise.
- Gathering the information from informative websites and creating a learning community to establish new knowledge about the chosen subjects and determine which target groups will benefit the most from the newly acquired information.
- Making sure that the managers visit those places that are deemed to be the most interesting in order to establish intensive contact with the local culture so that they can understand how new products can relate to customer needs.

Incubation

A company that starts with new product/market combinations based on an innovative business model often opts for radical new solutions: innovations related to areas such as production lines, business models and approaches to unknown branches of new target groups.

Significant risks are inherent in these types of solutions. During the development phase, many different ideas are embraced, often on the basis of conflicting information. Many assumptions are acted upon without sufficient research into their viability. For this reason an incubation period must be included as a part of the total development process.[57] It is irresponsible to promote radical new concepts without a planned incubation time.

The following questions should have a clear answer.

- What are the critical success factors?
- What barriers must be overcome in the target group before their needs can be converted into a purchasing pattern?

As they did for the scope expansion, Hart and Sharma[58] also determined an outline for the incubation or consolidation programmes. This outline also contains a goal and a procedure.

The goal would be to integrate the testing and the implementation of breakthrough innovations with the development of new business models.

And *the procedure* should contain the following four activities:

1. Organizing the stakeholders' dialogue between fringe stakeholders and all involved within the company including line managers, product developers and technicians.
2. Appointing the task groups to perform additional research on new, yet-to-be established research themes.
3. Conducting the tests and redefining the product concepts and the new business models.
4. Organizing the horizontal and vertical information channels to keep everyone informed.

Business Model Canvas[59]

Developing a business model is an important complementary activity for any new product market strategy.[60] It refers to which products and services are brought to the market, the values that customers associate with them and helps determine how the business is to be set up, finance and cash flow patterns, and the way in which incoming and outgoing streams of goods, services and communications are regulated.

To set up or improve a business model the concept of the Business Model Canvas can be used. The Business Model Canvas is a strategic business start-up template. The template describes nine relevant building blocks that form the basis for developing and documenting new or existing business models. The Business Model Canvas was developed by Alexander Osterwalder and Yves Pigneur working together with 470 professionals. The template allows people to set up operations on the basis of discussions between involved parties and the talks concerning the content of the building blocks give insight into the core elements of an enterprise. Dialogue for the nine building blocks becomes dialectic, with proposals and rebuttals and pros and cons receiving extra attention. The model is primarily intended to clarify new business intentions on a single sheet of paper and is used frequently by managers to express their thoughts with maximum efficiency. See figure 11.7 in which the template is partially filled in for Zipcar.

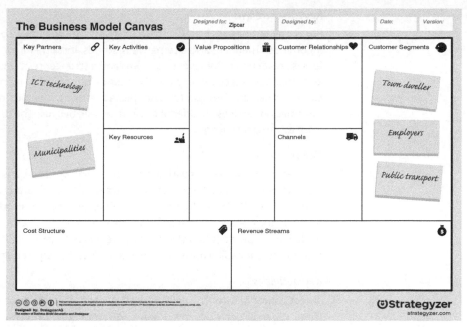

Figure 11.7 Some aspects of the business model of Zipcar[61]

Information about using the Business Model Canvas can be found on the website businessmodelgeneration.com. Here is a brief description of each of its nine blocks:

Customer segments

The customer segments building block provides information pertaining to the wish for a segmented operation and to what degree it is to be included in the operation. If the enterprise chooses customized segmentation, different value propositions, distribution channels and customer relations become important.

Value propositions

Value proposition is the interpretation of performance, customization, service and the positioning and the status of the brand name. Customer ease of use is also described as the way in which the product can assist the purchaser. Value proposition implies the way in which the product's values stand up to the price being asked, including its accessibility and meaning, and whether the product is financially appealing to the target group.

Channels

The business must determine the channels to be used for promotion, order information, delivery and after-sales service. Whether the channel is direct or indirect becomes an important choice. For promotion, a business can choose to cover a wide area using mass media or other methods such as direct mail, the website and social media. The direct or indirect choice also applies to the delivery. The goods and services can be supplied through company channels, retail and wholesale outlets or a combination.

Customer relationships

The field for determining customer relationships includes key words such as intimacy, pragmatism, self-motivation, efficiency and effectiveness. It addresses basic questions such as: 'How much time and attention is spent on the client?' and 'What is the function of the activities developed to clarify customer relationships?' Concepts that play a role in customer relationships include self-service, communities, co-creation and the degree of customers' personal commitment.

Revenue streams

For many businesses, billing or cash payments are the most common way of generating income but there are also alternative methods. Instalment payments, subscriptions and leases create repetitive revenue streams and a stronger relationship with the customer. In addition, businesses can explore the possibilities of involving partners to see if revenues can be obtained through, for example, advertising income. In this way, many internet information services are offered free to the user, because the company generates income from advertising sources.

Key resources

To effectively reach clients with a distinctive value proposal, it is important to have insight into the key resources the company has available to it, including transport and the production facilities, factory and/or the sales points necessary to produce the item and bring it to the market. A second aspect concerns the intellectual resources. It must be decided if trade names, product knowledge and patents are to be used. Adjacent to this, the size of the investment capital must be known as well as the required employee competence.

Key activities

To get a clear view of the new enterprise, core activities must be determined. There are three types of activities: production, generating solutions and linkage. An enterprise emphasizing production ensures that sufficient amounts of an acceptable quality are manufactured. Problem-solving businesses are concerned with management of, for example, advice offices, care and schools. Questions relating to quality and quantity are translated into employee experience and the number of people being employed. Organizations involved in linkage have a platform as the key resource for core activities in networking and matchmaking; examples are banks and auction houses. Linkage organizations rely heavily on software for effective and efficient processing.

Key partners

Who are the key partners, what role do they play and how do they contribute to the business? The answer to this question depends on the ascertaining of competence: who is best able to deal with involved risks, and which partners are best suited to performing activities to increase scale advantages. Increased ICT facilities make it possible to form alliances with small and large partners who feed on each other's strengths.

Cost structure

The first approach to determining cost spread is the question: 'How important is the price of an item in the value proposition being presented to the customer?' If the distinguishing capital of the business is based on low price, then a 'lean' approach is the best option. When luxury items, comfort and exclusivity are offered, the relation between cost and profit becomes more diffuse and establishing the exact value proposition becomes more important than efficiency. The relation between constant and variable costs also influences cost structure and questions arise as to the possibilities for variable expenses and which activities can be sourced out.

Using the Business Model Canvas

Brainstorming sessions using the nine blocks of the Business Model Canvas can give us valuable insights about setting up an enterprise.[62] The template provides those involved with the opportunity to decide which activities need more or less attention and which marketing strategy will have the most impact. The results of this type of brainstorming will be illustrated in the case study in Box 11.6: Peepoople.

Box 11.6   Peepoople[63]

Peepoople is a company that makes a simple biologically degradable plastic bag. The simplest business model would be a transfer, where the plastic bag is handed over to a customer in return for money. Anders Wilhelmson, the company's founder, had a different idea. He recognized a huge hygiene problem in the slums of developing countries because urine and excrement were not easily disposable, an unacceptable problem in this day and age with its link to infections from different diseases. Wilhelmson addressed this issue with his biologically disposable plastic bag, combining this with the opportunity provided by the fact that human waste forms good raw material for fertilizer. The waste has an economic value, the plastic bag is not expensive and combining the two elements can solve a serious hygiene problem. Additional research was carried out and the plastic bag came into being with the amusing trade name of Peepoo. Every bag contains several grams of ureum. This material converts the waste material into carbon dioxide, water and biomass and neutralizes harmful germs.

Business Model Canvas is an excellent instrument for developing this type of idea into a fully fledged business and there is a case study on the Internet by Alexander Osterwalder.[64]

During brainstorming sessions for the **revenue streams** building block, the company came up with the idea of selling the bags to mountain climbers. This group would theoretically be prepared to pay a hefty price because purchasing a Peepoo bag for climbing aids hygiene in remote and sparsely populated areas. Thus, the **customer segments** building block would not need to target slum residents only. There is also a premium segment that could benefit.

Many options also exist for the channels block. Collection and distribution, for example, could involve school children with the schools serving as collection points. The children could also fulfil a role in the **customer relationships** cornerstone. They could inform their own families about the plastic bags and convey the importance and necessity of good hygiene. The cornerstone **key partners** involves the school, but also additional stakeholders who offer government-sponsored programmes in the area of preventive health care. Lessons on proper hygiene are directly linked to changes in behaviour. During brainstorming sessions, a new channel could be created for 'micro-entrepreneurs' who have a commercial interest in selling and collecting Peepoos. By weighing advantages and disadvantages against each other, an effective well-thought out channel strategy can be put in place.

The block **value propositions** also offers a wide range of choices. Is it aimed at comfort for example, where indoor sanitation could replace a night-time visit to the latrine, or are there other economic advantages or hygiene improvements on offer? For a good interpretation of the value proposal is important to create an inventory of the taboos associated with human waste disposal, if any exist. The value proposition is also dependent on the **key partners** building block. Western sponsors assisting in emancipation of micro-entrepreneurs from the lowest levels of society will have a different proposition to that of a government-sponsored preventive health care programme.

Cost structure assumes importance for establishing the scale size of the initiative. If there are many permanent expenses, due to hygiene promotion campaigns being set up, and the enterprise is struggling with fluctuating profits of a few pennies, many risks can be involved. If the promotion campaign is a key element of

(Continued)

the concept, this has implications for the block **key partners**. To cover permanent expenses, a business could choose to work with charitable institutions who are willing to assume the recurring promotional costs.

With the interrelation of the cornerstones **key resources** and **core activities**, the new business set-up begins to take shape. Special attention must be paid to which core activities are being established. In some countries Peepoople can direct its efforts to promoting hygiene and can choose to offer production, distribution and collection to independent contractors. When this business model is chosen, it means that key resources rely on mass communication. The core activity of the business must be in tune with the current media in order to present its message in the most positive light.

The Business Model Canvas is intuitively easy to follow. If business is involved with new technology, an idea or even the physical development of an item, the Business Model Canvas is an inspiration because people are challenged to think about alternatives for filling in the blocks. Brainstorming about possible different key partners offers new horizons for setting up operations in a totally different manner. Which stakeholders benefit from the new technology, who can play a role in providing the service and what alternative channels are available to reach the consumer? By filling in the nine blocks in a different way, new businesses have a smoother sailing into the blue ocean. The blocks are there to educate people to take risks and play with different alternatives. One could be, for example, the idea of leasing instead of sales (Zipcar), which allows people to find companies with personally appealing features.

Conclusion

The distinctive value proposition, Stuart Hart's expansion of scope and the Business Model Canvas can be used for business development offering relevant products and services to society. The models invite us to think about the interests of the various stakeholders and assist in clarifying the possibilities of transactive links. A society looking for breakthrough innovations that give definitions to themes such as Cradle to Cradle, social cohesion, individualism, and efficiency and effectiveness, must be on the lookout for new business strategies.

 11.3 Case Study: Microcredit

Case prepared by Ankit Gaur

Microcredit programmes were initiated with the aim of providing small loans to impoverished and neglected sections of society by tailoring financial services to meet their specific needs and circumstances. The main beneficiaries of this scheme are usually borrowers who lack the ability to provide collateral and do not have steady employment and verifiable credit histories. The biggest beneficiaries of such schemes around the globe have been women from impoverished backgrounds. Since women in many traditional societies lack employment, education and access to finances, these microcredit programmes have been successful in improving their lot.[65]

One of the most successful cases of microcredit in the world can be traced to Bangladesh's Grameen Bank which was started in 1976. The bank was founded by Professor Muhammad Yunus who was the head of the Rural Economics Programme

(Continued)

at the University of Chittagong. By 1983, the Grameen Bank was given the title of an independent bank by the Bangladeshi government. In 2006, Muhammad Yunus and the bank were jointly awarded the Nobel Peace Prize for their work.[66] Today, 95% of the shares of the bank are owned by the borrowers and only 5% by the government. When it was founded, the main objective of the bank was to eliminate the exploitation of the lower sections of society at the hands of money lenders by providing easy banking facilities to these individuals. This project was also able to provide employment opportunities for a large number of people in Bangladesh.[67]

The main reason why the Grameen Bank initiative has been so valuable and successful in attracting a large number of customers is because it does not require the borrowers to provide collateral against the loan; neither does the borrower have to sign any legal document regarding the repayment of the loan. The only requirement is that the borrower must belong to a five-member group. However, the group does not have to provide any guarantee for the borrower and is not responsible or liable in any way for cases of non-payment. The group's responsibility is only to ensure that all the members and borrowers behave in a responsible manner. The philosophy behind this model is that creating groups helps overcome shortcomings at the individual level. Hence, group responsibility and peer pressure work effectively in ensuring that the members repay their loans on time.[68]

Another attractive feature of this initiative is the rate of interest that is charged by the bank. The interest rate of the loan is decided by the type of loan taken. Loans taken for income-generating projects have an interest rate of 20%, housing loans are 8%, student loans 5% and there is 0% interest for struggling members or beggars. All the interest is charged as simple interest, and the interest never exceeds the principal amount. Although the interest rates on loans are modest, the deposit rates are very attractive, ranging from 8.5% to 12%.[69]

The Grameen Bank initiative has been a profit-making scheme, and has made a profit every year from the day it was started except in 1983, 1991 and 1992. The main expenditure of the bank is in the form of the interest on the deposits, which account for 54% of the total expenditure. Deposits made by the borrowers are an important aspect of the business model because 100% of the loans that are financed by the bank are through its deposits. The second major expenditure of the bank is the salaries of the employees, accounting for 27% of the costs. The salaries are kept relatively low as the borrowers make up a large section of the employees themselves. Self-management is the keyword for borrowing groups. They select participants for new projects and determine the amount that can be borrowed responsibly. This helps to ensure proper and timely payment.[70]

Following the tremendous success of the Grameen Bank in Bangladesh, microcredit programmes have become popular in several parts of the world such the US, as well as India and China who are also following the footsteps of Grameen's initiative and are developing their own versions of microcredit.

Microcredit is evolving into a great stimulant for the economic development of countries. Investing in poor people supports them by providing them with a source of income, educating them and motivating them in turn to start a business and further employ others. It also helps to reduce the pressure on governments by decreasing the social assistance costs. These non-profit organizations provide microcredit options for new entrepreneurs, and once the loans are repaid the money is invested into new loans thereby expanding the pool of entrepreneurs that drive economic development.[71]

Case Study Questions

1. Research the Grameen Bank and establish the defining characteristics of the Business Model Canvas. Present your arguments.
2. Determine and identify the fringe stakeholders, who they are and their relation to the Grameen Bank. Present your findings.
3. Name three Bottom of the Pyramid principles discussed in Section 11.1.2 that have importance for the Grameen Bank. Present your arguments.

11.4   Learning tools

11.4.1 Summary

- A substantial number of people living close to the poverty line are increasingly becoming consumers of regular market goods resulting in a heavier ecological footprint.
- Internet and off-grid technology have resulted in small and medium enterprises now operating at international levels.
- Companies that realize a product and/or production innovation which results in a structural lower per capita cost and make a leap downward to appeal to the Bottom of the Pyramid (BoP) markets have a competitive advantage.
- Strategic approaches to generate profits in a BoP market include:

1. Capacity to consume
2. Hybrid innovation
3. Scale of operations
4. Sustainable development
5. Functionality for the BoP client
6. Supply chain innovation
7. Making better use of uneducated employees
8. Client empowerment
9. Integral approach.

- Stuart Hart uses the term greening for enterprises who use a stepwise improvement approach to achieve sustainability. The notion of Beyond Greening refers to those companies who use disruptive innovation to guide them forward.
- Good starting points in the search for Beyond Greening innovation are changes in:

1. Technology
2. Market
3. Partners
4. Needs
5. Stakeholders.

- Drivers for an innovative CSR Strategy are:

1. Cradle to Cradle
2. Sharing
3. Redesign of the supply chain
4. Human value management
5. Bottom of the Pyramid (BoP).

- Tools available for developing an innovative CSR Strategy are:

1. Distinctive value proposition (Blue Ocean Strategy/Kim and Maubornge)

(Continued)

2. Expansion of scope (Stuart Hart)
3. Business Model Canvas (Osterwalder and Pigneur).

- The distinctive value proposition is directed towards client values and focuses on new markets in order to stand out from the competition.
- To determine distinctive client values, Blue Ocean Strategy poses the following questions:

1. Which values must be weakened to a lower level than branch standards?
2. Which obvious branch values have to be eliminated?
3. Which values need to be strengthened to levels higher than branch standards?
4. Which values (that the branch has never offered) must be created?

- Stuart Hart's 'expansion of scope' makes use of three steps:

1. Transactive links
2. Renewed research fields
3. Incubation.

- The Business Model Canvas of Osterwalder and Pigneur consists of nine parts that have to be established when considering a business model. These are:
  - Customer segments
  - Value proposition
  - Channels
  - Customer relationships
  - Revenue streams
  - Key resources
  - Key activities
  - Key partners
  - Cost structure.

11.4.2 Further reading

Hart, S. L. (2007). *Capitalism at the Crossroads*. FT Press.

Kim, W. C. & Mauborgne, R. (2005). *Blue Ocean Strategy*. Boston, MA: Harvard Business School Press.

Prahalad, C. K. (2006). *Fortune at the Bottom of the Pyramid: Eradicating Poverty Through Profits*. Philadelphia, PA: Pearson Prentice Hall.

Prahalad, C. K. & Krishnan, M. S. (2008). *The New Age of Innovation: Driving Cocreated Value Through Global Networks*. New York, NY: McGraw-Hill Education.

Rumelt, R. (2011). *Good Strategy Bad Strategy: The Difference and Why It Matters*. New York, NY: Crown Business.

Senge, P. (2006). *The Fifth Discipline: The Art and Practice of The Learning Organization*. New York, NY: Doubleday.

11.4.3 Assignments

 Assignment 11.1

Future growth in developing countries will be less dependent on governments because they will no longer play a crucial role in the creation of infrastructure. Determine the 'for' and 'against' arguments for this statement and present your conclusions.

Assignment 11.2

Researching on the Internet, describe the way in which concrete manufacturer Cemex (Mexico) has implemented the ideas contained in the 'Bottom of the Pyramid' theory and determine the pillars that form the basis for 'economic responsibility'.

 Assignment 11.3

Find a company that you would like to be director of, because of the possibilities for success in applying concepts as sharing, Cradle to Cradle, human value approach, redesign of the supply chain and Bottom of the Pyramid. Look specifically for an enterprise that does not yet have a workable form of future-orientated business strategy. Show why the chosen company has a good chance of applying one of these concepts using technical and economic feasibility.

 Assignment 11.4

Describe the features of the business Aravind Eye Care by using Osterwalder's Business Model Canvas and by doing Internet research. Also, elaborate on how it has applied Bottom of the Pyramid principles.

11.4.4   Self-test questions

 Self-test Questions

1. Give an example of off-grid technology'. What consequences does this technology have for small and medium enterprises trying to establish themselves in fragile states? Present your arguments.
2. Provide an example of a Western company that owes it success to a 'great leap downward'. What is the economic basis that makes the company's leap downward profitable?
3. Prahalad states that in order to successfully serve the Bottom of the Pyramid, it is important to think about the concept 'create the capacity to consume'.
   a. Explain in detail 'create the capacity to consume'.
   b. Using an example, demonstrate how Prahalad's theory can be further embellished and expanded.
4. Describe the breakthrough driver 'sharing'. Give an example of a company that has used this theory as a base for its business model.
5. Describe and elaborate on Zipcar's business model using at least six building blocks of the Business Model Canvas.

12

THE CHALLENGE OF PROGRESS TOWARDS SUSTAINABLE DEVELOPMENT

Overview and learning objectives

Our world has experienced radical changes in the past 300 years. Administrative innovations such as trias politica, the market economy, democracy and human rights are now to some extent institutionalized in many parts of the world. The Age of Enlightenment became the harbinger of cultural change. Rationality, efficiency and well-being became the standards by which we measured our progress. The last few centuries have been characterized by an enormous increase in productivity fuelled by an abundance of natural resources. Now that purchasing power is being rapidly increased in the developing world, consumption demand keeps growing while natural resources keep dwindling. It is becoming clear that a circular economy might be the only viable alternative to progress towards a sustainable economy. Governments, business and citizens are on the brink of a new transformation process. Global businesses are already operating in a context of social, productive and technological transitions towards a new economy. Whether or not such new economy will be one where sustainable development represents the mainstream will depend on whether the transition follows a path of collective action between states, the private sector and civil society to achieve social and environmental goals. If vested interests and technological lock-in diverge us into a path of denial of social problems and a continuous overuse of natural resources, the transition might be towards the collapse of capitalism as we know it.

This final chapter therefore focuses on 'transitions' and look at the rules and criteria that play a role in institutionalizing sustainable development.

Learning objectives

This chapter will enable the student to:

- Understand that the effectiveness of managerial and administrative innovations depends on consideration of the complexity of the human psyche which is largely determined through a diversity of natural characteristics.
- Understand that institutionalizing of managerial and administrative innovations is a dynamic transition process.
- Understand the factors that can speed up the transition process towards a sustainable economy.

12.1   Spread of managerial innovations in the past

During the last few centuries, administrative innovations have had a huge impact on welfare and well-being. Social capital and productivity growth are correlated.[1] The policies put into place by governments for dealing with human nature have gained trust from the populace and this forms the basis of social capital.[2] As we have seen in Chapter 4, it is important for societies to deal with such human nature aspects as homo economicus, feelings of fairness, empathy, the exploratory impulse, respect for authority, status (reputation), conformism, aggression and kin selection. Homo economicus reacts favourably to a fair justice system, respect for property and a minimum of corruption.[3] Democracy and human rights provide people with a 'feeling of fairness'.[4, 5] The cry for revolutionary changes in the system becomes tempered, especially if 'status' and power are regulated.[6] Trias politica and countervailing power are probably the most relevant social innovations.[7] Politicians seeking power and authority but unable to justify unaccounted-for 'extras' will often be confronted with the outcry of public institutions when caught.

The past has shown us that good solutions were often at hand but could not be readily implemented. It sometimes happens that a significant drama must occur before appropriate measures are undertaken. A good example would be human rights. The call for 'human rights governance' gained strength after the Second World War.[8] The racial doctrine of Nazi Germany in the late 1930s whose beliefs about Aryan supremacy gave ideological legitimacy to the Holocaust led to the annihilation of six million Jews and other innocent people because of their race or religion. In the end, this human tragedy became a trigger for the institutionalizing of human rights.[9] The United Nations was founded in 1945, before the official Japanese surrender. The UN charter is the foundational treaty of this inter-governmental organization and human rights are an important aspect. After the Second World War, human rights played a pivotal role in political discourse and the way history developed; think only of the struggle against colonialism. Western countries prefer not to be seen on the wrong side of history and to know that their former dominance is no longer in sync with modern values. The indignation concerning South African apartheid and oppression in the former Soviet Union has made clear that human rights form an important part of the belief systems of publics worldwide. A study by Falk (2002) showed that the concept of human rights was far less prevalent in political thinking before WWII. Socio-economic development of the last 70 years has influenced cultural traditions and mass values have changed. The worldwide establishment can no longer cast a blind eye to the call for democracy, and the values of self-expression and freedom of choice have become ingrained in our culture. Inglehart and Welzel's (2005) study views democracy as the institutionalized form of self-expression and freedom of choice.[10]

Worldwide development can be partially seen as a result of steps taken for the institutionalization of human rights and the market economy. Nowadays the theme of sustainability is also a part of the political discourse. If institutionalizing on this subject fails, the world could be plunged into ecological disaster resulting from the consequences of climate change and natural resource exhaustion as described in Chapter 6, or ravaged by terrorism and civil war resulting from rampaging inequality as discussed in Chapters 1 and 8. Multilateral solutions for an inclusive circular economy are known, but when will the transition occur? A transformation can only be realized when individual parties are prepared to put their vested interests at stake and opt for exploratory, improvement-oriented deliberation.[11, 12]

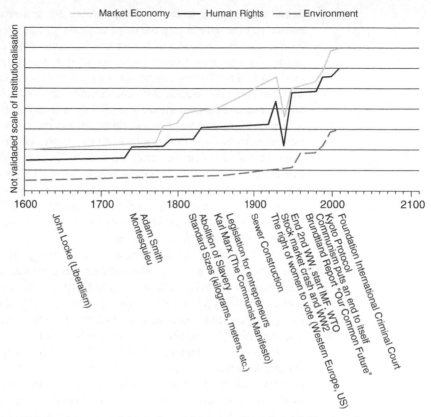

Figure 12.1   Intuitive, not-reliable and not-validated sketch of the intensification of institutionalization in three policy areas

12.2   Transition to sustainable development

Societal transition is a dynamic process through which the society structurally reforms in multiple areas such as technology, production facilities, infrastructure, regulations and values. The success of societal transition is dependent on the international context, government, civil society and business.[13] A transitional process has increased opportunity when a multi-dimensional approach is applied and also when the major participants (actors) in society are looking in the same direction.[14] Governments who enact legislation to weed out the 'bad guys' in a polluting economic sector, but who fail to take into account the socio-economic systems within society as a whole, may achieve short-term successes but they are devoid of any defining changes to society at large. Think only of the street protests in the Middle East and Russia which, in the end, have made no substantial improvements for the people in those areas. The situation in Egypt provides a cautionary example of a uni-dimensional approach to transitions. In Egypt, the transition from dictatorship to democracy was believed to be happening naturally with the replacement of an alleged tyrant with a democratically elected leader, without an actual change in the power structure that had supported the authoritarian government that was dethroned. The 2011 revolution in Cairo culminated in the election of President Morsi representing the Muslim Brotherhood, but tensions soon escalated sharply between the Sunni Muslims, the Coptic Christians, Shiites and the long-entrenched military regime.[15] In 2013, a year after Morsi's election, 14 million demonstrators took to the streets to protest his apparent grab for power. The army wasted no time in removing the democratically elected president from office and called for new elections in 2014 which were won by former army General Sisi. This latest power change has also raised some eyebrows as former president Morsi was sentenced to death in 2015 by the new regime, leaving no doubt that in Egypt, military power remains dominant over democratic principles. Democratic values have little impact on culture and democratic institutions are weak.[16] This raises a question about the role of Egypt's leaders in the inevitable changes taking place in the country. How can democracy and human rights become institutionalized in a country where its leaders have only known a system based on power struggles, mutual distrust and suppression? Transition to democracy becomes a multi-dimensional question. The existing literature points to political and socio-cultural factors which are not sufficiently embedded and institutionalized in society as being a reason for slow transition.[17] Under this heading a lack of independent courts, accepted democratic values and institutions for the enforcement of human rights can also be included.

If the transition towards democracy is challenging, the transition towards a sustainable society might be even more arduous. Research into the conditions necessary for this transition to happen have indicated that it only occurs when diverse players in society become involved. Government, citizens and business are dependent on each other and need to be engaged in transitions not only at the local and national level, but also increasingly at regional and global levels.[18] In the United Kingdom, for example, the transition to a sustainable society has a direct relationship with international relations specifically within the European continent.[19] The transition depends on socio-technical systems interacting between people, business, consumption patterns and production methods.[20] Additional factors include new legislation, new institutions and new regional infrastructure for diversity of items ranging from management and energy to the supply of raw materials.

The transition question also contains a global dimension. With a better investment climate in place for a number of developing and emerging countries coupled with increased product demand worldwide one might think of transition as a positive development, but for certain countries the quest for new roads to a circular economy has had a limited effect. A potential market share of 75% for California-produced batteries and hydrogen fuel cells for automobiles will have little effect on CO_2 emissions if other countries lag behind.[21] For countries in the first phases of economic development, increase in production is often the first priority so that their people can enjoy access to electricity, TV, mobile phones, motorcycles and fridges. Tim Jackson, a member of the UK's Sustainable Development Commission, has stated that transition only has a chance of success if the social logic of consumerism changes.[22] Many governments' attempts to achieve clean production costs with no regard for consumer lifestyle is starting to look like an untenable proposition. Jackson calls it the 'myth of decoupling'. In other words: growth and clean production are not simultaneously possible because the current increase in GDP is linked to a greater dependence on resources. The effort presently exerted to provide clean products is leading to a declining resource intensity per product while overall resource dependency is increasing. It is becoming evident that society will have to make some hard choices that will be more fundamental than renewing socio-technical systems, as long as this does not come together with other choices related to consumptive behaviour. Think, for example, of socio-technical systems where the concept of auto (car) ownership is abandoned and replaced by accessible and efficient public transport. The transition to a circular economy is inevitably linked to consumer lifestyle.

Societies in transition are searching for new value systems while previously held values are gradually abandoned.[23] Insecurity and turmoil can accompany transition and it is important that people are convinced of the necessity of change. Transition has more to do with evolution than revolution. It creates a fundamental shift in society which will take a generation or more.[24] The switch to sustainability differs from other societal transitions through the implementation of technique, with a prime example being the invention of the combustion engine which provides power for more than one billion cars worldwide.[25] The transition to sustainability differs from technical transitions because it is goal orientated with limited incentives for business, concerned as it is with the management of collective goods such as CO_2 emission reductions. The transition to sustainability searches for an answer to the tragedy of the commons. The 2005 study on sustainability transitions by Geels focused on a multi-level perspective with the results based on the interactions of the three domains: socio-technical regimes, radical technologies and landscapes.[26]

Socio-technical regimes have a determining role for the direct result of transition opportunities. The existing regulations, infrastructure, businesses and organizations that provide services in areas of food supply, transport, energy, communications and consumer durables are decisive for the success of transitions. These systems differ from country to country and certain conglomerates of socio-technical systems offer better possibilities to facilitate transition than others. The 'actors' like legislation, infrastructure, tech institutions and level of training are part of the systems and determine the possibilities of adopting new 'radical technologies'. Socio-technical regimes can in themselves also be an obstacle to transition. In the transport sector, for example, tax structure, garages, petrol stations, road networks, oil companies and car manufacturers geared to each other's needs in order to maintain the status quo are all examples of actors that can be immune to the prospect of transition if it threatens long-established patterns with vested interests. The feasibility of transition is both dependent on the current socio-technical systems and the landscape. The concept 'landscape' is broader in scope than the ideas behind the socio-technical regime and is especially concerned with the potential for change.[27] What are the values held by the people about sustainability? How has the political system been set up and can the government be effective in dealing with business and pressure groups to bring about new legislation?

Whether or not transitions proceed smoothly depends on these three levels and how they affect each other. Transition is thus not a clear, linear process. Sometimes good technologies are there for the asking, but society does not have the ability or willingness to incorporate the changes. Another element which plays a role in research on transitions is the aspect of unjustified 'techno optimism'. Alexander (2014) claims that radical technology must be realistically applied to socio-technical systems. Results will be based on good source analysis, good technique and – most importantly – the potential to trigger consumer lifestyle changes.[28]

For issues of sustainable development it is important to realize that there is a global question involving the participation of developed and developing countries, but also a division question whereby social capital becomes an important pillar for harmony, happiness and well-being. With more and more countries possessing the know-how and economic tools to create prosperity, it is conceivable that some values related to comfort, status and lifestyle are due for a redefinition, not only to allow for better distribution of scarce resources, but also to speed up the transition process and avoid unseen obstacles.

To stay focused on the issue of transition, we will delve further into the roles of government, people and business.

12.2.1   Transition and citizens

For a transition to occur, it is important that citizens in a society get linked to the values needed for sustainability. A crisis situation provides a good example of how this can have a positive effect. The 2008 financial crisis has led to society becoming more critical of competition and maximization of profits in the market economy.[29] A growing interest on the theme of sustainability has ensued. Research into 115 leading newspapers has shown that between 1990 and 2008, articles relating to sustainable development increased fourfold.[30] A trend analysis of citizens in Washington concluded that the majority of people realize that an attitude change is necessary.[31, 32] This is not to imply that transition happens from one day to the next. Researchers have stated that behavioural change in society is not only a question of an idea becoming widespread, but is also dependent on different groups in society approaching the problem with the same attitude (see Box 12.1).[33] White collar workers, blue collar workers and environmentalists must all be on a similar wavelength if transition is to occur. The process can be accelerated to reach more people when, in addition to broadsheet press coverage, social media and television make the case for environmental issues.

Box 12.1   Spreading ideas

Are tree-hugger ecologists the only ones concerned with the environment?

Applied mathematician Ugander and computer scientist Kleinberg argue that the likelihood of a new idea becoming dominant is not so much dependent on the number of people who are interested, but rather on the variety of different types of people advocating the idea and disseminating it. Ideas don't spread like contagious diseases. An epidemic begins with a small group and quickly spreads to the general public. To spread ideas successfully it works in another way. The diversity of people who take an interest at an early stage is of prime importance. If someone is presented an idea by four people from different groups, the chance that he/she will quickly warm to it is greater than if the idea is presented by four people from the same group. Ugander and Kleinberg proved their point with the help of Facebook. Working together with sociologists Backstrom and Marlow, they analysed 54 million email invitations. They showed that the same invitation had much more impact when sent from different sources. Professional journal *PNAS* claimed that the research can have profound influence for, among other things, health campaigns. To convince people to change their behaviour, they have to be encouraged by different sides. This attitude also has implications for the environment. If 'tree-hugger' environmentalists are the only ones advocating change, they will have little success.[34]

Improvements to society are not only dependent on a general spread of sustainability values. Protest groups are a healthy element in engaging in political debate. Just as the abolition of slavery in the US did not instantly eliminate the radical subordination of African Americans, it is a fairly safe assumption that the road to a sustainable society is going to take some time. In the 1950s and 60s Martin Luther King and the citizens' movement made important progress in closing the black–white divide. Protest is important to help shatter the status quo but remains sterile if it is not connected to values that are widespread in society.[35]

12.2.2   Transition and government

New government legislation comes into being as a result of the impact political conflicts have on cultural and ideological standpoints. The political struggle occurs within histori- cal and institutional boundaries.[36] Individual politicians and government organizations as a whole are important players on the football pitch of power.[37] A government has instruments at its disposal to speed up transition in a positive way. Economist Porter has claimed that environmental regulations contribute to innovation and are often coupled with improved competitive spirit.[38] His theories have become known as the Porter Hypothesis (see Figure 12.2). He states that waste and air pollution are the result of inefficient production and stringent regulations to counteract this can be a trigger for innovations. As explained in Chapter 6, in this context it is important that businesses are positively steered not only with command and control regulations, but also with market-based instruments as taxes, subsidies and caps and trade emissions. The Porter Hypothesis has become the subject of considerable research and it has been shown that society benefits by implementing a stricter environmental policy. It forces companies to be more innovative concerning environmental issues which in general leads to increased performance and better results. This is clearly a benefit to society as well, although the results for business in the analysis are variable.[39] There is no evidence that business benefits from stricter environmental policy. Nevertheless, those enterprises that view the fledgling policy as an opportunity and actively pursue innovative solutions often perform on a better-than-average scale. It is important that management believes in the win-win paradigm.[40] Businesses that opt for a defensive rather than a pro-active position with regard to their performance under new environmental regulation can end up in unclear territory. No positive correlation has been demonstrated between stricter envi- ronmental regulation and competitiveness.

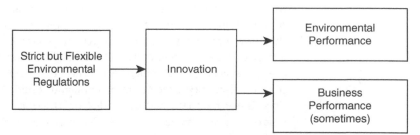

Figure 12.2   Porter Hypothesis[41]

12.2.3   Transition and business

An active government committed to transition creates a new playing field for business. Innovative companies, as opposed to those reliant on vested interests, see new regu- lations as an opportunity.[42] A country is well served when its policy is geared towards innovation.[43] Investment in new technologies, implementation of new business models and development of new markets take place when companies perceive an improve- ment in their current situation. Companies themselves defend new business strategies primarily from the standpoint of economic and legal responsibilities.[44] Van Bommel (2011) argues that organizations that have opted for a responsibly orientated business strategy have innovation at the heart of their core values, for the company as well as the employees.[45]

These companies benefit from societies that embrace transitional policy and the associated new socio-technical systems. They obtain extra economic freedom of movement because government regulation is on their side. Think of it as 'social capital' offered to companies with an exploratory nature. For the government it means that they must be open for measures that provide a direct stimulus to companies exploring the opportunities arising from sustainable transitions. This applies to restricting as well as facilitating policy. On the one hand, legislation must be developed that makes it more difficult to offer products with high externalities, but on the other hand transitions are dependent on new socio-technical systems that clash with older established ones. Roads, cable networks, public transport, property rights, working rights, social legislation, refuse disposal, subsidies and taxes are designed for a linear economy and these hamper transition. Existing socio-economic systems are equipped to facilitate the old, unsustainable market economy and have to be dismantled so that the new economy can emerge. Transition is about creative destruction and it faces resistance from ingrained vested interests.[46]

 12.3   Case Study: Germany's 'Renewable Energy Law'

In 2000 Germany adopted the 'Renewable Energy Law' which was designed to provide a sustainable energy production of 30% for the country by the year 2020. The law included a clause which stated the prices (feed-in tariff) energy providers could expect to receive for providing sustainable energy. German government chose the subsidized route for the long-term results and also because green energy was not yet capable of competing with traditional providers. The legislation was available to every investor and every supplier had access to the power grid.[47] The law proved to be a watershed for German society. Energy supply was no longer in the hands of a selected few, but was now linked to citizens and smaller competitors. In 2014 there were more than 1.5 million solar power plants with a million of these being connected to electricity supply networks. Between 2001 and 2013 the number of energy cooperatives grew from 66 to 888.[48, 49] Germany's 'Renewable Energy Law' gives citizens and small and medium enterprises the chance to contribute to sustainable development. Free access to the power grid coupled with a fixed price for electricity is seen as meaningful and considerate without incurring major risks. Research into the field concludes that this so-called 'creation of value' by business owners can also be seen as a social phenomenon. Entrepreneurship is a form of social participation and the creation of value becomes a challenge that is as much social as economic.[50]

The Renewable Energy Law has resulted in Germany being less dependent on foreign suppliers for gas and oil. In 2014, 31% of the locally supplied energy was sustainable with wind, biomass and solar energy being the biggest contributors. The future is looking bright for solar energy because installation costs are steadily decreasing. The feed-in tariffs per kilowatt-hour for the solar power plants (PV systems) built in 2013 are much lower than those of 2007. Government subsidies made it possible that network providers pay €0.47 per kWh for plants built in 2007. The feed-in tariff is guaranteed for 20 years and must be paid until 2027. For the plants built in 2013 the guaranteed price for twenty years is €0.12 per kWh, because solar systems costs have reduced substantially and this price is already sufficiently high to stimulate investors to build new solar power plants. The €0.12 per kWh price is not far from the standard free market price of €0.08 which is paid for solar energy. €0.12 per kWh is also in line with the €0.10 price which is the market price for fossil-nuclear energy when externalities are included in the price structure.[51]

Case Study Questions

1. Which market developments can currently be applied to the different forms of energy and to what extent are subsidies required for renewable energy markets? Choose a region/continent for further research.
2. Has the German 'Renewable Energy Law' dealt with the transition to sustainable energy in an effective and efficient way? Present your arguments.
3. Which government legislation would you champion to improve labour conditions worldwide? Present your arguments.

12.4   Learning tools 🔧

12.4.1   Summary

- The institutionalizing of social capital is dependent on rules and the enforcement of those rules that deal directly with human nature and related characteristics such as homo economicus, feelings of fairness, empathy, the exploratory impulse, and respect for authority, status and conformism, and those that are also able to react to issues concerning aggression and kin selection.
- Societal transition is a dynamic process whose outcome is based on the interactions of three domains: socio-technical regimes, radical technologies and landscapes.
- If ideas spread through different segments of society, there is an increased chance that government will turn them into legislation.
- Porter Hypothesis: legislation directed towards environmental improvement acts as a trigger for environmental innovation. The laws offer a better competitive position with regard to waste issues.
- To achieve transition, it is important that government makes use of facilitating policy and restrictive regulations.

12.4.2   Further reading

Grin, J., Rotmans, J. & Schot, J. (2010). *Transitions to Sustainable Development: New Directions in the Study of Long Term Transformative Change.* London and New York, Routledge.
Sen, A. (2000). *Development as Freedom.* New York, NY: Anchor.

12.4.3   Assignments

 Assignment 12.1

Search the Internet to find a recent scenario analysis concerning a sustainability theme like energy, poverty, health or deforestation which gives insight into development of the world or a certain region over a 20-year period or longer. Provide a brief summary of the analysis including strengths and weaknesses.

Assignment 12.2

Search the Internet to find an older 'sustainability' scenario analysis about a theme like energy, poverty, health or deforestation in the world or in a certain region that was written at least 10 years ago with development proposals for 15 years or longer. Provide a short summary and determine which scenario best relates to the current situation and how the predictions fit with or differ from the present.

12.4.4   Self-test questions

 Self-test Questions

1. What is the Porter Hypothesis?
2. Which four 'actors' influence societal transition?
3. What is the meaning of the concept institutionalizing?
4. Which transition did the citizens of Egypt try to achieve in 2011, and what are the causes of the failure of this transition?
5. Give an example of a facilitating policy which enabled the German government to take the first step towards the transition to sustainable energy.
6. Which socio-technical systems are a hindrance for the transition to a sustainable society?

NOTES

Prelims

1. Scholte, J. A. (2005) *Globalization: A Critical Introduction*. London: Palgrave.
2. Wanner, T. (2014). The new passive revolution of the green economy and growth discourse. *New Political Economy*. Published online DOI: 10.1080/13563467 .2013.866081.
3. Baker, S. (2005) *Sustainable Development*. London: Routledge.
4. Rodrik, D. (2012) *The Globalization Paradox: Why Markets, Globalization and Democracy Can't Coexist*. Oxford: Oxford University Press.
5. Stiglitz, J. (2010). *Making Globalization Work*. London: Penguin.
6. ibid.
7. Lichbach, M. & Zuckerman, A. (2002). *Comparative Politics: Rationality, Culture and Structure*. Cambridge: Cambridge University Press.
8. Wilson, E. O. (1996) *In Search of Nature*, London: Allen Lane.
9. Garrido-Azevedo, S., Brandenburg, M., Carvalho, H. & Cruz-Machado, V. (2014). *Eco-Innovation and the Development of Business Models*. London: Springer.

Chapter 1   The World Economy: Trends and Indicators

1. Cambridge Dictionaries Online. *GDP*. Retrieved from http://dictionary.cambridge .org/dictionary/english/gdp?q=GDP on 14 August 2015.
2. Stiglitz, J. E., Sen A., Fitoussi, J. P. (2010). *Mismeasuring our Lives: Why GDP Doesn't Add Up*. New York, NY: The New Press.
3. Stiglitz, J. (2012). *The Price of Inequality: How Today's Divided Society Endangers Our Future*. London: Penguin.
4. Kennedy, D. M. (1999). *Freedom From Fear: The American People in Depression and War, 1929–1945*. Oxford: Oxford University Press.
5. Hulme, D. (2009). The Millennium Development Goals (MDGs): A short history of the world's biggest promise. BWPI Working Paper 100, 8–12.
6. Groningen Growth & Development Centre (2008). The Maddison Project. Retrieved from www.ggdc.net/MADDISON/oriindex.htm on 8 October 2015.
7. Based on the data GDP and population of The Maddison Project: Groningen Growth & Development Centre (2008). *The Maddison Project*. Retrieved from www .ggdc.net/MADDISON/oriindex.htm on 8 October 2015.
8. Peet, R. (2008). *The Geography of Power: The Making of Global Economic Policy*. Oxford: Oxford University Press.
9. Rodrik, D. (2012). *The Globalization Paradox: Why Markets, Globalization and Democracy Can't Coexist*. Oxford: Oxford University Press.

10. Peet, R. (2008). *The Geography of Power: The Making of Global Economic Policy.* Oxford: Oxford University Press.

11. Hulme, D. (2009). *The Millennium Development Goals (MDGs): A short history of the world's biggest promise.* BWPI Working Paper 100, 8–12.

12. Stiglitz, J. (2012). *The Price of Inequality: How Today's Divided Society Endangers Our Future.* London: Penguin.

13. Rodrik, D. (2012). *The Globalization Paradox: Why Markets, Globalization and Democracy Can't Coexist.* Oxford: Oxford University Press.

14. Organisation for Economic Co-operation and Development; see website statistics in the years 2009–2013 for US, Europe, Japan: http://stats.oecd.org/Index.aspx?DatasetCode=SNA_TABLE1, Retrieved on 10 October 2015.

15. Organisation for Economic Co-operation and Development; see website statistics in the years 2009–2013 for Southeast Asia, China and India: http://stats.oecd.org/Index.aspx?DatasetCode=SNA_TABLE1, Retrieved on 10 October 2015.

16. Organisation for Economic Co-operation and Development. Retrieved from http://stats.oecd.org/Index.aspx?DatasetCode=SNA_TABLE1 on 10 October 2015.

17. Stiglitz, J. (2012). *The Price of Inequality: How Today's Divided Society Endangers Our Future.* London: Penguin.

18. Yang, X. & Luo, H. (2009). Migration, urbanization, and drug use and casual sex in China: a multilevel analysis. *Environment and Planning A, 41*(3), 581–597.

19. Bergheim, S. (2005). The growth of global wealth until 2020. The Capco Institute. *Journal of Financial Transformation, 15,* 128–133.

20. Siebert, H. (2003). Why Germany has such a weak growth performance (Kiel Working Paper 1182). In Kiel (ed.), *Institut für Weltwirtschaft.* Retrieved from http://hdl.handle.net/10419/3046 on 8 October 2015.

21. Organisation for Economic Co-operation and Development. (2013). *FDI in Figures.* Retrieved from http://www.oecd.org/daf/inv/FDI%20in%20figures.pdf on 8 October 2015.

22. Li, J. et al. (2008). The higher educational transformation of China and its global implications (Working Paper 13849). Cambridge, MA: National Bureau of Economic Research.

23. Hufbauer, G. (2007). *The US Congress and the Chinese Yuan.* Washington DC: Peterson Institute for International Economics.

24. ibid.

25. Euromoney (2015). Rising dollar makes renminbi second most overvalued currency. Retrieved from www.euromoney.com/Article/3427487/Rising-dollar-makes-renminbi-second-most-overvalued-currency.html on 8 October 2015.

26. Reuters. (2015). Surprised by global impact of yuan move, China looks to calm markets. Retrieved from www.reuters.com/article/2015/08/27/us-china-yuan-idUSKCN0QW09I20150827 on 8 October 2015.

27. Index Mundi. (2015). China natural resources. Retrieved from http://www.indexmundi.com/china/natural_resources.html on 8 October 2015.

28. Zeng, N. et al. (2008). Climate change – the Chinese challenge. *Science, 319,* 730–731.

29. Zheng, J. (2009). Can China's growth be sustained? A productivity perspective. *World Development, 37*(4), 874–888.

30. Short films relating to globalization and what developments we can expect in the future can be found on YouTube (www.youtube.co.uk) by typing 'shift happens' into the search field.

31. Mahbubani, K. (2008). *The New Asian Hemisphere: The Irresistible Shift of Global Power to the East* (pp. 144–150). New York, NY: Public Affairs.

32. Beina, X. (2014, 25 September). Media censorship in China. Council on Foreign Relations. Retrieved from www.cfr.org/china/media-censorship-china/p11515 on 8 October 2015.

33. Chin, D. & Chan, Y. (2012). Public service and individual rights: Striking the balance between order, development and freedom of speech in China. *Media Culture & Society, 34*(7), 898–891. London: Sage.

34. Yang, G. (2011). *The Power of the Internet in China: Citizen Activism Online.* New York, NY: Columbia University Press.

35. Givens, J. & MacDonald, A. (2013). The Internet with Chinese characteristics: Democratizing discourse but not politics (APSA 2013 Annual Meeting Paper). Pittsburgh, PA and Louisville, KY: Asian Studies Center, University of Pittsburgh and University of Louisville – Center for Asian Democracy.

36. ibid.

37. Morrisson, C. & Murtin, F. (2011). Average income inequality between countries (1700–2030) (Working Paper P25). Clermont-Ferrand: FERDI Fondation pour les études et recherches sur le développement international.

38. Stiglitz, J. (2012). *The Price of Inequality: How Today's Divided Society Endangers Our Future.* London: Penguin.

39. Stiglitz, J. (2015). *The Great Divide.* London: Penguin.

40. Meschi, E. & Vivarelli, M. (2009). Trade and income inequality in developing countries. *World Development, Elsevier, 37*(2), 287–302.

41. Piketty, T. (2014). *Capital in the Twenty-First Century.* Cambridge, MA: Harvard University Press.

42. Warner, D., Prasada Rao, D. S., Griffiths, W. E. & Chotikapanich, D. (2011). Global inequality: Levels and trends, 1993–2005 (Discussion Papers Series 436). Queensland: School of Economics, University of Queensland, Australia.

43. Centraal Bureau voor de Statistiek. (CBS) (2010, December). *Terugblikken, een eeuw in statistieken.* Den Haag/Heerlen: CBS.(Only available in Dutch.)

44. Mason, C. (2011, May). *Democracy in Tanzania?: The Role of NGOs in Fostering Government Accountability.* Bloomington: Department of Political Science, Indiana University.

45. Shmelev, S. E. (2011). Dynamic sustainability assessment: The case of Russia in the period of transition (1985–2008). *Ecological Economics, Elsevier, 70*(11), 2039–2049.

46. UN Millennium Project (2005). *Investing in Development: A Practical Plan to Achieve the Millennium Development Goals.* New York.

47. United Nations (2014). *The Millennium Development Goals Report 2014.* New York.

48. ibid.

49. Piketty, T. (2014). *Capital in the Twenty-First Century.* Cambridge, MA: Harvard University Press.

50. Stiglitz, J. (2015). *The Great Divide.* London: Penguin.

51. ibid.

52. Babatunde, A. S. (2012). The impact of tax incentives on foreign direct investment in the oil and gas sector in Nigeria. *OSR Journal of Business and Management, 6*(1), 1–15.

53. IPCC (2014). *Fifth Assessment Report (AR5) Climate Change 2014 Synthesis Report.* Retrieved from www.ipcc.ch/report/ar5/syr/ on 10 October 2015.

54. World Bank (2013). Africa continues to grow strongly but poverty and inequality remain persistently high. Retrieved from www.worldbank.org/en/news/press-release/2013/10/07/africa-continues-grow-strongly-poverty-inequality-persistently-high on 8 October 2015.

55. ibid.

56. United Nations Economic Commission for Africa (2011). *Minerals and Africa's Development: The International Study Group Report on Africa's Mineral Regimes.* Retrieved from www.africaminingvision.org/amv_resources/AMV/ISG%20Report_eng.pdf on 8 October 2015.

57. McElroy, C. (2013). *Hybridity, Learning, and the Performance of Corporate Foundations in the Mining Industry.*

58. United Nations Development Programme (2014). *Human Development Report 2014: Sustaining Human Progress: Reducing Vulnerabilities and Building Resilience* (p. 21 and p. 37). New York.

59. Tax Justice Network – Africa (2014). *Africa Rising? Inequalities and the Essential Role of Fair Taxation.* Retrieved from www.christianaid.org.uk/images/Africa-tax-and-inequality-report-Feb2014.pdf on 8 October 2015.

60. United Nations Economic Commission for Africa. *Economic Report on Africa 2012: Unleashing Africa's Potential as a Pole of Global Growth.* Retrieved from www.uneca.org/sites/default/files/PublicationFiles/era2012_eng_fin.pdf on 8 October 2015.

61. Bonsu, S. K. (2014). Governing the global periphery: Socio-economic development in service of the global core. In R. Westwood, G. Jack, F. R. Khan & M. Frenkel (eds), *Core-Periphery Relations and Organisation Studies* (pp. 121–138). London: Palgrave Macmillan.

62. Stiglitz, J. (2015). *The Great Divide.* London: Penguin.

63. ibid.

64. Bonsu, S. K. (2014). Governing the global periphery: Socio-economic development in service of the global core. In R. Westwood, G. Jack, F. R. Khan & M. Frenkel (eds), *Core–Periphery Relations and Organisation Studies* (pp. 121–138). London: Palgrave Macmillan.

Chapter 2 Market Economies and Governments

1. Weingast, B. R. (1995). The economic role of political institutions: Market-preserving federalism and economic development. *Journal of Law, Economics and Organization, 11*(1), 1–31.

2. Gilpin, R. (2011). *Global Political Economy: Understanding the International Economic Order.* Princeton, NJ: Princeton University Press.

3. Stiglitz, J. (2002). *Globalization and Its Discontents.* London: Penguin.

4. ibid.

5. Hetzel, R. L. (2012). *The Great Recession: Market Failure or Policy Failure?* New York: Cambridge University Press.

6. Navarro, V. (2007). Neoliberalism as a class ideology; or, the political causes of the growth of inequalities. *International Journal of Health Services, 37*(1), 47–62.

7. Liston-Heyes C. (2015). *International Business Economics.* London: University of London.

8. ibid.

9. ibid.

10. Roubini, N. & Mihn, S. (2011). *Crisis Economics: A Crash Course in the Future of Finance.* London: Penguin.

11. World Bank Report (1993). *The East Asian Miracle: Economic Growth and Public Policy.* New York: Oxford University Press for the World Bank.

12. There is strong controversy about whether Schumpeter should be considered a true member of the Austrian School but we endorse David Simpson's position. Simpson argues that despite differences on technical questions, Schumpeter and his Austrian economics colleagues shared very similar views on the substantive issues of their economic analysis. See Simpson, D. (1983). Joseph Schumpeter and the Austrian School of Economics. *Journal of Economic Studies, 10*(4), 15–28.

13. Szirmai, A. (2005). *The Dynamics of Socio-Economic Development* (p. 38). Cambridge: Cambridge University Press.

14. ibid.

15. Szirmai, A. (2005). *The Dynamics of Socio-Economic Development* (p. 35). Cambridge: Cambridge University Press.

16. Weber, M. (1905). *Die Protestantische Ethik und der Geist des Kapitalismus.* Weinheim: Beltz Athenäum Verlag.

17. Locke, J. & Macpherson, C. B. (1980). *Second Treatise of Government.* Indianapolis, IN: Hackett Publishing.

18. Smith, A. (1991). *The wealth of nations* (Vol. 3). A. S. Skinner (ed.) (p. 8). New York, NY: Prometheus Books.

19. Collins, D. (1988). Adam Smith's social contract. *Business and Professional Ethics Journal, 7*(3/4), 119–146.

20. Eaton, J. (1952). *Political Economy: a Marxist Textbook.* London: Farleigh Press Limited.

21. ibid.

22. ibid.

23. Marks, G. (1989). *Unions in Politics: Britain, Germany, and the United States in the Nineteenth and Early Twentieth Century.* Princeton, NJ: Princeton University Press.

24. Ó Riain, S. (2000). States and markets in an era of globalization. *Annual Review of Sociology, 26,* 187–213.

25. Hymer, S. & Resnick, S. (1969). A model of an agrarian economy with non-agricultural activities. *American Economic Review, 59*(4), 493–506.

26. Ma, G. & Yi, W. (2011). China's high saving rate: Myth and reality. *Economie Internationale, 122*(2), 5–39.

27. Van Der Velden, S. (2012). De lonen bij de dekenfabriek van Zaalberg te Leiden, 1896-1902. *Jaarboek der Sociale en Economische Geschiedenis van Leiden en Omstreken, 24,* 49–72. (Only available in Dutch.)

28. Scholliers, P. (1981). Arbeidersconsumptie in transitie, *1890*-1930. In J. Hannes (ed.), *Consumptiepatronen en prijsindexen* (pp. 30–36). Brussels: VUB-press. (Only available in Dutch.)

29. Vakbond Metaal en Techniek (2009). *Collectieve Arbeidsovereenkomst Kleinmetaal 2011.* (Only available in Dutch.)

30. Yao, S. (2002). Privilege and corruption: The problems of China's socialist market economy. *American Journal of Economics and Sociology, 61*(1), 279–299.

31. Tanzi, V. (1998). Corruption around the world: Causes, consequences, scope, and cures. *Staff Papers – International Monetary Fund, 45*(4), 559–594.

32. OECD (2006). *African Economic Outlook 2005/2006: Tanzania.* Retrieved from www.oecd.org/dev/emea/africaneconomicoutlook20052006.htm on 30 November 2015.

33. World Bank Group. *Doing Business.* Retrieved from www.doingbusiness.org/ on 31 August 2010.

34. Dubbink, W. (2003). Assisting the invisible hand: Contested relations between market, state and civil society. *Springer Science & Business Media, 18.*

35. Bishop, J. D. (1995). Adam Smith's invisible hand argument. *Journal of Business Ethics, 14*(3), 165–180.

36. Gu, Y. & Wenzel, T. (2011). Transparency, price-dependent demand and product variety. *Economics Letters, 110*(3), 216–219.

37. Krishna, P. & Mitra, D. (1998). Trade liberalization, market discipline and productivity growth: New evidence from India. *Journal of Development Economics, 56*(2), 447–462.

38. Kumar, U., Mishra, P. (2008). Trade liberalization and wage inequality: Evidence from India. *Review of Development Economics, 12*(2), 291–311.

39. Aghion, P., Dewatripont, M. & Rey, P. (1999). Competition, financial discipline and growth. *Review of Economic Studies, 66*, 825–852.

40. Szirmai, A. (2005). *The Dynamics of Socio-Economic Development.* (p. 106). Cambridge: Cambridge University Press.

41. Data 1870–2000: Obstfeld, M. & Taylor, A. M. (2004). *Global Capital Markets: Integration, Crisis and Growth.* Cambridge: Cambridge University Press / Data 2003: Lane, P. R. & Milesi-Ferretti, G. M. (2007). The External Wealth of Nations Mark II: Revised and extended estimates of foreign assets and liabilities, 1970–2004. *Journal of International Economics, 73*, 223–250.

42. WTO. *Who we are.* Retrieved from www.wto.org/english/thewto_e/whatis_e/who_we_are_e.htm on 11 July 2015.

43. Shaikh, A. (1996). Free trade, unemployment, and economic policy. In J. Eatwell (ed.) *Global Unemployment: Loss of Jobs in the '90s.* New York, Armonk: ME Sharpe.

44. As we will see in Chapter 8, empirical evidence does not show that poorer countries will simply improve their welfare with free trade; rather the opposite.

45. King, J. E. (2013). *David Ricardo.* Palgrave Macmillan.

46. Another international trade theory usually invoked to support free trade is the Heckscher–Ohlin factor-proportion theory of comparative advantage (H–O theory). H–O argues that international trade compensates geographical differences in the endowment of resources, thus a truly global market will lead to similar demand across countries and lower prices everywhere. The main insight of H–O is that traded products are actually bundles of factors of production (labour, capital, land). International trade transfers otherwise immobile factors of production from places where they are abundant to places where they are not. We do not discuss H–O in detail here since, as noted by Leamer (1995), empirical evidence provides a very strong and convincing case against its conclusions; however, with Learner we feel that 'it remains alive and well in every textbook written by authors fond of the artistic diagrams and simple theorems associated with H–O' (p. 2). Leamer, E. (1995). The Heckscher–Ohlin Model in theory and practice. *Princeton Studies in International Finance, 77*.

47. Boudreaux, D. J. Comparative advantage. *The Concise Encyclopedia of Economics.* Retrieved from www.econlib.org/library/Enc/ComparativeAdvantage.html on 26 November 2015.

48. Library of Economics and Liberty. Retrieved from www.econlib.org/library/Enc/ComparativeAdvantage.html on 7 July 2015.

49. Naughton, B. (2007). *The Chinese Economy: Transitions and Growth.* Cambridge, MA: MIT Press.

50. Stiglitz, D. J. (2009). Moving beyond market fundamentalism to a more balanced economy. *Annals of Public and Cooperative Economics 80*(3), 345–360.

51. Winston, C. (2007). *Government Failure Versus Market Failure: Microeconomics Policy Research and Government Performance.* Brookings Institution Press.

52. Stiglitz, J. E. (2000). Capital market liberalization, economic growth, and instability. *World Development, 28*(6), 1075–1086.
53. Weiss, A. (2005). *A Comparison of Economic Democracy and Participatory Economics.* Retrieved from http://nicomedia.math.upatras.gr/Econ-Dem/resources/Papers/Weiss_AComparisonOfEconomicDemocracy%26ParticipatoryEconomics.pdf on 26 November 2015.
54. Stiglitz, D. J. (2009). Moving beyond market fundamentalism to a more balanced economy. *Annals of Public and Cooperative Economics, 80*(3), 345–360.
55. Teo, T. S. H. & Yu, Y. (2005). Online buying behavior: a transaction cost economics perspective. *Omega, 33*(5), 451–465.
56. Ardichvili, A., Cardozo, R. & Ray, S. (2003). A theory of entrepreneurial opportunity identification and development. *Journal of Business Venturing 18*(1), 105–123.
57. Alleman, J. & Rappoport, P. (2005). Regulatory Failure: Time for a New Policy Paradigm. *Communications and Strategies, 60*(4), 105–121.
58. P. Desai, P. & Martin, R. (1983). Efficiency loss from resource misallocation in Soviet industry. *The Quarterly Journal of Economics, 98*(3), 441–456.
59. Viscusi, W. K., Harrington, J. E. & Vernon, J. M. (2005). *Economics of Regulation and Antitrust.* MIT Press.
60. Posner, R. (2009). *Antitrust Law.* Chicago: University of Chicago Press.
61. Hamilton, J. D. (2008). Understanding crude oil prices. *National Bureau of Economic Research, w. 14492.*
62. Meadows, D. H., Meadows, D. L., Randers, J. & Behrens, W. W. (1972). *The Limits to Growth.* New York, NY: Universe Books. Meadows, D. H., Randers, J. & Meadows, D. L. (2004). *Limits to Growth: The 30-Year Update.* White River Junction, VT: Chelsea Green Publishing.
63. Mullainathan, S. & Thaler, R. H. (2000). Behavioral economics (Working Paper 7948). *National Bureau of Economic Research.*
64. Keynes, J. M. (1935). *The General Theory of Employment, Interest and Money.* NY, Prometheus Books.
65. Farmer, R. E. A. & Guo, J. T. (1994). Real business cycles and the animal spirits hypothesis. *Journal of Economic Theory, 63*(1), 42–72.
66. Palley, T. (2011). America's flawed paradigm: Macroeconomic causes of the financial crisis and great recession. *Empirica, 38*(1), 3–17.
67. Jin, C., Soydemir, G. & Tidwell, A. (2014). The US housing market and the pricing of risk: Fundamental analysis and market sentiment. *Journal of Real Estate Research, 36*(2), 187–219.
68. Ferreira, R. D. S. & Dufourt, F. (2006). Free entry and business cycles under the influence of animal spirits. *Journal of Monetary Economics, 53*(2), 311–328.
69. Velzing, E. J. (2013). *Innovatiepolitiek: Een reconstructie van het innovatiebeleid van het ministerie van Economische Zaken van 1976 tot en met 2010* (Innovation Policy: A Reconstruction of the Innovation Policy of the Ministry of Economic Affairs from 1976 to 2010) (p. 327). Delft: Eburon.
70. Adler, P. S. (2001). Market, hierarchy, and trust: The knowledge economy and the future of capitalism. *Organization science, 12*(2), 215–234.
71. Ostrom, E. (2003). How types of goods and property rights jointly affect collective action. *Journal of Theoretical Politics, 15*(3), 239–270.
72. Krueger, A. B. & Lindahl, M. (2000). Education for growth: Why and for whom? *National Bureau of Economic Research, w. 7591.*
73. Kaul, I., Grunberg, I. & Stern, M. A. (1999). Defining global public goods. In I. Kaul, I. Grunberg & M. A. Stern (eds), *Global Public Goods: International Cooperation in the 21st Century,* 2–19.

74. Parry, I. W. H., Walls, M. & Harrington, W. (2007). Automobile externalities and policies. *Journal of Economic Literature*, 45(2), 373–399.

75. Chang, H. (2002). *Breaking the Mould: An Institutionalist Political Economy Alternative to the Neo-Liberal Theory of the Market and the State. Cambridge Journal of Economics*, 26(5), 539–559. doi: 10.1093/cje/26.5.539.

76. Wilkinson, R. G. & Pickett, K. E. (2006). Income inequality and population health: A review and explanation of the evidence. *Social Science & Medicine*, 62(7), 1768–1784.

77. Brush, J. (2007). Does income inequality lead to more crime? A comparison of cross-sectional and time-series analyses of United States counties. *Economics Letters*, 96(2), 264–268.

78. Szirmai, A. (2005). *The Dynamics of Socio-Economic Development* (p. 221). Cambridge: Cambridge University Press.

79. Tomasi, J. (2012). *Free Market Fairness*. Princeton: Princeton University Press.

80. Wilkinson, R. G. & Pickett, K. E. (2009). *The Spirit Level: Why More Equal Societies Almost Always Do Better* (pp. 129–145). London: Allen Lane.

81. Wilkinson, R. G. & Pickett, K. E. (2009). *The Spirit Level: Why More Equal Societies Almost Always Do Better* (p. 52). London: Allen Lane.

82. Finseraas, H. (2009). Income inequality and demand for redistribution: A multilevel analysis of European public opinion. *Scandinavian Political Studies*, 32(1), 94–119.

83. UNDP. *Human Development Report 2011: Statistical Annex*. Retrieved from www .undp.org/content/dam/undp/library/corporate/HDR/2011%20Global%20HDR/ English/HDR_2011_EN_Tables.pdf on 30 November 2015.

84. Sachs, J. D. (1995). Economic reform and the process of global integration. *Brookings Papers on Economic Activity*, 1, 1–118.

85. Blanchard, O. & Landier, A. (2002). The perverse effects of partial labour market reform: Fixed-term contracts in France. *The Economic Journal*, 112(480), F214–F244.

86. Low Pay Commission. National *Minimum Wage: Low Pay Commission Report 2009*. The Stationery Office.

87. Stiglitz, J. (2002, 12 May). Argentina, short-changed: Why the nation that followed the rules fell to pieces. *The Washington Post*.

88. Solanas, F. (2004). *A Social Genocide* [documentary motion picture]. Buenos Aires: Cinesur Producciones.

89. Hornbeck, J. (2002). *The Argentine Financial Crisis: A Chronology of Events*. CRS Report for US Congress.

90. Roubini, N. & Mihn, S. (2011). *Crisis Economics: A Crash Course in the Future of Finance*. London: Penguin.

91. ibid.

92. ibid.

93. Roubini, N. & Mihn, S. (2011). *Crisis Economics: A Crash Course in the Future of Finance*. London: Penguin.

94. ibid.

95. Davies, H. (2010). *The Financial Crisis: Who is to Blame?* London: Polity Press.

96. ibid.

97. Krugman, P. (2008). After the money's gone. In M. Lewis (ed.), *Panic!: The Story of Modern Financial Insanity*. London: Penguin.

98. ibid.

99. Cooper, G. (2008). *The Origin of Financial Crises: Central banks, Credit Bubbles and the Efficient Market Fallacy*. New York, NY: Vintage.

100. Stiglitz, J. (2010). *Freefall: Free Markets and the Sinking of the Global Economy*. London: Penguin.

101. Davies, H. (2010). *The Financial Crisis: Who is to Blame?* London: Polity Press.
102. Cooper, G. (2008). *The Origin of Financial Crises: Central banks, Credit Bubbles and the Efficient Market Fallacy.*
103. Stiglitz, J. (2002, May 12). Argentina, short-changed: Why the nation that followed the rules fell to pieces. *The Washington Post.*
104. *Newsweek* (2007, 23 September). A Candid Conversation with Alan Greenspan, by John Meachan.
105. Krugman, P. (2008). After the money's gone. In M. Lewis (ed.), *Panic!: The Story of Modern Financial Insanity.* London: Penguin.
106. Lewis, M. (ed.) (2008). *Panic!: The Story of Modern Financial Insanity.* London: Penguin.
107. ibid.
108. Stiglitz, J. (2010). *Freefall: Free Markets and the Sinking of the Global Economy.* London: Penguin.
109. ibid.

Chapter 3   Good Governance

1. Easterly, W. (2001). The middle class consensus and economic development. *Journal of Economic Growth* 6(4), 317–335.
2. The World Bank (2014). *What is Governance?* Retrieved from http://go.worldbank.org/G2CHLXX0Q0 on 1 December 2015.
3. ibid.
4. Strictly speaking, governance in the sense the World Bank understands the term was introduced in the 1990s. It is arguably a spin-off from the concept of governmentality, developed by Foucault to refer to the techniques and procedures designed to govern the conduct of both individuals and populations at every level, not just the administrative or political level. See: Foucault, M. (1991). Governmentality. In G. Burchell, C. Gordon & P. Miller (eds), *The Foucault Effect: Studies in Governmentality* (pp. 87–104). Chicago: University of Chicago Press.
5. O'Farrell, C. (2005). *Michel Foucault.* London: SAGE.
6. Bevir, M. (2013). *Key Concepts in Governance.* London: SAGE.
7. Stiglitz, J. (2010). *Freefall: Free Markets and the Sinking of the Global Economy.* London: Penguin.
8. Kerbo, H. R. (2006). *Social Stratification and Inequality: Class Conflict in Historical, Comparative, and Global Perspective* (p. 228). Boston: McGraw-Hill.
9. Cronin, C. (2003). Kant's politics of Enlightenment. *Journal of the History of Philosophy, 41*(1), 51–80.
10. Oakeshott, M. (1958). *Morality and Politics in Modern Europe.* New Haven, CT: Yale University Press. (Also see: Wansink, H. (2011, 8 October). *It's the philosophy, stupid! Volkskrant.* Retrieved from www.volkskrant.nl/archief/it-s-the-philosophy-stupid~a2958315/ on 30 November 2015.)
11. Shuger, D. K. (1997). *Habits of Thought in the English Renaissance: Religion, Politics, and the Dominant Culture.* Toronto: University of Toronto Press.
12. Moseley, A. (2014). *John Locke* (p. 25–29). Bloomsbury Publishing.
13. Rauscher, F. (2006). Kant on the edge. *The Philosophers' Magazine, 36,* 33–35.
14. Kant, I. (1784/2009). *An Answer to the Question: 'What is Enlightenment?'* trans. by D. F. Ferrer. London: Penguin.
15. Hobsbawm, E. (1995). *Age of Extremes: The Short Twentieth Century 1914–1991.* London: Abacus.

16. Inglehart, R. (2003, January). *How Solid is Mass Support for Democracy – And How Can We Measure It?* PSOnline. Retrieved from www.apsanet.org on 1 December 2015.

17. Lake, D. A. & Baum, M. (2001). The invisible hand of democracy: Political control and the provision of public services. *Comparative Political Studies, 34*(6), 587–621.

18. Acemoglu, D. (2006). *Economic Origins of Dictatorship and Democracy.* Cambridge: Cambridge University Press.

19. ibid.

20. Goldstein, R. J. (2013). *Political Repression in 19th Century Europe* (Routledge Library Editions: Political Science Volume 24). London and New York, Routledge.

21. Mair, P. (2005). *Democracy Beyond Parties* (CSD Working Paper 05/06). Irvine, CA: Center for the Study of Democracy, University of California.

22. Reybrouck, D. van (2013). *Tegen Verkiezingen* (Against Elections). Amsterdam: De Bezige Bij. (Only available in Dutch.)

23. ibid.

24. ibid.

25. Alonso, S., Keane, J. & Merkel, W. (2011). *The Future of Representative Democracy.* Cambridge: Cambridge University Press.

26. Humes, K. R., Jones, N. A. & Ramirez, R. R. (2011, March). *Overview of Race and Hispanic Origin: 2010. 2010 Census Briefs.* U.S. Census Bureau. Retrieved from www.census.gov/prod/cen2010/briefs/c2010br-02.pdf on 1 December 2015.

27. Fishkin, J. S. (1991). *Democracy and Deliberation: New Directions for Democratic Reform.* London: Yale University Press.

28. ibid.

29. Moravcsik, A. (1995). Explaining international human rights regimes: Liberal theory and Western Europe. *European Journal of International Relations, 1*(2), 157–189.

30. Davis, D. B. (2008). *Inhuman Bondage: The Rise and Fall of Slavery in the New World* (p. 238). New York, NY: Oxford University Press.

31. Bergman, M. P. (1991). Montesquieu's theory of government and the framing of the American constitution. *Pepperdine Law Review, 18*(1). Retrieved from: http://digitalcommons.pepperdine.edu/plr/vol18/iss1/3 on 1 December 2015.

32. Roberts, J. (2002). Building the complementary board. The work of the plc chairman. *Long Range Planning, 35*(5), 493–520.

33. Braithwaite, J. (1997). On speaking softly and carrying big sticks: Neglected dimensions of a republication separation of powers. *University of Toronto Law Journal,* 305–361.

34. Arndt, C. (2008). The politics of governance ratings. *International Public Management Journal, 11,* 275–297.

35. Karskens, M. L. J. (2000). What is civil society? In J. Gruppelaar (ed.), *Burgers en hun bindingen* (pp. 11–30). Best: Damon.

36. Fukuyama, F. (2004). *State Building: Governance and World Order in the 21st Century.* Ithaca, NY: Cornell University Press.

37. Weber, M. (2009). *From Max Weber: Essays in Sociology.* Routledge.

38. Elias, N. & Jephcott, E. (1982). *The Civilizing Process* (Vol. 2). New York: Pantheon Books.

39. Bevir, M. (2013). *Key Concepts in Governance.* London: SAGE.

40. World Bank (1989). *Sub-Saharan Africa: From Crisis to Sustainable Growth. A Long-Term Perspective Study.* Washington, DC: The World Bank.

41. Annan, K. (1999). *Preventing War and Disaster: A Growing Global Challenge* (p. 82). United Nations.

42. UNDP (1994). *Governance for Sustainable Human Development*. United Nations Development Programme.

43. From *Governance for Sustainable Human Development*, by United Nations Development Programme, © 1997 United Nations. Reprinted with the permission of the United Nations.

44. Fukuyama, F. (2004). *State Building: Governance and World Order in the 21st Century*. Ithaca, NY: Cornell University Press.

45. Dicken, P. (2011). *Global Shift: Mapping the Contours of the World Economy*. New York, NY: Guilford Press.

46. Stiglitz, J. (2010). *Freefall: Free Markets and the Sinking of the Global Economy*. London: Penguin. Stiglitz, J. (2012). *The Price of Inequality: How Today's Divided Society Endangers Our Future*. London: Penguin.

47. Krugman, P. (2007). *The Conscience of a Liberal*. New York, NY: W.W. Norton & Company. Krugman, P. (2013). *End This Depression Now!* New York, NY: W.W. Norton & Company.

48. Bevir, M. (2013). *Key Concepts in Governance* (p. 6). London: SAGE.

49. Dicken, P. (2011). *Global Shift: Mapping the Contours of the World Economy* (p. 170). New York, NY: Guilford Press.

50. British Economist John Maynard Keynes (1886–1946) revolutionized neo-classical economics claiming that markets were not efficient to assure full employment and indeed free markets led to cycles of economic boom and economic depression. Keynes was the architect of the world economy recovery after the great depression in the 1930s. He was also one of the ideologists behind the creation of the World Bank, International Monetary Fund and World Trade Organization. After his death, his ideas were misused to justify increasing government interference with markets (far beyond the levels of involvement advocated by Keynes).

51. Stiglitz, J. (2012). *The Price of Inequality: How Today's Divided Society Endangers Our Future*. London: Penguin.

52. Roubini, N. & Mihn, S. (2011). *Crisis Economics: A Crash Course in the Future of Finance*. London: Penguin.

53. Dicken, P. (2011). *Global Shift: Mapping the Contours of the World Economy*. New York, NY: Guilford Press.

54. Krugman, P. (2013). *End This Depression Now!* New York, NY: W.W. Norton & Company.

55. World Bank. (1997). *World Development Report 1997: The State in a Changing World*. New York, NY: Oxford University Press. © World Bank. Retrieved from https://openknowledge.worldbank.org/handle/10986/5980 on 30 March 2015. License: CC BY 3.0 IGO.

56. Hall, P. & Soskice, D. (2001). *Varieties of Capitalism: The Institutional Foundations of Comparative Advantage*. New York, NY: Oxford University Press.

57. World Bank (1997). *World Development Report 1997: The State in a Changing World*. New York, NY: Oxford University Press. © World Bank. Retrieved from https://openknowledge.worldbank.org/handle/10986/5980 on 30 March 2015. License: CC BY 3.0 IGO.

58. ibid.

59. Samuels, K. (2006, October). *Rule of Law Reform in Post-Conflict Countries: Operational Initiatives and Lessons Learnt* (Social Development Papers: Conflict Prevention and Reconstruction, Paper No. 37/2006). Washington DC: Social Development Department, The World Bank.

60. Schäfer, H. B. & Ott, C. (2004). *The Economic Analysis of Civil Law*. Northampton: Edward Elgar Publishing.

61. Mahoney, P. G. (2001). The common law and economic growth: Hayek might be right. *The Journal of Legal Studies*, 30(2), 503–525.

62. Hanninen, O., Farago, M. & Monos, E. (1983). Ignaz Philipp Semmelweis, the prophet of bacteriology. *Infection Control*, 4(5), 367–370.

63. Bodea, C. & Hicks, R. (2015). Price stability and central bank independence: Discipline, credibility, and democratic institutions. *International Organization*, 69(01), 35–61.

64. European Central Bank (2015). *Monetary Policy*. Retrieved from www.ecb.europa .eu/mopo/html/index.en.html on 27 July 2015.

65. Epstein, G. (2006). Central banks as agents of economic development (Research Paper 2006/54). UNU-WIDER, United Nations University (UNU).

66. Sveriges Riksbank. The Riksbank's banknote history – Tumba Bruk museum. Retrieved from www.riksbank.se/en/The-Riksbank/History/The-Riksbanks-banknote-history-Tumba-Bruk-museum/ on 15 August 2015. Sveriges Riksbank. Money and power – the history of Sveriges Riksbank. Retrieved from www.riksbank.se/en/The-Riksbank/History/Money-and-power-the-history-of-Sveriges-Riksbank/ on 15 August 2015.

67. Francis, J. H. (1888). *History of the Bank of England*. Chicago, IL: Euclid Publishing Co.

68. Fazio, A. (1991). Role and independence of central banks. In P. Downes & R. Vaez-Zadeh (eds), *The Evolving Role of Central Banks*, pp.121–139. Washington, DC: IMF.

69. International Monetary Fund (1996). *Balance of Payments Textbook*. Washington, DC: International Monetary Fund.

70. *Europa Nu*. Retrieved from http://www.europa-nu.nl/ on 28 July 2015. (Only available in Dutch.)

71. Ngai, V. (2012). Stability and growth pact and fiscal discipline in the eurozone (Working Paper 12-10). Wharton Financial Institutions Center, University of Pennsylvania.

72. Edwards, S. & Tabellini, G. (1991). Explaining fiscal policies and inflation in developing countries. *Journal of International Money and Finance*, 10, S16–S48.

73. Wijnbergen, S. Van (1986). Exchange rate management and stabilization policies in developing countries. *Journal of Development Economics*, 23(2), 227–247.

74. World Bank. (1997). *World Development Report 1997: The State in a Changing World*. New York, NY: Oxford University Press. © World Bank. https://openknowledge. worldbank.org/handle/10986/5980 License: CC BY 3.0 IGO.

75. ibid.

76. Beckert, J. (1996). What is sociological about economic sociology? Uncertainty and the embeddedness of economic action. *Theory and Society*, 25(6), 803–840.

77. Grootaert, C. (2001). Social capital: The missing link? In C. Grootaert (ed.), *Social Capital and Participation in Everyday Life*. London: Routledge.

78. Tanzi, V. (2005). The economic role of the state in the 21st century. *Cato J*, 25, 617.

79. Dowla, A. (2006). In credit we trust: Building social capital by Grameen Bank in Bangladesh. *The Journal of Socio-Economics*, 35(1), 102–122.

80. Holleran, E., Bredahl, M. E. & Zaibet, L. (1999). Private incentives for adopting food safety and quality assurance. *Food policy*, 24(6), 669–683.

81. World Bank (1997). *World Development Report 1997: The State in a Changing World*. New York, NY: Oxford University Press. © World Bank. https://openknowledge .worldbank.org/handle/10986/5980 License: CC BY 3.0 IGO.

82. Bardhan, P., Bowles, S. & Gintis, H. (2000). Wealth inequality, wealth constraints and economic performance. *Handbook of income distribution*, 1, 541–603.

83. Sokoloff, K. L. & Engerman, S. L. (2000). History lessons: Institutions, factors endowments, and paths of development in the new world. *The Journal of Economic Perspectives, 14*(3), 217–232.

84. ibid.

85. Stiglitz, J. (2012). *The Price of Inequality: How Today's Divided Society Endangers Our Future.* London: Penguin.

86. Stiglitz, J. (2002). *Globalization and its Discontents,* London: Penguin.

87. Dollar, D. & Sokoloff, K. L. (1994). Industrial policy, productivity, growth and structural change in the manufacturing industries: A comparison of Taiwan and South Korea. In J. D. Aberbach, D. Dollar & K. L. Soko (eds), *The Role of the State in Taiwan's Development* (pp. 8–11). New York: M.E. Sharpe.

88. Amsden, A. H. (1992). *Asia's Next Giant: South Korea and Late Industrialization.* New York, NY: Oxford University Press.

89. Cho, D. S. (2004). Design, economic development, and national policy: Lessons from Korea. *Design Management Review, 15*(4), 10–20.

90. Hellum, A. & Derman, B. (2004). Land reform and human rights in contemporary Zimbabwe: Balancing individual and social justice through an integrated human rights framework. *World Development, 32*(10), 1785–1805.

91. Bond, P. (2004). *Talk Left, Walk Right: South Africa's Frustrated Global Reforms.* London: Merlin Press.

92. Marais, H. (2011). *South Africa Pushed to the Limit: The Political Economy of Change.* London: Zed Books.

93. South African Government (2015). Black Business Supplier Development Programme (BBSDP). Retrieved from www.gov.za/services/business-incentives/black-business-supplier-development-programme-bbsdp on 30 July 2015.

94. Donnelly, J. (1998). Human rights: a new standard of civilization? *International Affairs, 74*(1), 1–23.

95. Central Intelligence Agency. *The World Factbook 2009.*

96. eMapsWorld. (2014). *Mozambique Location Map In Africa Black and White.* Retrieved from www.emapsworld.com/mozambique-location-map-in-africa-black-and-white.html on 30 March 2015. © MapsOpenSource. Retrieved from http://creativecommons.org/licenses/by/3.0/deed.en_US License: Creative Commons Attribution 3.0 Unported License on 30 March 2015.

97. Diffie, B. W. & Winius, G. D. (1973). *Foundations of the Portuguese Empire 1415–1580.* St. Paul: North Central Publishing Company.

98. Clarence-Smith, W. G. (1985). *The Third Portuguese Empire 1825–1975: A Study in Economic Imperialism.* Manchester: Manchester University Press.

99. Newitt, M. (1995). *A History of Mozambique.* London: C. Hurst & Co.

100. Birmingham, D. (2003). *A Concise History of Portugal.* Cambridge: Cambridge University Press.

101. SABC (2011). *Mozambique remembers Samora Machel.* Retrieved from http://www.sabc.co.za/news/a/d90ad38048be4eda9abd9aee2cb4f1d1/Mozambique-remembers-Samora-Machel-20111910 on 15 August 2015.

102. ibid.

103. Newitt, M. (1995). *A History of Mozambique.* London: C. Hurst & Co.

104. De Renzio, P. & Hanlon, J. (2007). *Contested Sovereignty in Mozambique: The Dilemmas of Aid Dependence.* Department of Politics and International Relations, Oxford: University College Oxford.

105. Roque, P. (2009). *China in Mozambique: A Cautious Approach: Country Case Study.* South African Institute of International Affairs.

106. BBC (2014). *Mozambique country profile – Overview*. Retrieved from www.bbc .co.uk/news/world-africa-13890416 on 15 August 2015.

107. AP (2014). *More than 300,000 face famine in Mozambique*. Retrieved from http:// bigstory.ap.org/article/more-300000-face-famine-mozambique on 15 August 2015.

108. Bill and Melinda Gates Foundation (2014). *Bio fuels and the poor: Case study Mozambique*. Retrieved from http://biofuelsandthepoor.com/case-study-mozambique/ #benefit on 15 August 2015.

109. Bill and Melinda Gates Foundation (2014). *Bio fuels and the poor: Case study Mozambique*. Retrieved from http://biofuelsandthepoor.com/case-study-mozambique/# benefit on 15 August 2015.

110. Arnall, A. & Talhada, S. (2014). Development, donors and direitos: interrogating the 'global land-grabbing' narrative in rural Mozambique (Conference Paper). Presented at University of Surrey, Land Grabbing Seminar on 1 December 2014.

111. Bill and Melinda Gates Foundation (2014). *Bio fuels and the poor: Case study Mozambique*. Retrieved from http://biofuelsandthepoor.com/case-study-mozambique/# benefit on 15 August 2015.

112. Arnall, A. & Talhada, S. (2014). *Development, donors and direitos: Interrogating the 'global land-grabbing' narrative in rural Mozambique* (Conference Paper). Presented at University of Surrey, Land Grabbing Seminar on 1 December 2014.

113. Donnelly, J. (1998). Human rights: A new standard of civilization? *International Affairs, 74*(1), 1–23.

114. O'Donnell, G., Schmitter, P. C. & Whitehead, L. (1986). *Transitions from Authoritarian Rule: Southern Europe*. The Woodrow Wilson International Center for Scholars.

115. Manuel, P. C. (2010). Portuguese exceptionalism and the return to Europe: the 25 April 1974 coup and democratization, 1974–2010 *CES Working Paper Series, 175*, 22.

116. Cahen, M. (1993). Check on socialism in Mozambique – What check? What socialism? *Review of African Political Economy, 20*(57), 46–59.

117. Bill and Melinda Gates Foundation (2014). *Bio fuels and the poor: Case study Mozambique*. Retrieved from http://biofuelsandthepoor.com/case-study-mozambique/#benefit on 15 August 2015.

118. Kant, I. (1784/2009). *An Answer to the Question: 'What is Enlightenment?'* trans. by D. F. Ferrer. London: Penguin (p. 4).

Chapter 4   Life in Modern Society

1. Blau, J. R. & Goodman, N. (eds) (1995). *Bovenkant formulier* Onderkant formulier *Social Roles and Social Institutions: Essays in Honor of Rose Laub Coser* (p. 20). New Brunswick, NJ: Transaction Publishers.

2. Unger, R. M. (1976). *Bovenkant formulier* Onderkant formulier *Law in Modern Society* (pp. 36–39). New York, NY: The Free Press.

3. ibid.

4. Hayek, F. A. (2013). *Bovenkant formulier Onderkant formulier Law, Legislation and Liberty*. London/New York: Routledge Classics.

5. Cunningham Wood, J. (ed.) (1996). *Adam Smith: Critical Assessments* (p. 209). London/New York: Routledge.

6. Post, J. M. (1993, March). Current concepts of the narcissistic personality. Implications for political psychology. *Political Psychology, 14*(1), 99–121.

7. Pervin, L. A. & John, O. P. (1999). *Handbook of Personality: Theory and Research* (pp. 251–252). New York, NY: The Guilford Press.

8. ibid.
9. Pusey, M. (1998). Economic rationalism, human rights and civil society. *Australian Journal of Human Rights, 4*(2), 131–153.
10. Bech, U. et al. (1994). *Reflexive Modernisation* (pp. 63–65). Cambridge: Polity.
11. Cloninger, C. R., Przybeck, T. R., Svrakic, D. M. & Wetzel, R. D. (1994). *The Temperament and Character Inventory (TCI): A Guide to its Development and Use.* St. Louis, MO: Center for Psychobiology and Personality, Washington University.
12. Brener, M.E. (2008). *Evolution and Empathy: The Genetic Factor in the Rise of Humanism.* Jefferson, NC: McFarland & Co.
13. *The Oxford Dictionary of Philosophy* (2015). *Homo economicus.* Retrieved from www.oxfordreference.com/view/10.1093/oi/authority.20110803095943203 on 27 February 2015.
14. Shoda, Y., Mischel, W. & Peake, P. K. (1990). Predicting adolescent cognitive and self-regulatory competencies from preschool delay of gratification: Identifying diagnostic conditions. *Developmental Psychology, 26,* 978–986.
15. Oxford Dictionaries (2015). Status. Retrieved from www.oxforddictionaries.com/definition/english/status on 27 February 2015.
16. Ministry of Home Affairs, Government of India (2015). Retrieved from www.mha.nic.in/awards_medals on 26 November 2015.
17. Financial Crimes Enforcement Network (2011, January). *Mortgage Loan Fraud Update: Suspicious Activity Report Fillings from July 1-September 30, 2010.* Retrieved from www.fincen.gov/news_room/rp/files/MLF_Update_3rd_Qtly_10_FINAL.pdf on 26 November 2015.
18. Oxford Dictionaries (2015). Aggression. Retrieved from www.oxforddictionaries.com/definition/english/aggression on 27 February 2015.
19. Haney, C., Banks, C. & Zimbardo, P. (1973). Study of prisoners and guards in a simulated prison. *Naval Research Reviews, 9,* 1–17.
20. Zimbardo, P. (2007). *The Lucifer Effect: Understanding How Good People Turn Evil.* New York, NY: Random House.
21. Giddens, A. (1997). *Sociology* (p. 581). London: Polity Press.
22. Tse, W. S. & Bond, A. J. (2002). Serotonergic intervention affects both social dominance and affiliative behaviour. *Psychopharmacology, 161,* 324–330.
23. Young, S. N. (2008). The neurobiology of human social behaviour: an important but neglected topic. *Journal of Psychiatry & Neuroscience, 33*(5), 391–392.
24. Jordan, A., Wurzel, R. K. W. & Zito, A. (2005). The rise of 'new' policy instruments in comparative perspective: Has governance eclipsed government? *Political Studies, 53*(3), 477–496.
25. Marcuse, H. (2002). *One-Dimensional Man: Studies in the Ideology of Advanced Industrial Society.* London: Routledge Classics.
26. Herzberg, T. (2006). *Hoe Warmer de Armen, hoe Wijder de Wereld: Over dwang en vrijheid in opvoeding en onderwijs* (The Warmer the Poor, the Wider the World: About coercion and freedom in upbringing and education). Retrieved from www.tamirherzberg.nl/Warme_armen_wijde_wereld.doc on 26 November 2015. (Only available in Dutch.)
27. Laevers, F. (1997). Welbevinden en betrokkenheid. Richtsnoeren voor een ervaringsgerichte onderwijspraktijk. In B. Van Oers & F. Janssen-Vos (eds), *Visies op onderwijs aan jonge kinderen* (Visions on teaching young children). Assen, the Netherlands: Koninklijke Van Gorcum BV. (Only available in Dutch.)
28. Laucht, M., Becker, K. & Schmidt, M. H. (2006). Visual exploratory behaviour in infancy and novelty seeking in adolescence: Two developmentally specific phenotypes of DRD4? *Journal of Child Psychology and Psychiatry, 47*(11), 1143–1151.

29. Dweck, C. S. (2006). *Mindset: The New Psychology of Success*. New York, NY: Random House.
30. Rosenberg, A. & Arp, R. (2009). *Philosophy of Biology: An Anthology and other* (pp. 99–102). Chichester: John Wiley & Sons.
31. Dingemanse, N. J. & Both, C. et al. (2004). Fitness consequences of avian personalities in a fluctuating environment. *Proceedings of the Royal Society B, 271*, 847–852.
32. De Waal, F. B. M. (2009). *The Age of Empathy: Nature's Lessons for a Kinder Society*. New York, NY: Harmony.
33. ibid.
34. Brosnan, S. F. & de Waal, F. B. M. (2003). Monkeys reject unequal pay. *Nature, 425*(6955), 297–299.
35. Brandts, J., Riedl, A. & van Winden, F. (2009). Competitive rivalry, social disposition, and subjective well-being: An experiment. *Journal of Public Economics, 93*, 1158–1167.
36. Asch, S. E. (1951). Effects of group pressure upon the modification and distortion of judgment. In H. Guetzkow (ed.), *Groups, Leadership and Men*. Pittsburgh, PA: Carnegie Press.
37. The Royal College of Physicians (2012). *Fifty Years Since: Smoking and Health: Progress, Lessons and Priorities for a Smoke-free UK*. Royal College of Physicians.
38. Klucharev, V., Hytönen, K., Rijpkema, M., Smidts, A. & Fernández, G. (2009). Reinforcement learning signal predicts social conformity. *Neuron, 61*(1), 140–151.
39. Buskes, C. (2006). *Evolutionair Denken: De Invloed van Darwin op ons Wereldbeeld* (*Evolutionary Thinking: Darwin's Influence on our View of the World*). Amsterdam, Nieuwezijds. (Only available in Dutch.)
40. Daly, M. & Wilson, M. (2001). An assessment of some proposed exceptions to the phenomenon of nepotistic discrimination against stepchildren. *Annales Zoologici Fennici, 38*(3–4), 287–296.
41. Buskes, C. (2013). Darwinism extended: A survey of how the idea of cultural evolution evolved. *Philosophia, 41*(3), 661–691.
42. Kessler, K. (1991). Teaching Holocaust literature. *English Journal, 80*(7), 29–32.
43. Baehr, P. R. & Castermans-Holleman, M. (2004). *The Role of Human Rights in Foreign Policy* (3rd ed.) (p. 11). New York, NY: Palgrave Macmillan.
44. de Bruin, E. (2010, 30 October). Ongeremd goed doen (interview with social psychologist Kees van den Bos). Rotterdam, *NRC*. (Only available in Dutch.)
45. Ashbrook, J. B. (ed.) (1996). *Brain, Culture, and the Human Spirit: Essays from an Emergent Evolutionary*. Lanham, MD: University Press of America.
46. Brothers, L. (1989). A biological perspective on empathy. *American Journal of Psychiatry, 146*(1), 10–19.
47. Decety, J. & Lamm, C. (2006). Human empathy through the lens of social neuroscience. *The Scientific World Journal, 6*, 1146–1163.
48. Buskes, C. (2006). *Evolutionair Denken: De invloed van Darwin op ons Wereldbeeld* (*Evolutionary Thinking: Darwin's Influence on our View of the World*). Amsterdam: Uitgeverij Niewezijds.
49. Gilligan, J. (2003). Shame, guilt, and violence. *Social Research, 70*(4), 1149–1180.
50. Trzesniewski, K. H., Donnellan, M. B., Moffitt, T. E., Robins, R. W., Poulton, R. & Caspi, A. (2006). Low self-esteem during adolescence predicts poor health, criminal behavior, and limited economic prospects during adulthood. *Developmental Psychology, 42*(2), 381–390.
51. Woods, N. (2000). The challenge of good governance for the IMF and the World Bank themselves. *World Development, Elsevier, 28*(5), 823–841.

52. Wollebæk, D. & Selle, P. (2007). Origins of social capital: Socialization and institutionalization approaches compared. *Journal of Civil Society*, *3*(1), 1–24.

53. Graham, A. (2008). Flexibility, friendship, and family. *Personal Relationships*, *15*(1), 1–16.

54. Triandis, H. C. (2000). Cultural syndromes and subjective well-being. In E. Diener & E. M. Suh (eds), *Culture and Subjective Well-Being* (pp. 13–36). Cambridge, MA: MIT Press.

55. Trompenaars, F. & Woolliams, P. (2003). *Business Across Cultures*. Chichester, Capstone.

56. Richter, F. D. & Tjosvold, D. (1980). Effects of student participation in classroom decision making on attitudes, peer interaction, motivation, and learning. *Journal of Applied Psychology*, *65*(1), 74–80.

57. Dahlgren, P. (2006). Civic participation and practices: Beyond 'deliberative democracy'. In N. Carpentier, P. Pruulmann-Vengerfeldt, K. Nordenstreng, M. Hartmann, P. Vihalemm & B. Cammaerts (eds), *Researching Media, Democracy and Participation: The Intellectual Work of the 2006 European Media and Communication Doctoral Summer School* (23–34). The researching and teaching communication series. Tartu: Tartu University Press.

58. Field, E. (2005). Property rights and investment in urban slums. *Journal of the European Economic Association*, *3*, 279–290.

59. Schock, K. (1999). People power and political opportunities: Social movement mobilization and outcomes in the Philippines and Burma. *Social Problems*, *46*(3), 355–375.

60. Sargent, T. J. (1982). The ends of four big inflations. In R. E. Hall (ed.), *Inflation: Causes and Effects*. Chicago, IL: University of Chicago Press.

61. Wright, R. (2000). *Nonzero: The Logic of Human Destiny*. New York, NY: Pantheon Books.

62. Honneth, A. (1995). *The Struggle for Recognition: The Moral Grammar of Social Conflicts*. Cambridge: Polity Press.

63. Winkler, P. (2006). Bedrijfsethiek (Business ethics). In L. Moratis & M. van der Veen (eds), *Basisboek MVO (The Basics of Corporate Social Responsibility)*. Assen, the Netherlands: Koninklijke van Gorcum BV. (Only available in Dutch.)

64. Paxton, P. (2002). Social capital and democracy: An interdependent relationship. *American Sociological Review*, *67*(2), 254–277.

65. Rex, J. (1996). National identity in the democratic multi-cultural state. *Sociological Research Online*, *1*(2), 1–12.

66. Sandel, M. J. (2010). *Justice: What's the Right Thing to Do?* London: Penguin.

67. Stuurman, S. (2009). *De Uitvinding van de Mensheid (The Invention of Mankind)*. Amsterdam: Uitgeverij Bert Bakker. (Only available in Dutch.)

68. Baurmann, M. (1997a). Liberal society and planned morality. In E. Morscher & O. Neumaier (eds) (1998), *Applied Ethics in a Troubled World* (203–223). Dordrecht: Springer.

69. Trompenaars, F. (1996). Resolving international conflict: Culture and business strategy. *Business Strategy Review*, *7*, 51–68. doi: 10.1111/j.1467-8616.1996.tb00132.x

70. Meyer, J. W., Boli, J., Thomas, G. M. & RamirezBovenkant formulier, F. O. (1997). World society and the nation-state. *American Journal of Sociology*, *103*(1), 144–181.

71. Geertz, C. (1966). Religion as a cultural system. In M. Banton (ed.), *Anthropological Approaches to the Study of Religion* (1–46). London: Routledge.

72. Irons, W. (2001). Religion as a hard-to-fake sign of commitment. In M. Randolph & M. D. Nesse (eds), *Evolution and the Capacity for Commitment* (292–309). New York, NY: Russell Sage Foundation.

73. Kant, I. (1998). *Religion Within the Boundaries of Mere Reason: And Other Writings.* Cambridge: Cambridge University Press.
74. Hamburger, P. (2009). *Separation of Church and State.* Cambridge, MA: Harvard University Press.
75. ibid.
76. Fuller, G. E. (2011). The future of political Islam: Its dilemmas and options. In F. Volpi (ed.), *Political Islam, A Critical Reader* (413–421). Routledge.
77. New Straits Times (2007, April 12). Lina Joy ruling the 'next change', says chief justice.
78. Brettschneider, C. L. (2013). *Democratic Persuasion and Freedom of Speech: A Response to Four Critics and Two Allies* (Working Paper). Providence, RI: Brown University, Department of Political Science.
79. Paulsen, M. S. (2014). Is religious freedom irrational? *Michigan Law Review, 112*(6), 1043–1070.
80. Stanford Encyclopedia of Philosophy (2012). *Virtue Ethics.* Retrieved from http://plato.stanford.edu/entries/ethics-virtue on 30 March 2015.
81. Bentham, J. (2009). *An Introduction to the Principles of Morals and Legislation.* Mineola, NY: Dover Publications Inc.
82. Stanford Encyclopedia of Philosophy (2014). *The History of Utilitarianism: 2.1 Jeremy Bentham.* Retrieved from http://plato.stanford.edu/entries/utilitarianism-history/#JerBen on 1 April 2015.
83. Sandel, M. J. (2010). *Justice: What's the Right Thing to Do?* London: Penguin.
84. ibid.
85. IPCC (2013). Summary for policymakers. In T. F. Stocker, D. Qin, G.-K. Plattner, M. Tignor, S. K. Allen, J. Boschung, A. Nauels, Y. Xia, V. Bex & P. M. Midgley (eds), *Climate Change 2013: The Physical Science Basis. Contribution of Working Group I to the Fifth Assessment Report of the Intergovernmental Panel on Climate Change* (3–32). Cambridge, UK and New York, NY: Cambridge University Press.
86. CoastalAdaptation.eu. Plan to Adapt to Coastal Climate Change. *Cork Harbour and Climate Change.* Retrieved from www.coastaladaptation.eu/index.php/en/9-experiences-3/cork-harbour/82-cork-harbour-climate-change-drivers-and-coastal-management on 26 November 2015.
87. Kant, I. (1993) [1785]. *Grounding for the Metaphysics of Morals* (trans. by James W. Ellington). Indianapolis, IN: Hackett Publishing Company, Inc.
88. Stanford Encyclopedia of Philosophy. Edward N. Zalta. Retrieved from https://mally.stanford.edu/zalta.html on 26 February 2015.
89. Menzel, D. C. (2005). Research on ethics and integrity in governance: A review and assessment. *Public Integrity, 1,* 239–264.
90. Fraser, N. & Honneth, A. (2003). *Redistribution or Recognition?: A Political–Philosophical Exchange* (p. 28). London/New York: Verso.
91. Wattles, J. (1996). *The Golden Rule* (p. 84). Oxford: Oxford University Press.
92. Athanassoulis, N. (2006). Virtue Ethics. *Internet Encyclopedia of Philosophy.* Retrieved from www.iep.utm.edu/virtue/ on 3 April 2015.
93. Hursthouse, R. (2012). Virtue Ethics. *The Stanford Encyclopedia of Philosophy.* Retrieved from http://plato.stanford.edu/archives/fall2013/entries/ethics-virtue/ on 14 April 2015.
94. Athanassoulis, N. (2006). Virtue Ethics. *Internet Encyclopedia of Philosophy.* Retrieved from www.iep.utm.edu/virtue/ on 3 April 2015.
95. MacIntyre, A. (1981). *After Virtue* (p. 201). Notre Dame, IN: University of Notre Dame Press.
96. Marenbon, J. (1997). *The Philosophy of Peter Abélard.* Cambridge: Cambridge University Press.

97. Stueber, K. R. (2009). Intentionalism, intentional realism, and empathy. *Journal of the Philosophy of History*, 3(3), 290–307.

98. Bennett, C. (1992). *Victorian Images of Islam*. London: Grey Seal.

99. Koçan, G. (2008). *Models of public sphere in political philosophy* (Online Working Paper 2). Eurosphere.

100. Mank, B. C. (1996). *Is a textualist approach to statutory interpretation pro-environmentalist?: Why pragmatic agency decisionmaking is better than judicial literalism* (Paper 140). Faculty Articles and Other Publications. Cincinnati, OH: University of Cincinnati College of Law.

101. Schmid, P. F. (2001). Comprehension: the art of not-knowing. Dialogical and ethical perspectives on empathy as dialogue in personal and person-centred relationships. *Empathy*, 2, 53–71.

102. Carr, L., Lacoboni, M., Dubeau, M. C., Mazziotta, J. C. & Lenzi, G. L. (2003). *Neural Mechanisms of Empathy in Humans: A Relay from Neural Systems for Imitation to Limbic Areas*. Proceedings of the National Academy of Sciences of US.

103. Stapert, W. (2010). De ontwikkeling van het geweten: stand van zaken van onderzoek en theorievorming (The development of conscience; progress of research and theory). *Tijdschrift voor Psychiatrie*, 52(7), 433–443. (Only available in Dutch.)

104. Arnhart, L. (1998). *Darwinian Natural Right: The Biological Ethics of Human Nature*. New York, NY: State University of New York Press.

105. Hudson, W. H. (2007). *The Book of a Naturalist* (173). Wildside Press.

106. Goleman, D. (1995). *Emotional Intelligence*. New York, NY: Bantam.

107. Witteman, H. (2008). Meer over het brein: Het emotionele geheugen (More about the brain: The emotional memory). *Onderwijsvanmorgen*. Retrieved from www.onderwijsvanmorgen.nl/meer-over-het-brein-het-emotionele-geheugen on 26 November 2015. (Only available in Dutch.)

108. Engel, J. A. (2009). *The Fall of the Berlin Wall: The Revolutionary Legacy of 1989*. Oxford: Oxford University Press.

109. Fukuyama, F. (1999). *Social Capital and Civil Society*. George Mason University. The Institute of Public Policy.

110. Pichler, F. & Wallace, C. (2007). Patterns of formal and informal social capital in Europe. *European Sociological Review*, 23, 423–435.

111. Boeck, T., Fleming, J. & Kemshall, H. (2006). The context of risk decisions: Does social capital make a difference? *Forum: Qualitative Social Research*, 7(1).

112. Trompenaars, F. & Woolliams, P. (2003). *Business Across Cultures*. Capstone.

113. Kleiner, A. (2001). The Dilemma Doctors. *Strategy+Business*. Retrieved from www.strategy-business.com/article/17251?gko=444c1 on 5 April 2015.

114. Cohen, J. L. (1992). *Civil Society and Political Theory*. Massachusetts Institute of Technology.

115. Collins English Dictionary. Civil society. Retrieved from www.collinsdictionary.com/dictionary/english/civil-society on 11 May 2015.

116. Hanke, S. H. & Walters, S. J. K. (1997). Economic freedom, prosperity, and equality: A survey. *The Cato Journal*, 17(2).

117. Porter, M. E. & Kramer, M. R. (2011). Creating shared value: How to reinvent capitalism and unleash a wave of innovation and growth. *Harvard Business Review*, 89(1), S. 62–77.

118. Meny, Y. & Surel, Y. (2001). *Democracies and the Populist Challenge*. Hampshire, Palgrave Macmillan.

119. Jacobs, A. M. (2011). *Governing for the Long Term: Democracy and the Politics of Investment*. Cambridge: Cambridge University Press.

120. Buskes, C. (2006). *Evolutionair Denken: De Invloed van Darwin op ons Wereldbeeld* (*Evolutionary Thinking: Darwin's Influence on our View of the World*). Amsterdam, Nieuwezijds (Only in available in Dutch.)

121. ibid.

122. Helve, H. (2015). Re-thinking youth and citizenship. Value groups and citizenship types of young Finns. *Italian Journal of Sociology of Education, 7*(1), 32–66.

Chapter 5   Sustainable Development: Environmental and Social Aspects

1. Campbell, C. (2005). *The Romantic Ethic and the Spirit of Modern Consumerism.* Writersprintshop.

2. World Commission on Environment and Development (1987). *Our Common Future* (p. 27). Oxford: Oxford University Press.

3. Elkington, J. (1997). *Cannibals with Forks: The Triple Bottom Line of Twenty-First Century Business.* Oxford: Capstone.

4. Organization for Economic Co-operation and Development. Green Growth and Sustainable Development. Retrieved from www.oecd.org/greengrowth/green-growth-key-documents.htm on 26 November 2015.

5. Vazquez-Brust, D., Smith, A. & Sarkis, J. (2014). Managing the transition to critical green growth: The green growth state. *Futures, 64*, 123–148.

6. United Nations Conference on Sustainable Development (2011). Retrieved from www.uncsd2012.org/ on 16 July 2014.

7. Steffen, W. et al (2015). Planetary boundaries: Guiding human development on a changing planet. *Science, 347*(6223) DOI:10.1126/science.1259855.

8. Revkin, A. C. (2015, 15 January). Can humanity's great acceleration be managed? *The New York Times.* Retrieved from http://dotearth.blogs.nytimes.com/2015/01/15/can-humanitys-great-acceleration-be-managed-and-if-so-how/?_r=0 on 26 November 2015.

9. Steffen, W. et al. (2015). Planetary boundaries: Guiding human development on a changing planet. *Science, 347*(6223) DOI:10.1126/science.1259855.

10. Stockholm Resilience Centre (2015). *Figures and data for the updated Planetary Boundaries.* Retrieved from www.stockholmresilience.org/21/research/research-programmes/planetary-boundaries/planetary-boundaries-data.html on 26 November 2015.

11. Strzelczyk, S. & Rothschild, R. (2009, 28 October). UN Agenda 21 – Coming to a neighborhood near you. *American Thinker.* Retrieved from www.americanthinker.com/articles/2009/10/un_agenda_21_coming_to_a_neigh.html on 26 November 2015.

12. Gerhardt, T. (2012, 20 June). Rio+20 kicks off. *The Progressive.* Retrieved from www.progressive.org/rio_20_kicks_off.html on 26 November 2015.

13. International Centre for Trade and Sustainable Development (2012, 21 June). *Agreement reached on weakened outcome text as leaders arrive for Rio Summit.* Retrieved from www.ictsd.org/bridges-news/biores/news/agreement-reached-on-weakened-outcome-text-as-leaders-arrive-for-rio-summit on 15 July 2014.

14. United Nations (2015). *Transforming our world: The post-2015 agenda for sustainable development.* Retrieved from https://sustainabledevelopment.un.org/post2015/transformingourworld on 26 November 2015.

15. International Council for Sciences and International Social Sciences Council (2015). Review of target for the SDG: The science perspective. Paris.

16. ibid.

17. Stockholm Resilience Centre (2015). *Figures and data for the updated Planetary Boundaries*. Retrieved from www.stockholmresilience.org/21/research/research-programmes/planetary-boundaries/planetary-boundaries-data.html on 26 November 2015.

18. US Geological Survey (2015). *Distribution of Earth's water*. Retrieved from http://ga.water.usgs.gov/edu/waterdistribution.html on 26 November 2015.

19. World Business Council for Sustainable Development (ed.) (2009). *Facts and Trends. Water* (Version 2). Geneva: World Business Council for Sustainable Development (WBDSC). Retrieved from www.sswm.info/sites/default/files/reference_attachments/WBCSD%202009%20Water%20Facts%20and%20Trends.pdf on 12 March 2009.

20. UN News Centre (2005, 24 February). World population to reach 9.1 billion in 2050, UN projects. Retrieved from www.un.org/apps/news/story.asp?NewsID=13451&Cr=population&Cr1 on 10 March 2009.

21. Ocean dumping of sewage sludge is prohibited in the US by the Marine Protection, Research, and Sanctuaries Act (MPRSA).

22. World Business Council for Sustainable Development (ed.) (2009). *Facts and Trends. Water* (Version 2). Geneva: World Business Council for Sustainable Development (WBDSC). Retrieved from www.sswm.info/sites/default/files/reference_attachments/WBCSD%202009%20Water%20Facts%20and%20Trends.pdf on 12 March 2009.

23. UN Water (2007). *World Water Day 2007. Coping with water scarcity: Challenge of the twenty-first century*. Retrieved from www.fao.org/nr/water/docs/escarcity.pdf on 26 November 2015.

24. The Earth Observatory (2014, 19 August). *World of Change: Shrinking Aral Sea*. Retrieved from http://earthobservatory.nasa.gov/Features/WorldOfChange/aral_sea.php on 26 November 2015.

25. Woodard, C. (2001, 4 September). Netherlands battens its ramparts against warming climate. *National Geographic: Christian Science Monitor*. Retrieved from http://news.nationalgeographic.com/news/2001/08/0829_wiredutch.html on 26 November 2015.

26. Knabb, R. D., Rhome, J. R. & Brown, D. P. (2005, 20 December). Tropical Cyclone Report: Hurricane Katrina: August 23–30, 2005. United States National Oceanic and Atmospheric Administration's National Weather Service. Retrieved from www.nhc.noaa.gov/data/tcr/AL122005_Katrina.pdf on 10 December 2013.

27. Goldenberg, S. (2009, 5 June). US urged to abandon ageing flood defences in favour of Dutch system. *The Guardian*.

28. Palca, J. (2008, 28 January). Dutch architects plan for a floating future [radio broadcast]. *National Public Radio, Washington DC*.

29. Meadows, D. H., Meadows, D. L., Randers, J. & Behrens, W. W. (1972). *The Limits to Growth*. New York, NY: Universe Books.

30. Brownstein, R. (2012). *Environment and Utopia: A Synthesis*. New York: Springer.

31. Meadows, D. H., Meadows, D. L., Randers, J. & Behrens, W. W. (1972). *The Limits to Growth*. New York, NY: Universe Books.

32. Jasinski, S. M. (2009). Phosphate rock. In US Geological Survey (ed.), *Mineral Commodity Summaries* (pp. 120–121). USGS.

33. Revkin, A. C. (2015) *Can humanity's great acceleration be managed?* Retrieved from http://dotearth.blogs.nytimes.com/2015/01/15/can-humanitys-great-acceleration-be-managed-and-if-so-how/?_r=0 on 26 November 2015.

34. Ashley, K. & Mavinic, D. (2009). *International Conference on Nutrient Recovery From Wastewater Streams Vancouver*. London: IWA Publishing.

35. Schipper, W., Klapwijk, A., Potjer, B., Rulkens, W. H., Temmink, B. G., Kiestra, F. D. G., Lijmbach, A. C. M. (2004). Phosphate recycling in the phosphorus industry. *Phosphorus Research Bulletin, 15*, 47–51.

36. Jasinski, S. M. (2009). Phosphate rock. In US Geological Survey (ed.), *Mineral Commodity Summaries* (120–121). USGS.

37. British Geological Survey. *World Mineral Production 2007–2011*. Keyworth, Nottingham: British Geological Survey.

38. Bloodworth, A. (2014). Resources: track flows to manage technology-metal supply. *Nature, 505*(7481), 19–20.

39. Jackson, B. & Mikolajczak, C. (2012). *Availability of Indium and Gallium*. Indium Corporation.

40. Allwood, J. M. & Cullen, J. M. (2012). *Sustainable Materials*. Cambridge: UIT Cambridge.

41. Umicore. *Recycling*. Retrieved from www.umicore.com/en/ourBusinesses/recycling/ on 26 November 2015.

42. Parker Price, E. *Recycling cell phones. Going Green today*. Retrieved from http://blog.goinggreentoday.com/recycling-cell-phones/ on 7 November 2013.

43. *Global Footprint Network* (2010). Retrieved from www.footprintnetwork.org/en/index.php/GFN/ on 26 November 2015.

44. *Global Footprint Network* (2010). Retrieved from www.footprintnetwork.org/en/index.php/GFN/ on 26 November 2015.

45. Maestre, F. T. (2012). Plant species richness and ecosystem multifunctionality in global drylands. *Science, 335*(6065), 214–218. DOI: 10.1126/science.1215442.

46. Tscharntke, T., Leuschner, C., Veldkamp, E., Faust, H. & Guhardja, E. (eds) (2010). *Tropical Rainforests and Agroforests Under Global Change* (270–271). Heidelberg, Springer.

47. Mongillo, J. F. & Zierdt-Warshaw, L. (2000). *Encyclopedia of Environmental Science* (p. 104). Rochester, NY: University of Rochester Press.

48. Forest Stewardship Council. Retrieved from https://us.fsc.org/ on 26 November 2015.

49. Jarvis, S. C., Murray, P. J. & Roker, J. A. (eds) (2005). *Optimisation of Nutrient Cycling and Soil Quality for Sustainable Grasslands*. Wageningen: Academic Publishers.

50. Stockholm Resilience Centre (2015). Retrieved from www.stockholmresilience.org/21/research/research-programmes/planetary-boundaries/planetary-boundaries-data.html on 26 November 2015.

51. World Wide Fund for Nature (2014). *Living Planet Report 2014*. Retrieved from http://wwf.panda.org/about_our_earth/all_publications/living_planet_report/ on 26 November 2015.

52. World Wide Fund for Nature (2014). *Living Planet Report 2014* (p. 16). Retrieved from http://wwf.panda.org/about_our_earth/all_publications/living_planet_report/ on 26 November 2015.

53. Strategic Plan for Biodiversity 2011–2020 and the Aichi Targets 'Living in Harmony with Nature'. Retrieved from www.cbd.int/doc/strategic-plan/2011-2020/Aichi-Targets-EN.pdf on 26 November 2015.

54. BP (2013). *Data workbook (xlsx) - Statistical Review of World Energy 2013*. London: BP.

55. Negishi, M. (2011, 12 April). Japan raises nuclear crisis severity to highest level. *Reuters*. Retrieved from www.trust.org/item/20110412021100-nz0tm?view=print on 12 November 2013.

56. Fraunhofer Institute for Solar Energy Systems ISE (2014, 29 December). *Electricity Production from Solar and Wind in Germany in 2014* (p. 5). Freiburg, Germany. Fraunhofer ISE. Retrieved from www.ise.fraunhofer.de/en/downloads-englisch/pdf-files-englisch/data-nivc-/electricity-production-from-solar-and-wind-in-germany-2014.pdf on 22 July 2014.

57. Renewable Fuels Association (2012, 6 March). *Accelerating Industry Innovation –
    2012 Ethanol Industry Outlook* (pp. 3, 8, 10, 22 and 23). Retrieved from www
    .ethanolrfa.org/wp-content/uploads/2015/09/2012-Ethanol-Industry-Outlook.pdf
    on 22 March 2012.

58. Global Wind Energy Council (2012). *Global Wind Report: Annual Market Update
    2012.* GWEC.

59. Aarts, P. & Janssen, D. (2003). Shades of opinion: the oil exporting countries and
    international climate politics. *The Review of International Affairs*, 3(2), 332–351.

60. Deffeyes, K. S. Current events – Join us as we watch the crisis unfolding. *Princeton
    University*. Retrieved from www.princeton.edu/hubbert/current-events.html on 27
    July 2008.

61. Laherrere, J. (2007, 24 April). *Uncertainty of data and forecasts for fossil fuels*
    (p. 32, figure A46). University of Castilla-La Mancha. Paper presented at the ASPO-5
    conference in San Rossore, Italy. Retrieved from www.hubbertpeak.com/laherrere/
    climatechange200704.pdf on 26 November 2015.

62. Laherrere, J. (2006, November). Oil and gas: what future? Paper presented at the
    Groningen Annual Energy Convention. World 1 (292,549) 534. Figure 33.

63. Pachauri, R. K. & Reisinger, A. (eds) (2007). *Climate Change 2007: Contribution of
    Working Groups I, II and III to the Fourth Assessment Report of the Intergovernmental
    Panel on Climate Change.* Geneva, Switzerland: IPCC.

64. ibid.

65. ibid.

66. Jansen, E. et al. (2007). Palaeoclimate. In S. Solomon, D. Qin, M. Manning et al.,
    *Climate Change 2007: The Physical Science Basis. Contribution of Working Group I
    to the Fourth Assessment Report of the Intergovernmental Panel on Climate Change*
    (433–497). Cambridge: Cambridge University Press.

67. Sen, A. K. (2000). The ends and means of sustainability. *Journal of Human Develop-
    ment and Capabilities: A Multi-Disciplinary Journal for People-Centered Development*,
    14(1), 6–20.

68. Source: James, P., Magee, L., Scerri, A. & Steger, M. (2015). *Urban Sustainability in
    Theory and Practice: Circles of Sustainability.* London: Routledge. Also available at
    www.circlesofsustainability.org (last accessed on 26 November 2015).

69. Raphael, D. (2014, 11 July) *Basic Concepts of Social Sustainability #4.* Retrieved from
    www.linkedin.com/pulse/20140711134858-49584789-basic-concepts-of-social-
    sustainability-4 on 26 November 2015.

70. Magee, L., Scerri, A., James, P., Thom, J. A., Padgham, L., Hickmott, S., Deng, H. &
    Cahill, F. (2013). Reframing social sustainability reporting: Towards an engaged
    approach. *Environment, Development and Sustainability*, 15, 225–243.

71. Oxfam (2012). A safe and just space for humanity: Can we live within the doughnut?
    Retrieved from http://policy-practice.oxfam.org.uk/publications/a-safe-and-just-
    space-for-humanity-can-we-live-within-the-doughnut-210490 on 26 November 2015.

72. McKendry, P. (2002). Energy production from biomass (part 1): Overview of
    biomass. *Bioresource Technology*, 83(1), 37–46.

73. Brennana, L. & Owendea, P. (2010). Biofuels from microalgae – a review of tech-
    nologies for production, processing, and extractions of biofuels and co-products.
    Renewable and Sustainable Energy Reviews, 14(2), 557–577.

74. Lee, R. A. & Lavoie, J. M. (2013). From first- to third-generation biofuels: Challenges
    of producing a commodity from a biomass of increasing complexity. *Animal Fron-
    tiers*, 3(2), 6–11.

75. Avery, D. T. (2006). *Biofuels, Food, Or Wildlife?: The Massive Land Costs of US Ethanol.*
    Washington, DC: Competitive Enterprise Institute.

76. Rosegrant, M. W. (2008, 7 May). *Biofuels and grain prices: Impacts and policy responses.* Testimony of the Director, Environment and Production Technology Division International Food Policy Research Institute for the US Senate Committee on Homeland Security and Governmental Affairs.

77. Sperling, D. & Gordon, D. (2009). *Two Billion Cars: Driving Toward Sustainability.* Oxford: Oxford University Press.

Chapter 6   Governance of Sustainability

1. MacNeill, J., Winsemius, P. & Yakushiji, T. (1991). *Beyond Interdependence: The Meshing of the World's Economy and the Earth's Ecology.* Oxford: Oxford University Press.

2. United Nations (2012, June 20–22). *Report of the United Nations Conference on Sustainable Development. Rio de Janeiro, Brazil.* New York: United Nations.

3. Bremmer, I. (2010). The end of the free market: who wins the war between states and corporations? *European View, 9*(2), 249–252.

4. Grimaud, A. & Rouge, L. (2008, December). Environment, directed technical change and economic policy. *Environmental and Resource Economics, 41*(4), 439–463.

5. Kemp, R., Parto, S. & Gibson, R.B. (2005). Governance for sustainable development: moving from theory to practice. *Journal of Sustainable Development, 8,* 18.

6. Ehrlich, P. R. (1968). *The Population Bomb.* New York, NY: Ballantine Books.

7. Koblitz, N. (1981). Mathematics as propaganda. In L. A. Steen (ed.), *Mathematics Tomorrow* (111–120). New York, NY: Springer Verlag.

8. Gardner, D. (2010). *Future Babble: Why Expert Predictions Fail – and Why We Believe Them Anyway.* McClelland & Stewart.

9. Grist Magazine (2004, August 10). *Paul Ehrlich, famed ecologist, answers questions.* Retrieved from http://grist.org/article/ehrlich/2/ on 26 November 2015.

10. Ehrlich, P. R. (1968). *The Population Bomb.* New York, NY: Ballantine Books.

11. Cleland, J., Bernstein, S., Ezeh, A., Faundes, A., Glasier, A. & Innis, J. (2006). Family planning: The unfinished agenda. *The Lancet, Elsevier, 368,* 1810–1827.

12. Pimentel, D. & Pimentel, M. (2006). Global environmental resources versus world population growth. *Ecological Economics, Elsevier, 59,* 195–198.

13. Wolfgang, L., Sanderson, W. & Scherbov, S. (2001). The end of world population growth. *Nature, 412,* 543–545.

14. Lee, R. (2007). The demographic transition: Three centuries of fundamental change. *Journal of Economic Perspectives, 17*(4), 167–190.

15. World Bank (2015). Population growth (annual %). Retrieved from http://data.worldbank.org/indicator/SP.POP.GROW/countries?display=default on 29 August 2015.

16. Freedman, L. P. & Isaacs, S. L. (1993). Human rights and reproductive choice. *Studies in Family Planning, 24*(1), 18–30.

17. Attane, I. (2002). China's family planning policy: An overview of its past and future. *Studies in Family Planning, 33*(1), 111.

18. Hesketh, T., Li Lu & Zhu, W.X. (2005). The effects of China's one-child family policy after 25 years. *The New England Journal of Medicine, 353*(11), 1171–1176.

19. Quandl. (2015). Fertility rate, total (births per woman) – China. From the database: World Bank Cross Country Data. Retrieved from www.quandl.com/WORLDBANK/CHN_SP_DYN_TFRT_IN-Fertility-rate-total-births-per-woman-China on 22 February 2015.

20. Greenhalgh, S. (2003). Science, modernity, and the making of China's one-child policy. *Population and Development Review, 29*(2), 163–196.

21. Cohen, S.A. (2011). US overseas family planning program, perennial victim of abortion politics, is once again under siege. *Guttmacher Policy Review, 14*(4), 7–13.
22. Sen, A. (1999). *Principles of Development as Freedom.* New York, NY: Anchor.
23. BBC News. (2000, 25 September). China steps up 'one child' policy. Retrieved from http://news.bbc.co.uk/2/hi/asia-pacific/941511.stm on 26 November 2015.
24. World Bank (2015). Retrieved from http://databank.worldbank.org/data/reports. aspx?source=Health%20Nutrition%20and%20Population%20Statistics:%20 Population%20estimates%20and%20projections on 29 August 2015.
25. Fasolo, L., Galetto, M. & Turina, E. (2013, February). A pragmatic approach to evaluate alternative indicators to GDP. *Quality & Quantity, Springer, 47*(2), 633–657.
26. Schepelmann, P., Goossens, Y. & Makipaa, A. (2009). *Towards Sustainable Development: Alternatives to GDP for Measuring Progress.* Wuppertal Spezial, Wuppertal Institut für Klima, Umwelt und Energie.
27. Vazquez-Brust, D. & Sarkis, J. (2010). *Green Growth: Managing the Transition to Sustainable Economies.* London: Springer.
28. Meadows, D. H., Meadows, D. L., Randers, J. & Behrens, W. W. (1972). *The Limits to Growth.* New York, NY: Universe Books.
29. ibid.
30. Dryzek, J. (2005) *The Politics of Earth: Environmental Discourses.* Oxford: Oxford University Press.
31. ibid.
32. Ekins, P. (1997). The Kuznets curve for the environment and economic growth: Examining the evidence. *Environment and Planning A, 29,* 805–830.
33. Stern, D. (2014) The rise and fall of the environmental Kuznets curve. *World Development, 32*(8), 1419–1439.
34. The 'Gift Economy' movement aims to eradicate money and land ownership and replace them with a fairer system, based on giving/receiving gifts and sharing. The Gift Economy. Retrieved from www.gifteconomymovement.org/ on 26 November 2015.
35. Haberl, H., Fischer-Kowalski, M., Krausmann, F., Weisz, H. & Winiwarter, V. (2004) Progress towards sustainability? What the conceptual framework of material and energy flow accounting (MEFA) can offer. *Land Use Policy, 21*(3), 199–213.
36. Eurostat (2015). *Resource productivity statistics.* Retrieved from http://ec.europa .eu/eurostat/statistics-explained/index.php/Resource_productivity_statistics on 26 November 2015.
37. Vázquez-Brust, D., Smith, A. & Sarkis, J. (2014). Managing the transition to critical green growth: The green growth state. *Futures, 64,* 123–148.
38. Jackson, T. (2009). *Prosperity Without Growth.* New York, NY: Routledge.
39. New Economics Foundation. (2012). *The Happy Planet Index: 2012 Report.* Retrieved from www.neweconomics.org/publications/entry/happy-planet-index-2012-report on 26 November 2015.
40. Layard, R. (2005). *Happiness: Lessons from a New Science.* London: Penguin Press.
41. Jackson, T. (2009). *Prosperity Without Growth.* New York, NY: Routledge.
42. World Economics (n.d.) *Maddison Historical GDP Data.* Retrieved from www .worldeconomics.com/Data/MadisonHistoricalGDP/Madison%20Historical%20 GDP%20Data.efp on 6 May 2015.
43. Veenhoven R. (2015). Happiness US 1946–2010 (unweighted average of the previous data) / Veenhoven. R. (n.d.). *Average Happiness in 149 Nations 2000–2009.* World Database of Happiness. Rank report average happiness. Retrieved from http:// worlddatabaseofhappiness.eur.nl/hap_nat/findingreports/RankReport_Average-Happiness.php on 1 March 2015.

44. Layard, R. (2005). *Happiness: Lessons from a New Science*. London: Penguin Press.

45. Bram van de Groes, cartoonist. Commissioned by Martin Oyevaar.

46. Layard, R. (2005). *Happiness: Lessons from a New Science* (p. 53). London: Penguin Press.

47. Helliwell, J.F. (2005, December). *Well-being, Social Capital and Public Policy: What's New?* (NBER Working Papers 11807). National Bureau of Economic Research, Inc.

48. Bjornskov, C., Dreher, A., Fischer, J.A.V., Schnellenbach, J. & Gehring, K. (2013). *Inequality and happiness: When perceived social mobility and economic reality do not match* (Discussion Paper 13/2). Freiburg Discussion Papers on Constitutional Economics, Walter Eucken Institut e.V.

49. World Bank. (2015). *Data: Indicators*. (Average 2000-2009: PPP constant 2011/ international $). Retrieved from http://data.worldbank.org/indicator/NY.GDP.PCAP.PP.KD on 22 February, 2015.

50. Veenhoven, R. (n.d.). *Average happiness in 149 nations 2000-2009*. World Database of Happiness. Rank report Average Happiness. Retrieved from http://worlddata baseofhappiness.eur.nl/hap_nat/findingreports/RankReport_AverageHappiness on 22 February 2015 (142 countries and 98% of World GDP (Data GDP 2011 World Bank constant 2005 / NY.GDP.MKTP.KD)).

51. New Economics Foundation. (2012). *The Happy Planet Index: 2012 Report*. Retrieved 2015-26-11 from http://www.neweconomics.org/publications/entry/happy-planet-index-2012-report

52. Layard, R. (2005). *Happiness: Lessons from a New Science*. London: Penguin Press.

53. New Economics Foundation. (2012). *The Happy Planet Index: 2012 Report*. Retrieved from www.neweconomics.org/publications/entry/happy-planet-index-2012-report on 26 November 2015.

54. IMF (2014, October). *World Economic Database (purchasing power parity US-dollar United States)*. Retrieved from www.imf.org/external/pubs/ft/weo/2014/02/weodata/download.aspx on 26 November 2015.

55. Rutjens, B.T., Harreveld, F. van, Pligt, J. van der, Elk, M. van & Pyszczynski, T. (2014). A march to a better world? Religiosity and the existential function of belief in social–moral progress. *International Journal for the Psychology of Religion*, in press.

56. Schmid, W. (2008). *Ökologische Lebenskunst: Was jeder Einzelne für das Leben auf dem Planeten tun kann (Organic Food Art: What individuals can do for life on the planet)*. Berlin: Suhrkamp Verlag. (Only available in German.)

57. Jonas, H. & Herr, D. (1979). *The Imperative of Responsibility: In Search of an Ethics for the Technological Age* (translation of Das Prinzip Verantwortung). Chicago & London: The University of Chicago Press.

58. Carter, R., Marks, R. & Hill, D. (1999). *Could a National Skin Cancer Primary Prevention Campaign in Australia be Worthwhile?: An Economic Perspective*. Oxford: Oxford University Press.

59. George Philander, S. (2012). *Encyclopedia of Global Warming and Climate Change* (2nd edition) (p. 958). Thousand Oaks, CA: Sage Publications.

60. Gilliam, H. C. & Rod Martin, J. (1975). Economic importance of antibiotics in feeds to producers and consumers of pork, beef and veal. *Journal of Animal Science*, 40(6), 1241–1255.

61. Marcus, A., Shrivastava, P., Sharma, S. & Pogutz, S. (2011). *Cross-Sector Leadership for the Green Economy*. New York, NY: Palgrave Macmillan.

62. Bell, D. V. J. (2002). *The Role of Government in Advancing Corporate Sustainability*. Vancouver: York University.

63. gDiapers (2015). *Getting Started.* Retrieved from http://www.gdiapers.com/getting-started/ on 2 December 2015.

64. Baumol, W. J. (2002). *The Free-market Innovation Machine: Analyzing the Growth Miracle of Capitalism.* Princeton, NJ: Princeton University Press.

65. Dean, T. J. & McMullen, J. S. (2007). Toward a theory of sustainable entrepreneurship: Reducing environmental degradation through entrepreneurial action. *Journal of Business Venturing, 22*, 29–49.

66. Kemp, R., Parto, S. & Gibson, R. B. (2005). Governance for sustainable development: moving from theory to practice. *International Journal of Sustainable Development, 8*(1–2), 12–30.

67. Hardin, G. (1968, 13 December). The tragedy of the commons. *Science, New Series, 162*(3859), 1243–1248.

68. ibid.

69. Tol, R. S. J. (2008). The social cost of carbon: Trends, outliers and catastrophes. *Economics: The Open-Access, Open-Assessment E-Journal, 2*(25), 1–22.

70. United Nations Treaty Collection. (2015). *Kyoto Protocol to the United Nations Framework Convention on Climate Change.* Retrieved from https://treaties.un.org/pages/ViewDetails.aspx?src=TREATY&mtdsg_no=XXVII-7-a&chapter=27&lang=en-title=UNTC-publisher=United on 14 April 2015.

71. Prescott, J. (2009). *The challenges posed by climate change* (Document 12002). Parliamentary Assembly Europe.

72. Dimitrov, R. S. (2010). Inside Copenhagen: The state of climate governance. *Global Environmental Politics, 10*(2), 18–24.

73. Kooten, G. C. van (1993). *Land Resource Economics and Sustainable Development: Economic Policies and the Common Good.* Vancouver: UBC Press.

74. Cornes, R. (1996). *The Theory of Externalities, Public Goods, and Club Goods.* Cambridge: Cambridge University Press.

75. Gordon, R. B., Bertram, M. & Graedel, T. E. (2006). Metal stocks and sustainability. *Proceedings of the National Academy of Sciences, 103*(5), 1209–1214.

76. Cornes, R. (1996). *The Theory of Externalities, Public Goods, and Club Goods.* Cambridge: Cambridge University Press.

77. Dunning, J. (2001). *Global Capitalism at Bay.* London and New York, Routledge.

78. Oorschot, K. van, Haverkamp, B., Steen, M. van der & Twist, M. van. (2013). *Choice Architecture* (NSOB Working Paper). The Hague: Nederlandse School voor Openbaar Bestuur.

79. Araujo, C., Araujo Bonjean, C., Combes, J-L., Combes Motel, P. & Reis, E. J. (2009, June). Property rights and deforestation in the Brazilian Amazon. *Ecological Economics, 68*(8–9), 2461–2468.

80. Nabuurs, G. J. et al. (2003). Temporal evolution of the European forest sector carbon sink from 1950 to 1999. *Global Change Biology, 9*, 152–160.

81. International Council on Clean Transportation (2014, January). *EU CO2 Emission Standards for Passenger Cars and Light-Commercial Vehicles.* ICCT.

82. Wadud, Z. (2014, November). New vehicle fuel economy in the UK: Impact of the recession and recent policies. *Energy Policy, 74*, 215–223.

83. Nystrom, S. M. A. & Zaidi, A. B. A. (2014, March). Environmental tax reform in California: Economic and climate impact of a carbon tax swap. Washington DC: Regional Economic Models, Inc.

84. Ekins, P., Pollitt H., Summerton, P. & Chewpreecha, U. (2011). Increasing carbon and material productivity through environmental tax reform. *Energy Policy, 42*(3), 365–376.

85. ibid.

86. European Parliament (2008, April 24). *Green Paper on Market-Based Instruments for Environment and Related Policy Purposes* (file number: ENVI/6/49275; non-legislative resolution).

87. House of Lords. European Union Committee (2006). *Including the Aviation Sector in the European Union Emissions Trading Scheme. 21st Report of Session 2005–06.* London: The Stationary Office Limited.

88. Wiesmeth, H. (2012). *Environmental Economics: Theory and Policy in Equilibrium.* Heidelberg, Dordrecht, London & New York: Springer.

89. ibid.

90. Montgomery, W. D. (1974). Artificial markets and the theory of games. *Public choice, 18*(1), 25–40.

91. UNFCCC. (2007, 20 November). Making Kyoto work: data, policies, infrastructures. Press Briefing, Deutsche Welle, Bonn, Germany.

92. Orths, A., Schmitt, A., Styczynski, Z. A. & Verstege, J. (2001). Multi-criteria optimization methods for planning and operation of electrical energy systems. *Electrical Engineering, 83,* 252.

93. Ruska, M. & Kiviluoma, J. (2011). *Renewable Electricity in Europe. Current State, Drivers, and Scenarios for 2020* (Research Notes 2584). Espoo, Finland: VTT Tiedot-teita.

94. Schaber, K., Steinke, F. & Hamacher, T. (2012). Transmission grid extensions for the integration of variable renewable energies in Europe: Who benefits where? *Energy Policy, 43,* 123–135.

95. New Scientist. (2012, 14 March). Energy without borders. *World Resources Simulation Center.* Retrieved from www.wrsc.org/story/energy-without-borders on 26 November 2015.

96. Meadowcroft, J. (2007). Who is in charge here? Governance for sustainable development in a complex world. *Journal of Environmental Policy & Planning, 9*(3–4), 299–314.

97. Pierre, J. & Peters, B. (2000). *Governance, Politics and the State.* Palgrave Macmillan.

98. Peters, B. G. & Pierre, J. (2001). Developments in intergovernmental relations: towards multi-level governance. *Policy & Politics, 29*(2), 131–135.

99. Mahbubani, K. (2008). *The New Asian Hemisphere: The Irresistible Shift of Global Power to the East.* New York, NY: PublicAffairs.

100. Vázquez-Brust, D., Smith, A. & Sarkis, J. (2014). *Managing the transition to critical green growth: The green growth state. Futures, 64,* 123–148.

101. Mahbubani, K. (2008). *The New Asian Hemisphere: The Irresistible Shift of Global Power to the East* (p. 66). New York, NY: PublicAffairs.

102. Collins, R. (2003). Market dynamics as the engine of historical change. *Sociological Theory, 8*(2), 111–135.

103. Chan, J. (2007). Democracy and meritocracy: Toward a Confucian perspective. *Journal of Chinese Philosophy, 34,* 179–193.

104. Tetlock, P. E. (2006). *How Accurate Are Your Pet Pundits?* Project Syndicate.

105. NASA Eclipse. *Catalog of Solar Eclipses: 2101 to 2200.* Retrieved from http://eclipse.gsfc.nasa.gov/SEcat5/SE2101-2200.html on 27 July 2009.

106. Tetlock, P. (2005). *Expert Political Judgment: How Good is It? How Can We Know?* Princeton, NJ: Princeton University Press.

107. Aroney, N. (2008). Four reasons for an upper house: Representative democracy, public deliberation, legislative outputs and executive accountability. *Adelaide Law Review, 29*(2), 205.

108. Fischer, F. (1990). *Technocracy and the Politics of Expertise*. Newbury Park, CA: SAGE.

109. Federico, A. (2005). Making do: George Orwell's *Coming Up For Air*. *Studies in the Novel, 37*(1), 50–63.

110. Easterley, W. (2001). *The Elusive Quest for Growth: Economists' Adventures and Misadventures in the Tropics*. Cambridge, MA: MIT Press.

111. Braithwaite, J. (1998). Institutionalizing distrust, enculturating trust. In B. V., & M. Levi (eds), *Trust and Governance* (p. 343). New York: Russell Sage Foundation.

112. Flyvbjerg, B. (1998). Habermas and Foucault: thinkers for civil society? *The British Journal of Sociology, 49*(2), 210–233.

113. Jacobs, L. R. & Soss, J. (2010). The politics of inequality in America: A political economy framework. *Annual Review of Political Science, 13*, 341–364.

114. Milner, H.V. (2005). Globalization, development, and international institutions: Normative and positive perspectives. *Perspectives on Politics, 3*(4), 833–854.

115. UNDP. *Human Development Report 1992: Global Dimensions of Human Development*. New York, Oxford: Oxford University Press.

116. Anderson, B. (2006). Transcending without transcendence: Utopianism and an ethos of hope. *Antipode, 38*(4), 691–710.

117. Ellen MacArthur Foundation (2012). *Towards the Circular Economy: an economic and business rationale for an accelerated transition*. Retrieved from www.ellen-macarthurfoundation.org/publications/towards-the-circular-economy-vol-1-an-economic-and-business-rationale-for-an-accelerated-transition on 20 November 2015.

118. ibid.

119. Smith, A., Stirling, A. & Berkhout, F. (2005). The governance of sustainable socio-technical transitions. *Research Policy, 34*(10), 1491–1510.

120. Davis, D. B. (2008). *Inhuman Bondage: The Rise and Fall of Slavery in the New World* (p. 238). New York, NY: Oxford University Press.

121. Feeny, D. et al. (1990). The tragedy of the commons: Twenty-two years later. *Human Ecology, 18*(1), 1–19.

122. Aarohi. (2002). *Community Forest Management in Kumaon: A Documentation of Aarohi's work: 1992–2002*. Aarohi.

123. Agrawal, A., Chhatre, A. & Hardin, R. (2008). Changing governance of the world's forests. *Science, 320*(5882), 1460–1462.

124. Agrawal, A. & Ostrom, E. (2001). Collective action, property rights, and decentralization in resource use in India and Nepal. *Politics & Society, 29*(4), 485–514.

125. Aarohi. (2002). *Community Forest Management in Kumaon: A Documentation of Aarohi's work: 1992–2002*. Aarohi.

Chapter 7   Globalization

1. McLuhan, H. M. (1962). *The Gutenberg Galaxy*. Toronto, Canada: University of Toronto Press.

2. Scholte, J. A. (2010). *Globalization: A Critical Introduction*. London: Palgrave.

3. ibid.

4. Dicken, P. (2014). *Global Shift: Mapping the Changing Contours of the World Economy* (p. 12). London: Paul Chapman.

5. Stiglitz, J. (2002). *Globalization and its Discontents* (p. 9). London: Penguin.

6. Dicken, P. (2014). *Global Shift: Mapping the Changing Contours of the World Economy*. London: Paul Chapman.

7. Scholte, J. A. (2010). *Globalization: A Critical Introduction.* London: Palgrave.
8. Chudnovsky, D. & López, A. (1999). Globalization and developing countries: Foreign direct investment and growth and sustainable human development. Working Paper prepared for the UNCTAD/UNDP Global Programme on Globalization, Liberalization and Sustainable Development.
9. ibid.
10. Wolf, M. (2004). *Why Globalisation Works.* New Haven, CT: Yale University Press.
11. World Bank (2014). *Migrations and Remittances: Recent Developments and Outlook.* Retrieved from http://siteresources.worldbank.org/INTPROSPECTS/Resources/334934-1288990760745/MigrationandDevelopmentBrief22.pdf on 1 September 2015.
12. Scholte, J. A. (2010). *Globalization: A Critical Introduction.* London: Palgrave.
13. ibid.
14. ibid.
15. Hirst, P. & Thompson, G. (2002). *Globalization in Question.* Cambridge: Polity Press.
16. ibid.
17. Dicken, P. (2014). *Global Shift: Mapping the Changing Contours of the World Economy.* London: Paul Chapman.
18. Hirst, P. & Thompson, G. (2002). *Globalization in Question.* Cambridge: Polity Press.
19. Ohmae, K. (1990). *The Borderless World.* London: Collins.
20. Giddens, A. (1996). Globalization: A Keynote Address. *UNRISD News, 15,* 4–5.
21. Hirst, P. & Thompson, G. (2002). *Globalization in Question.* Cambridge: Polity Press.
22. Jones, G. (1994). *The Evolution of International Business.* London: Routledge.
23. Rodrik, D. (2006). Goodbye Washington consensus, hello Washington confusion? *Journal of Economic Literature, 44,* 973–987.
24. Dicken, P. (2014). *Global Shift: Mapping the Changing Contours of the World Economy.* London: Paul Chapman.
25. ibid.
26. Held, D., McGrew, A., Goldblatt, D. & Perraton, J. (2009). *Global Transformations: Politics, Economics and Culture.* Stanford, CA: Stanford University Press.
27. Held, D., McGrew, A., Goldblatt, D. & Perraton, J. (2009). *Global Transformations: Politics, Economics and Culture* (p. 15). Stanford, CA: Stanford University Press.
28. ibid.
29. Stiglitz, J. (2007). *Making Globalization Work: The Next Steps to Global Justice.* London: Penguin.
30. Scholte, J. A. (2010). *Globalization: A Critical Introduction.* London: Palgrave.
31. ibid.
32. Hall, P. & Soskice, D. (2010). *Varieties of Capitalism: The Institutional Foundations of Comparative Advantage.* Oxford: Oxford University Press.
33. Amable, B. (2009). *The Diversity of Modern Capitalism.* Oxford: Oxford University Press.
34. ibid.
35. Serra, S. & Stiglitz, J. (2012). *The Washington Consensus Reconsidered.* Oxford: Oxford University Press.
36. Held, D., McGrew, A., Goldblatt, D. & Perraton, J. (2009). *Global Transformations: Politics, Economics and Culture.* Stanford, CA: Stanford University Press.
37. Nee, V. (1992). Organizational dynamics of market transition: Hybrid forms, property rights, and mixed economy in China. *Administrative Science Quarterly, 37,* 1–27.
38. Zhu, X. (2012). Understanding China's growth: Past, present, and future (Digest Summary). *Journal of Economic Perspectives, 26*(4), 103–124.

39. Ge, W. (1999). Special economic zones and the opening of the Chinese economy: Some lessons for economic liberalization. *World Development, 27*(7), 1267–1285.
40. Stiglitz, J. (2010). *Freefall: Free Markets and the Sinking of the Global Economy.* London: Penguin.
41. Cooper, G. (2008). *The Origin of Financial Crises: Central Banks, Credit Bubbles and the Efficient Market Fallacy.* New York, NY: Vintage Books.
42. Stiglitz, J. (2007). *Making Globalization Work: The Next Steps to Global Justice.* London: Penguin.
43. Solanas, F. (2004). *A Social Genocide.* Documentary motion picture. Buenos Aires: Cinesur Producciones
44. Stiglitz, J. (2002). *Globalization and its Discontents.* London: Penguin.
45. Davies, H. (2010). *The Financial Crisis: Who is to Blame?* London: Polity Press.
46. Australian Ministers for Trade (2010). Doorstop interview with World Trade Organization (WTO) Director-General, Pascal Lamy. Archive 1995 to 2010. Retrieved from http://trademinister.gov.au/transcripts/2010/100209_lamy.html on 1 August 2015.
47. Serra, S. & Stiglitz, J. (2012). *The Washington Consensus Reconsidered.* Oxford: Oxford University Press.
48. Dicken, P. (2014). *Global Shift: Mapping the Changing Contours of the World Economy.* London: Paul Chapman.
49. ibid.
50. Dunning, P. & Lundin, S. (2008). *Multinational Enterprise and the Global Economy.* London: Addison-Wesley.
51. Hirst, P. & Thompson, G. (2002). *Globalization in Question.* Cambridge: Polity Press.
52. Dicken, P. (2014). *Global Shift: Mapping the Changing Contours of the World Economy.* London: Paul Chapman.
53. Beugelsdijk, S., Brakman, S., Garretsen, H. & Van Marrewijk, C. (2013). *International Economics and Business: Nations and Firms in the Global Economy.* Cambridge: Cambridge University Press.
54. Dunning, P. & Lundin, S. (2008). *Multinational Enterprise and the Global Economy.* London: Addison-Wesley.
55. James, J. (2002). *Technology, Globalization and Poverty.* Cheltenham: Edward Elgar Publishing.
56. Fukuda-Parr, S., Lopes, C. & Malik, K. (2013). *Capacity for Development: New Solutions to Old Problems.* London: Routledge.
57. Busse, M. (2003). Tariffs, transport costs and the WTO Doha round: The case of developing countries. *Journal of International Law and Trade Policy, 4*(1), 15–31.
58. OECD (2007, July). *OECD Communications Outlook 2007* (p. 209).
59. Aker, J. C. & Mbiti, I. M. (2010). *Mobile phones and economic development in Africa* (CGD Working Paper 211). Washington DC: Center for Global Development.
60. Worldbank (2015). Data retrieved from http://data.worldbank.org/indicator/SP.POP.TOTL on 14 February 2015 (new
61. ITU World Telecommunication (2015). Retrieved from www.itu.int/en/ITU-D/Statistics/Pages/stat/default.aspx on 14 February 2015.
62. Carmel, E. & Tjia, P. (2005). *Offshoring Information Technology: Sourcing and Outsourcing to a Global Workforce* (p. 32). Cambridge: Cambridge University Press.
63. Information taken from interviews, Indian Dept. of Electronics annual reports and Dataquest (India) surveys.
64. Brini, M. (2003). *India as an IT Opportunity for European Companies*; US Delegation (2008). *The Competitiveness of India in the Global Economy.*

65. Port of Rotterdam. (2010). *Container Owner Association.* Promotional Leaflet.

66. Behar, A. & Venables, A. J. (2011). Transport costs and international trade. In A. De Palma, R. Lindsey, E. Quinet & R. Vickerman (eds), *A Handbook of Transport Economics* (pp. 97–115). Cheltenham: Edward Elgar.

67. Hummels, D. (2007). Transportation costs and international trade in the second era of globalization. *Journal of Economic Perspectives, American Economic Association, 21*(3), 131–154.

68. Vital Wave Consulting (2009). *Health for Development: The Opportunity of Mobile Technology for Healthcare in the Developing World* (p. 64). Washington, DC and Berkshire, UK: UN Foundation-Vodafone Foundation Partnership.

69. Celpay Zambia. *About us.* Retrieved from www.zm.celpay.com on 10 October 2014.

70. Blomström, M., Globerman, S. & Kokko, A. (2002). Regional integration and foreign direct investment. In J. H. Dunning (ed.), *Regions, Globalization, and the Knowledge-based Economy* (109–130). Oxford: Oxford University Press.

71. Krugman, P. (1991). The move toward free trade zones. In *Policy Implications of Trade and Currency Zones* (7–42). Symposium Proceedings, Jackson Hole: Federal Reserve Bank of Kansas City.

72. International Peace Research Institute Oslo (2011). *Conflict dataset 1948–2008.* Retrieved from http://www.pcr.uu.se/research/ucdp/datasets/ucdp_prio_armed_conflict_dataset/ on 15 August 2011.

73. Van Creveld, Martin (2009). *Transformation of war.* New York, Simon and Schuster.

74. Mickler, D. (2009, February). *China and Russia in the post-Cold War UN Security Council: Obstructors or sentinels of global security?* Paper presented at the annual meeting of the ISA's 50th Annual Convention: 'Exploring the past, anticipating the future', New York.

75. Panajoti, T. (2008). *Humanitarian Crises and World Politics: The Conflict between Ethics and Pragmatism in Humanitarian Intervention Decisions.* UN & Humanitarian Governance.

76. Akhavan, P. (2003). The International Criminal Court in context: Mediating the global and local in the age of accountability. *The American Journal of International Law, (97)*3, 712–721.

77. International Criminal Court. *ICC at a glance.* Retrieved from www.icc-cpi.int/en_menus/icc/about%20the%20court/icc%20at%20a%20glance/Pages/icc%20at%20a%20glance.aspx on 3 August 2015.

78. Human Security Report Project. *Human Security Report 2005: War and Peace in the 21st Century.* Oxford: Oxford University Press; Human Security Report Project. *Human Security Report 2009/2010: The Causes of Peace and the Shrinking Costs of War.* Oxford: Oxford University Press.

79. International Peace Research Institute Oslo (2011). Conflict dataset 1948–2008. Retrieved from http://www.pcr.uu.se/research/ucdp/datasets/ucdp_prio_armed_conflict_dataset/ on 15 August 2011.

80. Stiglitz, J. (2007). *Making Globalization Work: The Next Steps to Global Justice.* London: Penguin.

81. Stiglitz, J. (2002). *Globalization and its Discontents.* London: Penguin.

82. ibid.

83. Dimand, R. (1988). *The Origins of the Keynesian Revolution.* Stanford, CA: Stanford University Press.

84. Abel, A. & Bernanke, B. (2005). *Macroeconomics.* Pearson: Addison Weasley.

85. Markwell, D. (2006). *John Maynard Keynes and International Relations: Economic Paths to War and Peace.* Oxford: Oxford University Press.

86. IMF (2015). *IMF History*. Retrieved from www.imf.org/external/about/history.htm on 29 November 2015.
87. ibid.
88. Akyüz, Y. & Cornford, A. J. (2000). *Capital flows to developing countries and the reform of the international financial system* (Discussion Paper 190). United Nations University, World Institute for Development Economics Research.
89. Siamwalla, A., Vajragupta, Y. & Vichyanond, P. (1999). *Foreign Capital Flows to Thailand: Determinants and Impact* (4–5). Thailand Development Research Institute, Bangkok.
90. ibid. p. 38
91. Khan, M. & Sharma, S. (2003). IMF conditionality and country ownership of adjustment programs. *The World Bank Research Observer, 18*(2), 227–248.
92. Stiglitz, J. (2007). *Making Globalization Work: The Next Steps to Global Justice.* London: Penguin.
93. World Bank (2015). *Spotlight: Organizational Units*. Retrieved from www.worldbank.org/en/about on 1 September 2015.
94. ibid.
95. Beck, T. et al. (2008). *Bank Financing for SMEs around the World: Drivers, Obstacles, Business Models, and Lending Practices.* Washington, DC: World Bank.
96. World Bank. *Annual Report 2014.* Washington, DC: World Bank.
97. Ndizeye, P. (2008). *Feasibility study for setting up a small scale production of Portland cement in Burundi. Thesis for bachelor degree in business management Saxion University of Applied Sciences.*
99. World Bank. *Annual Report 2014.* Washington, DC: World Bank.
99. WTO (2015). *History*. Retrieved from www.wto.org/english/thewto_e/cwr_e/cwr_history_e.htm on 1 September 2015.
100. Ricardo, D. (1817). *On the Principles of Political Economy and Taxation.* London: John Murray
101. ibid.
102. Peet, R. (2003). *Unholy Trinity: The IMF, World Bank and WTO.* London: Zed Books.
103. WTO (2015). *Members and observers of the WTO.* Retrieved from www.wto.org/english/thewto_e/countries_e/org6_map_e.htm on 8 July 2015.
104. WTO (2015). *Principles of the trading system.* Retrieved from www.wto.org/english/thewto_e/whatis_e/tif_e/fact2_e.htm on 8 July 2015.
105. Ministry of Foreign Affairs of Denmark. *What is a trade barrier?* Retrieved from http://um.dk/en/tradecouncil/barriers/what-is/ on 3 August 2015.
106. Dee, P. S. & Ferrantino, M. J. (eds) (2005). *Quantitative Methods for Assessing the Effects of Nontariff Measures and Trade Facilitation.* Singapore: Asia-Pacific Economic Cooperation (APEC) and World Scientific.
107. ibid.
108. Hoekman, B. M., Mattoo, A. & English, P. (2002). *Bovenkant formulier* Onderkant formulier Development, Trade, and the WTO: A Handbook. Washington, DC: World Bank.
109. Borger, J., Watt, N. & Vidal, J. (2006, 8 February). US wins WTO backing in war with Europe over GM food. *The Guardian.*
110. WTO (2015). A unique contribution. Retrieved from www.wto.org/english/thewto_e/whatis_e/tif_e/disp1_e.htm on 8 July 2015.
111. Peet, R. (2003). *Unholy Trinity: The IMF, World Bank and WTO.* London: Zed Books.
112. ibid.

113. ibid.
114. Trebilcock, M. (2014). *Between theories of trade and development: The future of the World Trading System* (Law Working Paper Series 2014-10). Toronto, Canada: University of Toronto.
115. WTO (2015). *Principles of the trading system.* Retrieved from www.wto.org/english/thewto_e/whatis_e/tif_e/fact2_e.htm on 1 September 2015.
116. WTO (2015). Retrieved from www.wto.org/english/thewto_e/whatis_e/tif_e/org6_e.htm on 20 February 2015.
117. Ietto-Gillies, G. (1988). Different conceptual frameworks for the assessment of the degree of internationalization and empirical analysis of various indices for the top 100 transnational corporations. *Transnational Corporations, 7,* 19–38.
118. Sullivan, D. (1996). Measuring the degree of Internationalization of a firm. *Journal of International Business Studies, 27*(1), 179–192.
119. Ietto-Gillies, G. (1988). Different conceptual frameworks for the assessment of the degree of internationalization and empirical analysis of various indices for the top 100 transnational corporations. *Transnational Corporations, 7,* 19–38.

Chapter 8   The Impact of Globalization on Sustainable Development

1. Lloyd, C. (2009). *What on Earth Happened: The Complete Story of the Planet. Life and People, from the Big Bang Theory to the Present* (p. 7). London: Bloomsbury.
2. ibid.
3. Hertz, N. (2002). *The Silent Takeover: Global Capitalism and the Death of Democracy.* London: Arrow.
4. Scholte, J. A. (2007). *Globalization: A Critical Introduction.* London: Palgrave.
5. Stiglitz, J. (2002). *Globalization and its Discontents.* London: Penguin.
6. Lloyd, C. (2009). *What on Earth Happened: The Complete Story of the Planet. Life and People, from the Big Bang Theory to the Present.* London: Bloomsbury.
7. Peet, R. (2008). *The Geography of Power: The Making of Global Economic Policy.* Oxford: Oxford University Press.
8. Stiglitz, J. (2002). *Globalization and its Discontents* (p. 8). London: Penguin.
9. Stiglitz, J. (2002). *Globalization and its Discontents.* London: Penguin.
10. Djawoto, Munawar, I., Maskie, G. & Ashar, K. (2014). Keynes's view versus Solow. *Journal of Economics and Sustainable Development, 5*(16), 34–41.
11. Rodrik, D. (2006). Goodbye Washington Consensus, hello Washington confusion? *Journal of Economic Literature, 44,* 973–987.
12. Hanshaw, S. (2013). *The Dangers of Aggressive Trade Liberalization: Why the Washington Consensus is Not a Global Consensus* (Paper 1). Government, Politics & Global Studies Undergraduate Publications.
13. Peet, R. (2008). *The Geography of Power: The Making of Global Economic Policy.* Oxford: Oxford University Press.
14. ibid.
15. Williamson, J. (2000). What should the World Bank think about the Washington Consensus? *World Bank Research Observer, 15*(2), 251–64.
16. ibid.
17. Peet, R. (2008). *The Geography of Power: The Making of Global Economic Policy.* Oxford: Oxford University Press.

18. Stiglitz, J. (2010). *Freefall: Free Markets and the Sinking of the Global Economy*. London: Penguin.
19. Rich, B. (1996). World Bank: 50 years is enough. In Goddard et al. (eds), *International Political Economy*. London: Routledge.
20. Peet, R. (2008). *The Geography of Power: The Making of Global Economic Policy*. Oxford: Oxford University Press.
21. Stiglitz, J. (2002). *Globalization and its Discontents*. London: Penguin.
22. Rodrik, D. (2006). Goodbye Washington Consensus, hello Washington confusion? *Journal of Economic Literature, 44*, 973–987.
23. Stiglitz, J. (2002). *Globalization and its Discontents*. London: Penguin.
24. World Bank (2005). *Economic Growth in the 1990s: Learning from a Decade of Reform*. Washington, DC: World Bank.
25. Stiglitz, J. (2007). *Making Globalization Work: The Next Steps to Global Justice*. London: Penguin.
26. World Bank (2005). *Economic Growth in the 1990s: Learning from a Decade of Reform*. Washington, DC: World Bank.
27. Peet, R. (2008). *The Geography of Power: The Making of Global Economic Policy*. Oxford: Oxford University Press.
28. IMF (2015, May 29). *Debt Relief Under the Heavily Indebted Poor Countries (HIPC) Initiative*. Retrieved from www.imf.org/external/np/exr/facts/hipc.htm on 1 October 2015.
29. Peet, R. (2008). *The Geography of Power: The Making of Global Economic Policy*. Oxford: Oxford University Press.
30. Stiglitz, J. (2002). *Globalization and its Discontents*. London: Penguin.
31. World Bank. (2005). *Economic Growth in the 1990s: Learning from a Decade of Reform*. Washington, DC: World Bank.
32. Rodrik, D. (2006). Goodbye Washington Consensus, hello Washington confusion? *Journal of Economic Literature, 44*, 973–987.
33. IMF (2015, May 29). *Debt Relief Under the Heavily Indebted Poor Countries (HIPC) Initiative*. Retrieved from www.imf.org/external/np/exr/facts/hipc.htm on 29 May 2015.
34. Sachs, J. D., McArthur, J. W., Schmidt-Traub, G., Kruk, M., Bahadur, C., Faye, M. & McCord, G. (2004). Ending Africa's poverty trap. *Brookings Papers on Economic Activity, 1*, 117–216.
35. Peet, R. (2008). *The Geography of Power: The Making of Global Economic Policy*. Oxford: Oxford University Press.
36. Rodrik, D. (2006). Goodbye Washington Consensus, hello Washington confusion? *Journal of Economic Literature, 44*, 973–987.
37. Serra, S. & Stiglitz, J. (2013). *The Washington Consensus Reconsidered: Towards a New Governance*. Oxford: Oxford University Press.
38. Lateef, S. (1996). The World Bank: Its first half century. In Goddard et al. (eds), *International Political Economy*. London: Routledge.
39. Rodrik, D. (2006). Goodbye Washington Consensus, hello Washington confusion? *Journal of Economic Literature, 44*, 973–987.
40. Rich, B. (1996). World Bank: 50 years is enough. In Goddard et al. (eds), *International Political Economy*. London: Routledge.
41. World Bank Portfolio Management Task Force (1992). *Effective Implementation, Key to Development Impact Report*. Washington, DC: World Bank.
42. Peet, R. (2008). *The Geography of Power: The Making of Global Economic Policy*. Oxford: Oxford University Press.

43. Kilby, J. (2009). The political economy of conditionality: An empirical analysis of World Bank loan disbursements. *Journal of Development Economics, 89,* 51–61.

44. Rich, B. (1994). *Mortgaging the Earth: The World Bank, Environmental Impoverishment and the Crisis of Development.* Boston, MA: Bacon Press.

45. Hackett, S. (2011). *Environmental and Natural Resource Economics.* New York, NY: Sharpe.

46. Rich, B. (1996). World Bank: 50 years is enough. In Goddard et al. (eds), *International Political Economy.* London: Routledge.

47. Peet, R. (2003). *Unholy Trinity: The IMF, World Bank and WTO.* London: Zed Books.

48. Stiglitz, J. (2007). *Making Globalization Work: The Next Steps to Global Justice.* London: Penguin.

49. Evaluation Group. (2011). *Capturing Technology for Development: An Evaluation of World Bank Group Activities in Information and Communication Technologies. Volume 1. The Evaluation.* Washington, DC: World Bank. © World Bank. Retrieved from https://openknowledge.worldbank.org/handle/10986/2370 on 1 October 2015. License: Creative Commons Attribution CC BY 3.0.

50. Rodrik, D. (2006). Goodbye Washington Consensus, hello Washington confusion? *Journal of Economic Literature, 44,* 973–987.

51. Peet, R. (2008). *The Geography of Power: The Making of Global Economic Policy.* Oxford: Oxford University Press.

52. Wolf, M. (2004). *Why Globalization Works.* New Haven, CT: Yale University Press.

53. World Trade Organization (2012). *WTO Public Forum 2011: Seeking Answers to Global Trade Challenges.* Geneva: WTO. Retrieved from www.wto.org/english/res_e/booksp_e/public_forum11_e.pdf on on 1 October 2015.

54. ibid.

55. Hoekman, B. M. & Kostecki, M. M. (2010). *The Political Economy of the World Trading System: The WTO and Beyond.* Oxford: Oxford University Press.

56. Hoekman, B. (2011). *Proposal for WTO reform, a synthesis and assessment* (Policy Research Working Paper 5525). Washington: The World Bank Poverty Reduction and Economic Management Network.

57. Serra, S. & Stiglitz, J. (2013). *The Washington Consensus Reconsidered: Towards a New Governance.* Oxford: Oxford University Press.

58. Stern, D. (2014) The rise and fall of the Environmental Kuznets Curve. *World Development, 32*(8), 1419–1439.

59. Hackett, S. (2011). *Environmental and Natural Resource Economics.* New York, NY: Sharpe.

60. Peet, R. (2008). *The Geography of Power: The Making of Global Economic Policy.* Oxford: Oxford University Press.

61. Hackett, S. (2011). *Environmental and Natural Resource Economics.* New York, NY: Sharpe.

62. UNEP (1999). *Trade Liberalization and the Environment: Lessons learnt from Bangladesh, Chile, India, Philippines, Romania and Uganda* (p. 1). Geneva: United Nations.

63. Stiglitz, J. (2002). *Globalization and its Discontents.* London: Penguin.

64. Legrain, P. (2003). *Open World: The Truth about Globalisation.* London: Abacus.

65. Hertz, N. (2002). *The Silent Takeover: Global Capitalism and the Death of Democracy.* London: Arrow.

66. Legrain, P. (2003). *Open World: The Truth about Globalisation* (p. 258). London: Abacus.

67. Hoekman, B. M. & Kostecki, M. M. (2010). *The Political Economy of the World Trading System: the WTO and Beyond.* Oxford: Oxford University Press.

68. Serra, S. & Stiglitz, J. (2013). *The Washington Consensus Reconsidered: Towards a New Governance.* Oxford: Oxford University Press.

69. Legrain, P. (2003). *Open World: The Truth about Globalisation.* London: Abacus
70. ibid.
71. Hoekman, B. (2011) Proposal for WTO reform, a synthesis and assessment (Policy Research Working Paper 5525). Washington: The World Bank Poverty Reduction and Economic Management Network.
72. Hoekman, B. M. & Kostecki, M. M. (2010). *The Political Economy of the World Trading System: the WTO and Beyond.* Oxford: Oxford University Press.
73. Stiglitz, J. (2002). *Globalization and its Discontents.* London: Penguin.
74. Hertz, N. (2002).*The Silent Takeover: Global Capitalism and the Death of Democracy.* London: Arrow.
75. Corden, W. M. (1984). Boom sector and Dutch Disease economics: Survey and consolidation. *Oxford Economic Papers, 36,* 362.
76. The Economist (1977, 26 November). The Dutch Disease (82–83).
77. Lall, S. & Narulla, R. (2004). Foreign direct investment and its role in economic development: Do we need a new agenda? *The European Journal of Development Research, 16,* 447–464.
78. Davies, G.A. (1995). Learning to love the Dutch Disease: Evidence from the Mineral Economies. *World Development, 23*(10), 1765–1779.
79. Wolf, M. (2004). *Why Globalization Works.* New Haven, CT: Yale University Press.
80. Dicken, P. (2011). *Global Shift: Mapping the Changing Contours of the World Economy.* London: Paul Chapman.
81. Sloterdijk, P. (2003). In Soeterbeeck (Roman Catholic Church). (Only available in Dutch.)
82. Sloterdijk, P. (2005). Foreword to the Theory of Spheres. In M. O'Hanian & J. C. Royoux (eds), *Cosmograms* (223–241). New York, NY: Lukas and Sternberg.
83. ibid.
84. ibid.
85. Stimson, R. J., Stough, R. R. & Roberts, B. H. (2006). *Regional Economic Development: Analysis and Planning Strategy.* Springer Science & Business Media.
86. Baltagi, B. H., Egger, P. & Pfaffermayr, M. (2008). Estimating regional trade agreement effects on FDI in an interdependent world. *Journal of Econometrics, 145*(1), 194–208.
87. Dicken, P. (2011). *Global Shift: Mapping the Changing Contours of the World Economy.* London: Paul Chapman.
88. Stiglitz, J. (2007). *Making Globalization Work: The Next Steps to Global Justice.* London: Penguin.
89. Kuznets, S. (1955). Economic growth and income inequality. *American Economic Review, 35,* 1–28.
90. Foster, J. (2014). Joseph Schumpeter and Simon Kuznets: Comparing their evolutionary economic approaches to business cycles and economic growth. *Journal of Evolutionary Economics, 25*(1), 163–172. Published online 30 May 2014.
91. Piketty, T. (2014). *Capital in the Twenty-First Century.* Cambridge, MA: Harvard University Press.
92. Dicken, P. (2011). *Global Shift: Mapping the Changing Contours of the World Economy.* London: Paul Chapman.
93. Schumpeter, J. A. (1934). *The Theory of Economic Development.* New Brunswick: Transaction Publishers.
94. Vázquez-Brust, D. & Sarkis, J. (2010). *Green Growth: Transitions Towards a Sustainable Economy.* London: Springer.
95. ibid.
96. Stiglitz, J. (2012). *The Price of Inequality: How Today's Divided Society Endangers Our Future.* London: Penguin.

97. ibid.
98. Piketty, T. (2014). *Capital in the Twenty-First Century*. Cambridge, MA: Harvard University Press.
99. ibid.
100. ibid.
101. Gates, B. (2014, 13 October). Why inequality matters. *The Gates Notes*. Retrieved from www.gatesnotes.com/Books/Why-Inequality-Matters-Capital-in-21st-Century-Review on 8 October 2015.
102. Elliot, L. (2014, 29 May). FT economist accused of serious errors in Thomas Piketty's takedown. *The Guardian*. Retrieved from www.theguardian.com/business/economics-blog/2014/may/29/ft-journalist-errors-thomas-piketty-takedown on 8 October 2015.
103. Moore, H. (2014, 21 September). Why is Thomas Piketty's 700 pages book a bestseller? *The Guardian*. Retrieved from www.theguardian.com/money/2014/sep/21/-sp-thomas-piketty-bestseller-why on 8 October 2015.
104. Piketty, T. (2014). *Capital in the Twenty-First Century*. Cambridge, MA: Harvard University Press.
105. Gates, B. (2014, 13 October). Why inequality matters. *The Gates Notes*. Retrieved from www.gatesnotes.com/Books/Why-Inequality-Matters-Capital-in-21st-Century-Review on 8 October 2015.
106. Dolcerocca, A & Terzioglu, G. (2015) Interview: Thomas Piketty responds to criticisms from the left. *The Potemkin Review*, 1, 1, 12–16.
107. Stiglitz, J. (2012). *The Price of Inequality: How Today's Divided Society Endangers Our Future*. London: Penguin.
108. Stiglitz, J. (2015). *The Great Divide*. London: Penguin.
109. Piketty, T. (2014). *Capital in the Twenty-First Century*. Cambridge, MA: Harvard University Press.
110. Atkinson, A. (2015). *Inequality: What Can be Done?* Cambridge, MA: Harvard University Press.
111. ibid.
112. Vázquez-Brust, D., Smith, A. & Sarkis, J. (2014). Managing the transition to critical green growth: The green growth state. *Futures, 64*, 38–50.
113. Lloyd, C. (2009). *What on Earth Happened: The Complete Story of the Planet. Life and People, from the Big Bang Theory to the Present*. London: Bloomsbury.
114. Hertz, N. (2002). *The Silent Takeover: Global Capitalism and the Death of Democracy*. London: Arrow.
115. Stiglitz, J. (2012). *The Price of Inequality: How Today's Divided Society Endangers Our Future*. London: Penguin.
116. Dolcerocca, A & Terzioglu, G. (2015) Interview: Thomas Piketty responds to criticisms from the left, *The Potemkin Review*, 1, 1, 12–16.
117. Stiglitz, J. (2007). *Making Globalization Work: The Next Steps to Global Justice*. London: Penguin.
118. Stiglitz, J. (2010). *Freefall: Free Markets and the Sinking of the Global Economy*. London: Penguin.
119. ibid.
120. Stiglitz, J. (2002). *Globalization and its Discontents*. London: Penguin.
121. Stiglitz, J. (2010). *Freefall: Free Markets and the Sinking of the Global Economy*. London: Penguin.
122. Friedman, B. (2002). Globalization: Stiglitz's case. *The New York Review of Books, 49*(13), 48–53.

123. Friedman himself attempted a critique of Stiglitz in his book *The Moral Consequences of Economic Growth* (2005). Friedman makes a strong case for economic growth as primary policy objective. He argues that growth sustains modern society, as long as there is growth, morality, democracy and solidarity will flourish. When growth stops, even as result of economic stagnation, political democracy, individual liberty and social tolerance are at risk even in prosper countries. Unfortunately for Friedman, his arguments would be soon tested by the global depression that set in only two years after his book. In contradiction to his thesis, the aftermath of the crisis saw a tendency towards strengthened democracy, individuals' liberties and social sensibilities worldwide, with left-centrist governments replacing neoliberals, most notably in USA and France.

124. IDE-JETRO. (2014). *China in Africa: 11. The Role of China's Financial Institutions.* Retrieved from www.ide.go.jp/English/Data/Africa_file/Manualreport/cia_11.html on 1 October 2015.

125. Asongu, S. (2013). *A Development Consensus reconciling the Beijing Model and Washington.* Cameroon: Consensus: Views and Agenda, African Governance and Development Institute.

126. BNDES is the acronym for National Bank for Economic and Social Development in the Portuguese language.

127. Stiglitz, J. & Lin, J. (eds) (2013). *The Industrial Policy Revolution I: The Role of Government Beyond Ideology.* New York, Palgrave Macmillan.

128. The Economist. (2014, 11 November). Why China is creating a new 'World Bank' for Asia. Retrieved from www.economist.com/blogs/economist-explains/2014/11/economist-explains-6 on 1 October 2015.

129. GBN (2013, 2 May). How Ghana dumped World Bank for China Development Bank over gas infrastructure. Retrieved from www.ghanabusinessnews.com/2013/05/02/how-ghana-dumped-world-bank-for-china-development-bank-over-gas-infrastructure/ on 14 October 2015.

130. Osava, M. (2009). Brazil: Development Bank funds destructive projects, say activists. *Inter Press Service.* Retrieved from www.ipsnews.net/2009/11/brazil-development-bank-funds-destructive-projects-say-activists/ on 21 September 2015.

131. Bill and Melinda Gates Foundation. (2014). *Bio Fuels and the Poor: Case Study Mozambique.* Retrieved from http://biofuelsandthepoor.com/case-study-mozambique/#benefit on 11 October 2015.

132. Peet, R. (2008). *The Geography of Power: The Making of Global Economic Policy.* Oxford: Oxford University Press.

133. The Economist. (2014, 11 November). Why China is creating a new 'World Bank' for Asia? Retrieved from www.economist.com/blogs/economist-explains/2014/11/economist-explains-6 on 1 October 2015.

Chapter 9   Innovations in Global Supply Networks

1. Hulleman, W. & Marijs, A. J. (2014). *Internationale Economische Ontwikkelingen en Bedrijfsomgeving* (International Economic Trends and Business Environment). Noordhoff Uitgevers. (Only available in Dutch.)

2. Busse, M. (2003). Tariffs, Transport costs and the WTO Doha Round: The case of developing countries. *Journal of International Law and Trade Policy,* 4(1), 15–31.

3. Trapp, A. C., Konrad, R. A., Sarkis, J. & Zeng, A. Z. (2015). *Closing the Loop: Forging High-Quality Virtual Enterprises in a Reverse Supply Chain through Solution Portfolios.* Working Paper WP2-2015. Worcester, MA: WPI Center for Sustainability in Business.

4. Kumar, S. & Putnam, V. (2008). Cradle to cradle: Reverse logistics strategies and opportunities across three industry sectors. *International Journal of Production Economics, 115*(2), 305–315.

5. Kumar, S. & Putnam, V. (2008). Cradle to cradle: Reverse logistics strategies and opportunities across three industry sectors. *International Journal of Production Economics, 115*(2), 305–315

6. Hawks, K. What is Reverse Logistics? *Reverse Logistics Magazine,* Winter/Spring 2006.

7. Fleischmann, M. (2000). *Quantitative Models for Reverse Logistics* (TRAIL Research School Ph.D series T2000/3, ERIM Ph.D series Research in Management 2). Erasmus University Rotterdam.

8. PricewaterhouseCoopers. (2008, May). Reverse logistics: How to realise an agile and efficient reverse chain within the consumer electronics industry. *Integrated Supply Chain Solutions.*

9. Heijungs, R., Guinée, J. B., Huppes, G., Lankreijer, R. M., Udo de Haes, H. A., Wegener Sleeswijk, A., Ansems, A. M. M., Eggels, P. G., Duin, R. van, Goede & H. P. de (1992). *Environmental Life Cycle Assessment of Products: Guide and Backgrounds.* Leiden, the Netherlands: CML.

10. Goedkoop, M., Heijungs, R., Huijbregts, M. A. J., De Schryver, A., Struijs, J. & Van Zelm, R. (2009). *ReCiPe 2008, A life cycle impact assessment method which comprises harmonised category indicators at the midpoint and the endpoint level* (1st edition). Report I: Characterisation.

11. Bio Intelligence Service Comparative (2008). *Life Cycle Assessment of Tetra Pak packaging Synthesis.* Retrieved from www.biois.com/en/menu-en/publications-en/new-publications/comparative-life-cycle-assessment-of-tetra-pak-packaging.html on 26 November 2015.

12. Collado-Ruiz, D. & Ostad-Ahmad-Ghorabi, H. (2010). Comparing LCA results out of competing products: developing reference ranges from a product family approach. *Journal of Cleaner Production, 18*(4), 355–364.

13. International Organization for Standardization (2006). ISO 14040:2006: Environmental management – life cycle assessment – principles and framework. Retrieved from www.iso.org/iso/catalogue_detail%3Fcsnumber%3D37456 on 20 November 2014.

14. International Organization for Standardization (2006). ISO 14040:2006: Environmental management – life cycle assessment – principles and framework. Retrieved from www.iso.org/iso/catalogue_detail%3Fcsnumber%3D37456 on 20 November 2014. The figure taken from ISO 14040:2006: Environmental management – life cycle assessment – principles and framework is reproduced with the permission of the International Organization for Standardization, ISO. This standard can be obtained from any ISO member and from the website of the ISO Central Secretariat at the following address: www.iso.org. Copyright remains with ISO.

15. PRé Sustainability. *LCA methodology.* Retrieved from www.pre-sustainability.com/lca-methodology on 26 November 2015.

16. Muthu, S. S. (ed.) (2015) *Social Life Cycle Assessment: An Insight.* Heidelberg, Dordrecht, London & New York, Springer.

17. Product Social Impact Assessment. *Project.* Retrieved from http://product-social-impact-assessment.com/project/ on 26 November 2015.

18. Schneidewind, U. (2003). Symbols and substances: An interpretive supply chain management perspective. In S. Seuring, M. Müller, M. Goldbach & U. Schneidewind (eds), *Strategy and Organization in Supply Chains* (pp. 83–98). Physica-Verlag.

19. Halldórsson, A., Skjott-Larsen,T. & Kotzab, H. (2003). Interorganizational theories behind supply chain management. In S. Seuring, M. Müller, M. Goldbach, U. Schneidewind (eds.), *Strategy and Organization in Supply Chains* (pp. 31–46). Physica-Verlag.

20. Choi, T. Y., Dooley, K. J. & Rungtusanatham, M. (2001). Supply networks and complex adaptive systems: Control versus emergence. *Journal of Operations Management, 19*(3), 351–366.

21. Lambert, M. D. & Cooper, C. M. (2000). Issues in supply chain management. *Industrial Marketing Management, 29*, 65–83.

22. Gereffi, G. (1999). *A Commodity Chains Framework for Analyzing Global Industries.* Durham, NC: Duke University.

23. Chen, I. J. & Paulraj, A. (2004). Understanding supply chain management: Critical research and a theoretical framework. *International Journal of Production Research, 42*(1), 131–163.

24. Håkansson, H. & Snehota, I. (eds) (1995). *Developing Relationships in Business Networks.* London: Routledge.

25. Schrempf-Stirling, J. (2012). *The Delimitation of Corporate Social Responsibility: Upstream, Downstream, and Historic CSR.* University of Richmond, School of Business.

26. SOMO. Centre for Research on Multinational Corporations. (n.d.). Retrieved from www.somo.nl on 26 November 2015.

27. Cramer, J. (2006). *Corporate Social Responsibility and Globalization: An Action Plan for Business.* Greenleaf Publishing.

28. D. E. Master Blenders 1753. Our approach. Retrieved from www.demasterblenders1753.com/en/sustainability/Our-approach/ on 26 November 2015.

29. McDonald, H., London, T. & Hart, S. (2002). *Expanding the Playing Field: Nike's World Shoe Project (A).* World Resources Institute & Kenan-Flagler Business School at the University of North Carolina, Chapel Hill.

30. Van Bommel, H. (2011). A conceptual framework for analyzing sustainability strategies in industrial supply networks from an innovation perspective. *Journal of Cleaner Production, (19)*8, 895–904.

31. Seuring, S. & Müller, M. (2007). Integrated chain management in Germany – identifying schools of thought based on a literature review. *Journal of Cleaner Production, 15*, 699–710.

32. Hall, J. (2000). Environmental supply chain dynamics. *Journal of Cleaner Production, 8*(6), 455–471.

33. Pesonen, H-L. (2001). Environmental management of value chains: Promoting life-cycle thinking in industrial networks. *Greener Management International, 33*, 45–58.

34. Van Bommel, H. & Bugge, K-E. (1998). Product Oriented Environmental Management Systems (POEMS): How to integrate product development in environmental management systems. *ENTRÉE 98 Proceedings Innovation Strategies for Economy and Environment,* Deventer, the Netherlands.

35. Sarkis, J., Zhu, Q. & Lai, K. H. (2011). An organizational theoretic review of green supply chain management literature. *International Journal of Production Economics, 130*(1), 1–15.

36. Boons. F. (2002). Greening products: a framework for product chain management. *Journal of Cleaner Production, 10*, 495–505.

37. Kleindorfer, P. R., Singhal. K. & Wassenhove, L. N. van. (2005). Sustainable operations management. *Production and Operations Management, 14*(4), 482–492.

38. Cramer, J. M. (2008). Organising corporate social responsibility in international product chains. *Journal of Cleaner Production, 16*(3), 395–400.

39. Kortelainen, K. (2008). Global supply chains and social requirements: Case studies of labour condition auditing in the People's Republic of China. *Business Strategy and the Environment, 17*(7), 431–443.

40. Mamic, I. (2005). Managing global supply chain: The sports footwear, apparel and retail sectors. *Journal of Business Ethics, 59*(1–2), 81–100.

41. Carter, C. R. & Jennings, M. M. (2004). The role of purchasing in corporate social responsibility: A structural equation analysis. *Journal of Business Logistics, 25*(1), 145–186.

42. Braungart, M. & McDonough, W. (2002). *Remaking the Way We Make Things*. New York, NY: North Point Press.

43. Cradle to Cradle Products Innovation Institute. (2014). Retrieved from www.c2ccertified.org/ on 26 November 2015.

44. McDonough Braungart Design Chemistry (2015). *Cradle to Cradle*. Retrieved from www.mbdc.com/ on 26 November 2015.

45. Thornton, K. (1994, 11 October). Salvo in Germany – Reiner Pilz. *SalvoNEWS, 99,* 14.

46. Cradle to Cradle in Taiwan (2015). Cradle to Cradle Terms & Definitions. Retrieved from www.c2cplatform.tw/en/c2c.php?Key=3. © EPEA Internationale Umweltforschung GmbH on 12 August 2015.

47. Desso (2015). *The Road Less Travelled*. Retrieved from www.desso.com/c2c-corporate-responsibility/the-road-less-travelled/ on 26 November 2015.

48. McDonough Braungart Design Chemistry, LLC (2012). *Cradle to Cradle Certified Product Standard, version 3.0*. Retrieved from www.c2ccertified.org/images/uploads/C2CCertified_Product_Standard_V3_121112.pdf on 26 November 2015.

49. Cradle to Cradle Products Innovation Institute (2014). Retrieved from www.c2ccertified.org/ on 26 November 2015.

50. Cradle to Cradle Products Innovation Institute (2014). *Products*. Retrieved from www.c2ccertified.org/products on 26 November 2015.

51. Gijsbert Koren: Design, Strategy & Innovation. (2009). Cradle to Cradle. Retrieved from https://gijsbertkoren.wordpress.com/2009/04/03/cradle-to-cradle/ on 26 November 2015.

52. Ellen MacArthur Foundation (2012). *Towards the Circular Economy: An Economic and Business Rationale for an Accelerated Transition*. Retrieved from www.ellenmacarthurfoundation.org/publications/towards-the-circular-economy-vol-1-an-economic-and-business-rationale-for-an-accelerated-transition on 20 November 2015.

53. Ellen MacArthur Foundation (2015). *Circular Economy Reports*. Retrieved from www.ellenmacarthurfoundation.org/business/reports on 26 November 2015.

54. Jonker, J. (2012). New business models: An explorative study of changing transactions creating multiple value(s) (Working Paper). School of Management, Radboud University Nijmegen, the Netherlands.

55. Jonker, J. (2012). New business models: An explorative study of changing transactions creating multiple value(s) (Working Paper). School of Management, Radboud University Nijmegen, the Netherlands.

56. MUD Jeans (2015). *Why We're Here*. Retrieved from www.mudjeans.eu/about/ on 26 November 2015.

57. ibid.

58. Jonker, J. (2012). New business models: An explorative study of changing transactions creating multiple value(s) (Working Paper). School of Management, Radboud University Nijmegen, the Netherlands.

59. Christern, M. (2012, 19 May). John Elkington in an interview with Max Christern. *NRC*. (Only available in Dutch.)

60. Smith, A. (2014, 1 July). When grassroots innovation movements encounter mainstream institutions. Academic papers, GIHCP (Historical and Comparative Perspectives).

61. Burke, J. (2013, 6 June). Bangladesh factory collapse leaves trail of shattered lives. *The Guardian*. Retrieved from www.theguardian.com/world/2013/jun/06/bangladesh-factory-building-collapse-community on 11 August 2015.

62. *Business Social Compliance Initiative* (2015). Retrieved from http://www.bsci-intl.org/ on 26 November 2015.

63. *Fair Wear Foundation* (2009). Retrieved from www.fairwear.org/ on 26 November 2015.

64. Social Accountability International. (n.d.). *SA8000˚ Standard and Documents*. Retrieved from www.sa-intl.org/index.cfm?fuseaction=Page.ViewPage&PageID=937 on 26 November 2015.

65. Organic Cotton (n.d.). *Standards and Certification of Organic Cotton*. Retrieved from www.organiccotton.org/oc/Organic-cotton/Standards-and-certification/Standards-and-certification.php on 26 November 2015.

66. Van Bommel, H. & Goorhuis, M. (2014). *Design Jeans for Recycling. A Supply Chain Case Study in the Netherlands*. Waste Management Research, ISWA.

Chapter 10   Corporate Social Responsibility

1. Schafrat, W. H. A. & Stierhout, A. J. H. M. (1993). *Mens en Werk, een Kijk op Personeelsbeleid (Man and Work, a View of Human Resource Management)* (p. 51). Houten/Zaventem: Bohn Stafleu Van Loghum. (Only available in Dutch.)

2. Bulte, M. (2008). *Emmenaren op Drift: Tragiek en Achtergrond van de Massale Migratie uit Zuid-Oost Drenthe, 1924–1936* (Tragedy and Background of the Mass Migration from South-East Drenthe, 1924–1936) (p. 126). Leeuwarden: Friese Pers/Noordboek Uitgeverij. (Only available in Dutch.)

3. Hitt, M. A., Freeman, R. E. & Harrison, J. S. (2001). *Handbook of Strategic Management* (p. 189). Oxford: Blackwell Publishers.

4. Maessen, R., Seters, P. van & Rijckevorsel, E. van (2007). Circles of stakeholders: towards a relational theory of corporate social responsibility. *International Journal of Business Governance and Ethics*, 3(1), 77–94.

5. Löfstedt, R. E. (1996). The Brent Spar controversy: An example of risk communication gone wrong. *Risk Analysis, 17*(2), 131–6.

6. Winkler, P. (2005). *Organisatie-ethiek (Organizational ethics)* (44–46). Pearson Education. (Only available in Dutch.)

7. Bouchra A. (2009). Interview with Mr. C. Dutilh, sustainability manager of Unilever. Website Centrum de Baak. Retrieved from www.debaak.nl on 17 August 2010.

8. Scholtens, B. (2007). Financial and social performance of socially responsible investments in the Netherlands. *Corporate Governance: An International Review, 15*(6), 1090–1105.

9. Casimir, G. & Dutilh, C. (2003, September). Sustainability: A gender studies perspective. *International Journal of Consumer Studies, 27*(4), 316–325.

10. SER (Dutch Social Economic Council) (2000). *Advisory report on Corporate Social Responsibility: Summary of Conclusions*. Retrieved from www.ser.nl/~/media/files/internet/talen/engels/2000/2000_11.ashx on 26 November 2015.

11. Post, J. E., Preston, L. E. & Sachs, S. (2002). *Redefining the Corporation: Stakeholder Management and Organizational Wealth* (p. 19). Stanford, CA: Stanford University Press.

12. Mitchell, R. K., Agle, B. R. & Wood, D. J. (1997). Towards a theory of stakeholder identification and salience: Defining the principle of who is who and what really counts. *Academy of Management Review, 22*, 853–856.

13. Burgos-Jimenez, J., Vázquez-Brust, D., Plaza-Ubeda, J. (2011). Adaptability, entrepreneurship and stakeholder integration: Scenarios and strategies for environment and vulnerability. *Journal of Environmental Protection, 2*(10), 1375–1387.

14. Mil, F. van, Prillevitz, F. & Olof, A. (2009). Introduction on the theme 'power and ethics'. *Magazine Idea, Year 30*, 3. Published by social liberals. (Only available in Dutch.)

15. Zerk, J. A. (2006). *Multinationals and Corporate Social Responsibility. Limitations and Opportunities in International Law*. Cambridge: Cambridge University Press.

16. Mutti, D., Yakovleva, N. & Vazquez-Brust, D. (2011). Corporate social responsibility in the mining industry: Perspectives from stakeholder groups in Argentina. *Resources Policy, Special Issue: CSR in Developing Countries*.

17. Vandana, S. (1991). *The Violence of the Green Revolution: Third World Agriculture, Ecology and Politics*. London: Zed Books.

18. GMO Compass (2007). GMO cultivation area by crop. Retrieved from www.gmo-compass.org/eng/agri_biotechnology/gmo_planting/144.gmo_cultivation_area_crop.html on 28 June 2010.

19. European Commission Brussels (2011). *Opinion of the European Economic and Social Committee on the 'Communication from the Commission to the European Parliament, the Council, the European Economic and Social Committee and the Committee of the Regions – A Renewed EU strategy 2011–14 for Corporate Social Responsibility'.* COM (2011) 681 final.

20. Retrieved from www.bsr.org/en/our-insights/blog-view/bsr-and-the-state-of-csr-what-we-mean-when-we-say-csr on 1 December 2015.

21. Moratis, L. & Cochius, T. (2011, May). *ISO 26000: The Business Guide to the New Standard on Social Responsibility*. Greenleaf Publishing.

22. NEN Standards Committee 400178 on Social Responsibility (2011, November). *Dutch Summary Code of Practice NPR 9026: Guidance on Self-Declaration NEN-ISO 26000*. The Netherlands.

23. International Organization for Standardization *ISO 26000:2010(en). Guidance on Social Responsibility. Introduction.* Retrieved from www.iso.org/obp/ui/#iso:std:iso:26000:ed-1:v1:en in January 2014. This figure taken from ISO 26000:2010, Guidance on Social Responsibility and is reproduced with the permission of the International Organization for Standardization, ISO. This standard can be obtained from any ISO member and from the website of the ISO Central Secretariat at the following address: www.iso.org. Copyright remains with ISO.

24. Reed, R. (2012, February). The CSR performance ladder certification standards. *The Executive Times*, 13–15.

25. MVO Prestatieladder. (n.d.). *CSR Performance Ladder*. Retrieved from www.mvoprestatieladder.nl/en/csrperf.php on 26 November 2015.

26. European Commission (2015). *The EU Ecolabel*. Retrieved from http://ec.europa.eu/environment/ecolabel/ on 26 November 2015.

27. International Organization for Standardization (n.d.). *ISO 14000 – Environmental management*. Retrieved from www.iso.org/iso/iso14000 on 26 November 2015.

28. Social Accountability Initiative (n.d.). *SA8000° Standard and Documents*. Retrieved from www.sa-intl.org/index.cfm?fuseaction=Page.ViewPage&PageID=937 on 26 November 2015.

29. The Green Key: an eco-label for leisure organizations. *Baseline Criteria for Hotels, Youth Hostels, Conference and Holiday Centres 2009/2010.* Retrieved from www .kmvk.nl/cmslib/www.kmvk.nl/greenkeyorg/files/International_baseline_criteria_HOTELS_V1.2.doc. on 26 November 2015.

30. Business Social Compliance Initiative (2015). Retrieved from http://www.bsci-intl .org/ on 26 November 2015.

31. Young, T. (2008, 8 January). Denmark latest to pass CSR reporting law. BusinessGreen. Retrieved from www.businessgreen.com/bg/news/1801774/denmark-pass-csr-reporting-law on 26 November 2015.

32. Global Reporting Initiative (n.d.). About sustainability reporting. Retrieved from www.globalreporting.org/information/sustainability-reporting/Pages/default.aspx on 26 November 2015.

33. Ingram, V. J., Grip, K. de, Ruijter de Wildt, M. J. M. de, Ton, G., Douma, M., Boone, J. A., Hoeven & J. T. van (2013). *Corporate Social Responsibility: The Role of Public Policy.* A systematic literature review of the effects of government supported interventions on the corporate social responsibility (CSR) behaviour of enterprises in developing countries (IOB Study 377). Den Haag: Ministry of Foreign Affairs of the Netherlands.

34. Moratis, L. & Cochius, T. (2011, May). *ISO 26000: The Business Guide to the New Standard on Social Responsibility.* Greenleaf Publishing.

35. Orlitzky, M., Schmidt, F. L. & Rynes, S. L. (2003). Corporate social and financial performance: A meta-analysis. *Organization Studies, 24*(3), 403–441.

36. Burke, L. & Logsdon, J. M. (1999). How corporate social responsibility pays off. *Long Range Planning, 29*(4), 495–502.

37. Husted, B. W. (2003). Governance choices for corporate social responsibility: To contribute, collaborate or internalize? *Long Range Planning, 36*(5), 481–498.

38. Hollender, J. & Breen, B. (2010).*The Responsibility Revolution. How the Next Generation of Businesses Will Win.* San Fransisco: Jossey-Bass.

39. Beavis, L. (2012, 30 May). DESSO: recycling to infinity and beyond. *The Guardian.* Retrieved from www.theguardian.com/sustainable-business/best-practice-exchange /desso-recycling-infinity-and-beyond on 26 November 2015.

40. Towers Perrin (2007–2008). *Closing the Engagement Gap: A Road Map for Driving Superior Business Performance.* Towers Perrin Global Workforce Study.

41. Coughlan, R. (2005). Employee loyalty as adherence to shared moral values. *Journal of Managerial Issues, 17*(1), 43–57.

42. Schoemaker, M., Nijhof, A. & Jonker, J. (2006). Human value management: The influence of the contemporary developments of corporate social responsibility and social capital on HRM. *Management Revue, 17*(4), 448–465.

43. ibid.

44. Schoemaker, M., Nijhof, A. & Jonker, J. (2005). Human value management: The influence of the contemporary developments of corporate social responsibility and social capital on HRM. Article in monograph or in proceedings. New York: Proceedings of the 10th Annual Conference of The Reputation Institute.

45. Chartered Institute of Personnel and Development (2007). *Personnel Management: A Short History. Factsheet.* Retrieved from https://rapidbi.com/cipd-factsheets/# .VldxVNIvd0u on 26 November 2015.

46. Schoemaker, M., Nijhof, A. & Jonker, J. (2006). Human value management: The influence of the contemporary developments of corporate social responsibility and social capital on HRM. *Management Revue, 17*(4), 448–465.

47. ibid.

48. Schoemaker, M., Nijhof, A. & Jonker, J. (2006). Human value management: The influence of the contemporary developments of corporate social responsibility and social capital on HRM. *Management Revue, 17*(4), 448–465.

49. Retrieved from www.bbc.com/news/magazine-26671221 on 1 December 2015.

50. Hollender, J. & Breen, B. (2010). *The Responsibility Revolution: How the Next Generation of Businesses Will Win.* John Wiley & Sons.

51. Ubuntu Circle (2012). Citation Desmond Tutu / http://www.ubuntucircle.nl/ (last accessed 28 May 2012).

52. Burgos-Jimenez, J., Vazquez-Brust, D. & Plaza-Ubeda, J. (2011). Adaptability, entrepreneurship and stakeholder integration: Scenarios and strategies for environment and vulnerability. *Journal of Environmental Protection, 2*(10), 1375–1387.

53. Whitney, S. (n.d.) Our Journey & Commitment. *Timberland Responsibility.* Retrieved from http://responsibility.timberland.com/executive-commitment/ on 26 November 2015.

54. Traas, M. (1990). *Cultuur en Identiteit: Overleven in een Veranderende Wereld.* (Culture and Identity: Surviving in a Changing World). Nijkerk/Baarn: Intro. (Only available in Dutch.)

55. Erikson, E. H. (1982). *The Life Cycle Completed.* New York: W.W. Norton.

56. *UTZ Certified.* (2015). Retrieved from www.utzcertified.org/ on 26 November 2015.

57. Fombrun, C. J., Gardberg, N. A. & Sever, J. M. (2000). The Reputation Quotient[SM]: A multi-stakeholder measure of corporate reputation. *Journal of Brand Management, 7*(2000), 241–255. doi:10.1057/bm.2000.10

58. CorpWatch (2001). Greenwash fact sheet. Retrieved from www.corpwatch.org/article.php?id=242 on 26 November 2015.

59. Vázquez-Brust, D., Plaza-Ubeda, J., Burgos-Jimenez, J. & Natenzon, C. (2010). Stakeholder pressures and strategic prioritisation: An empirical analysis of environmental responses in Argentinean firms. *Journal of Business Ethics, 91*(2), Supplement, 171–192.

60. Idemudia (2008). Conceptualising the CSR and development debate: Bridging existing analytical gaps. *Journal of Corporate Citizenship, 29,* 91–110.

61. Yakovleva, N. & Vázquez-Brust, D. (2012) Stakeholder perspectives on CSR of mining MNCs in Argentina. *Journal of Business Ethics, 106*(2), 191–211.

62. Carroll, A. B. & Shabana, K. M. (2010). The business case for corporate social responsibility: A review of concepts, research and practice. *International Journal of Management Reviews, 12*(1), 85–105.

63. Yakovleva, N., Vázquez-Brust, D. (2012) Stakeholder perspectives on CSR of mining MNCs in Argentina. *Journal of Business Ethics, 106*(2), 191–211.

64. Carroll, A. B. (1991). The pyramid of corporate social responsibility: toward the moral management of organizational stakeholders. *Business Horizons,* July–August, 39–48.

65. Yakovleva, N. & Vazquez-Brust, D. (2012) Stakeholder perspectives on CSR of mining MNCs in Argentina. *Journal of Business Ethics, 106*(2), 191–211.

66. Westphalen, L. G. (2012). *Corporate Social Responsibility in the Mining Sector.* Fraser Institute. Retrieved from www.fraserinstitute.org/uploadedFiles/fraser-ca/Content/research-news/research/articles/corporate-social-responsibility-in-mining-sector-CSR.pdf on 26 November 2015.

67. Barry, C. (2012). IPolitics. *CIDA, NGOs and mining companies: The Good, the Bad and the Ugly.* Retrieved from http://ipolitics.ca/2012/05/08/barry-carin-cida-ngos-and-mining-companies-the-good-the-bad-and-the-ugly/ on 26 November 2015.

68. Africa – News and Analysis. (2013). Zambia – conflict between copper mining companies and communities. Retrieved from http://africajournalismtheworld. com/2013/10/22/zambia-conflict-between-copper-mining-companies-and-communities/ on 15 September 2014.

69. Hamann, Kapelus (2004). Corporate social responsibility in mining in Southern Africa: Fair accountability or just greenwash? *Development, 47*(3), 85–92.

70. Owen, J. R. & Kemp, D. (2013). Social licence and mining: A critical perspective. *Resources Policy, 38*(1), 29–35.

71. AllAfrica. (2015). *Zambia.* Retrieved from http://allafrica.com/zambia/ on 26 November 2015.

Chapter 11   Globalization and Strategy Development

1. Aker, J. C. & Mbiti, I. M. (2010). Mobile phones and economic development in Africa (CGD Working Paper 211). Washington, DC: Center for Global Development.

2. Muto, M. & Yamano, T. (2009). The impact of mobile phone coverage expansion on market participation: Panel data evidence from Uganda. *World Development, 37*(12), 1887–1896.

3. Masters, W. A. et al. (2013). Urbanization and farm size in Asia and Africa: Implications for food security and agricultural research. *Global Food Security, 2*(3), 156–165.

4. Hart, S. L. (2007). *Capitalism at the Crossroads.* Upper Saddle River, NJ: FT Press.

5. Sovacool, G. K. (2012). Deploying off-grid technology to eradicate energy poverty. *Science, 338,* 47–48.

6. Ellen MacArthur Foundation (2012). *Towards the Circular Economy: An Economic and Business Rationale for an Accelerated Transition.* Retrieved from www.ellen-macarthurfoundation.org/publications/towards-the-circular-economy-vol-1-an-economic-and-business-rationale-for-an-accelerated-transition on 20 November 2015.

7. O'Connor, G. C. (2008). *Grabbing Lightning: Building a Capability for Breakthrough Innovation.* San Francisco, CA: John Wiley & Sons.

8. Matlay, H., Ruzzier, M., Hisrich, R. D. & Antoncic, B. (2006). SME internationalization research: Past, present, and future. *Journal of Small Business and Enterprise Development, 13*(4), 476–497.

9. *Van den Berg Roses.* (n.d.). Retrieved from www.vandenbergroses.com on 28 August 2010.

10. De Bloemist. (2008, December). (Only available in Dutch.)

11. ibid.

12. Lewin, A. Y. & Peeters, C. (2006). Offshoring work: business hype or the onset of fundamental transformation? *Long Range Planning, 39*(3), 221–239.

13. Erber, G. & Sayed-Ahmed, A. (2005). Offshore outsourcing. *Intereconomics, 40*(2),100–112.

14. VROM-raad. (2008, January). *Een prijs voor elke reis: Een beleidsstrategie voor CO2-reductie in verkeer en vervoer.* (Only available in Dutch.)

15. Kievit, H. (2011). *Social Venturing Entrepreneurship – A Positioning* (p. 29). Breukelen: Nyenrode Business Universiteit.

16. Elkington, J. & Hartigan, P. (2013). *The Power of Unreasonable People: How Social Entrepreneurs Create Markets that Change the World.* Cambridge, MA: Harvard Business School Press.

17. Hessen, F. van (2011, 10 October). Interview by Martin Oyevaar.

18. Stichting Gambia Project. *Solar food dryer MAMA DIOP*. Retrieved from www .stichtinggambiaproject.nl/nl/solar-fruit-dryer.html on 17 February 2015. (Only available in Dutch.)

19. Anderson, J. & Markides, C. (2006, August). *Strategic Innovation at the Base of the Economic Pyramid*.

20. Prahalad, C. K. (2006). Part I: The Fortune at the Bottom of the Pyramid. In C. K. Prahalad, *The Fortune at the Bottom of the Pyramid: Eradicating Poverty Through Profits* (1–112). Philadelphia, PA: Pearson Prentice Hall.

21. ibid.

22. Hart, S. L. (2007). The Great Leap Downward. In S. L. Hart, *Capitalism at the Crossroads* (111–138). NJ, FT Press.

23. Prahalad, C. K. (2006). *The Fortune at the Bottom of the Pyramid: Eradicating Poverty Through Profits*. Philadelphia, PA: Pearson Prentice Hall.

24. Kanani, R. (2011, August 8). Jaipur Foot: One of the most technologically advanced social enterprises in the world. *Forbes/Leadership*. Retrieved from www.forbes .com/sites/rahimkanani/2011/08/08/jaipur-foot-one-of-the-most-technologically-advanced-social-enterprises-in-the-world/ on 17 June 2015.

25. Sadikot, S., Nigam, A. & Jain, A. (2007, September). The Jaipur Foot: An effective low-cost prosthesis for people with diabetes. *Diabetes Voice, 52*(3).

26. Prahalad, C. K. (2006). *The Fortune at the Bottom of the Pyramid: Eradicating Poverty Through Profits*. Philadelphia, PA: Pearson Prentice Hall.

27. Crabtree, A. (2007). *Evaluating 'The Bottom of the Pyramid' from a Fundamental Capabilities Perspective* (CBDS Working Paper nr. 1, 2007). Frederiksberg, Denmark: Copenhagen Business School, Centre for Business and Development Studies. Retrieved from http://openarchive.cbs.dk/bitstream/handle/10398/6755/wps-2007_no.1_andrew.crabtree.pdf?sequence=1 on 20 November 2015.

28. Prahalad, C. K. & Hammond, A. (2002). Serving the world's poor, profitably. *Strategy+Business, 26*, 54–67.

29. Carroll, A. B. & Shabana, K. M. (2010). The business case for corporate social responsibility: A review of concepts, research and practice. *International Journal of Management Reviews, 12*(1), 85–105.

30. Elkington, J. (2006). Governance for sustainability. *Corporate Governance: An International Review, 14*(6), 522–529.

31. Hart, S. L. (2007). *Capitalism at the Crossroads*. Upper Saddle River, NJ: FT Press.

32. Hart, S. L. (2005). Innovation, creative destruction and sustainability. *Research-Technology Management, 48*(5), 21–27.

33. Hockerts, K. & Wüstenhagen, R. (2010). Greening Goliaths versus emerging Davids: theorizing about the role of incumbents and new entrants in sustainable entrepreneurship. *Journal of Business Venturing, 25*(5), 481–492.

34. Halt, S. & Milstein, M. (1999). Global sustainability and the creative destruction of industries. *Sloan Management Review, 41*(1), 23–33.

35. DSM. About DSM: DSM – More than a century of evolution. Retrieved from www .dsm.com on 10 March 2010. (Only available in Dutch.)

36. Bos, K. (2013). *The History of Chemelot*. Geleen, The Netherlands: Chemelot.

37. John, C. H. S., Cannon, A. R. & Pouder, R. W. (2001). Change drivers in the new millennium: Implications for manufacturing strategy research. *Journal of Operations Management, 19*(2), 143–160.

38. Green, K., Morton, B. & New, S. (1996). Purchasing and environmental management: Interactions, policies and opportunities. *Business Strategy and the Environment, 5*(3), 188–197.

39. Toh, R. S., DeKay, C. F. & Raven, P. (2011). Travel planning: Searching for and booking hotels on the internet. *Cornell Hospitality Quarterly, 52*(4), 388–398.
40. Monsen, K. (2013). Buurtzorg Nederland. *The American Journal of Nursing, 113*(8), 55–59.
41. Heinrichs, H. (2013). Sharing economy: A potential new pathway to sustainability. *Gaia, 22*(4), 228.
42. Belk, R. (2014). You are what you can access: Sharing and collaborative consumption online. *Journal of Business Research, 67*(8), 1595–1600.
43. ibid.
44. de Bruin, E. (2010, October 30). Uninhibited do well/Pimp your mind. Interview with social psychologist Kees van den Bos. *NRC.* (Only available in Dutch.)
45. Jonker, J. (2012). New Business Models. An exploratory study of changing transactions creating multiple value(s) (Working Paper). Nijmegen, The Netherlands: Nijmegen School of Management, Radboud University Nijmegen.
46. Kim, W. C. & Mauborgne, R. (2005). *Blue Ocean Strategy.* Boston, MA: Harvard Business School Press.
47. Allio, R. J. & Fahey, L. (2012). Joan Magretta: What executives can learn from revisiting Michael Porter. *Strategy & Leadership, 40*(2), 5–10.
48. Porter, M. (2008). *Competitive Strategy: Techniques for Analyzing Industries and Competitors.* New York, NY: Simon and Schuster.
49. Kim, W. C. & Mauborgne, R. (2005). *Blue Ocean Strategy.* Boston, MA: Harvard Business School Press.
50. Zipcar (2015). zipcar overview. Retrieved from www.zipcar.co.uk/press/overview on 7 January 2015.
51. Timetric (2014, January 24). *How the shared economy is changing the car rental market.* Retrieved 06-01-2015 from https://timetric.com/info/media-center/expert-insight/2014/01/24/how-shared-economy-changing-car-rental-market/
52. ibid.
53. Hart, S. L. (2007). Chapter 7: Broadening the corporate bandwidth & Chapter 8: Developing native capability. In S. L. Hart, *Capitalism at the Crossroads* (169–222). Upper Saddle River, NJ: FT Press.
54. Santen, H. van (2010, 31 July). Bacterie spint rag net zo goed als een spin. *NRC Handelsblad.* (Only available in Dutch.)
55. Omenetto, F. G. & Kaplan, D. L. (2010). New opportunities for an ancient material. *Science, 329*(5991), 528–531.
56. Hart, S. L. & Sharma, S. (2004). Engaging fringe stakeholders for competitive imagination. *The Academy of Management Executive, 18*(1), 7–18.
57. Sherman, H. D. (1999). Assessing the intervention effectiveness of business incubation programs on new business start-ups. *Journal of Developmental Entrepreneurship, 4*(2), 117.
58. Hart, S. L. & Sharma, S. (2004). Engaging fringe stakeholders for competitive imagination. *The Academy of Management Executive, 18*(1), 7–18.
59. Osterwalder, A. & Pigneur, Y. (2010). *Business Model Generation.* Hoboken, NJ: John Wiley and Sons.
60. Zott, C. & Amit, R. (2008). The fit between product market strategy and business model: implications for firm performance. *Strategic Management Journal, 29*(1), 1–26.
61. Osterwalder, A. & Pigneur, Y. (2010). *Business Model Generation.* Hoboken, NJ: John Wiley and Sons. / Template: Strategyzer AG. *The Business Model Canvas.* Retrieved from www.businessmodelgeneration.com/downloads/business_model_canvas_poster.pdf on 14 February 2015.

62. Eppler, M. J., Hoffmann, F. & Bresciani, S. (2011). New business models through collaborative idea generation. *International Journal of Innovation Management*, *15*(6), 1323–1341.

63. *Peepoople*. (n.d.). Retrieved from www.peepoople.com on 11 November 2014.

64. Osterwalder, A. (2010, 5 August). *Combining business model prototyping, customer development, and social entrepreneurship. Business Model Alchemist*. Retrieved from http://businessmodelalchemist.com/blog/2010/08/combining-business-model-prototyping-customer-development-and-social-entrepreneurship.html on 30 November 2015.

65. Olivares, M. & Santos, S. (2009). *Market Solutions in Poverty: The Role of Microcredit in Development Countries with Financial Restrictions* (Working Paper 2009/12). Working Papers Department of Economics, from ISEG – School of Economics and Management, Department of Economics, University of Lisbon.

66. Yunus, M. (2014). Grameen Bank – Facts. *Nobel Media AB*. Retrieved from www.nobelprize.org/nobel_prizes/peace/laureates/2006/grameen-facts.html on 9 January 2015.

67. Grameen Bank. (2014, October 29). *Introduction*. Retrieved from www.grameen.com/index.php?option=com_content&task=view&id=16&Itemid=112 on 5 January 2015.

68. ibid.

69. ibid.

70. ibid.

71. About Microfinance (2015). *Microfinance in Asia*. Retrieved from www.aboutmicrofinance.com/latin-america-caribbean/asia on 5 January 2015.

Chapter 12   The Challenge of Progress Towards Sustainable Development

1. Westlund, H. & Adam, F. (2010). Social capital and economic performance: A meta-analysis of 65 studies. *European Planning Studies*, *18*(6), 893–919.

2. Misztal, B. (2013). *Trust in Modern Societies: The Search for the Bases of Social Order*. Oxford: John Wiley & Sons.

3. Parker, S. C. (2007). Law and the economics of entrepreneurship. *Comparative Labor Law & Policy Journal*, *28*(4).

4. Elster, J. (2011). Chapter 2: Indeterminacy of emotional mechanisms. In P. Demeulenaere, *Analytical Sociology and Social Mechanisms*. Cambridge: Cambridge University Press.

5. Yuval, F. & Herne, K. (2005). Sophisticated behavior under majoritarian and non-majoritarian voting procedures. *Political Behavior*, *27*(3), 217–237.

6. Alesina, A. & Perotti, R. (1994). The political economy of growth: a critical survey of the recent literature. *The World Bank Economic Review*, *8*(3), 351–371.

7. Turner, J. C. (2005). Explaining the nature of power: A three-process theory. *European Journal of Social Psychology*, *35*(1), 1–22.

8. Falk, R. A. (2000). *Human Rights Horizons: The Pursuit of Justice in a Globalizing World*. New York: Psychology Press.

9. Levy, D. & Sznaider, N. (2004). The institutionalization of cosmopolitan morality: The Holocaust and human rights. *Journal of Human Rights*, *3*(2), 143–157.

10. Inglehart, R. & Welzel, C. (2005). *Modernization, Cultural Change, and Democracy: The Human Development Sequence*. Cambridge: Cambridge University Press.

11. Barbier, E. B. (2011). Transaction costs and the transition to environmentally sustainable development. *Environmental Innovation and Societal Transitions*, *1*(1), 58–69.

12. Adger, W. N. et al. (2003). Governance for sustainability: Towards a 'thick' analysis of environmental decision making. *Environment and Planning A, 35*(6), 1095–1110.
13. Rotmans, J., Kemp, R. & Van Asselt, M. (2001). More evolution than revolution: Transition management in public policy. *foresight, 3*(1), 15–31.
14. Truffer, B. & Coenen, L. (2012). Environmental innovation and sustainability transitions in regional studies. *Regional Studies, 46*(1), 1–21.
15. Mohieddin, M. (2013). *No Change in Sight: The Situation of Religious Minorities in post-Mubarak Egypt.* Minority Rights Group International.
16. Block, M. (2014). *Reform Failure and Underdevelopment in Egypt: An Institutional Explanation.*
17. O'Donnell, G. & Schmitter, P. C. (2013). *Transitions from Authoritarian Rule: Tentative Conclusions about Uncertain Democracies.* MD, JHU Press.
18. Rotmans, J., Kemp, R. & Van Asselt, M. (2001). More evolution than revolution: Transition management in public policy. *foresight, 3*(1), 15–31.
19. Coenen, L., Benneworth, P. & Truffer, B. (2012). Toward a spatial perspective on sustainability transitions. *Research Policy, 41*(6), 968–979.
20. Ropohl, G. (1999). Philosophy of socio-technical systems. Retrieved from DLA EJournal http://scholar.lib.vt.edu/ejournals/SPT/v4_n3html/ROPOHL.html on 23 May 2015.
21. Greene, D. L., Park, S. & Liu, C. (2013). *Analyzing the Transition to Electric Drive in California.* Prepared for the International Council on Clean Transportation. Retrieved from http://bakercenter.utk.edu/wp-content/uploads/2013/06/Trans itionto-Electric-Drive-2013-report. FINAL.pdf on 20 November 2015.
22. Jackson, T. (2009). Prosperity without growth?: The transition to a sustainable economy. *Sustainable Development Commission.*
23. Grin, J., Rotmans, J. & Schot, J. (2010). *Transitions to Sustainable Development: New Directions in the Study of Long Term Transformative Change.* London and New York, Routledge.
24. Rotmans, J., Kemp, R. & Van Asselt, M. (2001). More evolution than revolution: Transition management in public policy. *foresight, 3*(1), 15–31.
25. Sousanis, J. (2011). *World Vehicle Population Tops 1 Billion Units.* Retrieved from http://wardsauto.com/ar/world_vehicle_population_110815 on 20 November 2015.
26. Geels, F. G. (2011). The multi-level perspective on sustainability transitions: Responses to seven criticisms. *Environmental Innovation and Societal Transitions, 1*(1), 24–40.
27. ibid.
28. Alexander, S. (2014). *A Critique of Techno-Optimism: Efficiency without Sufficiency is Lost* (Working Paper 1/14). Melbourne Sustainable Society Institute.
29. Grin, J., Rotmans, J. & Schot, J. (2010). *Transitions to Sustainable Development: New Directions in the Study of Long Term Transformative Change.* Routledge.
30. Barkemeyer, R. et al. (2009). What the papers say: Trends in sustainability. A comparative analysis of 115 leading national newspapers worldwide. *Journal of Corporate Citizenship, 33,* 68–86.
31. Dunlap, R. E., Van Liere, K. D., Mertig, A. & Jones, R. E. (2000). Measuring of the new ecological paradigm: A revised NEP scale (Question 15 NEP). *Journal of Social Issues, 56,* 425–442.
32. Hawcroft, L. J. & Milfont, T. L (2010). The use (and abuse) of the new environmental paradigm scale over the last 30 years: A meta-analysis. *Journal of Environmental Psychology 30*(2), 143–158.
33. Ugander, J., Backstrom, L., Marlow, C. & Kleinberg, J. (2012). Structural diversity in social contagion. *Proceedings of the National Academy of Sciences, 109*(16), 5962–5966.

34. Ugander, J., Backstrom, L., Marlow, C. & Kleinberg, J. (2012). Structural diversity in social contagion. *Proceedings of the National Academy of Sciences, 109*(16), 5962–5966.
35. Subašić, E., Reynolds, K. J. & Turner, J. C. (2008). The political solidarity model of social change: Dynamics of self-categorization in intergroup power relations. *Personality and Social Psychology Review, 12*(4), 330–352.
36. Lieberman, R. C. (2002). Ideas, institutions, and political order: Explaining political change. *American Political Science Review, 96*(04), 697–712.
37. Loorbach, D. (2007). Transition management: New mode of governance for sustainable development. *Dutch Research Institute for Transitions* (DRIFT).
38. Lanoie, P., Ambec, S., Cohen, M. A., & Elgie, S. (2010). The Porter Hypothesis at 20: Can environmental regulation enhance innovation and competitiveness? *CIRANO-Scientific Publications 2010s–29.*
39. ibid.
40. Burgos-Jiménez, J. de, Vázquez-Brust, D., Plaza-Úbeda, J. A. & Dijkshoorn, J. (2013). Environmental protection and financial performance: An empirical analysis in Wales. *International Journal of Operations & Production Management, 33*(8), 981–1018.
41. Lanoie, P., Ambec, S., Cohen, M. A., & Elgie, S. (2010). The Porter Hypothesis at 20: Can environmental regulation enhance innovation and competitiveness? *Lanoie, P., Ambec, S., Cohen, M. A., & Elgie, S. (2010). The Porter Hypothesis at 20: Can Environmental Regulation Enhance Innovation and Competitiveness?. CIRANO-Scientific Publications 2010s–29.*
42. Sharma, S. (2000). Managerial interpretations and organizational context as predictors of corporate choice of environmental strategy. *Academy of Management Journal, 43*(4), 681–697.
43. Moe, E. (2010). Energy, industry and politics: Energy, vested interests, and long-term economic growth and development. *Energy, 35*(4), 1730–1740.
44. Carroll, A. B. & Shabana, K. M. (2010). The business case for corporate social responsibility: A review of concepts, research and practice. *International Journal of Management Reviews, 12*(1), 85–105.
45. Bommel, H. W. M. van (2011). A conceptual framework for analyzing sustainability strategies in industrial supply networks from an innovation perspective. *Journal of Cleaner Production, 19*, 895–904.
46. Lovio, R., Mickwitz, P. & Heiskanen, E. (2011). Path dependence, path creation and creative destruction in the evolution of energy systems. *The Handbook of Research on Energy Entrepreneurship*, 274.
47. Ragwitz, M. & Huber, C. (2005). *Feed-In Systems in Germany and Spain and Slovenia: A Comparison.* Fraunhofer Institute Systems and Innovation Research.
48. Wirth, H. (2014, 15 May). *Recent Facts about Photovoltaics in Germany.* Fraunhofer Institute for Solar Energy Systems.
49. *Die Agentur für Erneuerbare Energien.* Retrieved from www.unendlich-viel-energie.de on 31 May 2015.
50. Korsgaard, S. (2011). *Enacting Entrepreneurship as Social Value Creation.* The Open Access Institutional Repository at Robert Gordon University.
51. Wirth, H. (2014, 15 May). *Recent Facts about Photovoltaics in Germany.* Fraunhofer Institute for Solar Energy Systems.

INDEX